XML Schema

XML Schema

Eric van der Vlist

O'REILLY®

Beijing · Cambridge · Farnham · Köln · Paris · Sebastopol · Taipei · Tokyo

XML Schema
by Eric van der Vlist

Copyright © 2002 O'Reilly Media, Inc. All rights reserved.
Printed in the United States of America.

Published by O'Reilly Media, Inc., 1005 Gravenstein Highway North, Sebastopol, CA 95472.

O'Reilly Media, Inc. books may be purchased for educational, business, or sales promotional use. On-line editions are also available for most titles (*safari.oreilly.com*). For more information, contact our corporate/institutional sales department: (800) 998-9938 or *corporate@oreilly.com*.

Editor:	Simon St.Laurent
Production Editor:	Darren Kelly
Cover Designer:	Hanna Dyer
Interior Designer:	David Futato

Printing History:

June 2002:	First Edition.

 This book uses RepKover,™ a durable and flexible lay-flat binding.

ISBN-10: 0-596-00252-1
ISBN-13: 978-0-596-00252-7
[C]

Table of Contents

Preface

As developers create new XML vocabularies, they often need to describe those vocabularies to share, define, and apply them. This book will guide you through W3C XML Schema, a set of Recommendations from the World Wide Web Consortium (W3C). These specifications define a language that you can use to express formal descriptions of XML documents using a generally object-oriented approach. Schemas can be used for documentation, validation, or processing automation. W3C XML Schema is a key component of Web Services specifications such as SOAP and WSDL, and is widely used to describe XML vocabularies precisely.

With this power comes complexity. The Recommendations are long, complex, and generally difficult to read. The Primer helps, of course, but there are many details and style approaches to consider in building schemas. This book attempts to provide an objective, and sometimes critical, view of the tools W3C XML Schema provides, helping you to discover the possibilities of schemas while avoiding potential minefields.

Who Should Read This Book?

Read this book if you want to:

- Create W3C XML Schema schemas using a text editor, XML editor, or a W3C XML Schema IDE or editor.
- Understand and modify existing W3C XML Schema schemas.

You should already have a basic understanding of XML document structures and how to work with them.

Who Should Not Read This Book?

If you are just using an XML application using a W3C XML Schema schema, you probably do not need to deal with the subtleties of the Recommendation.

About the Examples

All the examples in this book have been tested with the XSV and Xerces-J implementations of W3C XML Schema running Linux (the Debian "sid" distribution). I have chosen these tools for their high level of conformance to the Recommendation (the best ones according to the tests I have performed); the vast majority runs without error on these implementations—however, the Recommendation is sometimes fuzzy and difficult to understand, and there are some examples that give different results with different implementations. These conform to my own understanding of the Recommendation as discussed on the xmlschema-dev mailing list (the archives are available at *http://lists.w3.org/Archives/Public/xmlschema-dev*).

Organization of This Book

Chapter 1, *Schema Uses and Development*
> This chapter examines why we would want to bring a new XML Schema language onto the XML scene and what basic benefits W3C XML Schema offers.

Chapter 2, *Our First Schema*
> This chapter presents a first complete schema, introducing the basic features of the language in a very "flat" style.

Chapter 3, *Giving Some Depth to Our First Schema*
> With W3C XML Schema, style matters. This chapter gives a second example of a complete schema, describing the same class of documents, and written in a completely different style called "Russian doll design."

Chapter 4, *Using Predefined Simple Datatypes*
> W3C XML Schema also provides datatyping. In this chapter, we explore how these types can be bound to the content of our document.

Chapter 5, *Creating Simple Datatypes*
> This chapter guides you through the process of defining your own simple types.

Chapter 6, *Using Regular Expressions to Specify Simple Datatypes*
> This chapter explores how to constrain new datatypes using regular expressions.

Chapter 7, *Creating Complex Datatypes*
> Now that we know all about simple types, this chapter explores the different complex types that can be used to define structures within an XML document.

Chapter 8, *Creating Building Blocks*
> This chapter shows how to organize schema tools into reusable building blocks.

Chapter 9, *Defining Uniqueness, Keys, and Key References*
> In addition to content (simple types) and structure (complex types), W3C XML Schema can constrain the identifiers and references within a document. We explore this feature in this chapter.

Chapter 10, *Controlling Namespaces*

Support for XML namespaces is one of the top requirements of W3C XML Schema. This chapter explains how this requirement has been implemented and its implications.

Chapter 11, *Referencing Schemas and Schema Datatypes in XML Documents*

This chapter shows how schema information may be embedded in the XML instance documents.

Chapter 12, *Creating More Building Blocks Using Object-Oriented Features*

This chapter explains how more building blocks may be defined, by playing with namespaces and justifying the object-oriented qualification given to W3C XML Schema.

Chapter 13, *Creating Extensible Schemas*

This chapter gives some hints to write extensible and open schemas.

Chapter 14, *Documenting Schemas*

This chapter shows how schemas can be documented and made more readable, either by humans or programs.

Chapter 15, *Elements Reference Guide*

This is a quick reference guide to the elements used by W3C XML Schema.

Chapter 16, *Datatype Reference Guide*

This is a quick reference guide to the W3C XML Schema predefined types.

Appendix A, *XML Schema Languages*

W3C XML Schema is not the only language of its kind. Here we provide a short history of this not-so-new family and see some of its competitors.

Appendix B, *Work in Progress*

If you want to look ahead at what's to come from the W3C, you may be interested in this list of promising developments yet to be done in relation with W3C XML Schema.

Glossary

This provides short definitions for the main concepts and acronyms manipulated in the book.

Conventions Used in This Book

Constant Width

Used for attributes, datatypes, types, elements, code examples, and fragments.

Constant Width Bold

Used to highlight a section of code being discussed in the text.

Constant Width Italic

Used for replaceable elements in code examples.

This icon designates a note, which is an important aside to the nearby text.

 This icon designates a warning relating to the nearby text.

How to Contact Us

Please address comments and questions concerning this book to the publisher:

O'Reilly & Associates, Inc.
1005 Gravenstein Highway North
Sebastopol, CA 95472
(800) 998-9938 (in the United States or Canada)
(707) 829-0515 (international or local)
(707) 829-0104 (fax)

We have a web page for this book, where we list errata, examples, or any additional information. You can access this page at:

http://www.oreilly.com/catalog/xmlschema

To comment or ask technical questions about this book, send email to:

bookquestions@oreilly.com

For more information about our books, conferences, Resource Centers, and the O'Reilly Network, see our web site at:

http://www.oreilly.com

Acknowledgments

I would like to thank the contributors of xmlhack for their encouragements, and more specifically Simon St.Laurent, whose role has been aggravated by the fact that he has also been my editor for this book and has shown a remarkable level of helpfulness and patience. I'd also like to thank Edd Dumbill, who helped me set up Debian on the laptop on which this book was written.

I have been lucky enough to work with Jeni Tennison as a technical reviewer. Jeni's deep and thorough knowledge has been invaluable to my confidence in the deciphering of the Recommendation. Her friendly, yet accurate, reviews were my safety net while I was writing this book.

I am also very grateful to all the people who have answered my many nasty questions on the xmlschema-dev mailing list, especially Henry S. Thompson, Noah Mendelsohn, Ashok Malhotra, Priscilla Walmsley, and Jeni Tennison (yes, Jeni is helping people on this list too!).

Finally, I would like to thank my wife and children for their patience during the whole year I have spent writing this book. Hopefully, now that this work is over, they can retrieve their husband and father!

CHAPTER 1

Schema Uses and Development

XML, the Extensible Markup Language, lets developers create their own formats for storing and sharing information. Using that freedom, developers have created documents representing an incredible range of information, and XML can ease many different information-sharing problems. A key part of this process is formal declaration and documentation of those formats, providing a foundation on which software developers can build software.

What Schemas Do for XML

An XML schema language is a formalization of the constraints, expressed as rules or a model of structure, that apply to a class of XML documents. In many ways, schemas serve as design tools, establishing a framework on which implementations can be built. Since formalization is a necessary ground for software designers, formalizing the constraints and structures of XML instance documents can lead to very diverse applications. Although new applications for schemas are being invented every day, most of them can be classified as validation, documentation, query, binding, or editing.

Validation

Validation is the most common use for schemas in the XML world. There are many reasons and opportunities to validate an XML document: when we receive one, before importing data into a legacy system, when we have produced or hand-edited one, to test the output of an application, etc. In all these cases, a schema helps to accomplish a substantial part of the job. Different kinds of schemas perform different kinds of validation, and some especially complex rules may be better expressed in procedural code rather than in a descriptive schema, but validation is generally the initial purpose of a schema, and often the primary purpose as well.

Validation can be considered a "firewall" against the diversity of XML. We need such firewalls principally in two situations: to serve as actual firewalls when we receive documents from the external world (as is commonly the case with Web Services and other XML communications), and to provide check points when we design processes as pipelines of transformations. By validating documents against schemas, you can ensure that the documents' contents conform to your expected set of rules, simplifying the code needed to process them.

Validation of documents can substantially reduce the risk of processing XML documents received from sources beyond your control. It doesn't remove either the need to follow the administration rules of your chosen communication protocol or the need to write robust applications, but it's a useful additional layer of tests that fits between the communications interface and your internal code.

Validation can take place at several levels. Structural validation makes certain that XML element and attribute structures meet specified requirements, but doesn't clarify much about the textual content of those structures. Data validation looks more closely at the contents of those structures, ensuring that they conform to rules about what type of information should be present. Other kinds of validation, often called business rules, may check relationships between information and a higher level of sanity-checking, but this is usually the domain of procedural code, not schema-based validation.

XML is a good foundation for pipelines of transformations using widely available tools. Since each of these transformations introduces a risk of error, and each error is easier to fix when detected near its source, it is good practice to introduce check points in the pipeline where the documents are validated. Some applications will find that validating after each step is an overhead cost they can't bear, while others will find that it is crucial to detect the errors just as they happen, before they can cause any harm and when they are still easy to diagnose. Different situations may have different validation requirements, and it may make sense to validate more heavily during pipeline design than during production deployment.

Documentation

XML schemas are frequently used to document XML vocabularies, even when validation isn't a requirement. Schemas provide a formal description of the vocabulary with a precision and conciseness that can be difficult to achieve in prose. It is very unusual to publish the specification of a new XML vocabulary without attaching some form of XML schema.

The machine-readability of schemas gives them several advantages as documentation. Human-readable documentation can be generated from the schema's formal description. Schema IDEs, for instance, provide graphical views that help to understand the structure of the documents. Developers can also create XSLT transformations that generate a description of the structure. (This technique was used to generate the structure of Chapters 15 and 16 from the W3C XML Schema for W3C XML Schema published on the W3C web site.)

We will see, in Chapter 14, that W3C XML Schema has introduced additional facilities to annotate schemas with both structured or unstructured information, making it easier to use schemas explicitly as a documentation framework.

Querying Support

The first versions of XPath and XSLT were defined to work without any explicit understanding of the structure of the documents being manipulated. This has worked well, but has imposed performance and functionality limits. Knowledge of the document's structure could improve the efficiency of optimizers, and some functions, such as sorts and equality testing, may be improved by a datatype system. The second version of XPath and XSLT and the first version of XQuery (a new specification defining an XML query language that is still a work in progress) will rely on the availability of a W3C XML Schema for those features.

Data Binding

Although it isn't especially difficult to write applications that process XML documents using the SAX, DOM, and similar APIs, it is a low-level task, both repetitive and error-prone. The cost of building and maintaining these programs grows rapidly as the number of elements and attributes in a vocabulary grows. The idea of automating these through "binding" the information available in XML documents directly into the structures of applications (generally as objects or RDBMS tables) is probably as old as markup.

Ronald Bourret, who maintains a list of XML Data Binding Resources at *http://www.rpbourret.com/xml/XMLDataBinding.htm*, makes a distinction between design time and runtime binding tools. While runtime binding tools do their best to perform a binding based on the structure of the documents and applications discovered by introspection, design time binding tools rely on a model formalized in a schema of some kind. He describes this category as "usually more flexible in the mappings they can support."

Many different languages, either specific or general-purpose XML schema languages, define these bindings. W3C XML Schema has a lot of traction in this area; many data-binding tools were started to support W3C XML Schema for even its early releases, well before the specification was finalized.

Guided Editing

XML editors (and SGML editors before them) have long used schemas to present users with appropriate choices over the course of document creation and editing. While DTDs provided structural information, recent XML schema languages add more sophisticated structural information and datatype information.

The W3C is creating a standard API that can be used by guided editing applications to ask a schema processor which action can be performed at a certain location in a document—for instance: "Can I insert this new element here?", "Can I update this text node to this value?", etc. The Document Object Model (DOM) Level 3 Abstract Schemas and Load and Save Specification (which is still a work in progress) defines "Abstract Schemas" generic enough to cover both DTDs and W3C XML Schema (and potentially other schema languages as well). When finalized and widely adopted, this API should allow you to plug the schema processor of your choice into any editing application.

Another approach to editing applications builds editors from the information provided in schemas. Combined with information about presentation and controls, these tools let users edit XML documents in applications custom-built for a particular schema. For example, the W3C XForms specification (which is still a work in progress) proposes to separate the logic and layout of the form from the structure of the data to edit, and relies on a W3C XML Schema to define this structure.

W3C XML Schema

XML 1.0 included a set of tools for defining XML document structures, called Document Type Definitions (DTDs). DTDs provide a set of tools for defining which element and attribute structures are permitted in a document, as well as mechanisms for providing default values for attributes, defining reusable content (entities), and some kinds of metadata information (notations). While DTDs are widely supported and used, many XML developers quickly outgrew the capabilities DTDs provide. An alternative schema proposal, XML-Data, was even submitted to the W3C before XML 1.0 was a Recommendation.

The World Wide Web Consortium (W3C), keeper of the XML specification, sought to build a new language for describing XML documents. It needed to provide more precision in describing document structures and their contents, to support XML namespaces, and to use an XML vocabulary to describe XML vocabularies. The W3C's XML Schema Working Group spent two years developing two normative Recommendations, XML Schema Part 1: Structures, and XML Schema Part 2: Datatypes, along with a nonnormative Recommendation, XML Schema Part 0: Primer.

W3C XML Schema is designed to support all of these applications. An initial set of requirements, formally described in the XML Schema Requirements Note (*http:// www.w3.org/TR/NOTE-xml-schema-req*), listed a wide variety of usage scenarios for schemas as well as for the design principles that guided its creation.

In the rest of this book, we explore the details of W3C XML Schema and its many capabilities, focusing on how to apply it to specific XML document situations.

CHAPTER 2
Our First Schema

Starting with a simple example (a limited number of elements and attributes and containing no namespaces), we will see how a first schema can be simply derived from the document structure, using a catalog of the elements in a document as we write a DTD for this document.

The Instance Document

The instance document, which we use in the first part of this book, is a simple library file describing a book, its author, and its characters:

```
<?xml version="1.0"?>
<library>
  <book id="b0836217462" available="true">
    <isbn>
      0836217462
    </isbn>
    <title lang="en">
      Being a Dog Is a Full-Time Job
    </title>
    <author id="CMS">
      <name>
        Charles M Schulz
      </name>
      <born>
        1922-11-26
      </born>
      <dead>
        2000-02-12
      </dead>
    </author>
    <character id="PP">
      <name>
        Peppermint Patty
      </name>
      <born>
```

```
        1966-08-22
      </born>
      <qualification>
        bold, brash and tomboyish
      </qualification>
    </character>
    <character id="Snoopy">
      <name>
        Snoopy
      </name>
      <born>
        1950-10-04
      </born>
      <qualification>
        extroverted beagle
      </qualification>
    </character>
    <character id="Schroeder">
      <name>
        Schroeder
      </name>
      <born>
        1951-05-30
      </born>
      <qualification>
        brought classical music to the Peanuts strip
      </qualification>
    </character>
    <character id="Lucy">
      <name>
        Lucy
      </name>
      <born>
        1952-03-03
      </born>
      <qualification>
        bossy, crabby and selfish
      </qualification>
    </character>
  </book>
</library>
```

Our First Schema

We will see, in the course of this book, that there are many different styles for writing a schema, and there are even more approaches to deriving a schema from an instance document. For our first schema, we will adopt a style that is familiar to those of you who have already worked with DTDs. We'll start by creating a classified list of the elements and attributes found in the schema.

The elements existing in our instance document are author, book, born, character, dead, isbn, library, name, qualification, and title, and the attributes are available, id, and lang.

We will build our first schema by defining each element in turn under our schema document element (named, unsurprisingly, schema), which belongs to the W3C XML Schema namespace (*http://www.w3.org/2001/XMLSchema*) and is usually prefixed as "xs."

Before we start, we need to classify the elements and, for this exercise, give some key definitions for understanding how W3C XML Schema does this classification. (We will see these definitions in more detail in the chapters about simple and complex types.)

The content model characterizes the types of children elements and text nodes that can be included in an element (without paying any attention to the attributes).

The content model is said to be "empty" when no children elements nor text nodes are expected, "simple" when only text nodes are accepted, "complex" when only subelements are expected, and "mixed" when both text nodes and sub-elements can be present. Note that to determine the content model, we pay attention only to the element and text nodes and ignore any attribute, comment, or processing instruction that could be included. For instance, an element with some attributes, a comment, and a couple of processing instructions would have an "empty" content model if it has no text or element children.

Elements such as name, born, and title have simple content models:

```
.../...

<title lang="en">
  Being a Dog Is a Full-Time Job
</title>
.../...

<name>
  Charles M Schulz
</name>

<born>
  1922-11-26
</born>
.../...
```

Elements such as library or character have complex content models:

```
<library>
  <book id="b0836217462" available="true">
    .../...
  </book>
</library>
```

```
<character id="Lucy">
  <name>
    Lucy
  </name>
  <born>
    1952-03-03
  </born>
  <qualification>
    bossy, crabby and selfish
  </qualification>
</character>
```

Within elements that have a simple content model, we can distinguish those which have attributes and those which cannot have any attributes. Later chapters discuss how W3C XML Schema can also represent empty and mixed content models.

W3C XML Schema considers the elements that have a simple content model and no attributes "simple types," while all the other elements (such as simple content with attributes and other content models) are "complex types." In other words, when an element can only have text nodes and doesn't accept any child elements or attributes, it is considered a simple type; in all the other cases, it is a complex type.

Attributes always have a simple type since they have no children and contain only a text value.

In our example, elements such as author or title have a complex type:

```
<author id="CMS">
  <name>
    Charles M Schulz
  </name>
  <born>
    1922-11-26
  </born>
  <dead>
    2000-02-12
  </dead>
</author>
.../...

<title lang="en">
  Being a Dog Is a Full-Time Job
</title>
```

While elements such as born or qualification (and, of course, all the attributes) have a simple type:

```
<born>
  1922-11-26
</born>
.../...

<qualification>
  brought classical music to the Peanuts strip
```

```
</qualification>
.../...

<book available="true"/>
```

Now that we have criteria to classify our components, we can define each of them. Let's start with the simplest one by taking a type element, such as the name element that can be found in author or character:

```
<name>
  Charles M Schulz
</name>
```

To define such an element, we use an xs:element (global definition), included directly under the xs:schema document element:

```
<xs:schema xmlns:xs="http://www.w3.org/2001/XMLSchema">
  <xs:element name="name" type="xs:string"/>
  .../...
</xs:schema>
```

The value used to reference the datatype (xs:string) is prefixed by xs, the prefix associated with W3C XML Schema. This means that xs:string is a predefined W3C XML Schema datatype.

The same can be done for all the other simple types as well as for the attributes:

```
<xs:schema xmlns:xs="http://www.w3.org/2001/XMLSchema">
  <xs:element name="name" type="xs:string"/>
  <xs:element name="qualification" type="xs:string"/>
  <xs:element name="born" type="xs:date"/>
  <xs:element name="dead" type="xs:date"/>
  <xs:element name="isbn" type="xs:string"/>
  <xs:attribute name="id" type="xs:ID"/>
  <xs:attribute name="available" type="xs:boolean"/>
  <xs:attribute name="lang" type="xs:language"/>
  .../...
</xs:schema>
```

While we said that this design style would be familiar to DTD users, we must note that it is flatter than a DTD since the declaration of the attributes is done outside of the declaration of the elements. This results in a schema in which elements and attributes get fairly equal treatment. We will see, though, that when a schema describes an XML vocabulary that uses a namespace, this simple flat style is impossible to use most of time.

The assimilation of simple type elements and attributes is a simplification compared to the XPath, DOM, and Infoset data models. These consider a simple type element to be an item having a single child item of type "character," and an attribute to be an item having a normalized value. The benefit of this simplification is we can use simple datatypes to define simple type elements and attributes indifferently and write in a consistent fashion:

```
<xs:element name="isbn" type="xs:string"/>
```
or
```
<xs:attribute name="isbn" type="xs:string"/>
```

The order of the definitions in a schema isn't significant; we can now take the next step in terms of type complexity and define the title element that appears in the instance document as:

```
<title lang="en">
  Being a Dog Is a Full-Time Job
</title>
```

Since this element has an attribute, it has a complex type. Since it has only a text node, it is considered to have a simple content. We will, therefore, write its definition as:

```
<xs:element name="title">
  <xs:complexType>
    <xs:simpleContent>
      <xs:extension base="xs:string">
        <xs:attribute ref="lang"/>
      </xs:extension>
    </xs:simpleContent>
  </xs:complexType>
</xs:element>
```

The XML syntax makes it verbose, but this can almost be read as plain English as "the element named title has a complex type which is a simple content obtained by extending the predefined datatype xs:string by adding the attribute defined in this schema and having the name lang."

The remaining elements (library, book, author, and character) are all complex types with complex content. They are defined by defining the sequence of elements and attributes that will compose them.

The library element, the most straightforward of them, is defined as:

```
<xs:element name="library">
  <xs:complexType>
    <xs:sequence>
      <xs:element ref="book" maxOccurs="unbounded"/>
    </xs:sequence>
  </xs:complexType>
</xs:element>
```

This definition can be read as "the element named library is a complex type composed of a sequence of 1 to many occurrences (note the maxOccurs attribute) of elements defined as having a name book."

The element author, which has an attribute and for which we may consider the date of death as optional, could be:

```
<xs:element name="author">
  <xs:complexType>
    <xs:sequence>
      <xs:element ref="name"/>
      <xs:element ref="born"/>
      <xs:element ref="dead" minOccurs="0"/>
    </xs:sequence>
    <xs:attribute ref="id"/>
  </xs:complexType>
</xs:element>
```

This means the element named author is a complex type composed of a sequence of three elements (name, born, and dead), and id. The dead element is optional- it may occur zero times.

The minOccurs and maxOccurs attributes, which we have seen in a couple of previous elements, allow us to define the minimum and maximum number of occurrences. Their default value is 1, which means that when they are both missing, the element must appear exactly one time in the sequence. The special value "unbounded" may be used for maxOccurs when the maximum number of occurrences is unlimited.

The attributes need to be defined after the sequence. The remaining elements (book and character) can be defined in the same way, which leads us to the following full schema:

```
<?xml version="1.0"?>
<xs:schema xmlns:xs="http://www.w3.org/2001/XMLSchema">
  <xs:element name="name" type="xs:string"/>
  <xs:element name="qualification" type="xs:string"/>
  <xs:element name="born" type="xs:date"/>
  <xs:element name="dead" type="xs:date"/>
  <xs:element name="isbn" type="xs:string"/>
  <xs:attribute name="id" type="xs:ID"/>
  <xs:attribute name="available" type="xs:boolean"/>
  <xs:attribute name="lang" type="xs:language"/>
  <xs:element name="title">
    <xs:complexType>
      <xs:simpleContent>
        <xs:extension base="xs:string">
          <xs:attribute ref="lang"/>
        </xs:extension>
      </xs:simpleContent>
    </xs:complexType>
  </xs:element>
  <xs:element name="library">
    <xs:complexType>
```

```
        <xs:sequence>
          <xs:element ref="book" maxOccurs="unbounded"/>
        </xs:sequence>
      </xs:complexType>
    </xs:element>
    <xs:element name="author">
      <xs:complexType>
        <xs:sequence>
          <xs:element ref="name"/>
          <xs:element ref="born"/>
          <xs:element ref="dead" minOccurs="0"/>
        </xs:sequence>
        <xs:attribute ref="id"/>
      </xs:complexType>
    </xs:element>
    <xs:element name="book">
      <xs:complexType>
        <xs:sequence>
          <xs:element ref="isbn"/>
          <xs:element ref="title"/>
          <xs:element ref="author" minOccurs="0" maxOccurs="unbounded"/>
          <xs:element ref="character" minOccurs="0"
            maxOccurs="unbounded"/>
        </xs:sequence>
        <xs:attribute ref="id"/>
        <xs:attribute ref="available"/>
      </xs:complexType>
    </xs:element>
    <xs:element name="character">
      <xs:complexType>
        <xs:sequence>
          <xs:element ref="name"/>
          <xs:element ref="born"/>
          <xs:element ref="qualification"/>
        </xs:sequence>
        <xs:attribute ref="id"/>
      </xs:complexType>
    </xs:element>
  </xs:schema>
```

First Findings

Even in this very simple schema, we have learned a lot about what W3C XML
Schema has to offer.

W3C XML Schema Is Modular

In this example, we defined simple components (elements and attributes in this case,
but we will see in the next chapters how to define other kinds of components) that
we used to build more complex components. This is one of the key principles that

have guided the editors of W3C XML Schema. These editors have borrowed many concepts of object-oriented design to develop complex components.

If we draw a parallel between datatypes and classes, the elements and attributes can be compared to objects. Each of the component definitions that we included in our first schema is similar to an object. Referencing one of these components to build a new element is similar to creating a new object by cloning the already defined component.

In the next chapters, we will see how we can also create the components "in place" (where they are needed) as well as create datatypes from which we can derive elements and attributes the same way we can instantiate a class to create an object.

W3C XML Schema Is Both About Structure and Datatyping

Note also that W3C XML Schema is pursuing two different levels of validation in this first example: we have defined both rules about the structure of the document and rules above the content of leaf nodes of the document. The W3C Recommendation makes a clear distinction between these two levels by publishing the recommendation in two parts (Part 1: Structures and Part 2: Datatypes), which are relatively independent.

There is also a big difference between simple types, which are about datatyping and constraining the content of leaf nodes in the tree structure of an XML document, and complex types, which are about defining the structure of a document.

Flat Design, Global Components

Finally, note the flatness of this schema: each component (element or attribute) is defined directly under the xs:schema document element.

Components defined directly under the xs:schema document element are called "global" components. These have a couple of notable properties: they can be referenced anywhere in the schema as well as in the other schema that may include or import this schema (we will see in the next chapters how to import or include schemas), and all the global elements can be used as document root elements.

CHAPTER 3

Giving Some Depth to Our First Schema

Our first schema was very flat, and all its components were defined at the top level. Our second attempt will give it more depth and show how local components may be defined.

Working From the Structure of the Instance Document

For this second schema, we follow a style opposite from the one we used in Chapter 2, and we define all the elements and attributes locally where they appear in the document.

Following the document structure, we will start by defining our document element library. This element was defined in the earlier schema as:

```
<xs:element name="library">
  <xs:complexType>
    <xs:sequence>
      <xs:element ref="book" maxOccurs="unbounded"/>
    </xs:sequence>
  </xs:complexType>
</xs:element>
```

In our new schema, we will keep the same construct and the same structure, but we will replace the reference to the book element with the actual definition of this element:

```
<xs:element name="library">
  <xs:complexType>
    <xs:sequence>
      <xs:element name="book" maxOccurs="unbounded">
        <xs:complexType>
          <xs:sequence>
            <xs:element ref="isbn"/>
            <xs:element ref="title"/>
            <xs:element ref="author" minOccurs="0"
```

```
              maxOccurs="unbounded"/>
          <xs:element ref="character" minOccurs="0"
              maxOccurs="unbounded"/>
        </xs:sequence>
        <xs:attribute ref="id"/>
        <xs:attribute ref="available"/>
      </xs:complexType>
    </xs:element>
  </xs:sequence>
  </xs:complexType>
</xs:element>
```

Because the definition of the book element is contained inside the definition of the library element, other definitions of book elements could be done at other locations in the schema without any risk of confusion—except maybe by human readers.

If all the elements and attributes still referenced in this schema are defined as global, this piece of schema is valid and accurately describes our schema. The only differences between the first schema and this intermediary step are that the definition of the book element cannot be reused elsewhere, and the book element can no longer be a document element any longer.

We can also reiterate the same operation and perform the definitions of all the elements and all the attributes locally:

```
<?xml version="1.0"?>
<xs:schema xmlns:xs="http://www.w3.org/2001/XMLSchema">
  <xs:element name="library">
    <xs:complexType>
      <xs:sequence>
        <xs:element name="book" maxOccurs="unbounded">
          <xs:complexType>
            <xs:sequence>
              <xs:element name="isbn" type="xs:integer"/>
              <xs:element name="title">
                <xs:complexType>
                <xs:simpleContent>
                <xs:extension base="xs:string">
                <xs:attribute name="lang" type="xs:language"/>
                </xs:extension>
                </xs:simpleContent>
                </xs:complexType>
              </xs:element>
              <xs:element name="author" minOccurs="0"
                maxOccurs="unbounded">
                <xs:complexType>
                <xs:sequence>
                <xs:element name="name" type="xs:string"/>
                <xs:element name="born" type="xs:date"/>
                <xs:element name="dead" type="xs:date"/>
                </xs:sequence>
                <xs:attribute name="id" type="xs:ID"/>
                </xs:complexType>
```

```
      </xs:element>
      <xs:element name="character" minOccurs="0"
        maxOccurs="unbounded">
        <xs:complexType>
         <xs:sequence>
         <xs:element name="name" type="xs:string"/>
         <xs:element name="born" type="xs:date"/>
         <xs:element name="qualification" type="xs:string"/>
         </xs:sequence>
         <xs:attribute name="id" type="xs:ID"/>
        </xs:complexType>
      </xs:element>
     </xs:sequence>
     <xs:attribute name="id" type="xs:ID"/>
     <xs:attribute name="available" type="xs:boolean"/>
    </xs:complexType>
   </xs:element>
  </xs:sequence>
 </xs:complexType>
 </xs:element>
</xs:schema>
```

Apart from an obvious difference in style, this new schema is validating the same instance document as in Chapter 2. It is not, strictly speaking, equivalent to the first one: it is less reusable (the document element is the only one that could be reused in another schema) and more strict, since it validates only the documents that have a library document element. Chapter 2's schema must validate documents having any of the elements as a document element.

 The price we pay to constrain the value of the document root element with W3C XML Schema is a loss of reusability. This has been widely criticized without affecting the decision of its editors. We will see, fortunately, that there are some workarounds to limit this loss for applications that need to constrain the value of the document element.

New Lessons

Although this schema describes the same document as the one in Chapter 2, it illustrates very different aspects of W3C XML Schema.

Depth Versus Modularity?

Even though we will present features to balance this fact in the next chapters—xs: complexType and xs:group—we have sacrificed the modularity of our first schema to gain the depth and structure of the second one. This is a general tendency in W3C XML Schema.

In practice, you will probably want to keep a balance between these two opposite styles and allow a certain level of depth under several global elements.

There are two cases, however, in which these two styles are not equivalent. The first is when elements with the same name need to be defined with different contents at different locations. In this case, local element definitions should be used (at least at all the location except one) since the elements are identified by their names.

In our example, the element name appears both within author and character with the same datatype. We may want to define the element name with different content models in author and character, as in this instance document:

```
<?xml version="1.0"?>
<library>
  <book id="b0836217462" available="true">
    <isbn>
      0836217462
    </isbn>
    <title lang="en">
      Being a Dog Is a Full-Time Job
    </title>
    <author id="CMS">
      <name>
        <first>
          Charles
        </first>
        <middle>
          M.
        </middle>
        <last>
          Schulz
        </last>
      </name>
      <born>
        1922-11-26
      </born>
      <dead>
        2000-02-12
      </dead>
    </author>
    <character id="Snoopy">
      <name>
        Snoopy
      </name>
      <born>
        1950-10-04
      </born>
      <qualification>
        extroverted beagle
      </qualification>
    </character>
  </book>
</library>
```

Since we can define only one global element named name, we need to define at least one of the name elements locally under its parent.

The W3C Schema for XML Schema gives several examples of elements having different types depending on their location. We will see this used in the next section in our Russian doll schema: global definitions of elements have a different type in the schema for schema than local definitions or references, even though they use the same element name (xs:element).

 Whether defining elements with the same name and different datatypes is good practice or not is subject to discussion. It may be confusing for human authors and more difficult to document, but W3C XML Schema gives, through local definitions, a way to avoid any confusion for the applications that will process these documents. In our example, for instance, we have two occurrences of a name element under author and under character. It is perfectly possible to define different constraints and even contents on those two elements. Although this could be presented as overloaded element names ("character/name" versus "author/name"), I find this practice unreliable, since we often don't have a clear and simple way to identify those two contexts.

Another example is recursive schema, in which an element can be included within an element of the same type directly or indirectly in a child element. In this case, a flat design employing references must be used since the depth of these recursive structures is unlimited.

W3C XML Schema offers several examples of such elements with local definitions of elements that can be recursively nested, as is the case in our second schema. A flat design must be used since these elements need to be referenced if we don't want to limit the maximum depth of the structure, and the schema for schema uses a reference mechanism. (The actual mechanism used in this case involves an element group, a feature we have not seen yet but is equivalent to an actual reference to an element.)

Russian Doll and Object-Oriented Design

The style of defining elements and attributes locally is often called the Russian doll design, since the definition of each element is embedded in the definition of its parent, in the same way Russian dolls are embedded into each other.

If we look at the Russian dolls with our object-oriented lenses, we may say that the objects are now created locally where they are needed as opposed to being created globally and cloned when we need them (which was the case as in our first schema).

At this point, we still need to learn how we can create types that are the equivalent of classes of objects and containers, and that will let us manipulate sets of objects.

Where Have the Element Types Gone?

Those of you who are familiar with XML (or SGML) and its DTD are used to identifying the elements though the term "element type." The XML 1.0 Recommendation states that "each element has a type, identified by name." This is further disambiguated by the namespaces specification, which explain that "an XML namespace is a collection of names, identified by a URI reference [RFC2396], which are used in XML documents as element types and attribute names."

A surprising feature of our Russian doll schema is that this fundamental notion of element type has completely disappeared, and there is no way to tell which element type name is. Two different elements have been defined as having a name equal to name. These have an independent definition, which is identical in our example, but could be different—such as if we had decomposed the first, middle, and last names for authors, but not for characters. The notion of element type name doesn't mean anything if we do not specify in which context it is used.

This loss has such little importance that few people have even noticed it. There are some situations where we need to identify elements, though—for instance to document XML vocabularies. A convenient way to write a reference manual for a XML vocabulary is to write an index of the element names with their definition. This becomes much more complex when there is no clear match between element types and their definitions and content models.

 RDF is another application that relies on element types. RDF uses element types to identify elements as objects in its triples. The element "name" of the namespace *http://dyomedea.com/ns* is identified as *http://dyomedea.com/ns#name*. Cutting the link between element types and their schema definition makes it difficult, if not impossible, to answer basic questions, such as what's the content model of *http://dyomedea.com/ns#name*, and where can I find its definition.

I was confronted with this issue when writing the reference guide of this book since the W3C XML Schema for W3C XML Schema uses many local element definitions. I came to the conclusion that the fact that the same element type (such as xs: restriction, which we will see later on) can have different content models with a different semantic, depending on its location in a schema, adds a significant amount of difficulty in understanding the language and reading a schema.

CHAPTER 4

Using Predefined Simple Datatypes

W3C XML Schema provides an extensive set of predefined datatypes. W3C XML Schema derives many of these predefined datatypes from a smaller set of "primitive" datatypes that have a specific meaning and semantic and cannot be derived from other types. We will see how we can use these types to define our own datatypes by derivation to meet more specific needs in the next chapter.

Figure 4-1 provides a map of predefined datatypes and the relationships between them.

Lexical and Value Spaces

W3C XML Schema introduced a decoupling between the data, as it can be read from the instance documents (the "lexical space"), and the value, as interpreted according to the datatype (the "value space").

Before we can enter into the definition of these two spaces, we must examine the processing model and the transformations endured by a value written in a XML document before it is validated. Element and attribute content proceeds through the following steps during processing:

Serialization space
> The series of bytes that is actually stored in a document (either as the value of an attribute or as a text node) may be seen as belonging to a first space, which we may call the "serialization space."

Parsed space
> The XML 1.0 Recommendation makes it clear that the serialization space is not directly meaningful to applications, and a first transformation is performed on the value by conforming XML parsers before the value reaches an application: characters are converted into Unicode, and ends of lines (for text nodes and attributes) and whitespaces (only for attributes) are normalized. The result of

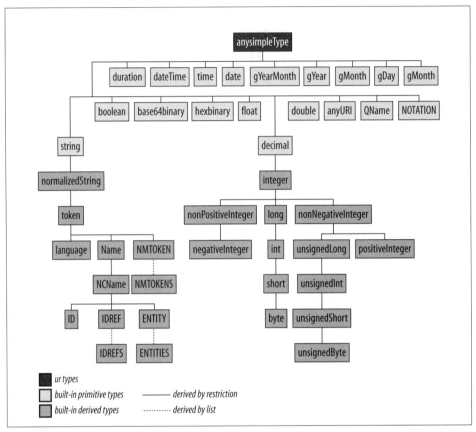

Figure 4-1. W3C XML Schema type hierarchy

this transformation is what reaches the applications—including schema processors—and belongs to what we may call the "parsed space."

Lexical space

Before doing any validation, W3C XML Schema performs a second round of whitespace processing on this value reported by the XML parser. This depends on the value's datatype and may either ignore, normalize, or collapse the whitespaces. The value after this whitespace processing belongs to the "lexical space" defined in the W3C XML Schema Recommendation.

Value space

W3C XML Schema considers an item from the lexical space to be a representation of an abstract value whose meaning or semantic is defined by its datatype and can be a piece of text, and also a number, a date, or qualified name. The ensemble of abstract values is defined as the "value space."

Each datatype has its own lexical and value spaces and its own rules to associate a lexical representation with a value; for many datatypes, a single value can have multiple lexical representations (for instance, the <xs:float> value "3.14116" can also be written equivalently as "03.14116," "3.141160," or ".314116E1"). This distinction is important since the basic operations performed on the values (such as equality testing or sorting) are done on the value space. "3.14116" is considered to be equal to "03.14116" when the type is xs:float and is different when the type is xs:string. The same applies to sort orders: some datatypes have a full order relation (every pair of values can be compared), others have no order relation at all, and the remaining types have a partial order relation (values cannot always be compared).

> Although future versions of APIs might send these values to the applications, the transformations between parsed, lexical, and value spaces are currently done for the sake of the validation only, and don't impact the values sent by a validating parser.

Whitespace Processing

The handling of special characters (tab, linefeeds, carriage returns and spaces, which are often used only to "pretty print" XML documents) has always been very controversial. W3C XML Schema has imposed a two-step generic algorithm, which is applied to most of the predefined datatypes (actually, on all of them except two, xs:string and xs:normalizedString).

Whitespace replacement
> This is the first step of whitespace processing applied to the parsed value. During whitespace replacement, all occurrences of any whitespace—#x9 (tab), #xA (linefeed), and #xD (carriage return)—are replaced with a space (#x20). The number of characters is not changed by this step, which is applied to all the predefined datatypes (except for xs:string, since no whitespace replacement is performed on the parsed value for this).

Whitespace collapse
> The second step removes the leading and trailing spaces, and replaces all contiguous occurrences of spaces by a single space character. This is applied on all the predefined datatypes (except for xs:string, since no whitespace replacement is performed on the parsed value for this, and for xs:normalizedString, in which whitespaces are only normalized).

> This notion of "normalized string" does not match the XPath function normalize-space( ), which corresponds with what W3C XML Schema calls whitespace collapsing. It is also different from the DOM normalize( ) method, which is a merge of adjacent text objects.

String Datatypes

This section discusses datatypes derived from the xs:string primitive datatype as well as other datatypes that have a similar behavior (namely, xs:hexBinary, xs:base64Binary, xs:anyURI, xs:QName, and xs:NOTATION). These types are not expected to carry any quantifiable value (W3C XML Schema doesn't even expect to be able to sort them) and their value space is identical to their lexical space except when explicitly described otherwise. One should note that even though they are grouped in this section because they have a similar behavior, these primitive datatypes are considered quite different by the Recommendation.

The datatypes covered in this section are shown in Figure 4-2.

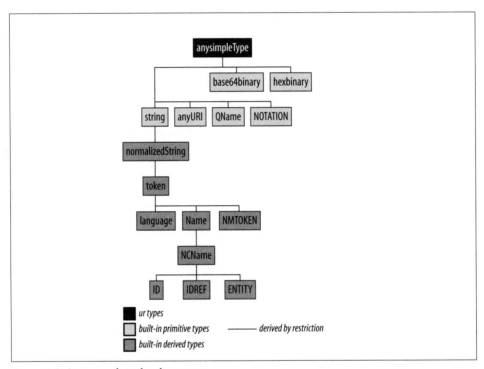

Figure 4-2. Strings and similar datatypes

The two exceptions in whitespace processing (xs:string and xs:normalizedString) are string datatypes. One of the main differences between these types is the applied whitespace processing. To stress this difference, we will classify these types by their whitespace processing.

No Whitespace Replacement

xs:string

> This string datatype is the only predefined datatype for which no whitespace replacement is performed. As we will see in the next chapter, the whitespace replacement performed on user-defined datatypes derived from this type can be defined without restriction. On the other hand, a user datatype cannot be defined as having no whitespace replacement if it is derived from any predefined datatype other than xs:string.
>
> As expected, a string is a set of characters matching the definition given by XML 1.0, namely, "legal characters are tab, carriage return, line feed, and the legal characters of Unicode and ISO/IEC 10646."
>
> The value of the following element:

```
<title lang="en">
    Being a Dog Is
    a Full-Time Job
</title>
```

> is the full string:

```
Being a Dog Is
a Full-Time Job
```

> with all its tabs, and CR/LF if the title element is a type xs:string.

Normalized Strings

xs:normalizedString

> The normalized string is the only predefined datatype in which whitespace replacement is performed without collapsing.
>
> The lexical space of xs:normalizedString is the same as the lexical space of xs:string from which it is derived—except that since any occurrence of #x9 (tab), #xA (linefeed), and #xD (carriage return) are replaced by a #x20 (space), these three characters cannot be found in its lexical and value spaces.
>
> The value of the same element:

```
<title lang="en">
    Being a Dog Is
    a Full-Time Job
</title>
```

> is now the string:

```
    Being a Dog Is    a Full-Time Job
```

> in which all the whitespaces have been replaced by spaces if the title element is a type xs:normalizedString.

There is no additional constraint on normalized strings. Any value that is valid as a xs:string is also valid as a xs:normalizedString but its tabs, linefeed and CR will be replaced by spaces. The difference is the whitespace processing that is applied when the lexical value is calculated.

Collapsed Strings

Whitespace collapsing is performed after whitespace replacement by trimming the leading and trailing spaces and replacing all the contiguous occurrences of spaces with a single space. All the predefined datatypes (except, as we have seen, xs:string and xs:normalizedString) are whitespace collapsed.

We will classify tokens, binary formats, URIs, qualified names, notations, and all their derived types under this category. Although these datatypes share a number of properties, we must stress again that this categorization is done for the purpose of explanation and does not directly appear in the Recommendation.

Tokens

xs:token

xs:token is xs:normalizedString on which the whitespaces have been collapsed. Since whitespaces are accepted in the lexical space of xs:token, this type is better described as a "tokenized" string than as a "token"!

The same element:

```
<title lang="en">
    Being a Dog Is
    a Full-Time Job
</title>
```

is still a valid xs:token, and its value is now the string:

```
Being a Dog Is a Full-Time Job
```

in which all the whitespaces have been replaced by spaces, any trailing spaces are removed, and contiguous sequences of spaces are replaced by single spaces.

As is the case with xs:normalizedString, there is no constraint on xs:token, and any value that is a valid xs:string is also a valid xs:token. The difference is the whitespace processing that is applied when the lexical value is calculated. This is not true of derived datatypes that have additional constraints on their lexical and value space. The restriction on the lexical spaces of xs:normalizedString is, therefore, a restriction by projection of their parsed space (different values of their parsed space are transformed into a single value of their lexical space), and not a restriction by invalidating values of their lexical space, as is the case for all the other predefined datatypes.

The predefined datatypes derived from xs:token are xs:language, xs:NMTOKEN, and xs:Name.

xs:language

This was created to accept all the language codes standardized by RFC 1766. Some valid values for this datatype are en, en-US, fr, or fr-FR.

xs:NMTOKEN

This corresponds to the XML 1.0 "Nmtoken" (Name token) production, which is a single token (a set of characters without spaces) composed of characters allowed in XML name. Some valid values for this datatype are "Snoopy", "CMS", "1950-10-04", or "0836217462". Invalid values include "brought classical music to the Peanuts strip" (spaces are forbidden) or "bold,brash" (commas are forbidden).

xs:Name

This is similar to xs:NMTOKEN with the additional restriction that the values must start with a letter or the characters ":" or "-". This datatype conforms to the XML 1.0 definition of a "Name." Some valid values for this datatype are Snoopy, CMS, or -1950-10-04-10:00. Invalid values include 0836217462 (xs:Name cannot start with a number) or bold,brash (commas are forbidden). This datatype should not be used for names that may be "qualified" by a namespace prefix, since we will see another datatype (xs:QName) that has a specific semantic for these values. The datatype xs:NCName is derived from xs:Name.

xs:NCName

This is the "noncolonized name" defined by Namespaces in XML1.0, i.e., a xs:Name without any colons (":"). As such, this datatype is probably the predefined datatype that is closest to the notion of a "name" in most of the programming languages, even though some characters such as "-" or "." may still be a problem in many cases. Some valid values for this datatype are Snoopy, CMS, -1950-10-04-10-00, or 1950-10-04. Invalid values include -1950-10-04:10-00 or bold:brash (colons are forbidden). xs:ID, xs:IDREF, and xs:ENTITY are derived from xs:NCName.

xs:ID

This is derived from xs:NCName. The one constraint added to its value space is that there must not be any duplicate values in a document. In other words, the values of attributes or simple type elements having this datatype can be used as unique identifiers, and this datatype emulates the XML 1.0 ID attribute type. We will see this feature in more detail in Chapter 9.

xs:IDREF

This is derived from xs:NCName. The constraint added to its value space is that it must match an ID defined in the same document. I will explain this feature in more detail in Chapter 9.

`xs:ENTITY`

Also provided for compatibility with XML 1.0 DTDs, this is derived from `xs:NCName` and must match an unparsed entity defined in a DTD.

 XML 1.0 gives the following definition of unparsed entities: "an unparsed entity is a resource whose contents may or may not be text, and if text, may be other than XML. Each unparsed entity has an associated notation, identified by name. Beyond a requirement that an XML processor make the identifiers for the entity and notation available to the application, XML places no constraints on the contents of unparsed entities." In practice, this mechanism has seldom been used, as the general usage is to define links to the resources that could be defined as unparsed entities.

Qualified names

`xs:QName`

Following Namespaces in XML 1.0, `xs:QName` supports the use of namespace-prefixed names. A namespace prefix xs:QName treats a shortcut to identify a URI. Each xs:QName effectively contains a set of tuples {namespace name, local part}, in which the namespace name is the URI associated to the prefix through a namespace declaration. Even though the lexical space of `xs:QName` is very close to the lexical space of `xs:Name` (the only constraint on the lexical space is that there is a maximum of one colon allowed in an `xs:QName`, which cannot be the first character), the value spaces of these datatypes are completely different (a scalar for `xs:Name` and a tuple for `xs:QName`) and `xs:QName` is defined as a primitive datatype. The constraint added by this datatype over an `xs:Name` is the prefix must be defined as a namespace prefix in the scope of the element in which this datatype is used.

W3C XML Schema itself has already given us some examples of QNames. When we write `<xs:attribute name="lang" type="xs:language"/>`, the type attribute is an `xs:QName` and its value is the tuple:

    {"http://www.w3.org/2001/XMLSchema", "language"}

because the URI:

    "http://www.w3.org/2001/XMLSchema"

was assigned to the prefix "xs:". If there is no namespace declaration for this prefix, the type attribute is considered invalid.

The prefix of an `xs:QName` is optional. We are also able to write:

    <xs:element ref="book" maxOccurs="unbounded"/>

in which the ref attribute is also a `xs:QName` and its value the tuple:

    {NULL, "book"}

because we haven't defined any default namespace. `xs:QName` does support default namespaces; if a default namespace is defined in the scope of this element, the value of its URI is used for this tuple.

URIs

`xs:anyURI`

This is another string datatype in which lexical and value spaces are different. This datatype tries to compensate for the differences of format between XML and URIs as specified in the RFCs 2396 and 2732. These RFCs are not very friendly toward non-ASCII characters and require many character escapings that are not necessary in XML. The W3C XML Schema Recommendation doesn't describe the transformation to perform, noting only that it is similar to what is described for XLink link locators.

As an example of this transformation, the `href` attribute of an XHTML link written as:

```
<a href="http://dmoz.org/World/Français/">
  Word/Français
</a>
```

would be converted to the value:

```
http://dmoz.org/World/Fran%c3%a7ais/
```

in the value space.

The `xs:anyURI` datatype doesn't pay any attention to `xml:base` attributes that may have been defined in the document.

Notations

`xs:NOTATION`

This is probably the most obscure of these string datatypes. This datatype was created to implement the XML 1.0 notations. It cannot be used directly in a schema; it must be used through user-defined derived datatypes. We will see more of it in the next chapter.

Binary string-encoded datatypes

XML 1.0 is unable to hold binary content, which must be string-encoded before it can be included in a XML document. W3C XML Schema has defined two primary datatypes to support two encodings that are commonly used (hexBinary and base64). These encodings may be used to include any binary content, including text formats whose content may be incompatible with the XML markup. Other binary text encodings may also be used (such as uuXXcode, Quote Printable, BinHex, aencode, or base85, to name a few), but their value would not be recognized by W3C XML Schema.

xs:hexBinary

This defines a simple way to code binary content as a character string by translating the value of each binary octet into two hexadecimal digits. This encoding is different from the encoding method called BinHex (introduced by Apple, described by RFC 1741, and includes a mechanism to compress repetitive characters).

A UTF-8 XML header such as:

```
<?xml version="1.0" encoding="UTF-8"?>
```

that is encoded as xs:hexBinary would be:

```
3f3c6d78206c657673726f693d6e3122302e20226e656f636964676e223d54552d4622383e3f
```

xs:base64Binary

This matches the encoding known as "base64" and is described in RFC 2045. It maps groups of 6 bits into an array of 64 printable characters.

The same header encoded as xs:base64Binary would be:

```
PD94bWwgdmVyc2lvbjOiMS4wIiBlbmNvZGluZzOiVVRGLTgiPz4NCg==
```

The W3C XML Schema Recommendation missed the fact that RFC 2045 requests a line break every 76 characters. This should be clarified in an errata. The consequence of these line breaks being thought of as optional by W3C XML Schema, is that the lexical and value spaces of xs:base64Binary cannot be considered identical.

Numeric Datatypes

The numeric datatypes are built on top of four primitive datatypes: xs:decimal for all the decimal types (including the integer datatypes, considered decimals without a fractional part), xs:double and xs:float for single and double precision floats, and xs:boolean for Booleans. Whitespaces are collapsed for all these datatypes.

The datatypes covered in this section are shown in Figure 4-3.

Decimal Types

All decimal types are derived from the xs:decimal primary type and constitute a set of predefined types that address the most common usages.

xs:decimal

This datatype represents the decimal numbers. The number of digits can be arbitrarily long (the datatype doesn't impose any restriction), but obviously, since a XML document has an arbitrary but finite length, the number of digits of the lexical representation of a xs:decimal value needs to be finite. Although the number of digits is not limited, we will see in the next chapter how the author of a schema can derive user-defined datatypes with a limited number of digits if needed.

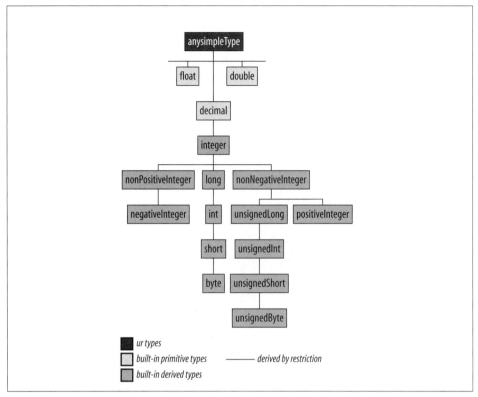

Figure 4-3. Numeric datatypes

Leading and trailing zeros are not significant and may be trimmed. The decimal separator is always a dot ("."); a leading sign ("+" or "-") may be specified and any characters other than the 10 digits (including whitespaces) are forbidden. Scientific notation ("E+2") is also forbidden and has been reserved to the float datatypes only.

Valid values for xs:decimal include:

```
123.456
+1234.456
-1234.456
-.456
-456
```

The following values are invalid:

```
1 234.456 (spaces are forbidden)
1234.456E+2 (scientific notation ("E+2") is forbidden)
+ 1234.456 (spaces are forbidden)
+1,234.456 (delimiters between thousands are forbidden)
```

xs:integer is the only datatype directly derived from xs:decimal.

xs:integer

This integer datatype is a subset of xs:decimal, representing numbers which don't have any fractional digits in its lexical or value spaces. The characters that are accepted are reduced to 10 digits and an optional leading sign. Like its base datatype, xs:integer doesn't impose any limitation on the number of digits, and leading zeros are not significant.

Valid values for xs:integer include:

```
123456
+00000012
-1
-456
```

The following values are invalid:

```
1 234 (spaces are forbidden)
1. (the decimal separator is forbidden)
+1,234 (delimiters between thousands are forbidden).
```

xs:integer has given birth to three derived datatypes: xs:nonPositiveInteger and xs:nonNegativeInteger (which have still an unlimited length) and xs:long (to fit in a 64-bit word).

xs:nonPositiveInteger *and* xs:negativeInteger

The W3C XML Schema Working Group thought that it would be more clear that the value "0" was included if they used litotes as names, and used xs:nonPositiveInteger if the integers are negative or null. xs:negativeInteger is derived from xs:nonPositiveInteger to represent the integers that are strictly negative. These two datatypes allow integers of arbitrary length.

xs:nonNegativeInteger *and* xs:positiveInteger

Similarly, xs:nonNegativeInteger is the integers that are positive or equal to zero and xs:positiveInteger is derived from this type. The "unsigned" family branch (xs:unsignedLong, xs:unsignedInt, xs:unsignedShort, and xs:unsignedByte) is also derived from xs:nonNegativeInteger.

xs:long, xs:int, xs:short, *and* xs:byte.

The datatypes we have seen up to now have an unconstrained length. This approach isn't very microprocessor-friendly. This subfamily represents signed integers that can fit into 8, 16, 32, and 64-bit words. xs:long is defined as all of the integers between -9223372036854775808 and 9223372036854775807, i.e., the values that can be stored in a 64-bit word. The same process is applied again to derive xs:int with a range between -2147483648 and 2147483647 (32 bits), to derive xs:short with a range between -32768 and 32767 (16 bits), and to derive xs:byte with a range between -128 and 127 (8 bits).

xs:unsignedLong, xs:unsignedInt, xs:unsignedShort, *and* xs:unsignedByte.

The last of the predefined integer datatypes is the subfamily of unsigned (i.e., positive) integers that can fit into 8, 16, 32, and 64-bit words. xs:unsignedLong is defined as the integers in a range between 0 and 18446744073709551615, i.e., the values that can be stored in a 64-bit word. The same process is applied again to derive xs:unsignedInt with a range between 0 and 4294967295 (32 bits), to derive xs:unsignedShort with a range between 0 and 65535 (16 bits), and to derive xs:unsignedByte with a range between 0 and 255 (8 bits).

Float Datatypes

xs:float *and* xs:double

> xs:float and xs:double are both primitive datatypes and represent IEEE simple (32 bits) and double (64 bits) precision floating-point types. These store the values in the form of mantissa and an exponent of a power of 2 (m $\times$ 2^e), allowing a large scale of numbers in a storage that has a fixed length. Fortunately, the lexical space doesn't require that we use powers of 2 (in fact, it doesn't accept powers of 2), but instead lets us use a traditional scientific notation with integer powers of 10. Since the value spaces (powers of 2) don't exactly match the values from the lexical space (powers of 10), the recommendation specifies that the closest value is taken. The consequence of this approximate matching is that float datatypes are the domain of approximation; most of the float values can't be considered exact, and are approximate.

> These datatypes accept several "special" values: positive zero (0), negative zero (-0) (which is greater than positive 0 but less than any negative value), infinity (INF) (which is greater than any value), negative infinity (-INF) (which is less than any float, and "not a number" (NaN).

> Valid values for xs:float and xs:double include:

```
123.456
+1234.456
-1.2344e56
-.45E-6
INF
-INF
NaN
```

The following values are invalid:

```
1234.4E 56  (spaces are forbidden)
1E+2.5  (the power of 10 must be an integer)
+INF  (positive infinity doesn't expect a sign)
NAN  (capitalization matters in special values)
```

xs:boolean

xs:boolean

> This is a primitive datatype that can take the values true and false (or 1 and 0).

Date and Time Datatypes

The datatypes covered in this section are shown in Figure 4-4.

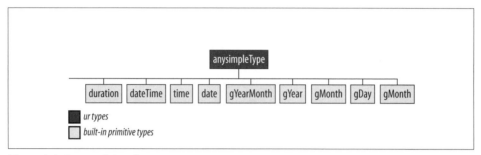

Figure 4-4. Date and time datatypes

The Realm of ISO 8601

The W3C Recommendation, "XML Schema Part 2: Datatypes," provides new confirmation of how difficult it is to fix time.

The support for date and time datatypes relies entirely on a subset of the ISO 8601 standard, which is the only format supported by W3C XML Schema. The purpose of ISO 8601 is to eliminate the risk of confusion between the various date and time formats used in different countries. In other words, W3C XML Schema does not support these local date and time formats, and imposes the usage of ISO 8601 for any datatype that has the semantic of a date or time. While this is a good thing for interchange formats, this is more questionable when XML is used to define user interfaces, since we will see that ISO 8601 is not very user friendly. The variations using the names of the months or different orders between year, month, and day are not the only victims of this decision: ISO 8601 imposes the usage of the Gregorian (Christian) calendar to the exclusion of calendars used by other cultures or religions.

ISO 8601 describes several formats to define date, times, periods, and recurring dates, with different levels of precision and indetermination. After many discussions, W3C XML Schema selected a subset of these formats and created a primitive datatype for each format that is supported.

The indeterminacy allowed in some of these formats adds a lot of difficulty, especially when comparisons or arithmetic are involved. For instance, it is possible to define a point in time without specifying the time zone, which is then considered undetermined. This undetermined time zone is identical all over the document (and between the schema and the instance documents) and it's not an issue to compare two datetimes without a time zone. The problem arises when you need to compare two points in time, one with a time zone and the other without. The result of this comparison will be undetermined if these values are too close, since one of them may be between -13 hours and +12 hours of Coordinated Universal Time (UTC). Thus, the support of these datetime datatypes introduces a notion of "partial order relation."

Another caveat with ISO 8601 is that time zones are only supported through the time difference from UTC, which ignores the notion of summer time. For instance, if an application working in British Summer Time (BST) wants to specify the time zone— and we have seen that this is necessary to be able to compare datetimes—the application needs to know if a date is in summer (the time zone will be one hour after UTC) or in winter (the time zone would then be UTC). ISO 8601 ignores the "named time zones" using the summer saving times (such as PST, BST, or WET) that we use in our day-to-day life; ignoring the time zones can be seen as a somewhat dangerous shortcut to specify that a datetime is on your "local time," whatever it is.

Datatypes

Point in time: `xs:dateTime`

The `xs:dateTime` datatype defines a "specific instant of time." This is a subset of what ISO 8601 calls a "moment of time." Its lexical value follows the format "CCYY-MM-DDThh:mm:ss," in which all the fields must be present and may optionally be preceded by a sign and leading figures, if needed, and followed by fractional digits for the seconds and a time zone. The time zone may be specified using the letter "Z," which identifies UTC, or by the difference of time with UTC.

 The value space of `xs:dateTime` is considered to be the moment of time itself. The time zone that defines the value (when there is one) is considered meaningless, which is a problem for some applications that complain that even though `2002-01-18T12:00:00+00:00` and `2002-01-18T11:00:00-01:00` refer to the same "moment of time," they carry different time zone information, which should make its way into the value space.

Valid values for `xs:dateTime` include:

```
2001-10-26T21:32:52
2001-10-26T21:32:52+02:00
2001-10-26T19:32:52Z
2001-10-26T19:32:52+00:00
-2001-10-26T21:32:52
2001-10-26T21:32:52.12679
```

The following values are invalid:

```
2001-10-26  (all the parts must be specified)
2001-10-26T21:32  (all the parts must be specified)
2001-10-26T25:32:52+02:00  (the hours part (25) is out of range)
```

01-10-26T21:32 (all the parts must be specified)

In the valid examples given above, three of them have identical value spaces:

```
2001-10-26T21:32:52+02:00
2001-10-26T19:32:52Z
2001-10-26T19:32:52+00:00
```

The first one (2001-10-26T21:32:52), which doesn't include a time zone specification, is considered to have an indeterminate value between 2001-10-26T21:32:52-14:00 and 2001-10-26T21:32:52+14:00. With the usage of summer saving time, this range is subject to national regulations and may change. The range was between -13:00 and +12:00 when the Recommendation was published, but the Working Group has kept a margin to accommodate possible changes in the regulations.

Despite the indeterminacy of the time zone when none is specified, the W3C XML Schema Recommendation considers that the values of datetimes without time zones implicitly refer to the same undetermined time zone and can be compared between them. While this is fine for "local" applications that operate in a single time zone, this is a source of potential confusion and errors for world-wide applications or even for applications that calculate a duration between moments belonging to different time saving seasons within a single time zone.

Periods of time: xs:date, xs:gYearMonth *and* xs:gYear.

The lexical space of xs:date datatype is identical to the date part of xs:dateTime. Like xs:dateTime, it includes a time zone that should always be specified to be able to compare two dates without ambiguity. As defined per W3C XML Schema, a date is a period one day in its time zone, "independent of how many hours this day has." The consequence of this definition is that two dates defined in a different time zone cannot be equal except if they designate the same interval (2001-10-26+12:00 and 2001-10-25-12:00, for instance). Another consequence is that, like with xs:dateTime, the order relation between a date with a time zone and a date without a time zone is partial.

Valid values for xs:date include:

```
2001-10-26
2001-10-26+02:00
2001-10-26Z
2001-10-26+00:00
-2001-10-26
-20000-04-01
```

The following values are invalid:

```
2001-10 (all the parts must be specified)
2001-10-32 (the days part (32) is out of range)
2001-13-26+02:00 (the month part (13) is out of range)
```

01-10-26 (the century part is missing)

xs:date represents a day identified by a Gregorian calendar date (and could have been called "gYearMonthDay"). xs:gYearMonth ("g" for Gregorian) is a Gregorian calendar month and xs:gYear is a Gregorian calendar year. These three datatypes are fixed periods of time and optional time zones may be specified for each of them. The only differences between them really are their length (1 day, 1 month, and 1 year) and their format (i.e., their lexical spaces).

The format of xs:gYearMonth is the format of xs:date without the day part. Valid values for xs:gYearMonth include:

```
2001-10
2001-10+02:00
2001-10Z
2001-10+00:00
-2001-10
-20000-04
```

The following values are invalid:

2001 (the month part is missing)
2001-13 (the month part is out of range)
2001-13-26+02:00 (the month part is out of range)
01-10 (the century part is missing)

The format of xs:gYear is the format of xs:gYearMonth without the month part. Valid values for xs:gYear include:

```
2001
2001+02:00
2001Z
2001+00:00
-2001
-20000
```

The following values are invalid:

01 (the century part is missing)
2001-13 (the month part is out of range)

This support of time periods is very restrictive: these periods can only match the Gregorian calendar day, month, or year, and cannot have an arbitrary length or start time.

Recurring point in time: xs:time

The lexical space of xs:time is identical to the time part of xs:dateTime. The semantic of xs:time represents a point in time that recurs every day; the meaning of 01:20:15 is "the point in time recurring each day at 01:20:15 am." Like xs:date and xs:dateTime, xs:time accepts an optional time zone definition. The same issue arises when comparing times with and without time zones.

Despite the fact that: 01:20:15 is commonly used to represent a duration of 1 hour, 20 minutes, and 15 seconds, a different format has been chosen to represent a duration.

Valid values for xs:time include:

```
21:32:52
21:32:52+02:00
19:32:52Z
19:32:52+00:00
21:32:52.12679
```

The following values are invalid:

```
21:32 (all the parts must be specified)
25:25:10 (the hour part is out of range)
-10:00:00 (the hour part is out of range)
1:20:10 (all the digits must be supplied)
```

This support of a recurring point in time is also very limited: the recursion period must be a Gregorian calendar day and cannot be arbitrary.

Recurring period of time: xs:gDay, xs:gMonth, *and* xs:gMonthDay.

We have already seen points in times and periods, as well as recurring points in time. This wouldn't be complete without a description of recurring periods. W3C XML Schema supports three predefined recurring periods corresponding to Gregorian calendar months (recurring every year) and days (recurring each month or year). The support of recurring periods is restricted both in terms of recursion (the recursion period can only be a Gregorian calendar year or month) and period (the start time can only be a Gregorian calendar day or month, and the duration can only be a Gregorian calendar month or day).

xs:gDay is a period of a Gregorian calendar day recurring each Gregorian calendar month. The lexical representation of xs:gDay is ---DD with an optional time zone specification. Valid values for xs:gDay include:

```
---01
---01Z
---01+02:00
---01-04:00
---15
---31
```

The following values are invalid:

```
--30- (the format must be "---DD")
---35 (the day is out of range)
---5 (all the digits must be supplied)
15 (missing the leading "---")
```

The rules of arithmetic between dates and durations apply in this case, and days are "pinned" in the range for each month. In our example, --31, the selected dates will be January 31st, February 28th (or 29th), March 31st, April 30th, etc.

xs:gMonthDay is a period of a Gregorian calendar day recurring each Gregorian calendar year. The lexical representation of xs:gMonthDay is --MM-DD with an optional time zone specification. Valid values for xs:gMonthDay include:

    --05-01
    --11-01Z
    --11-01+02:00
    --11-01-04:00
    --11-15
    --02-29

The following values are invalid:

    -01-30- (the format must be --MM-DD)
    --01-35 (the day part is out of range)
    --1-5 (one part is missing)
    01-15 (the leading -- is missing)

xs:gMonth is a period of a Gregorian calendar month recurring each Gregorian calendar year. The lexical representation of xs:gMonth defined in the Recommendation is --MM-- with an optional time zone specification. The W3C XML Schema Working Group has acknowledged that this was an error and that the format --MM defined by ISO 8061 should be used instead. It has not been decided yet if the format described in the Recommendation will be forbidden or only deprecated, but it is advised to use the format --MM (assuming that the tools you are using already support it). Valid values for xs:gMonth include:

    --05
    --11Z
    --11+02:00
    --11-04:00
    --02

The following values are invalid:

    -01- (the format must be --MM)
    --13 (the month is out of range)
    --1 (both digits must be provided)
    01 (the leading -- is missing)

xs:duration

Naive programmers who think that the concept of duration is simple should read the Recommendation, which states: "xs:duration is defined as a six-dimensional space!" Mathematicians would object that this is not absolutely true since most of the axes of these dimension are parallel, but the fact is that when these programmers say that a development will last one month and 3 days, they define a duration that is comprised of between 31 and 34 days. The attempt of W3C XML Schema to deal with these issues on top of ISO 8601 has introduced a degree of indeterminacy in the comparisons between durations.

The lexical space of xs:duration is the format defined by ISO 8601 under the form PnYnMnDTnHnMnS, in which the capital letters are delimiters that can be omitted when the corresponding member is not used. An important difference with the format used for xs:dateTime is none of these members are mandatory and none of them are restricted to a range. This gives flexibility to choose the units that will be used and to combine several of them—for instance, P1Y2MT123S (1 year, 2 months, and 123 seconds). This flexibility has a price; such a duration is not completely defined: a year may have 365 or 366 days, and a period of two months lasts between 59 and 62 days. Durations cannot always be compared and the order between durations is partial. We will see, in the next chapter, that user-defined datatypes can be derived from xs:duration, which can restrict the components used to express durations and insure that these indeterminations do not happen.

Since the value of a duration is fixed as soon as you give it a starting point, the schema Working Group has identified four datetimes:

```
1696-09-01T00:00:00Z
1697-02-01T00:00:00Z
1903-03-01T00:00:00Z
1903-07-01T00:00:00Z
```

These cause the greatest deviations when durations mixing day, month, and other components are added. The Working Group has determined that the comparison of durations is undefined if—and only if—the result of the comparison is different when each of these dates is used as a starting point.

Valid values for xs:duration include:

```
PT1004199059S
PT130S
PT2M10S
P1DT2S
-P1Y
P1Y2M3DT5H20M30.123S
```

The following values are invalid:

```
1Y (the leading P is missing)
P1S (the T separator is missing)
P-1Y (all parts must be positive)
P1M2Y (the parts order is significant and Y must precede M)
P1Y-1M (all parts must be positive)
```

List Types

These datatypes are lists of whitespace-separated items. The type of these items (called the item type) is defined during the derivation process (which we will see in the next chapter) and list datatypes can be derived from any simple type. Three predefined datatypes are lists (xs:NMTOKENS, xs:IDREFS, and xs:ENTITIES). For all the list datatypes, the items must be separated by one or more whitespaces.

xs:NMTOKENS

> This is a whitespace-separated list of xs:NMTOKEN. Each item of the list must be in the lexical space of xs:NMTOKEN.

xs:IDREFS

> This is a whitespace-separated list of xs:IDREF. Each item of the list must be in the lexical space of xs:IDREF and must reference an existing xs:ID in the same document.

xs:ENTITIES

> This is a whitespace-separated list of xs:ENTITY. Each item of the list must be in the lexical space of xs:ENTITY and must match an unparsed entity defined in a DTD.

What About anySimpleType?

We have now covered all the predefined datatypes except one, which is an atypical type: anySimpleType. This datatype is a kind of wildcard, which means, as expected, that any value is accepted and doesn't add any constraint on the lexical space.

anySimpleType has two other characteristics that make it unique among simple types: users' simple types cannot be derived from it and its properties, and its canonical form is not defined in the Recommendation! These characteristics make it a type that should be avoided, except when the rules of a derivation (which we will see in the next chapter) require its usage.

Back to Our Library

If we look back with a critical eye at our library, we see we used the following simple datatypes:

```
<xs:element name="name" type="xs:string"/>

<xs:element name="qualification" type="xs:string"/>

<xs:element name="born" type="xs:date"/>

<xs:element name="dead" type="xs:date"/>

<xs:element name="isbn" type="xs:string"/>
```

```
<xs:attribute name="id" type="xs:ID"/>

<xs:attribute name="available" type="xs:boolean"/>

<xs:attribute name="lang" type="xs:language"/>
```

We are lucky that the elements born and dead are ISO 8601 dates. The ISBN number is composed of numeric digits and a final character which can be either a digit or the letter "x"–and is therefore represented as a string. We also did a good job with the datatypes for the id, available and lang attributes, but the choice of xs:string for the elements name and qualification is more controversial. They appear in the instance document as:

```
<name>
  Charles M Schulz
</name>
                      .../...


<qualification>
  bold, brash and tomboyish
</qualification>
```

This formatting suggests that whitespaces are probably not significant and should be collapsed. This can be done by choosing the datatype xs:token instead of xs:string; the same applies to the title element, which is a simple content derived from xs:string that would be better derived from xs:token. This change will not have any impact on the validation with our schema, but the document is more precisely described and future derivations would be more easily built on xs:token than on xs:string. The other datatype that could have been chosen better is isbn, which can be represented as xs:NMTOKEN. The new schema would then be:

```
<?xml version="1.0"?>
<xs:schema xmlns:xs="http://www.w3.org/2001/XMLSchema">
  <xs:element name="name" type="xs:token"/>
  <xs:element name="qualification" type="xs:token"/>
  <xs:element name="born" type="xs:date"/>
  <xs:element name="dead" type="xs:date"/>
  <xs:element name="isbn" type="xs:NMTOKEN"/>
  <xs:attribute name="id" type="xs:ID"/>
  <xs:attribute name="available" type="xs:boolean"/>
  <xs:attribute name="lang" type="xs:language"/>
  <xs:element name="title">
    <xs:complexType>
      <xs:simpleContent>
        <xs:extension base="xs:token">
          <xs:attribute ref="lang"/>
        </xs:extension>
      </xs:simpleContent>
    </xs:complexType>
  </xs:element>
  <xs:element name="library">
```

```
    <xs:complexType>
      <xs:sequence>
        <xs:element ref="book" maxOccurs="unbounded"/>
      </xs:sequence>
    </xs:complexType>
  </xs:element>
  <xs:element name="author">
    <xs:complexType>
      <xs:sequence>
        <xs:element ref="name"/>
        <xs:element ref="born"/>
        <xs:element ref="dead" minOccurs="0"/>
      </xs:sequence>
      <xs:attribute ref="id"/>
    </xs:complexType>
  </xs:element>
  <xs:element name="book">
    <xs:complexType>
      <xs:sequence>
        <xs:element ref="isbn"/>
        <xs:element ref="title"/>
        <xs:element ref="author" minOccurs="0" maxOccurs="unbounded"/>
        <xs:element ref="character" minOccurs="0"
          maxOccurs="unbounded"/>
      </xs:sequence>
      <xs:attribute ref="id"/>
      <xs:attribute ref="available"/>
    </xs:complexType>
  </xs:element>
  <xs:element name="character">
    <xs:complexType>
      <xs:sequence>
        <xs:element ref="name"/>
        <xs:element ref="born"/>
        <xs:element ref="qualification"/>
      </xs:sequence>
      <xs:attribute ref="id"/>
    </xs:complexType>
  </xs:element>
</xs:schema>
```

CHAPTER 5

Creating Simple Datatypes

So far, we have used only predefined datatypes. In this chapter, we will see how to create new simple types, taking advantage of the different derivation mechanisms and facets of derivation by restriction.

W3C XML Schema has defined three independent and complementary mechanisms for defining our own custom datatypes, using existing datatypes as starting points. These new user datatypes that are built upon existing predefined datatypes or on other user datatypes are called "derivation."

The three derivation methods are derivation by restriction (where constraints are added on a datatype without changing its original semantic or meaning), derivation by list (where new datatypes are defined as being lists of values belonging to a datatype and take the semantic of list datatypes), and derivation by union (where new datatypes are defined as allowing values from a set of other datatypes and lose most of their semantic).

As with the xs:complexType, definitions (which we saw in our Russian doll design) and xs:simpleType can be either named or anonymous. Despite this similarity, simple and complex types are very different. A simple type is a restriction on the value of an element or an attribute (i.e., a constraint on the content of a set of documents) while a complex type is a definition of a content model (i.e., a constraint on the markup). This is why the derivation methods for simple and complex types are very different, even though W3C XML Schema used the same element name (xs: restriction) for both. This is a common source of confusion.

These derivation methods are flexible and powerful. However, that W3C XML Schema needs many different primary datatypes can be seen as proof that they are not sufficient to create a new primary datatype. The reason being that the derivation methods are only acting on the value space or on the lexical space (as defined in Chapter 4), but they cannot modify the relations between these two spaces, nor create new value or lexical spaces. This subject has been debated by the W3C XML Schema Working Group, which has not found an agreement for ways to define an abstract datatype system that would allow definition of several lexical representations. The most obvious consequence of this decision is that, despite the protestation from the W3C I18N Working Group, *W3C XML Schema* doesn't allow the definition of localized decimal or date datatypes.

Derivation By Restriction

Restriction is probably the most commonly used and natural derivation method. Datatypes are created by restriction by adding new constraints to the possible values. *W3C XML Schema* itself has been using derivation by restriction to define most of derived predefined datatypes, such as xs:positiveInteger, which is a derivation by restriction of xs:integer. The restrictions can be defined along different aspects or axes that *W3C XML Schema* calls "facets."

A derivation by restriction is done using a xs:restriction element and each facet is defined using a specific element embedded in the xs:restriction element. The datatype on which the restriction is applied is called the base datatype, which can be referenced through a <base> attribute or defined in the xs:restriction element:

```
<xs:simpleType name="myInteger">
  <xs:restriction base="xs:integer">
    <xs:minInclusive value="-2"/>
    <xs:maxExclusive value="5"/>
  </xs:restriction>
</xs:simpleType>
```

It can also be defined in two steps using an embedded xs:simpleType anonymous definition:

```
<xs:simpleType name="myInteger">
  <xs:restriction>
    <xs:simpleType>
      <xs:restriction base="xs:integer">
        <xs:maxExclusive value="5"/>
      </xs:restriction>
    </xs:simpleType>
    <xs:minInclusive value="-2"/>
  </xs:restriction>
</xs:simpleType>
```

The xs:minInclusive and xs:maxExclusive elements are two facets that can be applied to an integer datatype. As can be guessed from their names, they specify the minimum inclusive (i.e., that can be reached) and maximum exclusive (i.e., that is not allowed) values. We will introduce the list of facets in the next section. Depending on the facet, each acts directly either on the value space or on the lexical space of the datatype, and the same facet may have different effects depending on the datatype on which it is applied.

Whatever facet is being applied on a datatype, the semantic of its primitive type is unchanged, the list of facets that can be applied cannot be extended, and one must be careful to choose, when possible, a datatype whose primitive type matches the purpose of the node in which it will be used. For instance, while it is possible to constrain a string datatype to match non-ISO 8601 dates using patterns, this solution should be used only when absolutely required since this datatype would still be considered a string and lack facets, such as xs:minInclusive or xs:maxExclusive that are defined on date datatypes but that have no meaning (for W3C XML Schema) on a string.

 The impact of the "right" choice of the base datatype with a semantic as close as possible to its actual usage in the instance documents will become more critical when W3C XML Schema aware applications become available. Such applications will have a different behavior depending on the datatype information found in the PSVI. A "wrong" choice will have side effects. For instance, the first drafts of XPath 2.0 propose to interpret values according to predefined datatypes and the results of equality tests on values or the sort orders would depend on the datatypes.

Facets

Before we start looking at the list of facets, we'll discuss the way they work. They may be classified into three categories: xs:whiteSpace defines the whitespace processing that happens between the parser and lexical spaces—but can be used only on xs:string and xs:normalizedString. xs:pattern works on the lexical space; all the other facets constrain the value space. The availability of the facets and their effect depend on the datatype on which they are applied. We will see them in the context of groups of datatypes sharing the same set of facets.

Whitespace collapsed strings

These datatypes share the fact that they are character strings (even though technically W3C XML Schema doesn't consider all of them as derived from the xs:string datatypes) and that whitespaces are collapsed before validation, as defined in the Recommendation, "all occurrences of #x9 (tab), #xA (line feed), and #xD (carriage return) are replaced with #x20 (space) and then, contiguous sequences of #x20s are collapsed to a single #x20, and initial and/or final #x20s are deleted."

Those datatypes are: xs:ENTITY, xs:ID, xs:IDREF, xs:language, xs:Name, xs:NCName, xs:NMTOKEN, xs:token, xs:anyURI, xs:base64Binary, xs:hexBinary, xs:NOTATION, and xs:QName. Their facets are explained in the next section:

xs:enumeration. xs:enumeration allows definition of a list of possible values. Here's an example:

```
<xs:simpleType name="schemaRecommendations">
  <xs:restriction base="xs:anyURI">
    <xs:enumeration value="http://www.w3.org/TR/xmlschema-0/"/>
    <xs:enumeration value="http://www.w3.org/TR/xmlschema-1/"/>
    <xs:enumeration value="http://www.w3.org/TR/xmlschema-2/"/>
  </xs:restriction>
</xs:simpleType>
```

This facet is constraining the value space. For most of the string (and assimilated) datatypes, lexical and values are identical and this doesn't make any difference; however, it does make a difference for xs:anyURI, xs:base64Binary, and xs:QName. For instance, *"http://dmoz.org/World/Français/"* and *"http://dmoz.org/World/Fran%c3%a7ais/"* would be considered equal for xs:anyURI, the line breaks would be ignored for xs:base64Binary, and the match would be done on the tuples {namespace URI, local name} for xs:QName, ignoring the prefix used in the schema and instance documents.

One should also note that xs:anyURI datatypes are not "absolutized" by W3C XML Schema and do not support xml:base. This means that if the "schemaRecommendations" defined in the previous example is assigned to a XLink href attribute, it must fail to validate the following instance element:

```
<a xml:base="http://www.w3.org/TR/" href="xmlschema-1/">
  XML Schema Part 2: Datatypes
</a>
```

We cannot leave this section without discussing xs:NOTATION. This datatype is the only case of a predefined datatype that cannot be used directly in a schema and must be used through derived types specifying a set of xs:enumeration facets. Even though notations are very seldom used in real-life applications, this book wouldn't be complete without at least an example of notations. If we take the usual example of a picture using a notation in an attribute to qualify the content of a binary field as follows:

```
<?xml version="1.0"?>
<picture type="png">
```

    iVBORw0KGgoAAAANSUhEUgAAAAoAAAAKCAIAAAACUFjqAAAABmJLR0QA/wD/AP+gvaeTAAAA
    CXBIWXMAAAsSAAALEgHS3X78AAAAB3RJTUUH0QofESYx2JhwGwAAAFZJREFUeNqlj8ENwDAI
    A6HqGDCWp2QQ2AP2oI9IbaQm/dRPn9EJ7m7a56DPPDgiIoKIzGyBM9Pdx+4ueXabWVUBEJHR
    nLNJVbfuqspMAE0xw09r/vX3BTEnKRXtqqslAAAAAElFTkSuQmCC

```
</picture>
```

The schema might be written as (note how the notations need to be declared in the schema to be used in an xs:enumeration facet):

```
<?xml version="1.0"?>
<xs:schema xmlns:xs="http://www.w3.org/2001/XMLSchema">
  <xs:notation name="jpeg" public="image/jpeg"
    system="file:///usr/bin/xv"/>
  <xs:notation name="gif" public="image/gif"
    system="file:///usr/bin/xv"/>
  <xs:notation name="png" public="image/png"
    system="file:///usr/bin/xv"/>
  <xs:notation name="svg" public="image/svg"
    system="file:///usr/bin/xsmiles"/>
  <xs:notation name="pdf" public="application/pdf"
    system="file:///usr/bin/acroread"/>
  <xs:simpleType name="graphicalFormat">
    <xs:restriction base="xs:NOTATION">
      <xs:enumeration value="jpeg"/>
      <xs:enumeration value="gif"/>
      <xs:enumeration value="png"/>
      <xs:enumeration value="svg"/>
      <xs:enumeration value="pdf"/>
    </xs:restriction>
  </xs:simpleType>
  <xs:element name="picture">
    <xs:complexType>
      <xs:simpleContent>
        <xs:extension base="xs:base64Binary">
          <xs:attribute name="type" type="graphicalFormat"/>
        </xs:extension>
      </xs:simpleContent>
    </xs:complexType>
  </xs:element>
</xs:schema>
```

xs:length. xs:length defines a fixed length measured in number of characters (general case) or bytes (xs:hexBinary and xs:base64Binary):

```
<xs:simpleType name="standardNotations">
  <xs:restriction base="xs:NOTATION">
    <xs:length value="8"/>
  </xs:restriction>
</xs:simpleType>
```

This facet also constrains the value space. For xs:anyURI, this may be difficult to predict since the length is checked after the character normalization. For xs:QName, this is even worse since the W3C XML Schema recommendation has not given any definition of the length of an xs:QName tuple. Fortunately, in practice, constraining the length of these datatypes doesn't seem to be very useful, and it's a good idea to avoid using these constraints on these datatypes. The same restriction applies to the next two facets.

xs:maxLength. xs:maxLength defines a maximum length measured in number of characters (general case) or bytes (xs:hexBinary and xs:base64Binary):

```
<xs:simpleType name="binaryImage">
  <xs:restriction base="xs:hexBinary">
    <xs:maxLength value="1024"/>
  </xs:restriction>
</xs:simpleType>
```

xs:minLength. xs:minLength defines a minimum length measured in number of characters (general case) or bytes (hexBinary and base64Binary):

```
<xs:simpleType name="longName">
  <xs:restriction base="xs:NCName">
    <xs:minLength value="6"/>
  </xs:restriction>
</xs:simpleType>
```

xs:pattern. xs:pattern defines a pattern that must be matched by the string (we will explore patterns in more detail in the next chapter) :

```
<xs:simpleType name="httpURI">
  <xs:restriction base="xs:anyURI">
    <xs:pattern value="http://.*"/>
  </xs:restriction>
</xs:simpleType>
```

Several pattern facets can be defined in a single derivation step. They are then merged together through a logical "or" (a value will match the restricted datatype if it matches one of the patterns).

Because of the impossibility of defining a single order that would be useful for all the regional alphabets, *W3C XML Schema* has decided to handle the string datatypes as being unordered. The consequence is there are no facets to define minimal or maximal values for string datatypes.

Other strings

The whitespaces of these other strings are not collapsed before validation, and a new facet (xs:whiteSpace) is available, in addition to the facets just described, to specify the treatment to apply on whitespaces for the user-defined datatypes derived from them.

Those datatypes are: xs:normalizedString and xs:string.

xs:whiteSpace. xs:whiteSpace defines the way to handle whitespaces—i.e., #x20 (space), #x9 (tab), #xA (linefeed), and #xD (carriage return)—for this datatype:

```
<xs:simpleType name="CapitalizedNameWS">
  <xs:restriction base="xs:string">
```

```
      <xs:whiteSpace value="collapse"/>
      <xs:pattern value="([A-Z]([a-z]*) ?)+"/>
    </xs:restriction>
  </xs:simpleType>
```

The values of an xs:whiteSpace facet are "preserve" (whitespaces are kept unchanged), "replace" (all the instances of any whitespace are replaced with a space), and "collapse" (leading and trailing whitespaces are removed and all the other sequences of contiguous whitespaces are replaced by a single space). This facet is atypical since it specifies a treatment to be done on a value before applying any validation test on this value. In the earlier example, setting whitespace to "collapse" allows testing of a single space character in the pattern (" ?"). This ensures the whitespaces are collapsed before the pattern is tested and will match any number of whitespaces.

The whitespace behavior cannot be relaxed during a restriction: if a datatype has a whitespace set as "preserve," its derived datatypes can have any whitespace behavior; if its whitespace is set as "replace," its derived datatypes can only have whitespace equal to "replace" or "collapse"; if its whitespace is "collapse," all its derived datatypes must have the same behavior. This means xs:string is the only datatype that can be used to derive datatypes without any whitespace processing and xs:string and xs:normalizedString are the only datatypes that can be used to derive datatypes normalizing the whitespaces.

In practice, this facet isn't really useful for user-defined datatypes since the whitespace processing largely dictates the choice of the predefined datatype to use. When we need a datatype that does no whitespace processing, we must use xs:string and not xs:whiteSpace. When we need a datatype that normalizes the whitespaces, instead of using xs:string and applying a xs:whiteSpace facet, we can use xs:normalizedString directly, which has the same effect. When we need a datatype that collapses the whitespaces, we can use xs:token if it's a string—since, again, xs:token is not a token in the usual meaning of the word but rather a "tokenized string"—as well as any nonstring datatype. The whitespace processing will already be set to "collapse" without any need to use xs:whiteSpace. The previous example given is then equivalent to:

```
  <xs:simpleType name="CapitalizedNameWS">
    <xs:restriction base="xs:token">
      <xs:pattern value="([A-Z]([a-z]*) ?)+"/>
    </xs:restriction>
  </xs:simpleType>
```

 Technically speaking, the W3C Working Group hasn't "fixed" the xs:whiteSpace facet for xs:token and its derived datatypes. However, xs:whiteSpace has been set to "collapse" for xs:token; since the facet can't be relaxed in further restriction, this value cannot be changed in any datatype derived from these datatypes.

Float datatypes

The facets of: `xs:double` and `xs:float` are described in the next sections.

xs:enumeration. `xs:enumeration` allows definition of a list of possible values and operates on the value space—for example:

```
<xs:simpleType name="enumeration">
  <xs:restriction base="xs:float">
    <xs:enumeration value="-INF"/>
    <xs:enumeration value="1.618033989"/>
    <xs:enumeration value="3e3"/>
  </xs:restriction>
</xs:simpleType>
```

This simple type will match literals such as:

```
<enumeration>
  1.618033989
</enumeration>

<enumeration>
  3e3
</enumeration>

<enumeration>
  003000.0000
</enumeration>
```

This example shows (as we've briefly seen with `xs:anyURI`, `xs:QName`, and `xs:base64Binary`) two different lexical representations ("3e3" and "003000.0000") for the same value. It also shows, as expected, that all the lexical representations have the same value, so one of the enumerated values will be accepted.

xs:maxExclusive. `xs:maxExclusive` defines a maximum value that cannot be reached:

```
<xs:simpleType name="maxExclusive">
  <xs:restriction base="xs:float">
    <xs:maxExclusive value="10"/>
  </xs:restriction>
</xs:simpleType>
```

This datatype validates "9.999999999999999," but not "10."

The `xs:maxExclusive` facet is especially useful for datatypes such as `xs:float`, `xs:double`, `xs:decimal`, or even for datetime types that can cope with infinitesimal values and in which it is not possible to determine the greatest value that is smaller than a value.

xs:maxInclusive. `xs:maxInclusive` defines a maximum value that can be reached:

```
<xs:simpleType name="thousands">
  <xs:restriction base="xs:double">
    <xs:maxInclusive value="1e3"/>
```

```
    </xs:restriction>
  </xs:simpleType>
```

xs:minExclusive. `xs:minExclusive` defines a minimum value that cannot be reached:

```
<xs:simpleType name="strictlyPositive">
  <xs:restriction base="xs:double">
    <xs:minExclusive value="0"/>
  </xs:restriction>
</xs:simpleType>
```

xs:minInclusive. `xs:minInclusive` defines a minimum value that can be reached:

```
<xs:simpleType name="positive">
  <xs:restriction base="xs:double">
    <xs:minInclusive value="0"/>
  </xs:restriction>
</xs:simpleType>
```

xs:pattern. `xs:pattern` defines a pattern that must be matched by the lexical value of the datatype:

```
<xs:simpleType name="nonScientific">
  <xs:restriction base="xs:float">
    <xs:pattern value="[^eE]*"/>
  </xs:restriction>
</xs:simpleType>

<xs:simpleType name="noLeading0">
  <xs:restriction base="xs:float">
    <xs:pattern value="[^0].*"/>
  </xs:restriction>
</xs:simpleType>
```

This example shows how a pattern, acting on the lexical value of the float, can disable the use of scientific notation (xxxEyyy) or leading zeros.

 The xs:pattern is the only facet that directly acts on the lexical space of the datatype.

Date and time datatypes

These datatypes are partially ordered, and bounds can be defined even though some restrictions apply. These datatypes are: `xs:date`, `xs:dateTime`, `xs:duration`, `xs:gDay`, `xs:gMonth`, `xs:gMonthDay`, `xs:gYear`, `xs:gYearMonth`, and `xs:time` and their facets are the same as those of the float datatypes, as shown in the next sections.:

xs:enumeration. `xs:enumeration` allows definition of a list of possible values as well as works on the value space—for example:

```
<xs:simpleType name="ModernSwissHistoricalDates">
  <xs:restriction base="xs:gYear">
    <xs:enumeration value="1864"/>
    <xs:enumeration value="1872"/>
    <xs:enumeration value="1914"/>
    <xs:enumeration value="1939"/>
    <xs:enumeration value="1971"/>
    <xs:enumeration value="1979"/>
    <xs:enumeration value="1992"/>
  </xs:restriction>
</xs:simpleType>
```

This simple type will match literals such as:

```
1939
```

Since no time zone is specified for the dates in the enumeration, the time zone is undetermined. These dates do not match any date with a time zone specified, such as:

```
1939Z
```

or:

```
1939+10:00
```

The same issue appears if enumerations include a time zone, such as in:

```
<xs:simpleType name="wakeUpTime">
  <xs:restriction base="xs:time">
    <xs:enumeration value="07:00:00-07:00"/>
    <xs:enumeration value="07:15:00-07:00"/>
    <xs:enumeration value="07:30:00-07:00"/>
    <xs:enumeration value="07:45:00-07:00"/>
    <xs:enumeration value="08:00:00-07:00"/>
  </xs:restriction>
</xs:simpleType>
```

This new datatype matches:

```
07:00:00-07:00
```

as well as:

```
11:00:00-04:00
```

and even:

```
07:15:00-07:15
```

but will not validate any time with a time zone.

Even though handling both times with and without time zones is problematic and questionable, it is possible to mix enumerations of values with and without time zones, such as:

```
<xs:simpleType name="sevenOClockPST">
  <xs:restriction base="xs:time">
    <xs:enumeration value="07:00:00-07:00"/>
```

```
      <xs:enumeration value="07:00:00"/>
    </xs:restriction>
  </xs:simpleType>
```

xs:maxExclusive. `xs:maxExclusive` defines a maximum value that can be reached: *NOT*

```
<xs:simpleType name="beforeY2K">
  <xs:restriction base="xs:dateTime">
    <xs:maxExclusive value="2000-01-01T00:00:00Z"/>
  </xs:restriction>
</xs:simpleType>
```

This datatype validates any date strictly less than Y2K UTC, such as:

```
1999-12-31T23:59:59Z
```

or:

```
1999-12-31T23:59:59.999999999999Z
```

It will also validate the following; even if expressed using any other time zone, such as:

```
2000-01-01T11:59:59+12:00
```

It doesn't validate:

```
2000-01-01T00:00:00Z
```

The interval of indeterminacy of +/-14 hours is applied when compared to datetimes without a time zone. The greatest datetime without a time zone (without counting the fractions of seconds) is therefore:

```
1999-12-31T09:59:59
```

xs:maxInclusive. `xs:maxInclusive` defines a maximum value that can be reached:

```
<xs:simpleType name="AQuarterOrLess">
  <xs:restriction base="xs:duration">
    <xs:maxInclusive value="P3M"/>
  </xs:restriction>
</xs:simpleType>
```

This datatype validates all the durations less than or equal to 3 months. Durations such as P2M (2 months) or P3M (3 months) qualify. If both months and days are used, P2M30D (2 months and 30 days) will be valid, but P2M31D (2 months and 31 days), or even P2M30DT1S (2 months, 30 days and 1 second), will be rejected because of the indetermination of the actual duration when parts from year/month on one side and day/hours/minutes/seconds on the other side are used.

xs:minExclusive. `xs:minExclusive` defines a minimum value that can be reached: *NOT*

```
<xs:simpleType name="afterTeaTimeInParisInSummer">
  <xs:restriction base="xs:time">
    <xs:minExclusive value="17:00:00+02:00"/>
```

```
    </xs:restriction>
  </xs:simpleType>
```

xs:minInclusive. `xs:minInclusive` defines a minimum value that can be reached:

```
<xs:simpleType name="afterOrOnThe20th">
  <xs:restriction base="xs:gDay">
    <xs:minInclusive value="---20"/>
  </xs:restriction>
</xs:simpleType>
```

We can also take back our example using durations and define:

```
<xs:simpleType name="AQuarterOrMore">
  <xs:restriction base="xs:duration">
    <xs:minInclusive value="P3M"/>
  </xs:restriction>
</xs:simpleType>
```

This datatype validates all durations that are more than or equal to 3 months. Durations such as P4M (4 months) or P3M (3 months) will qualify. If both months and days are used, P2M31D (2 months and 31 days) will be valid, but P2M30D (2 months and 30 days), or even P2M30DT23H59M59S (2 months, 30 days, 23 hours, 59 minutes and 59 seconds), will be rejected because of the indetermination of the actual duration.

Because of this indeterminacy, W3C XML Schema considers our third month to have 30 days when we apply `xs:minInclusive`, and 31 days when we apply `xs:maxInclusive`. In practice, it may be wise to invalidate the usage of combinations allowing such an indeterminacy. We will see in the next chapter how to do it with a pattern.

xs:pattern. `xs:pattern` defines a pattern that must be matched by the lexical value of the datatype. We will see patterns in detail in the next chapter. To get an idea of what they look like, look at the following datatype. It forbids usage of a time zone by an `xs:dateTime` datatype:

```
<xs:simpleType name="noTimeZone">
  <xs:restriction base="xs:dateTime">
    <xs:pattern value=".*T[^Z+-]*"/>
  </xs:restriction>
</xs:simpleType>
```

Integer and derived datatypes

These datatypes are: `xs:byte`, `xs:int`, `xs:integer`, `xs:long`, `xs:negativeInteger`, `xs:nonNegativeInteger`, `xs:nonPositiveInteger`, `xs:positiveInteger`, `xs:short`, `xs:unsignedByte`, `xs:unsignedInt`, `xs:unsignedLong`, and `xs:unsignedShort`.

They accept the same facets of float datatypes as datetime of float datatypes, which we just saw, plus an additional facet to constrain the number of digits, as shown next.

xs:totalDigits. `xs:totalDigits` defines the maximum number of decimal digits:

```
<xs:simpleType name="totalDigits">
  <xs:restriction base="xs:integer">
    <xs:totalDigits value="5"/>
  </xs:restriction>
</xs:simpleType>
```

This datatype accepts only integers with up to five decimal digits.

`xs:totalDigits` acts on the value space, which means that the integer "000012345," whose canonical value is "12345," matches the datatype defined previously.

Decimals

This single datatype (`xs:decimal`) accepts all the facets of the integers and an additional facet to define the number of fractional digits as shown next.

xs:fractionDigits. `xs:fractionDigits` specifies the maximum number of decimal digits in the fractional part (after the dot) :

```
<xs:simpleType name="fractionDigits">
  <xs:restriction base="xs:decimal">
    <xs:fractionDigits value="2"/>
  </xs:restriction>
</xs:simpleType>
```

`xs:fractionDigits` acts on the value space, which means that the integer "1.12000," whose canonical value is "1.12," matches the datatype defined previously.

Booleans

With only one facet allowed, as far as restriction facets are concerned, the simplest datatype is `xs:boolean`. The value space of this simple datatype is limited to "true" and "false," but its lexical space also includes "0" and "1." The `xs:pattern` facet can be used to exclude one of these formats.

xs:pattern. The functionality of `xs:pattern` is usually very rich; however, given the limited number of values of the `xs:boolean`, its only use here appears to be to fix a format:

```
<xs:simpleType name="trueOrFalse">
  <xs:restriction base="xs:boolean">
    <xs:pattern value="true"/>
    <xs:pattern value="false"/>
  </xs:restriction>
</xs:simpleType>
```

List datatypes

The available facets for the list datatypes (`xs:IDREFS`, `xs:ENTITIES`, and `xs:NMTOKENS`) are the facets available for all the datatypes that are derived by list, as we will see in the next section.

Multiple Restrictions and Fixed Attribute

New restrictions can be applied to datatypes that are already derived by restriction from other types.

When the new restrictions are done on facets that have not yet been constrained, the new facets are just added to the set of facets already defined. The value and lexical spaces of the new datatype are the intersection of all the restrictions. Things become more complex when the same facets are being redefined, and restricting facets can extend the value space.

As far as multiple facet definitions are concerned, we can classify the facets into four categories, described in the next sections.

Facet that can be changed but needs to be more restrictive

This is the general case. xs:enumeration, xs:fractionDigits, xs:maxExclusive, xs:maxInclusive, xs:maxLength, xs:minExclusive, xs:minInclusive, xs:minLength, and xs:totalDigits are in this case.

For all these facets, it is forbidden to add a facet that expands the value space of the base datatype. The following examples demonstrate such errors:

```
<xs:simpleType name="minInclusive">
  <xs:restriction base="xs:float">
    <xs:minInclusive value="10"/>
  </xs:restriction>
</xs:simpleType>

<xs:simpleType name="minInclusive2">
  <xs:restriction base="minInclusive">
    <xs:minInclusive value="0"/>
  </xs:restriction>
</xs:simpleType>
```

or:

```
<xs:simpleType name="enumeration">
  <xs:restriction base="xs:float">
    <xs:enumeration value="-INF"/>
    <xs:enumeration value="1.618033989"/>
    <xs:enumeration value="3e3"/>
  </xs:restriction>
</xs:simpleType>

<xs:simpleType name="enumeration2">
  <xs:restriction base="enumeration">
    <xs:enumeration value="0"/>
  </xs:restriction>
</xs:simpleType>
```

Facet that cannot be changed

The `xs:length` facet is the only one in this category. The length of a derived datatype cannot be redefined if the length of its parent has been defined.

`xs:length` can be seen as a shortcut for assigning an equal value to `xs:maxLength` and `xs:minLength`. This behavior is coherent with what happens if these two facets are both used with the same value: further values of `xs:maxLength` must be inferior or equal to the length, and further values of `xs:minLength` must be greater than or equal to the length. Since `xs:minLength` must also be smaller than or equal to `xs:maxLength`, the only possibility is that they all need to stay equal to the length as previously defined.

Facet that performs the intersection of the lexical spaces

The `xs:pattern` facet is the only facet that can be applied multiple times. It always restricts the lexical space by performing a straight intersection of the lexical spaces. The following `noScientificNoLeading0` datatype will try to match the patterns for both the base datatype and the new restriction:

```
<xs:simpleType name="nonScientific">
  <xs:restriction base="xs:float">
    <xs:pattern value="[^eE]*"/>
  </xs:restriction>
</xs:simpleType>

<xs:simpleType name="noScientificNoLeading0">
  <xs:restriction base="nonScientific">
    <xs:pattern value="[^0].*"/>
  </xs:restriction>
</xs:simpleType>
```

Facet that does its job before the lexical space

`xs:whiteSpace` is a remarkable exception. This facet defines the whitespace processing and can actually expand the set of accepted instance documents during a "restriction," as shown in the following example:

```
<xs:simpleType name="greetings">
  <xs:restriction base="xs:string">
    <xs:whiteSpace value="replace"/>
    <xs:enumeration value="hi"/>
    <xs:enumeration value="hello"/>
    <xs:enumeration value="how do you do?"/>
  </xs:restriction>
</xs:simpleType>

<xs:simpleType name="restricted-greetings">
  <xs:restriction base="greetings">
    <xs:whiteSpace value="collapse"/>
  </xs:restriction>
</xs:simpleType>
```

While the first datatype ("greetings") accepts:

    how do you do?

but rejects a string such as:

    how do   you do?

the type issued from the "restriction" accepts both.

Fixed facets

Each facet (except xs:enumeration and xs:pattern) includes a fixed attribute which, when set to true, disables the possibility of modifying the facet during further restrictions by derivation.

If we want to make sure that the minimum value of our minInclusive cannot be modified, we write:

```
<xs:simpleType name="minInclusive">
  <xs:restriction base="xs:float">
    <xs:minInclusive value="10" fixed="true"/>
  </xs:restriction>
</xs:simpleType>
```

> This is the method used by the schema for *W3C XML Schema* to fix the value of the facets used to derive predefined datatypes. For instance, the type xs:integer is derived from xs:decimal through:
>
> ```
> <xs:simpleType name="integer" id="integer">
>   <xs:restriction base="xs:decimal">
>     <xs:fractionDigits value="0" fixed="true"/>
>   </xs:restriction>
> </xs:simpleType>
> ```

<xs:enumeration> and <xs:pattern> cannot be fixed.

Derivation By List

Derivation by list is the mechanism by which a list datatype can be derived from an atomic datatype. All the items in the list need to have the same datatype.

List Datatypes

List datatypes are special cases in which a structure is defined within the content of a single attribute or element. This practice is usually discouraged since applications do not have access to the atomic values through the current XML APIs, XPath expressions, or in the Infoset. This situation might change in the future since these datatypes should be adopted by XPath 2.0, which will likely provide some kind of mechanism to access to the items within these lists.

This feature appears to have been introduced to maintain compatibility with SGML and XML DTD IDREFS, but *W3C XML Schema* has been cautious and doesn't allow definition of the list separator or complex lists with complex types or heterogeneous members. Among the constructs that can be seen in some XML vocabularies and cannot be described by XML Schema (except by using regular expressions as a partial workaround) are comma-separated lists of values, and lists with heterogeneous members, such as values with units:

```
<commaSeparated>
  1, 2, 25
</commaSeparated>

<valueWithUnit>
  10 em
</valueWithUnit>
```

Whitespace-separated lists and split XML elements or attributes are preferred:

```
<commaSeparated>
  1 2 25
</commaSeparated>

<valueWithUnit unit="em">
  10
</valueWithUnit>

<valueWithUnit>
  10em
</valueWithUnit>
```

IDREFS, ENTITIES, and NMTOKENS are predefined list datatypes that are derived from atomic types using this method.

As we have seen with these three datatypes, all the list datatypes that can be defined must be whitespace-separated. No other separator is accepted.

With this restriction, defining a list is very simple, and *W3C XML Schema* has defined two syntaxes. Both use a xs:list element, which allows a definition by reference to existing types or embeds a type definition (these two syntaxes cannot be mixed).

The definition of a list datatype by reference to an existing type is done through a itemType attribute:

```
<xs:simpleType name="integerList">
  <xs:list itemType="xs:integer"/>
</xs:simpleType>
```

This datatype can be used to define attributes or elements that accept a whitespace-separated list of integers such as: "1 -25000 1000."

The definition of a list datatype can also be done by embedding a xs:simpleType element:

```
<xs:simpleType name="myIntegerList">
  <xs:list>
    <xs:simpleType>
      <xs:restriction base="xs:integer">
        <xs:maxInclusive value="100"/>
      </xs:restriction>
    </xs:simpleType>
  </xs:list>
</xs:simpleType>
```

This datatype can be used to define attributes or elements that accept a whitespace-separated list of integers smaller than or equal to 100 such as: "1 -25000 100."

List datatypes have their own value space that can be constrained using a set of specific facets that is common to all of them.

These facets are xs:length, xs:maxLength, xs:minLength, xs:enumeration and xs:whiteSpace. The unit used to measure the length of a list type is always the number of elements in the list.

To apply these facets to a user-defined list type, we need to follow two steps. We first define the list datatype, and then define a datatype to constrain the list datatype. The reason for this is each xs:simpleType (global definition) accepts only one derivation method chosen between the three existing methods.

In this process, the derivation by restriction has to be done first, since a list datatype loses the facets of its atomic type and has the only five facets just described that have a meaning that is specific to list types.

Derivation By Union

Derivation by union allows defining datatypes by merging the lexical spaces of several predefined or user datatypes.

As we've seen with the derivation by list, *W3C XML Schema* has defined two syntaxes, both using a xs:union element, allowing a definition by reference to existing types or by embedding type definition (these two syntaxes can be mixed). The definition of a union datatype by reference to existing types is done through a memberType attribute containing a whitespace-separated list of datatypes:

```
<xs:simpleType name="integerOrDate">
  <xs:union memberTypes="xs:integer xs:date"/>
</xs:simpleType>
```

The definition of a union datatype can also be done by embedding one or more <xs:simpleType> elements:

```
<xs:simpleType name="myIntegerUnion">
  <xs:union>
```

```
      <xs:simpleType>
        <xs:restriction base="xs:integer"/>
      </xs:simpleType>
      <xs:simpleType>
        <xs:restriction base="xs:NMTOKEN">
          <xs:enumeration value="undefined"/>
        </xs:restriction>
      </xs:simpleType>
    </xs:union>
  </xs:simpleType>
```

Both styles can be mixed and the previous example can be written as:

```
<xs:simpleType name="myIntegerUnion">
  <xs:union memberTypes="xs:integer">
    <xs:simpleType>
      <xs:restriction base="xs:NMTOKEN">
        <xs:enumeration value="undefined"/>
```

```
        </xs:restriction>
      </xs:simpleType>
    </xs:union>
  </xs:simpleType>
```

The resulting datatype is a merge that, as a whole, has lost the semantical meaning—and facets—from the member types. In the earlier example, we couldn't constrain the myIntegerUnion type to be either less than 100 or undefined except by defining a pattern. To do so, we can create a type derived by restriction from a built-in type to be less than 100, and perform the union to allow the value to be "undefined" afterward. The only two facets that can be applied to a union datatype are xs:pattern and xs:enumeration.

Those two facets are the only facets that are common to *almost* all the datatypes. The only exception is xs:enumeration, which is not allowed for xs:boolean. Defining a "dummy" union over an xs:boolean could be a workaround to define an xs:enumeration facet over this type.

Some Oddities of Simple Types

While simple types are structurally simple, they still have some complications worth watching for.

Beware of the Order

The order of the different derivation methods (restriction, list, or union) is significant.

We have already seen that derivation by list and union lose the semantic meaning of the types and their facets, which are replaced by a common set of facets with their own meaning (xs:length, xs:maxLength, xs:minLength, xs:enumeration, and xs:whiteSpace for derivation by list, and xs:pattern and xs:enumeration for derivation by union).

This means that all the restrictions on the atomic or member types must be done before the derivation by list or members (as we have seen in the corresponding sections for the facets) and that a new restriction can then be performed using the common set of facets.

The order between derivation by list and derivation by union depends on the result to achieve, as a list of unions is different from a union of lists, as one might expect:

```
<xs:simpleType name="listOfUnions">
  <xs:list>
    <xs:simpleType>
      <xs:union memberTypes="xs:date xs:integer"/>
    </xs:simpleType>
  </xs:list>
</xs:simpleType>
```

```
<xs:simpleType name="UnionOfLists">
  <xs:union>
    <xs:simpleType>
      <xs:list itemType="xs:date"/>
    </xs:simpleType>
    <xs:simpleType>
      <xs:list itemType="xs:integer"/>
    </xs:simpleType>
  </xs:union>
</xs:simpleType>
```

These two datatypes match the following:

```
<UnionOfLists>
  2001-01-01 2001-01-02
</UnionOfLists>

<UnionOfLists>
  1 2 3
</UnionOfLists>

<ListOfUnions>
  2001-01-01 2001-01-02
</ListOfUnions>

<ListOfUnions>
  1 2 3
</ListOfUnions>

<ListOfUnions>
  2001-01-01 1 2
</ListOfUnions>
```

But don't match:

```
<UnionOfLists>
  2001-01-01 1 2
</UnionOfLists>
```

This requires all the items of the list to have the same member type.

The order in which a set of derivation by restriction is completed is also significant when the same facets are being redefined, since we have seen that there are some restrictions that depend on the facets being used.

Using or Abusing Lists to Change the Behavior of Length Constraining Facets

We have seen that a derivation by list impacts not only the value space of the item types, but also their meaning. We have also seen that their set of facets is replaced by a generic set.

In the case of length-constraining facets, the length unit is generally a number of characters (in the general case) or bytes (binary types) before a derivation by list and becomes a number of whitespace-separated values for any list datatype.

A restriction by list then allows constraint of the number of whitespace-separated "words" on any datatype. For instance, if we want to define a string datatype of 100 and 200 words, each having a length of less than 15 characters and using only basic Latin characters, we can write:

```
<xs:simpleType name="word">
  <xs:list>
    <xs:simpleType>
      <xs:restriction base="xs:string">
        <xs:maxLength value="15"/>
        <xs:pattern value="\p{IsBasicLatin}*"/>
      </xs:restriction>
    </xs:simpleType>
  </xs:list>
</xs:simpleType>

<xs:simpleType name="story">
  <xs:restriction base="word">
    <xs:minLength value="100"/>
    <xs:maxLength value="200"/>
  </xs:restriction>
</xs:simpleType>
```

The first definition defines the constraint on the words and the second adds the constraint on the string itself, which is seen here as a list of words. However, one should note that in this example we have no way to define a constraint on the total number of characters of the "story." The next chapter will demonstrate that these two constraints can be defined using a set of patterns on the string itself.

Back to Our Library

Let's see how we can improve our schema by adding constraints on our datatypes with what we have learned in this chapter:

```
<xs:element name="name" type="xs:token"/>

<xs:element name="qualification" type="xs:token"/>

<xs:element name="born" type="xs:date"/>

<xs:element name="dead" type="xs:date"/>

<xs:element name="isbn" type="xs:NMTOKEN"/>

<xs:attribute name="id" type="xs:ID"/>

<xs:attribute name="available" type="xs:boolean"/>

<xs:attribute name="lang" type="xs:language"/>
```

First, we may want to limit the size of our strings—for instance, if they must be stored into fixed-length columns in an RDBMS. Here, we will consider that the name needs to fit in a string of 32 characters, and the title and qualification need to fit in strings of 255 characters. We create two simple datatypes for this:

```
<xs:simpleType name="string255">
  <xs:restriction base="xs:token">
    <xs:maxLength value="255"/>
  </xs:restriction>
</xs:simpleType>

<xs:simpleType name="string32">
  <xs:restriction base="xs:token">
    <xs:maxLength value="32"/>
  </xs:restriction>
</xs:simpleType>
```

Then, we may want to add some constraints on the ISBN number. The best we can do without using the patterns (we will see how to do this in the next chapter) is to limit the number of characters to 10 using xs:length. This facet is a number of characters and acts on the value space. This, therefore, does not eliminate instances such as ABCDEFGHIJ, but this is probably the best we can do for the moment:

```
<xs:simpleType name="isbn">
  <xs:restriction base="xs:NMTOKEN">
    <xs:length value="10"/>
  </xs:restriction>
</xs:simpleType>
```

We may finally want to limit the languages in which the title may be written. If our library only has titles in English and Spanish, we can add the following restriction:

```
<xs:simpleType name="supportedLanguages">
  <xs:restriction base="xs:language">
    <xs:enumeration value="en"/>
    <xs:enumeration value="es"/>
  </xs:restriction>
</xs:simpleType>
```

Our new schema is then:

```
<?xml version="1.0"?>
<xs:schema xmlns:xs="http://www.w3.org/2001/XMLSchema">
  <xs:simpleType name="string255">
    <xs:restriction base="xs:token">
      <xs:maxLength value="255"/>
    </xs:restriction>
  </xs:simpleType>
  <xs:simpleType name="string32">
    <xs:restriction base="xs:token">
      <xs:maxLength value="32"/>
    </xs:restriction>
  </xs:simpleType>
  <xs:simpleType name="isbn">
```

```
      <xs:restriction base="xs:NMTOKEN">
        <xs:length value="10"/>
      </xs:restriction>
    </xs:simpleType>
    <xs:simpleType name="supportedLanguages">
      <xs:restriction base="xs:language">
        <xs:enumeration value="en"/>
        <xs:enumeration value="es"/>
      </xs:restriction>
    </xs:simpleType>
    <xs:element name="name" type="string32"/>
    <xs:element name="qualification" type="string255"/>
    <xs:element name="born" type="xs:date"/>
    <xs:element name="dead" type="xs:date"/>
    <xs:element name="isbn" type="isbn"/>
    <xs:attribute name="id" type="xs:ID"/>
    <xs:attribute name="available" type="xs:boolean"/>
    <xs:attribute name="lang" type="supportedLanguages"/>
    <xs:element name="title">
      <xs:complexType>
        <xs:simpleContent>
          <xs:extension base="string255">
            <xs:attribute ref="lang"/>
          </xs:extension>
        </xs:simpleContent>
      </xs:complexType>
    </xs:element>
    <xs:element name="library">
      <xs:complexType>
        <xs:sequence>
          <xs:element ref="book" maxOccurs="unbounded"/>
        </xs:sequence>
      </xs:complexType>
    </xs:element>
    <xs:element name="author">
      <xs:complexType>
        <xs:sequence>
          <xs:element ref="name"/>
          <xs:element ref="born"/>
          <xs:element ref="dead" minOccurs="0"/>
        </xs:sequence>
        <xs:attribute ref="id"/>
      </xs:complexType>
    </xs:element>
    <xs:element name="book">
      <xs:complexType>
        <xs:sequence>
          <xs:element ref="isbn"/>
          <xs:element ref="title"/>
          <xs:element ref="author" minOccurs="0" maxOccurs="unbounded"/>
          <xs:element ref="character" minOccurs="0"
            maxOccurs="unbounded"/>
        </xs:sequence>
        <xs:attribute ref="id"/>
```

```
          <xs:attribute ref="available"/>
      </xs:complexType>
  </xs:element>
  <xs:element name="character">
    <xs:complexType>
      <xs:sequence>
        <xs:element ref="name"/>
        <xs:element ref="born"/>
        <xs:element ref="qualification"/>
      </xs:sequence>
      <xs:attribute ref="id"/>
    </xs:complexType>
  </xs:element>
</xs:schema>
```

CHAPTER 6

Using Regular Expressions to Specify Simple Datatypes

Among the different facets available to restrict the lexical space of simple datatypes, the most flexible (and also the one that we will often use as a last resort when all the other facets are unable to express the restriction on a user-defined datatype) is based on regular expressions.

The Swiss Army Knife

Patterns (and regular expressions in general) are like a Swiss army knife when constraining simple datatypes. They are highly flexible, can compensate for many of the limitations of the other facets, and are often used to define user datatypes on various formats such as ISBN numbers, telephone numbers, or custom date formats. However, like a Swiss army knife, patterns have their own limitations.

Multirange datatypes (such as integers between -1 and 5 or 10 and 15) can be defined as a union of datatypes meeting the different ranges (in this case, we could perform a union between a datatype accepting integers between -1 and 5 and a second datatype accepting integers between 10 and 15); however, after the union, the resulting datatype loses its semantic of integer and cannot be constrained using integer facets any longer. Using patterns to define multirange datatypes is therefore an option: although less readable than using an union, it preserves the semantic of the base type.

Cutting a tree with a Swiss army knife is long, tiring, and dangerous. Writing regular expressions may also become long, tiring, and dangerous when the number of combinations grows. One should try to keep them as simple as possible.

A Swiss army knife cannot change lead into gold, and no facet can change the primary type of a simple datatype. A string datatype restricted to match a custom date format will still retain the properties of a string and will never acquire the facets of a datetime datatype. This means that there is no effective way to express localized date formats.

The Simplest Possible Patterns

In their simplest form, patterns may be used as enumerations applied to the lexical space rather than on the value space.

If, for instance, we have a byte value that can only take the values "1," "5," or "15," the classical way to define such a datatype is to use the xs:enumeration facet:

```
<xs:simpleType name="myByte">
  <xs:restriction base="xs:byte">
    <xs:enumeration value="1"/>
    <xs:enumeration value="5"/>
    <xs:enumeration value="15"/>
  </xs:restriction>
</xs:simpleType>
```

This is the "normal" way of defining this datatype if it matches the lexical space and the value space of an xs:byte. It gives the flexibility to accept the instance documents with values such as "1," "5," and "15," but also "01" or "0000005." One of the particularities of xs:pattern is it must be the only facet constraining the lexical space. If we have an application that is disturbed by leading zeros, we can use patterns instead of enumerations to define our datatype:

```
<xs:simpleType name="myByte">
  <xs:restriction base="xs:byte">
    <xs:pattern value="1"/>
    <xs:pattern value="5"/>
    <xs:pattern value="15"/>
  </xs:restriction>
</xs:simpleType>
```

This new datatype is still derived from xs:byte and has the semantic of a byte, but its lexical space is now constrained to accept only "1," "5," and "15," leaving out any variation that has the same value but a different lexical representation.

> This is an important difference from Perl regular expressions, on which W3C XML Schema patterns are built. A Perl expression such as /15/ matches any string containing "15," while the W3C XML Schema pattern matches only the string equal to "15." The Perl expression equivalent to this pattern is thus /^15$/.

This example has been carefully chosen to avoid using any of the meta characters used within patterns, which are: ".", "\", "?", "*", "+", "{", "}", "(", ")", "[", and "]". We will see the meaning of these characters later in this chapter; for the moment, we just need to know that each of these characters needs to be "escaped" by a leading "\" to be used as a literal. For instance, to define a similar datatype for a decimal when lexical space is limited to "1" and "1.5," we write:

```
<xs:simpleType name="myDecimal">
  <xs:restriction base="xs:decimal">
```

```
        <xs:pattern value="1"/>
        <xs:pattern value="1\.5"/>
      </xs:restriction>
    </xs:simpleType>
```

A common source of errors is that "normal" characters should not be escaped: we will see later that a leading "\" changes their meaning (for instance, "\s" matches all the XML whitespaces and not the character "s").

Quantifying

Despite an apparent similarity, the xs:pattern facet interprets its value attribute in a very different way than xs:enumeration does. xs:enumeration reads the value as a lexical representation, and converts it to the corresponding value for its base datatype, while xs:pattern reads the value as a set of conditions to apply on lexical values. When we write:

```
    <xs:pattern value="15"/>
```

we specify three conditions (first character equals "1," second character equals "5," and the string must finish after this). Each of the matching conditions (such as first character equals "1" and second character equals "5") is called a piece. This is just the simplest form to specify a piece.

Each piece in a pattern is composed of an atom identifying a character, or a set of characters, and an optional quantifier. Characters (except special characters that must be escaped) are the simplest form of atoms. In our example, we have omitted the quantifiers. Quantifiers may be defined using two different syntaxes: either a special character (* for 0 or more, + for one or more, and ? for 0 or 1) or a numeric range within curly braces ({n} for exactly n times, {n,m} for between n and m times, or {n,} for n or more times).

Using these quantifiers, we can merge our three patterns into one:

```
    <xs:simpleType name="myByte">
      <xs:restriction base="xs:byte">
        <xs:pattern value="1?5?"/>
      </xs:restriction>
    </xs:simpleType>
```

This new pattern means there must be zero or one character ("1") followed by zero or one character ("5"). This is not exactly the same meaning as our three previous patterns since the empty string "" is now accepted by the pattern. However, since the empty string doesn't belong to the lexical space of our base type (xs:byte), the new datatype has the same lexical space as the previous one.

We could also use quantifiers to limit the number of leading zeros—for instance, the following pattern limits the number of leading zeros to up to 2:

```
    <xs:simpleType name="myByte">
      <xs:restriction base="xs:byte">
```

```
    <xs:pattern value="0{0,2}1?5?"/>
  </xs:restriction>
</xs:simpleType>
```

More Atoms

By this point, we have seen the simplest atoms that can be used in a pattern: "1,"
"5," and "\." are atoms that exactly match a character. The other atoms that can be
used in patterns are special characters, a wildcard that matches any character, or predefined and user-defined character classes.

Special Characters

Table 6-1 shows the list of atoms that match a single character, exactly like the characters we have already seen, but also correspond to characters that must be escaped
or (for the first three characters on the list) that are just provided for convenience.

Table 6-1. Special characters

\n	New line (can also be written as "
" since we are in a XML document).
\r	Carriage return (can also be written as "").
\t	Tabulation (can also be written as "	")
\\	Character "\"
|	Character "|"
\.	Character "."
\-	Character "-"
\^	Character "^"
\?	Character "?"
*	Character "*"
\+	Character "+"
\{	Character "{"
\}	Character "}"
\(	Character "("
\)	Character ")"
\[	Character "["
\]	Character "]"

Wildcard

The character "." has a special meaning: it's a wildcard atom that matches any XML
valid character except newlines and carriage returns. As with any atom, "." may be
followed by an optional quantifier and ".*" is a common construct to match zero or

more occurrences of any character. To illustrate the usage of ".*" (and the fact that xs:pattern is a Swiss army knife), a pattern may be used to define the integers that are multiples of 10:

```
<xs:simpleType name="multipleOfTen">
  <xs:restriction base="xs:integer">
    <xs:pattern value=".*0"/>
  </xs:restriction>
</xs:simpleType>
```

Character Classes

W3C XML Schema has adopted the "classical" Perl and Unicode character classes (but not the POSIX-style character classes also available in Perl).

Classical Perl character classes

W3C XML Schema supports the classical Perl character classes plus a couple of additions to match XML-specific productions. Each of these classes are designated by a single letter; the classes designated by the upper- and lowercase versions of the same letter are complementary:

\s

Spaces. Matches the XML whitespaces (space #x20, tabulation #x09, line feed #x0A, and carriage return #x0D).

\S

Characters that are not spaces.

\d

Digits ("0" to "9" but also digits in other alphabets).

\D

Characters that are not digits.

\w

Extended "word" characters (any Unicode character not defined as "punctuation", "separator," and "other"). This conforms to the Perl definition, assuming UTF8 support has been switched on.

\W

Nonword characters.

\i

XML 1.0 initial name characters (i.e., all the "letters" plus "-"). This is a W3C XML Schema extension over Perl regular expressions.

\I

Characters that may not be used as a XML initial name character.

`\c`

> XML 1.0 name characters (initial name characters, digits, ".", ":", "-", and the characters defined by Unicode as "combining" or "extender"). This is a W3C XML Schema extension to Perl regular expressions.

`\C`

> Characters that may not be used in a XML 1.0 name.

These character classes may be used with an optional quantifier like any other atom. The last pattern that we saw:

```
<xs:pattern value=".*0"/>
```

constrains the lexical space to be a string of characters ending with a zero. Knowing that the base type is a xs:integer, this is good enough for our purposes, but if the base type had been a xs:decimal (or xs:string), we could be more restrictive and write:

```
<xs:pattern value="-?\d*0"/>
```

This checks that the characters before the trailing zero are digits with an optional leading - (we will see later on in the section "Fixed format" how to specify an optional leading - or +).

Unicode character classes

Patterns support character classes matching both Unicode categories and blocks. Categories and blocks are two complementary classification systems: categories classify the characters by their usage independently to their localization (letters, uppercase, digit, punctuation, etc.), while blocks classify characters by their localization independently of their usage (Latin, Arabic, Hebrew, Tibetan, and even Gothic or musical symbols).

The syntax \p{Name} is similar for blocks and categories; the prefix Is is added to the name of categories to make the distinction. The syntax \P{Name} is also available to select the characters that do not match a block or category. A list of Unicode blocks and categories is given in the specification. Table 6-2 shows the Unicode character classes and Table 6-3 shows the Unicode character blocks.

Table 6-2. Unicode character classes

Unicode Character Class	Includes	Unicode Character Class	Includes
C	Other characters (non-letters, non symbols, non-numbers, non-separators)	Ll	Lowercase letters
Cc	Control characters	Lm	Modifier letters
Cf	Format characters	Lo	Other letters
Cn	Unassigned code points	Lt	Titlecase letters
Co	Private use characters	Lu	Uppercase letters
L	Letters	M	All Marks

Table 6-2. Unicode character classes (continued)

Unicode Character Class	Includes	Unicode Character Class	Includes
No	Other numbers	Pi	Initial quotes (may behave like Ps or Pe)
P	Punctuation	Po	Other forms of punctuation
Pc	Connector punctuation	Ps	Opening punctuation
Pd	Dashes	S	Symbols
Pe	Closing punctuation	Sc	Currency symbols
Pf	Final quotes (may behave like Ps or Pe)	Sk	Modifier symbols
Mc	Spacing combining marks	Sm	Mathematical symbols
Me	Enclosing marks	So	Other symbols
Mn	Non-spacing marks	Z	Separators
N	Numbers	Zl	Line breaks
Nd	Decimal digits	Zp	Paragraph breaks
Nl	Number letters	Zs	Spaces

Table 6-3. Unicode character blocks

AlphabeticPresentationForms	Arabic	ArabicPresentationForms-A
ArabicPresentationForms-B	Armenian	Arrows
BasicLatin	Bengali	BlockElements
Bopomofo	BopomofoExtended	BoxDrawing
BraillePatterns	ByzantineMusicalSymbols	Cherokee
CJKCompatibility	CJKCompatibilityForms	CJKCompatibilityIdeographs
CJKCompatibilityIdeographsSupplement	CJKRadicalsSupplement	CJKSymbolsandPunctuation
CJKUnifiedIdeographs	CJKUnifiedIdeographsExtensionA	CJKUnifiedIdeographsExtensionB
CombiningDiacriticalMarks	CombiningHalfMarks	CombiningMarksforSymbols
ControlPictures	CurrencySymbols	Cyrillic
Deseret	Devanagari	Dingbats
EnclosedAlphanumerics	EnclosedCJKLettersandMonths	Ethiopic
GeneralPunctuation	GeometricShapes	Georgian
Gothic	Greek	GreekExtended
Gujarati	Gurmukhi	HalfwidthandFullwidthForms
HangulCompatibilityJamo	HangulJamo	HangulSyllables
Hebrew	HighPrivateUseSurrogates	HighSurrogates
Hiragana	IdeographicDescriptionCharacters	IPAExtensions
Kanbun	KangxiRadicals	Kannada
Katakana	Khmer	Lao
Latin-1Supplement	LatinExtended-A	LatinExtendedAdditional
LatinExtended-B	LetterlikeSymbols	LowSurrogates
Malayalam	MathematicalAlphanumericSymbols	MathematicalOperators

Table 6-3. Unicode character blocks

MiscellaneousSymbols	MiscellaneousTechnical	Mongolian
MusicalSymbols	Myanmar	NumberForms
Ogham	OldItalic	OpticalCharacterRecognition
Oriya	PrivateUse	PrivateUse
PrivateUse	Runic	Sinhala
SmallFormVariants	SpacingModifierLetters	Specials
Specials	SuperscriptsandSubscripts	Syriac
Tags	Tamil	Telugu
Thaana	Thai	Tibetan
UnifiedCanadianAboriginalSyllabics	YiRadicals	YiSyllables

We don't yet know how to specify intersections between a block and a category in a single pattern, or how to specify that a datatype must be composed of only basic Latin letters. So, to "cross" these classifications and define the intersection of the block L (all the letters) and the category BasicLatin (ASCII characters below #x7F), we can perform two successive restrictions:

```
<xs:simpleType name="BasicLatinLetters">
  <xs:restriction>
    <xs:simpleType>
      <xs:restriction base="xs:token">
        <xs:pattern value="\p{IsBasicLatin}*"/>
      </xs:restriction>
    </xs:simpleType>
    <xs:pattern value="\p{L}*"/>
  </xs:restriction>
</xs:simpleType>
```

User-defined character classes

These classes are lists of characters between square brackets that accept - signs to define ranges and a leading ^ to negate the whole list—for instance:

```
[azertyuiop]
```

to define the list of letters on the first row of a French keyboard,

```
[a-z]
```

to specify all the characters between "a" and "z",

```
[^a-z]
```

for all the characters that are not between "a" and "z," but also

```
[-^\\]
```

to define the characters "-," "^," and "\," or

```
[-+]
```

to specify a decimal sign.

These examples are enough to see that what's between these square brackets follows a specific syntax and semantic. Like the regular expression's main syntax, we have a list of atoms, but instead of matching each atom against a character of the instance string, we define a logical space. Between the atoms and the character class is the set of characters matching any of the atoms found between the brackets.

We see also two special characters that have a different meaning depending on their location! The character -, which is a range delimiter when it is between a and z, is a normal character when it is just after the opening bracket or just before the closing bracket ([+-] and [-+] are, therefore, both legal). On the contrary, ^, which is a negator when it appears at the beginning of a class, loses this special meaning to become a normal character later in the class definition.

We also notice that characters may or must be escaped: "\\" is used to match the character "\". In fact, in a class definition, all the escape sequences that we have seen as atoms can be used. Even though some of the special characters lose their special meaning inside square brackets, they can always be escaped. So, the following:

    [-^\\]

can also be written as:

    [\-\^\\]

or as:

    [\^\\-]

since the location of the characters doesn't matter any longer when they are escaped.

Within square brackets, the character "\" also keeps its meaning of a reference to a Perl or Unicode class. The following:

    [\d\p{Lu}]

is a set of decimal digits (Perl class \d) and uppercase letters (Unicode category "Lu").

Mathematicians have found that three basic operations are needed to manipulate sets and that these operations can be chosen from a larger set of operations. In our square brackets, we already saw two of these operations: union (the square bracket is an implicit union of its atoms) and complement (a leading ^ realizes the complement of the set defined in the square bracket). W3C XML Schema extended the syntax of the Perl regular expressions to introduce a third operation: the difference between sets. The syntax follows:

    [set1-[set2]]

Its meaning is all the characters in set1 that do not belong to set2, where set1 and set2 can use all the syntactic tricks that we have seen up to now.

This operator can be used to perform intersections of character classes (the intersection between two sets A and B is the difference between A and the complement of B), and we can now define a class for the BasicLatin Letters as:

```
[\p{IsBasicLatin}-[^\p{L}]]
```

Or, using the \P construct, which is also a complement, we can define the class as:

```
[\p{IsBasicLatin}-[\P{L}]]
```

The corresponding datatype definition would be:

```
<xs:simpleType name="BasicLatinLetters">
  <xs:restriction base="xs:token">
    <xs:pattern value="[\p{IsBasicLatin}-[\P{L}]]*"/>
  </xs:restriction>
</xs:simpleType>
```

Oring and Grouping

In our first example pattern, we used three separate patterns to express three possible values. We can condense this definition using the "|" character, which is the "or" operator when used outside square brackets. The simple type definition is then:

```
<xs:simpleType name="myByte">
  <xs:restriction base="xs:byte">
    <xs:pattern value="1|5|15"/>
  </xs:restriction>
</xs:simpleType>
```

This syntax is more concise, but whether or not it's more readable is subject to discussion. Also, these "ors" would not be very interesting if it were not possible to use them in conjunction with groups. Groups are complete regular expressions, which are, themselves, considered atoms and can be used with an optional quantifier to form more complete (and complex) regular expressions. Groups are enclosed by brackets ("(" and ")"). To define a comma-separated list of "1," "5," or "15," ignoring whitespaces between values and commas, the following pattern could be used:

```
<xs:simpleType name="myListOfBytes">
  <xs:restriction base="xs:token">
    <xs:pattern value="(1|5|15)( *, *(1|5|15))*"/>
  </xs:restriction>
</xs:simpleType>
```

Note how we have relied on the whitespace processing of the base datatype (xs: token collapses the whitespaces). We have not tested leading and trailing whitespaces that are trimmed and we have only tested single occurrences of spaces with the following atom:

```
run back " * " run back
```

before and after the comma.

Common Patterns

After this overview of the syntax used by patterns, let's see some common patterns that you may have to use (or adapt) in your schemas or just consider as examples.

String Datatypes

Regular expressions treat information in its textual form. This makes them an excellent mechanism for constraining strings.

Unicode blocks

Unicode is a great asset of XML; however, there are few applications able to process and display all the characters of the Unicode set correctly and still fewer users able to read them! If you need to check that your string datatypes belong to one (or more) Unicode blocks, you can derive them from basic types such as:

```
<xs:simpleType name="BasicLatinToken">
  <xs:restriction base="xs:token">
    <xs:pattern value="\p{IsBasicLatin}*"/>
  </xs:restriction>
</xs:simpleType>

<xs:simpleType name="Latin-1Token">
  <xs:restriction base="xs:token">
    <xs:pattern value="[\p{IsBasicLatin}\p{IsLatin-1Supplement}]*"/>
  </xs:restriction>
</xs:simpleType>
```

Note that such patterns do not impose a character encoding on the document itself and that, for instance, the Latin-1Token datatype could validate instance documents using UTF-8, UTF-16, ISO-8869-1 or other encoding. (This assumes the characters used in this string belong to the two Unicode blocks BasicLatin and Latin-1Supplement.) In other words, working on the lexical space, i.e., after the transformations have been done by the parser, these patterns do not control the physical format of the instance documents.

Counting words

We have already seen a trick to count the words using a dummy derivation by list; however, this derivation counts only whitespace-separated "words," ignoring the punctuation that was treated like normal characters. We can limit the number of words using a couple of patterns. To do so, we can define an atom, which is a sequence of one or more "word" characters (\w+) followed by one or more nonword characters (\W+), and control its number of occurrences. If we are not very strict on the punctuation, we also need to allow an arbitrary number of nonword characters at the beginning of our value and to deal with the possibility of a value ending with a word (without further separation). One of the ways to avoid any ambiguity at the end of the string is to dissociate the last occurrence of a word to make the trailing separator optional:

```
<xs:simpleType name="story100-200words">
  <xs:restriction base="xs:token">
    <xs:pattern value="\W*(\w+\W+){99,199}\w+\W*"/>
  </xs:restriction>
</xs:simpleType>
```

URIs

We have seen that xs:anyURI doesn't care about "absolutizing" relative URIs and it may be wise to impose the usage of absolute URIs, which are easier to process. Furthermore, it can also be interesting for some applications to limit the accepted URI schemes. This can easily be done by a set of patterns such as:

```
<xs:simpleType name="httpURI">
  <xs:restriction base="xs:anyURI">
    <xs:pattern value="http://.*"/>
  </xs:restriction>
</xs:simpleType>
```

Numeric and Float Types

While numeric types aren't strictly text, patterns can still be used appropriately to constrain their lexical form.

Leading zeros

Getting rid of leading zeros is quite simple but requires some precautions if we want to keep the optional sign and the number "0" itself. This can be done using patterns such as:

```
<xs:simpleType name="noLeadingZeros">
  <xs:restriction base="xs:integer">
    <xs:pattern value="[+-]?([1-9][0-9]*|0)"/>
  </xs:restriction>
</xs:simpleType>
```

Note that in this pattern, we chose to redefine all the lexical rules that apply to an integer. This pattern would give the same lexical space applied to a xs:token datatype as on a xs:integer. We could also have relied on the knowledge of the base datatype and written:

```
<xs:simpleType name="noLeadingZeros">
  <xs:restriction base="xs:integer">
    <xs:pattern value="[+-]?([^0].*|0)"/>
  </xs:restriction>
</xs:simpleType>
```

Relying on the base datatype in this manner can produce simpler patterns, but can also be more difficult to interpret since we would have to combine the lexical rules of the base datatype to the rules expressed by the pattern to understand the result.

Fixed format

The maximum number of digits can be fixed using xs:totalDigits and xs:fractionDigits. However, these facets are only maximum numbers and work on the value space. If we want to fix the format of the lexical space to be, for instance, "DDDD.DD", we can write a pattern such as:

```
<xs:simpleType name="fixedDigits">
  <xs:restriction base="xs:decimal">
    <xs:pattern value="[+-]?.{4}\..{2}"/>
  </xs:restriction>
</xs:simpleType>
```

Datetimes

Dates and time have complex lexical representations. Patterns can give developers extra control over how they are used.

Time zones

The time zone support of W3C XML Schema is quite controversial and needs some additional constraints to avoid comparison problems. These patterns can be kept relatively simple since the syntax of the datetime is already checked by the schema validator and only simple additional checks need to be added. Applications which require that their datetimes specify a time zone may use the following template, which checks that the time part ends with a "Z" or contains a sign:

```
<xs:simpleType name="dateTimeWithTimezone">
  <xs:restriction base="xs:dateTime">
    <xs:pattern value=".+T.+(Z|[+-].+)"/>
  </xs:restriction>
</xs:simpleType>
```

Still simpler, applications that want to make sure that none of their datetimes specify a time zone may just check that the time part doesn't contain the characters "+", "-", or "Z":

```
<xs:simpleType name="dateTimeWithoutTimezone">
  <xs:restriction base="xs:dateTime">
    <xs:pattern value=".+T[^Z+-]+"/>
  </xs:restriction>
</xs:simpleType>
```

In these two datatypes, we used the separator "T". This is convenient, since no occurrences of the signs can occur after this delimiter except in the time zone definition. This delimiter would be missing if we wanted to constrain dates instead of datetimes, but, in this case, we can detect the time zones on their ":" instead:

```
<xs:simpleType name="dateWithTimezone">
  <xs:restriction base="xs:date">
    <xs:pattern value=".+[:Z].*"/>
  </xs:restriction>
</xs:simpleType>

<xs:simpleType name="dateWithoutTimezone">
  <xs:restriction base="xs:date">
    <xs:pattern value="[^:Z]*"/>
  </xs:restriction>
</xs:simpleType>
```

Applications may also simply impose a set of time zones to use:

```
<xs:simpleType name="dateTimeInMyTimezones">
  <xs:restriction base="xs:dateTime">
    <xs:pattern value=".+\+02:00"/>
    <xs:pattern value=".+\+01:00"/>
    <xs:pattern value=".+\+00:00"/>
    <xs:pattern value=".+Z"/>
    <xs:pattern value=".+-04:00"/>
  </xs:restriction>
</xs:simpleType>
```

We promised earlier to look at xs:duration and see how we can define two datatypes that have a complete sort order. The first datatype will consist of durations expressed only in months and years, and the second will consist of durations expressed only in days, hours, minutes, and seconds. The criteria used for the test can be the presence of a "D" (for day) or a "T" (the time delimiter). If neither of those characters are detected, then the datatype uses only year and month parts. The test for the other type cannot be based on the absence of "Y" and "M", since there is also an "M" in the time part. We can test that, after an optional sign, the first field is either the day part or the "T" delimiter:

```
<xs:simpleType name="YMduration">
  <xs:restriction base="xs:duration">
    <xs:pattern value="[^TD]+"/>
  </xs:restriction>
</xs:simpleType>

<xs:simpleType name="DHMSduration">
  <xs:restriction base="xs:duration">
    <xs:pattern value="-?P((\d+D)|T).*"/>
  </xs:restriction>
</xs:simpleType>
```

Back to Our Library

Let's see where we can use our Swiss army knife in our library. The first datatype, which we promised to improve at the end of the last chapter, is the ISBN number. Without fiddling the details of the constitution of an ISBN number (which can't be fully checked with W3C XML Schema), we can check that the total number of characters actually used is 10 and limit its contents to digits and the letter "X.":

```
<xs:simpleType name="isbn">
  <xs:restriction base="xs:NMTOKEN">
    <xs:length value="10"/>
    <xs:pattern value="[0-9]{9}[0-9X]"/>
  </xs:restriction>
</xs:simpleType>
```

 You may wonder why we kept the xs:length, since as far as validation is concerned, it is less constraining than the xs:pattern that we added. This is a question worth asking, but it doesn't have a complete answer yet. However, applications which use the PSVI as a source of meta information may or may not be able to deduce from a pattern that the length of a string has been fixed. It might be good practice to keep redundant facets to provide extra information to these future applications.

W3C XML Schema doesn't allow expression of the fact that the book ID is the same value as the ISBN number with a "b" used as a prefix, but we can still define that it is a "b" with 9 digits and a trailing digit or "X":

```
<xs:simpleType name="bookID">
  <xs:restriction base="xs:ID">
    <xs:pattern value="b[0-9]{9}[0-9X]"/>
  </xs:restriction>
</xs:simpleType>
```

To use this new datatype, we must be aware that we are using a global attribute that was referenced in the element book, but that was also referenced in the elements character and author, which do not have the same format. This is the main limitation in using global elements and attributes: they can be referenced only if they have the same types at all the locations in which they appear. We can work around this problem by creating a local attribute definition for the id attribute of book with the new datatype.

The last things we may want to constrain are the dates for which no time zones are needed and which, in fact, could just be a potential source of issues if we need to compare them:

```
<xs:simpleType name="date">
  <xs:restriction base="xs:date">
    <xs:pattern value="[^:Z]*"/>
  </xs:restriction>
</xs:simpleType>
```

Our new schema is then:

```
<?xml version="1.0"?>
<xs:schema xmlns:xs="http://www.w3.org/2001/XMLSchema">
  <xs:simpleType name="string255">
    <xs:restriction base="xs:token">
      <xs:maxLength value="255"/>
    </xs:restriction>
  </xs:simpleType>
  <xs:simpleType name="string32">
    <xs:restriction base="xs:token">
      <xs:maxLength value="32"/>
    </xs:restriction>
  </xs:simpleType>
  <xs:simpleType name="isbn">
    <xs:restriction base="xs:NMTOKEN">
      <xs:length value="10"/>
      <xs:pattern value="[0-9]{9}[0-9X]"/>
    </xs:restriction>
  </xs:simpleType>
  <xs:simpleType name="bookID">
    <xs:restriction base="xs:ID">
      <xs:pattern value="b[0-9]{9}[0-9X]"/>
    </xs:restriction>
  </xs:simpleType>
  <xs:simpleType name="supportedLanguages">
    <xs:restriction base="xs:language">
      <xs:enumeration value="en"/>
      <xs:enumeration value="es"/>
    </xs:restriction>
  </xs:simpleType>
  <xs:simpleType name="date">
    <xs:restriction base="xs:date">
      <xs:pattern value="[^:Z]*"/>
    </xs:restriction>
  </xs:simpleType>
  <xs:element name="name" type="string32"/>
  <xs:element name="qualification" type="string255"/>
  <xs:element name="born" type="date"/>
  <xs:element name="dead" type="date"/>
  <xs:element name="isbn" type="isbn"/>
  <xs:attribute name="id" type="xs:ID"/>
  <xs:attribute name="available" type="xs:boolean"/>
  <xs:attribute name="lang" type="supportedLanguages"/>
  <xs:element name="title">
    <xs:complexType>
      <xs:simpleContent>
        <xs:extension base="string255">
          <xs:attribute ref="lang"/>
        </xs:extension>
      </xs:simpleContent>
    </xs:complexType>
  </xs:element>
  <xs:element name="library">
```

```
        <xs:complexType>
          <xs:sequence>
            <xs:element ref="book" maxOccurs="unbounded"/>
          </xs:sequence>
        </xs:complexType>
      </xs:element>
      <xs:element name="author">
        <xs:complexType>
          <xs:sequence>
            <xs:element ref="name"/>
            <xs:element ref="born"/>
            <xs:element ref="dead" minOccurs="0"/>
          </xs:sequence>
          <xs:attribute ref="id"/>
        </xs:complexType>
      </xs:element>
      <xs:element name="book">
        <xs:complexType>
          <xs:sequence>
            <xs:element ref="isbn"/>
            <xs:element ref="title"/>
            <xs:element ref="author" minOccurs="0" maxOccurs="unbounded"/>
            <xs:element ref="character" minOccurs="0"
              maxOccurs="unbounded"/>
          </xs:sequence>
          <xs:attribute name="id" type="bookID"/>
          <xs:attribute ref="available"/>
        </xs:complexType>
      </xs:element>
      <xs:element name="character">
        <xs:complexType>
          <xs:sequence>
            <xs:element ref="name"/>
            <xs:element ref="born"/>
            <xs:element ref="qualification"/>
          </xs:sequence>
          <xs:attribute ref="id"/>
        </xs:complexType>
      </xs:element>
    </xs:schema>
```

CHAPTER 7

Creating Complex Datatypes

We have seen how to create simple datatypes that can be applied to attributes or simple type elements. It's now time to learn how complex types can be created.

Simple Versus Complex Types

Before we start diving into complex types, I would like to reiterate the fundamental difference between simple and complex types. The simple datatypes that we saw in the previous chapters describe the content of a text node or an attribute value. They are completely independent of the other nodes and, therefore, independent of the markup. The same datatype system can be used to describe the content of any format, even if it is not XML but an RDBMS (Relational DataBase Management System), CSV (Comma Separated Values), or a fixed-sized text format.

The complex types discussed in this chapter (and, more specifically, the complex content models) are, on the contrary, a description of the markup structure. They use simple datatypes to describe their leaf element nodes and attribute values, but have no other links with simple datatypes. Keep this in mind, especially when we study the derivation methods for complex datatypes. Even though the names (and elements) are sometimes the same as those we've seen for simple datatypes, their meaning, usage, and content models are different. When we discuss the xs: restriction element, for instance, you will see that this element has a different meaning and content model for simple types than it does for complex types. (In fact, this element even has two different content models for complex types, depending on its context.) Among the different content models composing complex types, the simple and mixed content models are special cases in which elements may have text nodes.

There is a kind of no man's land between simple types and complex contents, where the distinction between data and markup (or datatypes and structures) becomes fuzzier for W3C XML Schema. This ambiguity is a frequent source of confusion and complexity for human readers, but also for W3C XML Schema editing software and reference guides.

Examining the Landscape

W3C XML Schema has introduced many different ways of reaching your information modeling goals, and we will try to draw a global picture of the landscape to avoid getting lost! We have to make two key choices: which content model to use, and whether to create new types or to derive them from previously defined types.

Content Models

Let's go back over the definition of the content models and try to illustrate the different cases in Table 7-1. It shows the relationship between content model and child text and element nodes.

Table 7-1. Content models

Content model	Mixed	Complex	Simple	Empty
Child elements	Yes	Yes	No	No
Child text	Yes	No	Yes	No

W3C XML Schema provides two main ways to define complex types: one for complex content models and one for simple content models. It also offers several tricks for piggybacking the definition of mixed and empty contents on these definitions (through a `mixed` attribute on a complex type definition for mixed contents, and by omitting the option to declare elements or assigning a simple content that imposes a null value for empty contents).

Named Versus Anonymous Types

Like simple datatypes, complex datatypes can be either named (i.e., global) or anonymous (i.e., local). Global definitions must have a name and be a top-level element that is included directly in the `xs:schema` document element. The global definitions can then be referenced directly in an element definition using the element type attribute; new complex types can be derived from the global definitions. Local complex types are defined directly where they are needed in a schema; they are anonymous (i.e., no name attribute); and they have a local scope.

Creation Versus Derivation

For simple datatypes, there is no choice: you cannot create new primitive datatypes and we must define them by derivation. For complex datatypes, the situation is the opposite: there are no primitive complex types, and complex types must be created before we can do any derivation. When we create our first complex types, we have the choice of defining new content models from scratch or deriving them by extension or restriction from previously defined complex types. This makes it possible for libraries of complex datatypes to be reused within a schema or between different schemas. As far as validation is concerned, these derivations do not change anything compared to simpler definitions: they allow definition of exactly the same models applying to the same instance documents. On the other hand, some applications might be able to draw conclusions from the chain of derivations.

Simple Content Models

We will start by looking at complex types containing simple content because they are closest to simple types, which we've seen recently, and they also provide an easier transition to the more complex world of complex contents. We will not discuss the creation and derivation of simple types, already covered in Chapter 5, but instead will focus on complex types' simple content models (i.e., elements having only text nodes and attributes) and study how they are created and derived.

Creation of Simple Content Models

Complex types with simple content models are created by adding a list of attributes to a simple type. The operation of adding attributes to a simple type to create a simple content complex type is called an extension of the simple type. The syntax is straightforward and we have already seen examples of such creation in Chapter 4:

```
<xs:element name="title">
  <xs:complexType>
    <xs:simpleContent>
      <xs:extension base="string255">
        <xs:attribute ref="lang"/>
      </xs:extension>
    </xs:simpleContent>
  </xs:complexType>
</xs:element>
```

The only things that need to change here are that the definition of the simple type cannot be directly embedded in the xs:extension (complex content) and that it needs to be referenced through its base attribute.

This same syntax, with the same meaning, can be used to create global complex types, which can be used to define elements:

```
<xs:complexType name="tokenWithLang">
  <xs:simpleContent>
    <xs:extension base="xs:token">
      <xs:attribute ref="lang"/>
    </xs:extension>
```

```
    </xs:simpleContent>
  </xs:complexType>

<xs:element name="title" type="tokenWithLang"/>
```

Derivation from Simple Contents

Complex types provide a number of options for extending simple content models.

Derivation by extension

Derivation by extension is reserved for complex types and has no equivalent for simple types. It increases the number of child node elements or attributes allowed or expected in the complex type. For simple content complex types, child elements cannot be added and we stay with an extension that is identical to the method used to create a simple content complex type from a simple type. To add an attribute to the complex type tokenWithLang, just shown in the previous example, we could write:

```
<xs:element name="title">
  <xs:complexType>
    <xs:simpleContent>
      <xs:extension base="tokenWithLang">
        <xs:attribute name="note" type="xs:token"/>
      </xs:extension>
    </xs:simpleContent>
  </xs:complexType>
</xs:element>
```

Derivation by restriction

The derivation by restriction of simple content complex types is a feature at the border between the two parts of W3C XML Schema (Part 1: Structure and Part 2: Datatypes). It's also very similar to the derivation by restriction of simple datatypes, discussed in Chapter 6. The only difference between the derivations by restriction in these two contexts is that the derivation by restriction of a simple content complex type allows not only restriction of the scope of the text node, but also the restriction of the scope of the attribute. This restriction follows the same principle as the restriction of a simple type: any instance structure deemed valid per the restricted type must also be valid per the base type (with the exception already mentioned for the xs:whiteSpace facet).

The syntax used to restrict the text child is the same as the syntax used to derive simple types by restriction. The facets are the same as well. These facets must be followed by the new list of attributes, which may have different types as long as they are derived from the types of the attributes from the base type. Attributes that are not mandatory in the base type can be specified in the new list as "prohibited," and attributes that are not included are considered unchanged. Following are some examples of derivations that start from a simple content datatype equivalent to the content model just shown:

```
<xs:complexType name="tokenWithLangAndNote">
  <xs:simpleContent>
    <xs:extension base="xs:token">
      <xs:attribute name="lang" type="xs:language"/>
      <xs:attribute name="note" type="xs:token"/>
    </xs:extension>
  </xs:simpleContent>
</xs:complexType>
```

We can first show how to restrict the length of the text node, as we've done for simple types:

```
<xs:element name="title">
  <xs:complexType>
    <xs:simpleContent>
      <xs:restriction base="tokenWithLangAndNote">
        <xs:maxLength value="255"/>
         <xs:attribute name="lang" type="xs:language"/>
        <xs:attribute name="note" type="xs:token"/>
      </xs:restriction>
    </xs:simpleContent>
  </xs:complexType>
</xs:element>
```

To remove the note attribute from the element title, we declare note to be prohibited in the list of attributes in the restriction:

```
<xs:element name="title">
  <xs:complexType>
    <xs:simpleContent>
      <xs:restriction base="tokenWithLangAndNote">
        <xs:maxLength value="255"/>
        <xs:attribute name="lang" type="xs:language"/>
        <xs:attribute name="note" use="prohibited"/>
      </xs:restriction>
    </xs:simpleContent>
  </xs:complexType>
</xs:element>
```

We can also restrict the datatype by restricting its attributes. For instance, if we want to restrict the number of possible languages, we can do it directly in the definition of the lang attribute in the derived type:

```
<xs:element name="title">
  <xs:complexType>
    <xs:simpleContent>
      <xs:restriction base="tokenWithLangAndNote">
        <xs:maxLength value="255"/>
        <xs:attribute name="lang">
          <xs:simpleType>
            <xs:restriction base="xs:language">
              <xs:enumeration value="en"/>
```

```
                <xs:enumeration value="es"/>
              </xs:restriction>
            </xs:simpleType>
          </xs:attribute>
        </xs:restriction>
      </xs:simpleContent>
    </xs:complexType>
  </xs:element>
```

Comparison of these two methods

Despite apparent similarities, derivations by extension and restriction do not have much more in common than deriving new simple content types from base types! Derivation by extension can only add new attributes. It can neither change the datatype of the text node nor the type of an attribute defined in its base type. Derivation by restriction appears to be more flexible and can restrict the datatype of the text node and of the attributes of the base type. It can also remove attributes that are not mandatory in its base type.

Complex Content Models

Restricting or extending simple content models is useful, but XML is not very useful without more complex models.

Creation of Complex Content

Complex contents are created by defining the list (and order) of its elements and attributes. We have already seen a couple of examples of complex content models, defined as local complex types in Chapter 1 and Chapter 2:

```
<xs:element name="library">
  <xs:complexType>
    <xs:sequence>
      <xs:element ref="book" maxOccurs="unbounded"/>
    </xs:sequence>
  </xs:complexType>
</xs:element>

<xs:element name="author">
  <xs:complexType>
    <xs:sequence>
      <xs:element ref="name"/>
      <xs:element ref="born"/>
      <xs:element ref="dead" minOccurs="0"/>
    </xs:sequence>
    <xs:attribute ref="id"/>
  </xs:complexType>
</xs:element>
```

These examples show the basic structure of a complex type with complex content definition: the xs:complexType element is holding the definition. Here, this definition is local (xs:complexType is not top-level since it is included under an xs:element element) and, thus, anonymous. Under xs:complexType, we find the sequence of children elements (xs:sequence) and the list of attributes.

Compositors and particles

In these examples, the xs:sequence elements have a role as "compositors" and the xs:element elements, which are included in xs:sequence, play a role of "particle." This simple scenario may be extended using other compositors and particles.

W3C XML Schema defines three different compositors: xs:sequence, to define ordered lists of particles; xs:choice, to define a choice of one particle among several; and xs:all, to define nonordered list of particles. The xs:sequence and xs:choice compositors can define their own number of occurrences using minOccurs and maxOccurs attributes and they can be used as particles (some important restrictions apply to xs:all, which cannot be used as a particle, as we will see in the next section).

The particles are xs:element, xs:sequence, xs:choice, plus xs:any and xs:group, which we will see later in the section. The ability to include compositors within compositors is key to defining complex structures, although it is unfortunately subject to the allergy of W3C XML Schema for "nondeterminism."

To give an idea of the kind of structures that can be defined, let's suppose that the names in our library may be expressed in two different ways: either as a name element, as we have shown up to now, or as three different elements to define the first, middle, and last name (the middle name should be optional). Names could then be expressed as one of the three following combinations:

```
<first-name>
  Charles
</first-name>
     <middle-name>
  M
</middle-name>
      <last name>
  Schulz
</last-name>
```

or:

```
<first-name>
  Peppermint
</first-name>
     <last-name>
  Patty
</last-name>
```

or:

```
<name>
  Snoopy
</name>
```

To describe this, we will replace the reference to the name element with a choice between either a name element or a sequence of first-name, middle-name (optional), and last-name. The definition of author then becomes:

```
<xs:element name="author">
  <xs:complexType>
    <xs:sequence>
      <xs:choice>
        <xs:element ref="name"/>
        <xs:sequence>
          <xs:element ref="first-name"/>
          <xs:element ref="middle-name" minOccurs="0"/>
          <xs:element ref="last-name"/>
        </xs:sequence>
      </xs:choice>
      <xs:element ref="born"/>
      <xs:element ref="dead" minOccurs="0"/>
    </xs:sequence>
    <xs:attribute ref="id"/>
  </xs:complexType>
</xs:element>
```

The name element also appears in the character element, and a copy/paste can be used to replace it with the xs:choice structure, but we would rather take this opportunity to introduce a new feature that is very handy to manipulating reusable sets of elements.

Element and attribute groups

Element and attribute groups are containers in which sets of elements and attributes may be embedded and manipulated as a whole. These simple and flexible structures are very convenient for defining bits of content models that can be reused in multiple locations, such as the xs:choice structure that we created for our name.

The first step is to define the element group. The definition needs to be named and global (i.e., immediately under the xs:schema element) and has the following form:

```
<xs:group name="name">
  <xs:choice>
    <xs:element ref="name"/>
    <xs:sequence>
      <xs:element ref="first-name"/>
      <xs:element ref="middle-name" minOccurs="0"/>
      <xs:element ref="last-name"/>
    </xs:sequence>
  </xs:choice>
</xs:group>
```

These groups can then be used by reference as particles within compositors:

```
<xs:element name="author">
  <xs:complexType>
    <xs:sequence>
      <xs:group ref="name"/>
      <xs:element ref="born"/>
      <xs:element ref="dead" minOccurs="0"/>
    </xs:sequence>
    <xs:attribute ref="id"/>
  </xs:complexType>
</xs:element>

<xs:element name="character">
  <xs:complexType>
    <xs:sequence>
      <xs:group ref="name"/>
      <xs:element ref="born"/>
      <xs:element ref="qualification"/>
    </xs:sequence>
    <xs:attribute ref="id"/>
  </xs:complexType>
</xs:element>
```

Groups of attributes can be created in the same way using xs:attributeGroup:

```
<xs:attributeGroup name="bookAttributes">
  <xs:attribute name="id" type="xs:ID"/>
  <xs:attribute name="available" type="xs:boolean"/>
</xs:attributeGroup>

<xs:element name="book">
  <xs:complexType>
    <xs:sequence>
      <xs:element ref="isbn"/>
      <xs:element ref="title"/>
      <xs:element ref="author" minOccurs="0" maxOccurs="unbounded"/>
      <xs:element ref="character" minOccurs="0"
        maxOccurs="unbounded"/>
    </xs:sequence>
    <xs:attributeGroup ref="bookAttributes"/>
  </xs:complexType>
</xs:element>
```

Unique Particle Attribution Rule

Let's try a new example to illustrate one of the most constraining limitations of W3C XML Schema. We may want to describe all the pages of our books and to have a different description using different elements, such as odd-page and even-page for odd and even pages that require a different pagination. We can try to describe the new content model in the following group:

```
<xs:group name="pages">
  <xs:sequence>
```

```
      <xs:sequence minOccurs="0" maxOccurs="unbounded">
        <xs:element ref="odd-page"/>
        <xs:element ref="even-page"/>
      </xs:sequence>
      <xs:element ref="odd-page" minOccurs="0"/>
    </xs:sequence>
  </xs:group>
```

This seems like a simple, smart way to describe the sequences of odd and even pages: a sequence of odd and even pages eventually followed by a last odd page. The model covers books with an odd or even number of pages as well as tiny booklets with a single page. Neither XSV not Xerces appear to enjoy it, though:

```
XSV:

vdv@evlist:~/w3c-xml-schema/user/examples/complex-types$ xsd -n first-ambigous.xsd
first-ambigous.xml
using xsv (default)
<?xml version='1.0'?>
<xsv docElt='{None}library' instanceAssessed='true' instanceErrors='0'
rootType='[Anonymous]' schemaDocs='first-ambigous.xsd' schemaErrors='1'
target='/home/vdv/w3c-xml-schema/user/examples/complex-types/first-ambigous.xml'
validation='strict' version='XSV 1.203.2.20/1.106.2.11 of 2001/11/01 17:07:43'
xmlns='http://www.w3.org/2000/05/xsv'>
<schemaDocAttempt URI='/home/vdv/w3c-xml-schema/user/examples/complex-types/first-
ambigous.xsd'
outcome='success' source='command line'/>
<schemaError char='7' line='65' phase='instance'
resource='file:///home/vdv/w3c-xml-schema/user/examples/complex-types/first-ambigous.
xsd'>
non-deterministic content model for type None: {None}:odd-page/{None}:odd-page</
schemaError>
</xsv>


Xerces:

vdv@evlist:~/w3c-xml-schema/user/examples/complex-types$ xsd -n first-ambigous.xsd
-p xerces-cvs first-ambigous.xml
using xerces-cvs
startDocument
[Error] first-ambigous.xml:2:10: Error: cos-nonambig: (,odd-page)
and (,odd-page) violate the "Unique Particle Attribution" rule.
endDocument
```

Misled by the apparent flexibility of construction with compositors and particles, we violated an ancient taboo known in SGML as "ambiguous content models," which was imported into XML's DTDs as "nondeterministic content models," and preserved by W3C XML Schema as the "Unique Particle Attribution Rule."

In practice, this rule adds a significant amount of complexity to writing a W3C XML Schema, since it must be matched after all the many features, which allow you to define, redefine, derive, import, reference, and substitute complex types, have been resolved by the schema processor. The Recommendation recognizes that "given the presence of element substitution groups and wildcards, the concise expression of this constraint is difficult." When these features have been resolved, the remaining constraint requires that a schema processor should never have any doubt about which branch it is in while doing the validation of an element and looking only at this element. Applied to the previous example, which was as simple as possible, there is a problem. When a schema processor meets the first odd-page element, it has no way of knowing if the page will be followed by an even-page element without first looking ahead to the next element. This is a violation of the Unique Particle Attribution Rule.

This example, adapted from an example describing a chess board, is one of the famous instances in which the content model cannot be written in a "deterministic" way. This is not always the case, and many nondeterministic constructions describe content models that may be rewritten in a deterministic fashion. We should differentiate those that are fundamentally nondeterministic from those that are only "accidentally" nondeterministic. Let's go back to our example with a "name" sequence that can have two different content models, and imagine that instead of using first-name, we reused the name name. The content model is now either name or a sequence of name, "middle-name," and "last-name":

```
<xs:group name="name">
  <xs:choice>
    <xs:element ref="name"/>
    <xs:sequence>
      <xs:element ref="name"/>
      <xs:element ref="middle-name" minOccurs="0"/>
      <xs:element ref="last-name"/>
    </xs:sequence>
  </xs:choice>
</xs:group>

<xs:element name="author">
  <xs:complexType>
    <xs:sequence>
      <xs:group ref="name"/>
      <xs:element ref="born"/>
      <xs:element ref="dead" minOccurs="0"/>
    </xs:sequence>
    <xs:attribute ref="id"/>
  </xs:complexType>
</xs:element>
```

Here again, when the processor meets a name element, it has no way of knowing (without looking ahead) if this element matches the first or the second branch of the choice. In this case, though, the content model may be simplified if we note that the name element is common to both branches and that, in fact, we now have a mandatory name element followed by an optional sequence of an optional middle-name and a mandatory last-name. The content model can then be rewritten in a deterministic way as:

```
<xs:group name="name">
  <xs:sequence>
    <xs:element ref="name"/>
    <xs:sequence minOccurs="0">
      <xs:element ref="middle-name" minOccurs="0"/>
      <xs:element ref="last-name"/>
    </xs:sequence>
  </xs:sequence>
</xs:group>
```

This is a slippery path, though, which frequently depends on slight nuances in the content model and leads to schemas that are very difficult to maintain and may require nonsatisfactory compromises. If the requirement for the content model we have just written is changed and the name element in the second branch is no longer mandatory, then we are in trouble. The new content model is as follows:

```
<xs:group name="name">
  <xs:choice>
    <xs:element ref="name"/>
    <xs:sequence>
      <xs:element ref="name" minOccurs="0"/>
      <xs:element ref="middle-name" minOccurs="0"/>
      <xs:element ref="last-name"/>
    </xs:sequence>
  </xs:choice>
</xs:group>
```

But this model is nondeterministic for the same reason that the previous one was, and we need to reevaluate the different possible combinations to find that the new content model can now be expressed as:

```
<xs:group name="name">
  <xs:choice>
    <xs:sequence>
      <xs:element ref="name"/>
      <xs:sequence minOccurs="0">
        <xs:element ref="middle-name" minOccurs="0"/>
        <xs:element ref="last-name"/>
      </xs:sequence>
    </xs:sequence>
    <xs:sequence>
      <xs:element ref="middle-name" minOccurs="0"/>
      <xs:element ref="last-name"/>
    </xs:sequence>
  </xs:choice>
</xs:group>
```

Formal theories and algorithms can rewrite nondeterministic content models in a deterministic way when possible. Hopefully, W3C XML Schema development tools will integrate some of these algorithms to propose an alternative when a schema author creates nondeterministic content models.

Ambiguous content models were already a controversial issue in the 90s among the SGML community, and the restriction has been maintained in XML DTDs under the name "nondeterministic content models" despite the dissent of Tim Bray, Jean Paoli, and Peter Sharpe, three influential members of the XML Special Interest Group who wanted to maintain a compatibility with SGML parsers. The motivation to maintain the restriction in W3C XML Schema is to keep schema processors simple to implement and to allow implementations through finite state machines (FSM). The execution time of these automatons could grow exponentially when the Unique Particle Attribution Rule is violated. This decision has been heavily criticized by experts including Joe English, James Clark, and Murata Makoto, who have proved that other simple algorithms might be used that keep the processing time linear when this rule is not met. This is also one of the main differences between the descriptive powers of schema languages, such as RELAX, TREX, and RELAX NG, which do not impose this rule, and W3C XML Schema.

Consistent Declaration Rule

Although not related, strictly speaking, the Unique Particle Attribution Rule and the Consistent Declaration Rule are often associated, since, in practice, when the Consistent Declaration Rule is violated, the Unique Particle Attribution Rule is often violated too. This new rule is much easier to explain and understand, since it only states that W3C XML Schema explicitly forbids choices between elements with the same name and different types, such as in the following:

```
<xs:choice>
  <xs:element name="name" type="xs:string"/>
  <xs:element name="name">
    <xs:complexType>
      <xs:sequence>
        <xs:element ref="first-name"/>
        <xs:element ref="middle-name"/>
        <xs:element ref="last-name"/>
      </xs:sequence>
    </xs:complexType>
  </xs:element>
</xs:choice>
```

We will see a workaround using the xsi:type attribute, which may be used by some applications, in Chapter 11.

Limitations on unordered content models

While useful, unordered content models have their own sets of limitations.

Limitations of xs:all. Unordered content models (i.e., content models that do not impose any order on the children elements) not only increase the risks of nondeterministic content models, but are also an important complexity factor for schema processors. For the sake of implementation simplicity, the Recommendation has imposed huge limitations on the xs:all element, which makes it hardly usable in practice. xs:all cannot be used as a particle, but as a compositor only; xs:all cannot have a number of occurrences greater than one; the particles included within xs:all must be xs:element; and these particles must not specify numbers of occurrences greater than one.

To illustrate these limitations, let's imagine we have decided to simplify the life of document producers and want to create a vocabulary that doesn't care about the relative order of children elements. With a simple vocabulary such as the one defined in our first schema, this wouldn't add a big burden to the applications handling our vocabulary. When you think about it, there is no special reason to impose the definition of the title of a book after its ISBN number or the definition of the list of authors before the list of characters. The first content model that may be affected by this decision is the content model of the book element:

```
<xs:element name="book">
  <xs:complexType>
    <xs:sequence>
      <xs:element ref="isbn"/>
      <xs:element ref="title"/>
      <xs:element ref="author" minOccurs="0" maxOccurs="unbounded"/>
      <xs:element ref="character" minOccurs="0"
          maxOccurs="unbounded"/>
    </xs:sequence>
    <xs:attribute ref="id"/>
    <xs:attribute ref="available"/>
  </xs:complexType>
</xs:element>
```

Unfortunately, here the xs:sequence cannot be replaced by xs:all, since two of the children elements (author and character) have a maximum number of occurrences that is "unbounded" and thus higher than one. The second group of candidates includes the content models of author and character, which are relatively similar:

```
<xs:element name="author">
  <xs:complexType>
    <xs:sequence>
      <xs:element ref="name"/>
      <xs:element ref="born"/>
      <xs:element ref="dead" minOccurs="0"/>
    </xs:sequence>
    <xs:attribute ref="id"/>
```

```
      </xs:complexType>
    </xs:element>

    <xs:element name="character">
      <xs:complexType>
        <xs:sequence>
          <xs:element ref="name"/>
          <xs:element ref="born"/>
          <xs:element ref="qualification"/>
        </xs:sequence>
        <xs:attribute ref="id"/>
      </xs:complexType>
    </xs:element>
```

The good news here is that both author and character match the criteria for xs:all, so we can write:

```
    <xs:element name="author">
      <xs:complexType>
        <xs:all>
          <xs:element ref="name"/>
          <xs:element ref="born"/>
          <xs:element ref="dead" minOccurs="0"/>
        </xs:all>
        <xs:attribute ref="id"/>
      </xs:complexType>
    </xs:element>

    <xs:element name="character">
      <xs:complexType>
        <xs:all>
          <xs:element ref="name"/>
          <xs:element ref="born"/>
          <xs:element ref="qualification"/>
        </xs:all>
        <xs:attribute ref="id"/>
      </xs:complexType>
    </xs:element>
```

We can have two elements (author and character) in which the order of children elements is not significant. One may question, though, whether this is very interesting since this independence is not consistent throughout the schema. More importantly, we must note that we have lost a great deal of flexibility and extensibility by using a xs:all compositor. Since the maximum number of occurrences for each child element needs to be one, we can no longer, for instance, change the number of occurrences of the qualification element to accept several qualifications in different languages. And since the particles used in xs:all cannot be compositors or groups, we can't extend the content model to accept both name and the sequence first-name, middle-name, and last-name either.

Since `xs:all` appears to be pretty ineffective in general, there are a couple of workarounds that may be proposed for people who would like to develop order-independent vocabularies.

Adapting the structure of your document. The first workaround, which may be used only if you are creating your own vocabulary from scratch, is to adapt the structures of your document to the constraint of `xs:all`. In practice, this means that each time we have to use a `xs:choice`, a `xs:sequence`, or include elements with more than one occurrence, we will add a new element as a container. For instance, we will create containers named authors and characters that will encapsulate the multiple occurrences of author and character. The result is instance documents such as:

```
<?xml version="1.0"?>
<library>
  <book id="b0836217462" available="true">
    <title lang="en">
      Being a Dog Is a Full-Time Job
    </title>
    <isbn>
      0836217462
    </isbn>
    <authors>
      <author id="CMS">
        <born>
          1922-11-26
        </born>
        <dead>
          2000-02-12
        </dead>
        <name>
          Charles M Schulz
        </name>
      </author>
    </authors>
    <characters>
      <character id="PP">
        <name>
          Peppermint Patty
        </name>
        <qualification>
          bold, brash and tomboyish
        </qualification>
        <born>
          1966-08-22
        </born>
      </character>
      <character id="Snoopy">
        <born>
          1950-10-04
        </born>
        <name>
```

```
        Snoopy
      </name>
      <qualification>
        extroverted beagle
      </qualification>
    </character>
    <character id="Schroeder">
      <qualification>
        brought classical music to the Peanuts strip
      </qualification>
      <name>
        Schroeder
      </name>
      <born>
        1951-05-30
      </born>
    </character>
    <character id="Lucy">
      <name>
        Lucy
      </name>
      <born>
        1952-03-03
      </born>
      <qualification>
        bossy, crabby and selfish
      </qualification>
    </character>
  </characters>
 </book>
</library>
```

This instance document defined by a full schema, which could be:

```
<?xml version="1.0"?>
<xs:schema xmlns:xs="http://www.w3.org/2001/XMLSchema">
  <xs:element name="name" type="xs:token"/>
  <xs:element name="qualification" type="xs:token"/>
  <xs:element name="born" type="xs:date"/>
  <xs:element name="dead" type="xs:date"/>
  <xs:element name="isbn" type="xs:NMTOKEN"/>
  <xs:attribute name="id" type="xs:ID"/>
  <xs:attribute name="available" type="xs:boolean"/>
  <xs:attribute name="lang" type="xs:language"/>
  <xs:element name="title">
    <xs:complexType>
      <xs:simpleContent>
        <xs:extension base="xs:token">
          <xs:attribute ref="lang"/>
        </xs:extension>
      </xs:simpleContent>
    </xs:complexType>
  </xs:element>
  <xs:element name="library">
```

```
    <xs:complexType>
      <xs:sequence>
        <xs:element ref="book" maxOccurs="unbounded"/>
      </xs:sequence>
    </xs:complexType>
  </xs:element>
  <xs:element name="authors">
    <xs:complexType>
      <xs:sequence>
        <xs:element ref="author" minOccurs="0" maxOccurs="unbounded"/>
      </xs:sequence>
    </xs:complexType>
  </xs:element>
  <xs:element name="author">
    <xs:complexType>
      <xs:all>
        <xs:element ref="name"/>
        <xs:element ref="born"/>
        <xs:element ref="dead" minOccurs="0"/>
      </xs:all>
      <xs:attribute ref="id"/>
    </xs:complexType>
  </xs:element>
  <xs:element name="book">
    <xs:complexType>
      <xs:all>
        <xs:element ref="isbn"/>
        <xs:element ref="title"/>
        <xs:element ref="authors"/>
        <xs:element ref="characters"/>
      </xs:all>
      <xs:attribute ref="id"/>
      <xs:attribute ref="available"/>
    </xs:complexType>
  </xs:element>
  <xs:element name="characters">
    <xs:complexType>
      <xs:sequence>
        <xs:element ref="character" minOccurs="0"
          maxOccurs="unbounded"/>
      </xs:sequence>
    </xs:complexType>
  </xs:element>
  <xs:element name="character">
    <xs:complexType>
      <xs:all>
        <xs:element ref="name"/>
        <xs:element ref="born"/>
        <xs:element ref="qualification"/>
      </xs:all>
      <xs:attribute ref="id"/>
    </xs:complexType>
  </xs:element>
</xs:schema>
```

This adaptation of the instance document will be more painful if we want to implement our alternative "name" content model. Since we cannot include a xs:choice in a xs:all compositor, we have to add a first level of container, which is always the same, and a second level of container, which contains only the choice that would lead to instance documents such as:

```
<?xml version="1.0"?>
<library>
  <book id="b0836217462" available="true">
    <title lang="en">
      Being a Dog Is a Full-Time Job
    </title>
    <isbn>
      0836217462
    </isbn>
    <authors>
      <author id="CMS">
        <born>
          1922-11-26
        </born>
        <dead>
          2000-02-12
        </dead>
        <name>
          <complex-name>
            <last-name>
              Schulz
            </last-name>
            <first-name>
              Charles
            </first-name>
            <middle-name>
              M
            </middle-name>
          </complex-name>
        </name>
      </author>
    </authors>
    <characters>
      <character id="PP">
        <name>
          <complex-name>
            <first-name>
              Peppermint
            </first-name>
            <last-name>
              Patty
            </last-name>
          </complex-name>
        </name>
        <qualification>
          bold, brash and tomboyish
        </qualification>
```

```
      <born>
        1966-08-22
      </born>
    </character>
    <character id="Snoopy">
      <born>
        1950-10-04
      </born>
      <name>
        <simple-name>
          Snoopy
        </simple-name>
      </name>
      <qualification>
        extroverted beagle
      </qualification>
    </character>
    <character id="Schroeder">
      <qualification>
        brought classical music to the Peanuts strip
      </qualification>
      <name>
        <simple-name>
          Schroeder
        </simple-name>
      </name>
      <born>
        1951-05-30
      </born>
    </character>
    <character id="Lucy">
      <name>
        <simple-name>
          Lucy
        </simple-name>
      </name>
      <born>
        1952-03-03
      </born>
      <qualification>
        bossy, crabby and selfish
      </qualification>
    </character>
  </characters>
</book>
</library>
```

The adaptation of the schema is then straightforward and could be (keeping a flat design):

```
<?xml version="1.0"?>
<xs:schema xmlns:xs="http://www.w3.org/2001/XMLSchema">
  <xs:element name="simple-name" type="xs:token"/>
  <xs:element name="first-name" type="xs:token"/>
```

```
<xs:element name="middle-name" type="xs:token"/>
<xs:element name="last-name" type="xs:token"/>
<xs:element name="qualification" type="xs:token"/>
<xs:element name="born" type="xs:date"/>
<xs:element name="dead" type="xs:date"/>
<xs:element name="isbn" type="xs:NMTOKEN"/>
<xs:attribute name="id" type="xs:ID"/>
<xs:attribute name="available" type="xs:boolean"/>
<xs:attribute name="lang" type="xs:language"/>
<xs:element name="name">
  <xs:complexType>
    <xs:choice>
      <xs:element ref="simple-name"/>
      <xs:element ref="complex-name"/>
    </xs:choice>
  </xs:complexType>
</xs:element>
<xs:element name="complex-name">
  <xs:complexType>
    <xs:all>
      <xs:element ref="first-name"/>
      <xs:element ref="middle-name" minOccurs="0"/>
      <xs:element ref="last-name"/>
    </xs:all>
  </xs:complexType>
</xs:element>
<xs:element name="title">
  <xs:complexType>
    <xs:simpleContent>
      <xs:extension base="xs:token">
        <xs:attribute ref="lang"/>
      </xs:extension>
    </xs:simpleContent>
  </xs:complexType>
</xs:element>
<xs:element name="library">
  <xs:complexType>
    <xs:sequence>
      <xs:element ref="book" maxOccurs="unbounded"/>
    </xs:sequence>
  </xs:complexType>
</xs:element>
<xs:element name="authors">
  <xs:complexType>
    <xs:sequence>
      <xs:element ref="author" minOccurs="0" maxOccurs="unbounded"/>
    </xs:sequence>
  </xs:complexType>
</xs:element>
<xs:element name="author">
  <xs:complexType>
    <xs:all>
      <xs:element ref="name"/>
      <xs:element ref="born"/>
```

```
        <xs:element ref="dead" minOccurs="0"/>
      </xs:all>
      <xs:attribute ref="id"/>
    </xs:complexType>
  </xs:element>
  <xs:element name="book">
    <xs:complexType>
      <xs:all>
        <xs:element ref="isbn"/>
        <xs:element ref="title"/>
        <xs:element ref="authors"/>
        <xs:element ref="characters"/>
      </xs:all>
      <xs:attribute ref="id"/>
      <xs:attribute ref="available"/>
    </xs:complexType>
  </xs:element>
  <xs:element name="characters">
    <xs:complexType>
      <xs:sequence>
        <xs:element ref="character" minOccurs="0"
          maxOccurs="unbounded"/>
      </xs:sequence>
    </xs:complexType>
  </xs:element>
  <xs:element name="character">
    <xs:complexType>
      <xs:all>
        <xs:element ref="name"/>
        <xs:element ref="born"/>
        <xs:element ref="qualification"/>
      </xs:all>
      <xs:attribute ref="id"/>
    </xs:complexType>
  </xs:element>
</xs:schema>
```

This process may be generalized and used for purposes other than adapting instance documents to the constraints of xs:all. It is interesting to note that we have "externalized" the complexity, which was previously hidden from the instance document in the schema, to bring the full structure of the content model into the instance document itself. The choices and sequences (an element with multiple occurrences is nothing more than an implicit sequence) are now expressed through containers in the instance documents. Since the structure is more apparent in the instance documents, it can be considered more readable; some people find it a good practice to use such container.

Using xs:choice instead of xs:all. When it is not possible or not practical to adapt the structure of a document to the limitations of xs:all, another workaround that may be used is to replace xs:all compositors by xs:choice, when possible. This trick is far less generic than the adaptation of structures we just saw, and it may be surprising that two compositors with a very different meaning could be "interchanged." This applies only when a loose control on the number of occurrences can be applied, such as in a container that accepts both author and character elements in any order with any number of occurrences. Such a container can be defined as:

```
<xs:element name="persons">
  <xs:complexType>
    <xs:choice minOccurs="0" maxOccurs="unbounded">
      <xs:element ref="author"/>
      <xs:element ref="character"/>
    </xs:choice>
  </xs:complexType>
</xs:element>
```

This definition has the same meaning as the following xs:all (outside a group) definition, which is forbidden:

```
<xs:element name="persons">
  <xs:complexType>
    <xs:all>
      <xs:element ref="author" minOccurs="0" maxOccurs="unbounded"/>
      <xs:element ref="character" minOccurs="0"
        maxOccurs="unbounded"/>
    </xs:all>
  </xs:complexType>
</xs:element>
```

Derivation of Complex Content

Complex contents can also be derived, by extension or by restriction, from complex types. Before we see the details of these mechanisms, note that they are not symmetrical and their semantic is very different. The derivation of a complex content by restriction is a restriction of the set of matching instances. All the instance structures that match the restricted complex type must also match the base complex type. The derivation of a complex content by extension of a complex type is an extension of the content model by addition of new particles. A content that matches the base type does not necessarily match the extended complex type. This also means that there is no "roundtrip": in the general case, neither a restricted complex type nor an extended type can be extended or restricted back into its base type.

Derivation by extension

Derivation by extension is similar to the extension of simple content complex types. It is functionally very similar to joining groups of elements and attributes to create a new complex type. The idea behind this feature is to let people add new elements and attributes after those already defined in the base type. This is virtually equivalent to creating a sequence with the current content model followed by the new content model. Let's go back to our library to illustrate this. The content models of our elements author and character are relatively similar: author expects name, born, and dead, while character expects name, born, and qualification. If we want to use a derivation by extension, we can first create a base type that contains the first elements common to the content model of both elements:

```
<xs:complexType name="basePerson">
  <xs:sequence>
    <xs:element ref="name"/>
    <xs:element ref="born"/>
  </xs:sequence>
  <xs:attribute ref="id"/>
</xs:complexType>
```

It is then possible to use derivations by extension to append new elements (dead for author and qualification for character) after those that have already been defined in the base type:

```
<xs:element name="author">
  <xs:complexType>
    <xs:complexContent>
      <xs:extension base="basePerson">
        <xs:sequence>
          <xs:element ref="dead" minOccurs="0"/>
        </xs:sequence>
      </xs:extension>
    </xs:complexContent>
  </xs:complexType>
</xs:element>

<xs:element name="character">
  <xs:complexType>
    <xs:complexContent>
      <xs:extension base="basePerson">
        <xs:sequence>
          <xs:element ref="qualification"/>
        </xs:sequence>
      </xs:extension>
    </xs:complexContent>
  </xs:complexType>
</xs:element>
```

Technically, the meaning of this derivation is equivalent to creating a sequence containing the compositor used to define the base type as well as the base type included in the xs:extension element. Thus, the content models of these elements are similar to the content models defined as:

```
<xs:element name="author">
  <xs:complexType>
    <xs:sequence>
      <xs:sequence>
        <xs:element ref="name"/>
        <xs:element ref="born"/>
      </xs:sequence>
      <xs:sequence>
        <xs:element ref="dead" minOccurs="0"/>
```

```
          </xs:sequence>
        </xs:sequence>
        <xs:attribute ref="id"/>
      </xs:complexType>
    </xs:element>

    <xs:element name="character">
      <xs:complexType>
        <xs:sequence>
          <xs:sequence>
            <xs:element ref="name"/>
            <xs:element ref="born"/>
          </xs:sequence>
          <xs:sequence>
            <xs:element ref="qualification"/>
          </xs:sequence>
        </xs:sequence>
        <xs:attribute ref="id"/>
      </xs:complexType>
    </xs:element>
```

This equivalence clearly shows the feature of this derivation mechanism. As stated in the introduction of complex content derivation mechanisms, this is not an extension of the set of valid instance structures. An element character, with its mandatory qualification, cannot have a valid basePerson content model but rather the merge of two content models. This merge itself is subject to limitations: you cannot choose the point where the new content model is inserted; this addition is always done by appending the new compositor after the one of the base type. In our example, if the common elements name and born were not the first two elements, we couldn't have used a derivation by extension.

Another caveat in derivations by extension is we can't choose the compositor that is used to merge the two content models. This means that when we derive content models using xs:choice as compositors, it is not the scope of the choices that is extended, but rather the choices that are included in a xs:sequence. We could, for instance, extend the content model of the element persons, which we just created and which could be defined as a global complex type:

```
<xs:complexType name="basePersons">
  <xs:choice minOccurs="0" maxOccurs="unbounded">
    <xs:element ref="author"/>
    <xs:element ref="character"/>
  </xs:choice>
</xs:complexType>
```

If we add a new element using a derivation by extension:

```
<xs:complexType name="persons">
  <xs:complexContent>
    <xs:extension base="basePersons">
      <xs:sequence>
        <xs:element name="editor" type="xs:token" minOccurs="0"
```

```
          maxOccurs="unbounded"/>
      </xs:sequence>
    </xs:extension>
  </xs:complexContent>
</xs:complexType>
```

The result is a content type that is equivalent to:

```
<xs:complexType name="personsEquivalent">
  <xs:sequence>
    <xs:choice minOccurs="0" maxOccurs="unbounded">
      <xs:element ref="author"/>
      <xs:element ref="character"/>
    </xs:choice>
    <xs:sequence>
      <xs:element name="editor" type="xs:token" minOccurs="0"
        maxOccurs="unbounded"/>
    </xs:sequence>
  </xs:sequence>
</xs:complexType>
```

There is no way to obtain an extension of the xs:choice such as:

```
<xs:complexType name="personsAsWeWouldHaveLiked">
  <xs:choice minOccurs="0" maxOccurs="unbounded">
    <xs:element ref="author"/>
    <xs:element ref="character"/>
    <xs:element name="editor" type="xs:token"/>
  </xs:choice>
</xs:complexType>
```

The situation with xs:all is even worse: the restrictions on the composition of xs:all still apply. This means you can't add any content to a complex type defined with a xs:all—although you can still add new attributes—and also you can only use a xs:all compositor in a derivation by extension if the base type has an empty content model.

Derivation by restriction

Whereas derivation by extension is similar to merging two content models through a xs:sequence (outside a group) compositor, derivation by restriction is a restriction of the number of instance structures matching the complex type. In this respect, it is similar to the derivation by restriction of simple datatypes or simple content complex types (even though we've seen that a facet such as xs:whiteSpace expanded the number of instance documents matching a simple type). Note that this is the only similarity between derivations by restriction of simple and complex datatypes. This is highly confusing, since W3C XML Schema uses the same word and even the same element name in both cases, but these words have a different meaning and the content models of the xs:restriction elements are different.

Unlike simple type derivation, there are no facets to apply to complex types, and the derivation is done by defining the full content model of the derived datatype, which must be a logical restriction of the base type. Any instance structure valid per the derived datatype must also be valid per the base datatype. The W3C XML Schema specification does not define the derivation by restriction in these terms, but defines a formal algorithm to be followed by schema processors, which is roughly equivalent.

The derivation by restriction of a complex type is a declaration of intention that the derived type is a subset of the base type. (Rather than a derivation we've seen for simple types, this declaration is needed for features allowing substitutions and redefinitions of types, which we will see in Chapter 8 and Chapter 12 and which may provide useful information used by some applications.) When we derive simple types, we can take a base type without having to care about the details of the facets that are already applied, and just add our own set of facets. Here, on the contrary, we need to provide a full definition of a content model, except for attributes that can be declared as "prohibited" to be excluded from the restriction, something we have seen for the restriction of complex types with simple contents.

Moving on, let's try to find a base from which we can derive both the author and character elements by restriction. This time, we can be sure that such a complex type exists since all the complex types can be derived from an abstract xs:anyType, allowing any elements and attributes. In practice, however, we will try to find the most restrictive base type that can accommodate our needs. Since the name and born elements are present in both author and character, with the same number of occurrences, we can keep them as they appear. We then have two elements (dead and qualification, which appear only in one of the two elements author and character). Since both author and character will need to be valid per the base type, we will take both of them in the base type but make them optional by giving them a minOccurs attribute equal to 0. Our base type can then be:

```
<xs:complexType name="person">
  <xs:sequence>
    <xs:element ref="name"/>
    <xs:element ref="born"/>
    <xs:element ref="dead" minOccurs="0"/>
    <xs:element ref="qualification" minOccurs="0"/>
  </xs:sequence>
  <xs:attribute ref="id"/>
</xs:complexType>
```

The derivations are then done by defining the content model within a xs:restriction element (note that we have not repeated the attribute declarations which are not modified):

```
<xs:element name="author">
  <xs:complexType>
    <xs:complexContent>
      <xs:restriction base="person">
        <xs:sequence>
          <xs:element ref="name"/>
```

```
            <xs:element ref="born"/>
            <xs:element ref="dead" minOccurs="0"/>
          </xs:sequence>
        </xs:restriction>
      </xs:complexContent>
    </xs:complexType>
  </xs:element>

  <xs:element name="character">
    <xs:complexType>
      <xs:complexContent>
        <xs:restriction base="person">
          <xs:sequence>
            <xs:element ref="name"/>
            <xs:element ref="born"/>
            <xs:element ref="qualification"/>
          </xs:sequence>
        </xs:restriction>
      </xs:complexContent>
    </xs:complexType>
  </xs:element>
```

We see here that the syntax of a derivation by restriction is more verbose than the syntax of the straight definition of the content model. The purpose of this derivation is not to build modular schemas, but rather to give applications that use this schema the indication that there is some commonality between the content models, and if they know how to handle the complex type "person," they can handle the elements author and character. We will see W3C XML Schema features that rely on this derivation method in Chapter 8 and Chapter 12.

Changing the number of occurrences of particles is not the only modification that can be done during a derivation by restriction. Other operations that result in a reduction of the number of valid instance structures are also possible, such as changing a simple type to a more restrictive one or fixing values. The main constraint in this mechanism is that each particle of the derived type must be an explicit derivation of the corresponding particle of the base type. The effect of this statement is to limit the "depth" of the restrictions that can be performed in a single step, and when we need to restrict particles at a deeper level of imbrication, we may have to transform local definitions into global ones. We will see a concrete example in the section "Creating Mixed Content Models," which are similar in this respect.

Asymmetry of these two methods

We now have all the elements we need to look back at the claim about the asymmetry of these derivation methods. This lack of symmetry is not a defect as such, but studying it is a good exercise to understanding the meaning of these two derivation methods. Let's examine the derivation by extension of basePerson into the character element:

```
<xs:complexType name="basePerson">
  <xs:sequence>
```

```
      <xs:element ref="name"/>
      <xs:element ref="born"/>
    </xs:sequence>
    <xs:attribute ref="id"/>
  </xs:complexType>

<xs:element name="character">
  <xs:complexType>
    <xs:complexContent>
      <xs:extension base="basePerson">
        <xs:sequence>
          <xs:element ref="qualification"/>
        </xs:sequence>
      </xs:extension>
    </xs:complexContent>
  </xs:complexType>
</xs:element>
```

The content model of character contains a mandatory qualification element. Valid characters are not valid per basePerson; thus, there is no hope to be able to derive character back into basePerson by restriction, since all the instance structures that are valid per the derived type must be valid per the base type in a derivation by restriction.

Let's look back at the derivation by restriction of the person base type into a character element:

```
<xs:complexType name="person">
  <xs:sequence>
    <xs:element ref="name"/>
    <xs:element ref="born"/>
    <xs:element ref="dead" minOccurs="0"/>
    <xs:element ref="qualification" minOccurs="0"/>
  </xs:sequence>
  <xs:attribute ref="id"/>
</xs:complexType>

<xs:element name="character">
  <xs:complexType>
    <xs:complexContent>
      <xs:restriction base="person">
        <xs:sequence>
          <xs:element ref="name"/>
          <xs:element ref="born"/>
          <xs:element ref="qualification"/>
        </xs:sequence>
      </xs:restriction>
    </xs:complexContent>
  </xs:complexType>
</xs:element>
```

Again, it is not possible to derive the complex type of character into person, since it means changing the number of minimum occurrences of qualification from 1 to 0

---

and adding an optional dead element between born and qualification. None of these operations are possible during a derivation by extension, which can only append new content after the content of the base type, and can't update an existing particle (to change the number of occurrences) nor insert a new particle between two existing particles.

Mixed Content Models

Although W3CXML Schema permits mixed content models and describes them better than in XML DTDS, W3CXML Schema treats them as an add-on plugged on top of complex content models. The good news is that this allows control of children elements exactly as we've just seen for complex contents. The bad news is that we abandon any control over the child text nodes whose values cannot be constrained at all, and, of course, the descriptions of the child elements are subject to the same limitations as in the case of complex content models. The limitations on unordered content models are probably even more unfriendly for mixed content models, which are more "free style," than the limitation is for complex content models.

Creating Mixed Content Models

This add-on is implemented through a mixed attribute in the xs:complexType (global definition), which is otherwise used exactly as we've seen for complex content models. The effect of this attribute when its value is set to "true" is to allow any text nodes within the content model, before, between, and after the child elements. The location, the whitespace processing, and the datatype of these text nodes cannot be restricted in any way.

Let's go back to the definition of our title element and change it to accept a reduced version of XHTML with the a link and an em element to highlight some parts of its text. The definition, which was previously done by extending a simple type to create a simple content complex type, needs to be re-written as a complex content definition with a mixed attribute set to "true". The full definition, including the definition of the a element, the definition of a markedText complex type and its usage to define the title element, could be:

```
<xs:element name="a">
  <xs:complexType>
    <xs:simpleContent>
      <xs:extension base="xs:string">
        <xs:attribute name="href" type="xs:anyURI"/>
      </xs:extension>
    </xs:simpleContent>
  </xs:complexType>
</xs:element>

<xs:complexType name="markedText" mixed="true">
  <xs:choice minOccurs="0" maxOccurs="unbounded">
```

```
    <xs:element name="em" type="xs:token"/>
    <xs:element ref="a"/>
  </xs:choice>
  <xs:attribute ref="lang"/>
</xs:complexType>

<xs:element name="title" type="markedText"/>
```

This definition matches elements such as:

```
<title lang="en">
  Being a
  <a href="http://dmoz.org/Shopping/Pets/Dogs/">
    Dog
  </a>
  Is a
  <em>
    Full-Time
  </em>
  Job
</title>
```

Note that the length of the title can no longer be restricted.

Derivation of Mixed Content Models

Mixed content models are derived exactly like the complex content models on which they have been plugged. The semantic of both methods stays exactly the same.

Derivation by extension

Mixed contents complex types can be derived by extension from other complex content complex types and the meaning will be the same. If I want to add a strong element to my markedText mixed content type, I can define the following content model:

```
<xs:element name="title">
  <xs:complexType mixed="true">
    <xs:complexContent mixed="true">
      <xs:extension base="markedText">
        <xs:choice minOccurs="0" maxOccurs="unbounded">
          <xs:element name="strong" type="xs:string"/>
        </xs:choice>
      </xs:extension>
    </xs:complexContent>
  </xs:complexType>
</xs:element>
```

One must note, though, that this extension is equivalent to:

```
<xs:complexType name="resultingType" mixed="true">
  <xs:sequence>
    <xs:choice minOccurs="0" maxOccurs="unbounded">
      <xs:element name="em" type="xs:token"/>
```

```
      <xs:element ref="a"/>
    </xs:choice>
    <xs:choice minOccurs="0" maxOccurs="unbounded">
      <xs:element name="strong" type="xs:string"/>
    </xs:choice>
  </xs:sequence>
  <xs:attribute ref="lang"/>
</xs:complexType>
```

This is probably not what we would like to see in practice since this content model expects to see all the occurrences of a and em before any instance of strong. We will see later, in Chapter 12, that this specific issue can be solved using a feature named "substitution groups" instead of using xs:choice.

Derivation by restriction

The derivation of mixed content models by restriction is also done using the method defined for complex content models, with the same constraint that each particle must be an explicit derivation of the corresponding particle of the base type. To illustrate the consequences of this constraint, let's look again at the definition and the use of our markedText:

```
<xs:element name="a">
  <xs:complexType>
    <xs:simpleContent>
      <xs:extension base="xs:string">
        <xs:attribute name="href" type="xs:anyURI"/>
      </xs:extension>
    </xs:simpleContent>
  </xs:complexType>
</xs:element>

<xs:complexType name="markedText" mixed="true">
  <xs:choice minOccurs="0" maxOccurs="unbounded">
    <xs:element name="em" type="xs:token"/>
    <xs:element ref="a"/>
  </xs:choice>
  <xs:attribute ref="lang"/>
</xs:complexType>

<xs:element name="title" type="markedText"/>
```

If we want to forbid em elements in our title, force the href to be an http absolute URI, and require the lang attribute to be either en or es, we need to do some refactoring to show that the a element included in our title is an explicit derivation of the general definition of a. We also need to use a global complex type definition for a instead of the previous anonymous definition:

```
<xs:element name="a" type="link"/>
```

We can now either derive a new global complex type from the new link complex type or embed its derivation in the definition of our title element:

```
<xs:element name="title">
  <xs:complexType mixed="true">
    <xs:complexContent mixed="true">
      <xs:restriction base="markedText">
        <xs:choice minOccurs="0" maxOccurs="unbounded">
          <xs:element name="a">
            <xs:complexType>
              <xs:simpleContent>
                <xs:restriction base="link">
                <xs:attribute name="href">
                <xs:simpleType>
                <xs:restriction base="xs:anyURI">
                <xs:pattern value="http://.*"/>
                </xs:restriction>
                </xs:simpleType>
                </xs:attribute>
                </xs:restriction>
              </xs:simpleContent>
            </xs:complexType>
          </xs:element>
        </xs:choice>
        <xs:attribute name="lang">
          <xs:simpleType>
            <xs:restriction base="xs:language">
              <xs:enumeration value="en"/>
              <xs:enumeration value="es"/>
            </xs:restriction>
          </xs:simpleType>
        </xs:attribute>
      </xs:restriction>
    </xs:complexContent>
  </xs:complexType>
</xs:element>
```

This example is a caricature. In practice it would be more readable to create an intermediate global type definition to avoid embedding several derivations, but it provides an overview of this derivation process.

Derivation between complex and mixed content models

Since complex and mixed content models are built using the same mechanism, one may wonder what the possibilities are for deriving complex contents from mixed contents and vice versa. The answer to this question lurks in the semantic of these two derivation methods.

Derivation by extension appends new content after the content of the base type and the structure of the base type is kept unchanged. It is therefore not possible to derive a mixed content model from complex content model. When a content model is mixed, the position of the text nodes cannot be constrained, and this permits text nodes within the base type at any location. For the same reason, it is impossible to extend a mixed content model into a complex content model because the text nodes that are allowed in the base type would become forbidden.

Derivation by restriction defines a subset of the base type. It is forbidden to derive a mixed content model from a complex content model. The resulting type would allow text nodes that are forbidden in the base type and would expand rather than restrict the content model. There is one workable possibility, however. The last combination is the only possible one: a mixed content model can be restricted into a complex content model. Forbidding the text nodes of a mixed content model is a valid restriction and can be done by setting the mixed attribute to "false" in the xs:complexType definition. It is even possible to derive a simple content model into a mixed content model since this is, in fact, a restriction removing the sibling elements and keeping the text nodes. This assumes, of course, that the sibling elements are optional; i.e., they have a minOccurs attribute equal to 0.

Empty Content Models

Empty content models are elements that can only accept attributes. W3C XML Schema does not include any special support for empty content models, which can be considered either complex content models without elements or simple content models with a value restricted to the null string.

Creation of Empty Content Models

W3C XML Schema considers empty content models to be the intersection between complex content models (in the case in which no compositors are specified) and simple content models (in the case in which no text nodes are expected, which W3C XML Schema handles as if an empty text node was found). We will, therefore, be able to choose between the two methods to create an empty content model. Where we extended our title element to become mixed content, we carefully avoided adding empty elements, such as the HTML img or br. Let's see how we could define a br element with its id and class attributes using both methods.

As simple content models

This is done by defining a simple type that can only accept the empty string as a value. Strictly speaking, empty content models do not accept any whitespace between their start and end tags. Since we want to control this, we must use a datatype that does not alter the whitespaces, i.e., xs:string. Our empty content model is then derived by extension from this simple type:

```
<xs:simpleType name="empty">
  <xs:restriction base="xs:string">
    <xs:enumeration value=""/>
  </xs:restriction>
</xs:simpleType>

<xs:element name="br">
  <xs:complexType>
```

```
        <xs:simpleContent>
          <xs:extension base="empty">
            <xs:attribute name="id" type="xs:ID"/>
            <xs:attribute name="class" type="xs:NMTOKEN"/>
          </xs:extension>
        </xs:simpleContent>
      </xs:complexType>
    </xs:element>
```

As complex content models

The other (more straightforward) way to do this is to create a complex content model without any subelements:

```
<xs:element name="br">
  <xs:complexType>
    <xs:attribute name="id" type="xs:ID"/>
    <xs:attribute name="class" type="xs:NMTOKEN"/>
  </xs:complexType>
</xs:element>
```

Derivation of Empty Content Models

Each of the two empty content types keeps the derivation methods of its content model (simple or complex). The main difference between these two methods is essentially a matter of which derivations may be applied on the base type and what effect it will have.

Derivation by extension

If we try to remember and compare what we've learned about deriving complex and simple contents by extension, we can see that both allow addition of new attributes to the complex type. However, while we can add new subelements to complex content, we cannot change the type of the text node for a simple content model. Thus, this is the first difference between the two methods: when the empty content model is built on a simple type, it will not be possible to add anything other than attributes, while if it is built on top of a complex type, it will be possible to extend it to accept elements.

Derivation by restriction

At first glance, it seems that there are fewer differences here. The restriction methods of both simple and complex contents allow the restriction the scope of the attributes; restricting the content, which is already empty, doesn't seem to be very interesting. It's time, though, to remember what we've learned about a simple type derivation facet, which actually extends the set of valid instance documents! The "empty" simple type that we created to derive our empty simple content model has a base type equal to xs:string. When this simple type is derived through xs:

whiteSpace, the result may be an expansion of the sets of valid instance structures. In our case, setting xs:whiteSpace to "collapse" has the effect of accepting any sequence of whitespaces between the start and closing tags. This new type is not "empty," strictly speaking, but may be useful for some (if not for most) applications that are normalizing the whitespaces and do not make any difference between these two cases. Such a derivation can be done on the simple content complex type like this:

```
<xs:simpleType name="empty">
  <xs:restriction base="xs:string">
    <xs:enumeration value=""/>
  </xs:restriction>
</xs:simpleType>

<xs:complexType name="emptyBr">
  <xs:simpleContent>
    <xs:extension base="empty">
      <xs:attribute name="id" type="xs:ID"/>
      <xs:attribute name="class" type="xs:NMTOKEN"/>
    </xs:extension>
  </xs:simpleContent>
</xs:complexType>

<xs:complexType name="allmostEmptyBr">
  <xs:simpleContent>
    <xs:restriction base="emptyBr">
      <xs:whiteSpace value="collapse"/>
      <xs:attribute name="id" type="xs:ID"/>
      <xs:attribute name="class" type="xs:NMTOKEN"/>
    </xs:restriction>
  </xs:simpleContent>
</xs:complexType>
```

Simple or Complex Content Models for Empty Content Models?

As we have seen, choosing a simple or complex type doesn't make an awful lot of difference, except for extensibility. If we want to keep the possibility of adding subelements by derivation in the content model, we'd better choose an empty complex content model. However, if we want to be able to accept whitespaces in a derived type, an empty simple content model is a better bet.

Back to Our Library

We've covered so much ground in this chapter that it's not obvious which features could be the most beneficial! This choice also depends on external factors such as the level of W3C XML Schema support available from the tools that will be used. For instance, some tools that produce Java classes or binding may take advantage of complex type derivation by restriction. This is the path we will follow for now. We will create a complex type complex content, which will be a superset of the content models of author and character, which we will derive by restriction. First, we can also define an empty content model with an id attribute, which can be derived by extension for all the content models that have an id attribute:

```
<xs:complexType name="elementWithID">
  <xs:attribute ref="id"/>
</xs:complexType>
```

Note that we cannot use this type directly to define the book element, since its id attribute is a restriction of xs:ID:

```
<xs:element name="book">
  <xs:complexType>
    <xs:sequence>
      <xs:element ref="isbn"/>
      <xs:element ref="title"/>
      <xs:element ref="author" minOccurs="0" maxOccurs="unbounded"/>
      <xs:element ref="character" minOccurs="0"
        maxOccurs="unbounded"/>
    </xs:sequence>
    <xs:attribute name="id" type="bookID"/>
    <xs:attribute ref="available"/>
  </xs:complexType>
</xs:element>
```

To use our elementWithID complex type to define the book element, we need to derive by extension a complex type corresponding to the complex type of book without the restriction on the id attribute. The following code is quite verbose, but it is shown here as an exercise:

```
<xs:complexType name="bookTmp">
  <xs:complexContent>
    <xs:extension base="elementWithID">
      <xs:sequence>
        <xs:element ref="isbn"/>
        <xs:element ref="title"/>
        <xs:element ref="author" minOccurs="0"
          maxOccurs="unbounded"/>
        <xs:element ref="character" minOccurs="0"
          maxOccurs="unbounded"/>
      </xs:sequence>
      <xs:attribute ref="available"/>
    </xs:extension>
  </xs:complexContent>
</xs:complexType>

<xs:element name="book">
  <xs:complexType>
    <xs:complexContent>
      <xs:restriction base="bookTmp">
        <xs:sequence>
          <xs:element ref="isbn"/>
          <xs:element ref="title"/>
```

```
        <xs:element ref="author" minOccurs="0"
          maxOccurs="unbounded"/>
        <xs:element ref="character" minOccurs="0"
          maxOccurs="unbounded"/>
      </xs:sequence>
      <xs:attribute name="id" type="bookID"/>
      <xs:attribute ref="available"/>
    </xs:restriction>
  </xs:complexContent>
</xs:complexType>
</xs:element>
```

A more concise option is to derive by restriction first:

```
<xs:complexType name="elementWithBookID">
  <xs:complexContent>
    <xs:restriction base="elementWithID">
      <xs:attribute name="id" type="bookID"/>
    </xs:restriction>
  </xs:complexContent>
</xs:complexType>


<xs:complexType name="book">
  <xs:complexContent>
    <xs:extension base="elementWithBookID">
      <xs:sequence>
        <xs:element ref="isbn"/>
        <xs:element ref="title"/>
        <xs:element ref="author" minOccurs="0"
          maxOccurs="unbounded"/>
        <xs:element ref="character" minOccurs="0"
          maxOccurs="unbounded"/>
      </xs:sequence>
      <xs:attribute ref="available"/>
    </xs:extension>
  </xs:complexContent>
</xs:complexType>
```

Using the elementWithID to derive by extension a personType, which can then be used
to derive the author and character elements by restriction, is straightforward, if not
concise. We have already seen this example. The full schema is then:

```
<?xml version="1.0"?>
<xs:schema xmlns:xs="http://www.w3.org/2001/XMLSchema">
  <xs:simpleType name="string255">
    <xs:restriction base="xs:token">
      <xs:maxLength value="255"/>
    </xs:restriction>
  </xs:simpleType>
  <xs:simpleType name="string32">
    <xs:restriction base="xs:token">
      <xs:maxLength value="32"/>
    </xs:restriction>
  </xs:simpleType>
```

```
<xs:simpleType name="isbn">
  <xs:restriction base="xs:NMTOKEN">
    <xs:totalDigits value="10"/>
    <xs:pattern value="[0-9]{9}[0-9X]"/>
  </xs:restriction>
</xs:simpleType>
<xs:simpleType name="bookID">
  <xs:restriction base="xs:ID">
    <xs:pattern value="b[0-9]{9}[0-9X]"/>
  </xs:restriction>
</xs:simpleType>
<xs:simpleType name="supportedLanguages">
  <xs:restriction base="xs:language">
    <xs:enumeration value="en"/>
    <xs:enumeration value="es"/>
  </xs:restriction>
</xs:simpleType>
<xs:simpleType name="date">
  <xs:restriction base="xs:date">
    <xs:pattern value="[^:Z]*"/>
  </xs:restriction>
</xs:simpleType>
<xs:element name="name" type="string32"/>
<xs:element name="qualification" type="string255"/>
<xs:element name="born" type="date"/>
<xs:element name="dead" type="date"/>
<xs:element name="isbn" type="isbn"/>
<xs:attribute name="id" type="xs:ID"/>
<xs:attribute name="available" type="xs:boolean"/>
<xs:attribute name="lang" type="supportedLanguages"/>
<xs:complexType name="elementWithID">
  <xs:attribute ref="id"/>
</xs:complexType>
<xs:complexType name="bookTmp">
  <xs:complexContent>
    <xs:extension base="elementWithID">
      <xs:sequence>
        <xs:element ref="isbn"/>
        <xs:element ref="title"/>
        <xs:element ref="author" minOccurs="0"
          maxOccurs="unbounded"/>
        <xs:element ref="character" minOccurs="0"
          maxOccurs="unbounded"/>
      </xs:sequence>
      <xs:attribute ref="available"/>
    </xs:extension>
  </xs:complexContent>
</xs:complexType>
<xs:complexType name="personType">
  <xs:complexContent>
    <xs:extension base="elementWithID">
      <xs:sequence>
        <xs:element ref="name"/>
        <xs:element ref="born"/>
```

```
            <xs:element ref="dead" minOccurs="0"/>
            <xs:element ref="qualification" minOccurs="0"/>
        </xs:sequence>
      </xs:extension>
    </xs:complexContent>
</xs:complexType>
<xs:element name="title">
  <xs:complexType>
    <xs:simpleContent>
      <xs:extension base="string255">
        <xs:attribute ref="lang"/>
      </xs:extension>
    </xs:simpleContent>
  </xs:complexType>
</xs:element>
<xs:element name="library">
  <xs:complexType>
    <xs:sequence>
      <xs:element ref="book" maxOccurs="unbounded"/>
    </xs:sequence>
  </xs:complexType>
</xs:element>
<xs:element name="book">
  <xs:complexType>
    <xs:complexContent>
      <xs:restriction base="bookTmp">
        <xs:sequence>
          <xs:element ref="isbn"/>
          <xs:element ref="title"/>
          <xs:element ref="author" minOccurs="0"
            maxOccurs="unbounded"/>
          <xs:element ref="character" minOccurs="0"
            maxOccurs="unbounded"/>
        </xs:sequence>
        <xs:attribute name="id" type="bookID"/>
        <xs:attribute ref="available"/>
      </xs:restriction>
    </xs:complexContent>
  </xs:complexType>
</xs:element>
<xs:element name="author">
  <xs:complexType>
    <xs:complexContent>
      <xs:restriction base="personType">
        <xs:sequence>
          <xs:element ref="name"/>
          <xs:element ref="born"/>
          <xs:element ref="dead" minOccurs="0"/>
        </xs:sequence>
        <xs:attribute ref="id"/>
      </xs:restriction>
    </xs:complexContent>
  </xs:complexType>
</xs:element>
```

```
<xs:element name="character">
  <xs:complexType>
    <xs:complexContent>
      <xs:restriction base="personType">
        <xs:sequence>
          <xs:element ref="name"/>
          <xs:element ref="born"/>
          <xs:element ref="qualification"/>
        </xs:sequence>
        <xs:attribute ref="id"/>
      </xs:restriction>
    </xs:complexContent>
  </xs:complexType>
</xs:element>
</xs:schema>
```

Derivation or Groups

Since the derivation methods for complex types do not widen the scope of structures that can be defined by W3C XML Schema and are rather complex, their usage is controversial. Kohsuke Kawaguchi has published a convincing article on *XML.com (http://www.xml.com/pub/a/2001/06/06/schemasimple.html)* that explains how to avoid using complex type derivations without losing much in modularity.

CHAPTER 8

Creating Building Blocks

We have already seen most of the basic building blocks: elements, attributes, simple and complex types, element and attribute groups. In this chapter, we will see how we can reuse these building blocks between schemas. In doing so, we will see how schemas can be included and redefined to create schema libraries.

Schema Inclusion

The first and most straightforward way to build schema libraries is through inclusion, a feature similar to the inclusion in traditional programming languages, such as C. Compared to a "physical" inclusion, such as the result of expanding an external entity reference, or using XInclude (described in the section "XInclude," later in this chapter), schema inclusion is a "logical" inclusion, which can control the semantic of the inclusion. Schema inclusion may also be seen as a specific form of schema redefinition (seen in the next section). Note that a schema inclusion or redefinition is restricted to the definition of a single namespace (or lack of namespace) and that another mechanism (schema import), which is discussed in Chapter 10, must be used to import definitions for other namespaces.

Schema inclusions must be top-level elements, children of the xs:schema element. Their effect is to include all the top-level declarations of the included schema (which doesn't need to be a complete schema). The included top-level elements are then considered top-level elements of the resulting schema. There are no priority or precedence rules and the conflicts that may arise if a local definition is duplicated in both schemas are considered errors. We could use this feature to locate all our simple type definitions in a separate schema. This sub-schema would look like:

```
<?xml version="1.0"?>
<xs:schema xmlns:xs="http://www.w3.org/2001/XMLSchema">
  <xs:simpleType name="string255">
    <xs:restriction base="xs:token">
      <xs:maxLength value="255"/>
    </xs:restriction>
```

```
    </xs:simpleType>
    <xs:simpleType name="string32">
      <xs:restriction base="xs:token">
        <xs:maxLength value="32"/>
      </xs:restriction>
    </xs:simpleType>
    <xs:simpleType name="isbn">
      <xs:restriction base="xs:NMTOKEN">
        <xs:totalDigits value="10"/>
        <xs:pattern value="[0-9]{9}[0-9X]"/>
      </xs:restriction>
    </xs:simpleType>
    <xs:simpleType name="bookID">
      <xs:restriction base="xs:ID">
        <xs:pattern value="b[0-9]{9}[0-9X]"/>
      </xs:restriction>
    </xs:simpleType>
    <xs:simpleType name="supportedLanguages">
      <xs:restriction base="xs:language">
        <xs:enumeration value="en"/>
        <xs:enumeration value="es"/>
      </xs:restriction>
    </xs:simpleType>
    <xs:simpleType name="date">
      <xs:restriction base="xs:date">
        <xs:pattern value="[^:Z]*"/>
      </xs:restriction>
    </xs:simpleType>
  </xs:schema>
```

And then include it in our main schema using:

```
<xs:include schemaLocation="simple-types.xsd"/>
```

In this example, there is a one-way dependency: the simple types are defined in
simple-types.xsd and used in our main schema. The included schema is not very useful by itself. It has no element declaration, and cannot be used as a standalone
schema, since it couldn't validate any instance document. However, this is a complete schema that doesn't contain any reference except to predefined simple types.
This completeness of the included schema is not a requirement, as we see if we do
the same for our complex type definitions:

```
<?xml version="1.0"?>
<xs:schema xmlns:xs="http://www.w3.org/2001/XMLSchema">
  <xs:complexType name="elementWithID">
    <xs:attribute ref="id"/>
  </xs:complexType>
  <xs:complexType name="bookTmp">
    <xs:complexContent>
      <xs:extension base="elementWithID">
        <xs:sequence>
          <xs:element ref="isbn"/>
          <xs:element ref="title"/>
          <xs:element ref="author" minOccurs="0"
```

```
        maxOccurs="unbounded"/>
      <xs:element ref="character" minOccurs="0"
        maxOccurs="unbounded"/>
    </xs:sequence>
    <xs:attribute ref="available"/>
  </xs:extension>
</xs:complexContent>
</xs:complexType>
<xs:complexType name="personType">
  <xs:complexContent>
    <xs:extension base="elementWithID">
      <xs:sequence>
        <xs:element ref="name"/>
        <xs:element ref="born"/>
        <xs:element ref="dead" minOccurs="0"/>
        <xs:element ref="qualification" minOccurs="0"/>
      </xs:sequence>
    </xs:extension>
  </xs:complexContent>
</xs:complexType>
</xs:schema>
```

We can now include both these fragments in our main schema:

```
<xs:include schemaLocation="simple-types.xsd"/>
<xs:include schemaLocation="complex-types.xsd"/>
```

We now have an included schema (complex-types.xsd), which references elements (such as author, character, or dead), that are defined in the main schema using datatypes defined in either *simple-types.xsd* or *complex-types.xsd*. This combination is perfectly valid for W3C XML Schema since the schema processor collects all the pieces it needs (or at least most of the pieces it needs since wildcards may introduce exceptions, discussed in Chapter 12) before checking the references. This flexibility is powerful, handy for building flexible libraries, and eventually error-prone: a complex datatype, such as *personType*, will have the same children elements but these elements will have a different content model depending on the schema in which *complex-types.xsd* is included. While using these mechanisms, one must take care to keep track of the interdependencies that will be created!

Schema Inclusion with Redefinition

Inclusion does not provide any means to modify the definitions that are being included, and since they are considered global definitions after the import, they can't be modified afterward either. W3C XML Schema contains a feature that allows derivation of global types and group definitions during an inclusion; it keeps the same name after the derivation. Thus, the semantic of these redefinitions is "take this definition instead of the one you've found in the included schema, but make sure that it's a valid derivation so that applications are not too surprised about the change." These are implemented using the xs:redefine element with a schemaLocation attribute (like xs:include). Its children are component definitions that replace the definition found in the included schema. The definitions that are not included in the xs:redefine element are kept unchanged, which means that a xs:redefine with no child element is strictly equivalent to xs:include.

It is noteworthy that the effect of the redefinition is global to the resulting schema. References made to redefined components are all impacted by the modifications made to these components, even if they are made within the redefined schema.

Redefining of Simple and Complex Types

Simple and complex types are redefined by deriving them (by restriction for simple types and by restriction or extension for complex types) inside the xs:redefine element. We can apply this to our last example. The definition of bookTmp is currently used to describe the book element though derivation:

```
<xs:element name="book">
  <xs:complexType>
    <xs:complexContent>
      <xs:restriction base="bookTmp">
        <xs:sequence>
          <xs:element ref="isbn"/>
          <xs:element ref="title"/>
          <xs:element ref="author" minOccurs="0"
            maxOccurs="unbounded"/>
          <xs:element ref="character" minOccurs="0"
            maxOccurs="unbounded"/>
        </xs:sequence>
        <xs:attribute name="id" type="bookID"/>
        <xs:attribute ref="available"/>
      </xs:restriction>
    </xs:complexContent>
  </xs:complexType>
</xs:element>
```

Instead of doing this, we can also redefine the definition of the book complex type. The new schema to define the complex types is then:

```
<?xml version="1.0"?>
<xs:schema xmlns:xs="http://www.w3.org/2001/XMLSchema">
  <xs:complexType name="elementWithID">
    <xs:attribute ref="id"/>
  </xs:complexType>
  <xs:complexType name="book">
    <xs:complexContent>
      <xs:extension base="elementWithID">
        <xs:sequence>
          <xs:element ref="isbn"/>
          <xs:element ref="title"/>
          <xs:element ref="author" minOccurs="0"
            maxOccurs="unbounded"/>
          <xs:element ref="character" minOccurs="0"
```

```
              maxOccurs="unbounded"/>
        </xs:sequence>
        <xs:attribute ref="available"/>
      </xs:extension>
    </xs:complexContent>
  </xs:complexType>
  <xs:complexType name="personType">
    <xs:complexContent>
      <xs:extension base="elementWithID">
        <xs:sequence>
          <xs:element ref="name"/>
          <xs:element ref="born"/>
          <xs:element ref="dead" minOccurs="0"/>
          <xs:element ref="qualification" minOccurs="0"/>
        </xs:sequence>
      </xs:extension>
    </xs:complexContent>
  </xs:complexType>
</xs:schema>
```

The redefinition–note how a book complex type is redefined using a base type with the same name, which would be forbidden anywhere else—and usage of the book element looks like:

```
<xs:redefine schemaLocation="complex-types2.xsd">
  <xs:complexType name="book">
    <xs:complexContent>
      <xs:restriction base="book">
        <xs:sequence>
          <xs:element ref="isbn"/>
          <xs:element ref="title"/>
          <xs:element ref="author" minOccurs="0"
            maxOccurs="unbounded"/>
          <xs:element ref="character" minOccurs="0"
            maxOccurs="unbounded"/>
        </xs:sequence>
        <xs:attribute name="id" type="bookID"/>
        <xs:attribute ref="available"/>
      </xs:restriction>
    </xs:complexContent>
  </xs:complexType>
</xs:redefine>

<xs:element name="book" type="book"/>
```

Redefinition of Element and Attribute Groups

The redefinition of complex and simple types seems quite natural and should not be much of a surprise, since it builds on things we've discussed in detail in previous chapters. The new part of xs:redefine is that element and attribute groups—which cannot be derived—can also be redefined. Redefinition of element and attribute groups is done without any special schema element: a group redefinition that contains a reference to itself is considered an extension; otherwise, it's considered a restriction. These two methods have their own rules and semantics, which are similar but not identical to the rules and semantics of the derivation of complex types. These deserve a specific description. As we will see, the general principles are the same, and the asymmetry between extension and restriction is preserved for group redefinitions.

Extension

Group extensions are done by referencing the group somewhere in its redefinition. The semantic is, therefore, similar to the semantic of the derivation by extension of complex content complex types (some new content is added to the base type) with more flexibility. The location where the content of the base type is added may not be chosen during the extension of a complex content complex type, and the new content is always appended after the content of the base type. If we have, for instance, a group definition such as:

```
<?xml version="1.0"?>
<xs:schema xmlns:xs="http://www.w3.org/2001/XMLSchema">
  <xs:group name="character">
    <xs:sequence>
      <xs:element ref="born"/>
      <xs:element ref="qualification"/>
    </xs:sequence>
  </xs:group>
</xs:schema>
```

We can redefine it to add the name element, which is missing at the beginning of the content:

```
<xs:redefine schemaLocation="character-group.xsd">
  <xs:group name="character">
    <xs:sequence>
      <xs:element ref="name"/>
      <xs:group ref="character"/>
    </xs:sequence>
  </xs:group>
</xs:redefine>

<xs:element name="character">
  <xs:complexType>
    <xs:group ref="character"/>
    <xs:attribute ref="id"/>
  </xs:complexType>
</xs:element>
```

We see that we have been able to choose the insertion point of the content of the base group, which is after the name element. The name element has been added; this is an enhancement over complex content complex type derivation.

This method of extending element or attribute groups is clearly underspecified in the Recommendation and should be used in its simplest form with caution to avoid interoperability issues. The Recommendation specifies that the `minOccurs` and `maxOccurs` attributes of the reference need to be exactly one, which shows a wish to include the content of the base group during an extension exactly one time. However, the wording of the Recommendation does not forbid inclusion of this reference in a branch that has a different number of occurrences, such as:

```
<xs:redefine schemaLocation="bar.xsd">
  <xs:group name="foo">
    <xs:sequence>
      <xs:sequence minOccurs="0">
        <xs:group ref="foo"/>
      </xs:sequence>
      <xs:element ref="bar"/>
    </xs:sequence>
  </xs:group>
</xs:redefine>
```

This is functionally equivalent to having `minOccurs` equal to zero on the group reference and allows content models without any occurrences of the base group. Since this is contrary to the philosophy behind derivations by extension, these kinds of structures shouldn't be used. Similarly, the Recommendation does not forbid the use of another compositor other than a `xs:sequence` to redefine a group. However, since using `xs:choice` instead of `xs:sequence` leads to redefined groups in which the content of the base can be omitted, this is certainly something to avoid.

The references used to extend groups during a redefinition must be done at the top level of the group definition. The last thing to note about element group extensions is that even though its syntax uses a group reference to the group being defined, self references cannot be used in regular global group definitions for defining recursive content models. These need to be done at a lower level, such as:

```
<xs:group name="group">
  <!-- This group definition is *not* valid -->
  <xs:sequence>
    <xs:element name="foo">
      <xs:complexType>
        <xs:group ref="group" minOccurs="0"/>
      </xs:complexType>
    </xs:element>
    <xs:element name="bar" type="xs:token"/>
  </xs:sequence>
</xs:group>
```

Restriction

The redefinition of attribute and element groups by restriction is similar, in principle, to a derivation of a complex content complex type by restriction. A new definition of the group is given; this new definition must match the same criteria as that of a complex content complex type restriction, and must be a valid restriction of the base group. A content that matches the redefined group must always match the base group and the elements used by the new definition must be explicit restrictions of the elements used in the base group. If we have a group definition available, such as:

```
<?xml version="1.0"?>
<xs:schema xmlns:xs="http://www.w3.org/2001/XMLSchema">
  <xs:group name="author">
    <xs:sequence>
      <xs:element ref="name"/>
      <xs:element ref="born"/>
      <xs:element ref="dead" minOccurs="0"/>
      <xs:element name="nationality" type="xs:NMTOKEN" minOccurs="0"/>
    </xs:sequence>
  </xs:group>
</xs:schema>
```

We can redefine it to remove the element nationality, which is optional:

```
<xs:redefine schemaLocation="author.xsd">
  <xs:group name="author">
    <xs:sequence>
      <xs:element ref="name"/>
      <xs:element ref="born"/>
      <xs:element ref="dead" minOccurs="0"/>
    </xs:sequence>
  </xs:group>
</xs:redefine>

<xs:element name="author">
  <xs:complexType>
    <xs:group ref="author"/>
    <xs:attribute ref="id"/>
  </xs:complexType>
</xs:element>
```

Before we leave this subject, we need to note that the rules for restricting attribute groups are different than the rules for restricting complex types. The list of attributes must include all the attributes that are kept. (This is unlike complex type restrictions in which attributes that are not mentioned are considered unchanged.) If we have an attribute group such as:

```
<xs:attributeGroup name="commonAttributes">
  <xs:attribute name="id" type="xs:ID"/>
  <xs:attribute name="available" type="xs:boolean"/>
  <xs:attribute name="lang" type="xs:language"/>
</xs:attributeGroup>
```

If we want to restrict it to remove the available attribute through a redefinition, we then must repeat the definitions of the two other attributes:

```
<xs:redefine schemaLocation="attributes.xsd">
  <xs:attributeGroup name="commonAttributes">
    <xs:attribute name="id" type="xs:ID"/>
```

```
      <xs:attribute name="lang" type="xs:language"/>
    </xs:attributeGroup>
  </xs:redefine>
```

Other Alternatives

The `xs:include` and `xs:redefine` elements are features which provide a safe way to include "pieces" of schemas. Their processing model is designed to provide a result that is a coherent schema. However, the price for this safety is a certain rigidity: only full schema documents can be included and the insertion can only occur at a global level in a schema. (It is not possible, for instance, to pick a couple of definitions in a schema without including the others.) These rules mean that these features cannot be used to include local elements, such as annotations or commonly used facets. Let's imagine, for instance, that we want to require that all our dates and related datatypes specify a time zone, and that we have worked very hard to define a generic pattern to use to enforce this constraint. This can be something such as:

```
<xs:pattern value=".+(Z|[+-].{5})"/>
```

We could derive user-defined datatypes for each of the eight primitive times—which can have a time zone using this pattern—and ask to our schema designers to use only these datatypes in their schemas. However, we may prefer to give them this pattern as a tool, which they can use in their schemas by reference instead of copying it (we may want to keep the possibility of modifying the pattern without having to update all the schemas). In this case, `xs:include` and `xs:redefine` cannot be used, and we must consider using one of the generic XML inclusion methods, which are external parsed entities and XInclude.

External Parsed Entities

External parsed entities are one of the SGML features inherited by XML though its DTD. As the name indicates, these are entities (i.e., something you need to declare in the DTD and can reference later on in your document) that are external (i.e., their replacement value is read from an external file when they are referenced) and parsed (i.e., their content is parsed and merged into the infoset of the including document).

To use external parsed entities, we will create an XML document with the pattern we want to include:

```
<?xml version="1.0"?>
<xs:pattern value=".+(Z|[+-].{5})"
  xmlns:xs="http://www.w3.org/2001/XMLSchema"/>
```

Note that including a namespace declaration in this file (which will be used as an external parsed entity) is not strictly mandatory, if we are sure that this entity will always be used in documents in which the namespace has already been defined with the same prefix. However, even in this case, the redefinition of the namespace is allowed though it will have no effect. Defining it will guarantee that if another prefix has been used in the included document, the snippet that we include will still be understood as belonging to the W3C XML Schema namespace. To use this entity, it must be declared in the internal or external DTD of our schema and referred to in our derivations:

```
<?xml version="1.0"?>
<!DOCTYPE xs:schema[
<!ENTITY TZ-pattern SYSTEM "pattern.ent">
]>
<xs:schema xmlns:xs="http://www.w3.org/2001/XMLSchema">
        <xs:simpleType name="myDate">
                <xs:restriction base="xs:date">
                        &TZ-pattern;
                </xs:restriction>
        </xs:simpleType>
        <xs:element name="myDate" type="myDate"/>
</xs:schema>
```

The interesting thing here is we have a finer granularity than we could have achieved using the W3C XML Schema inclusion mechanisms, which manipulate only global components. The price for using a general purpose inclusion mechanism such as external parsed entities (or XInclude, discussed in the next section) is that this mechanism doesn't implement any of the semantics of W3C XML Schema and doesn't allow any redefinition. Beyond this simple example, other DTD features, such as internal parsed entities, and even parameter entities can be used in conjunction with W3C XML Schema to produce innovative combinations!

XInclude

Currently a W3C Candidate Recommendation, XInclude is a XML application that relies on XPointer. XInclude will eventually replace external parsed entities and can be used in a similar way; the main difference is that a XInclude reference doesn't need to be declared prior to its use and can include a fragment of a XML document. The same example can then be implemented using XInclude, taking advantage of its feature to fetch our pattern by its `id` even if it is defined within a more complete schema such as:

```
<?xml version="1.0"?>
<xs:schema xmlns:xs="http://www.w3.org/2001/XMLSchema">
  <xs:simpleType name="date">
    <xs:restriction base="xs:date">
      <xs:pattern value=".+(Z|[+-].{5})" id="TZ-pattern"/>
    </xs:restriction>
  </xs:simpleType>
  <xs:element name="myDate" type="myDate"/>
</xs:schema>
```

Now that the `id` attribute of the `xs:pattern` element is defined, we can use the XPointer "bare names" syntax, which allows us to use the value of an `id` as a fragment identifier. In our case, the XPointer reference to our xs:pattern definition is thus pattern.xsd#TZ-pattern. We can write:

```
<?xml version="1.0"?>
<xs:schema xmlns:xs="http://www.w3.org/2001/XMLSchema"
  xmlns:xi="http://www.w3.org/2001/XInclude">
  <xs:simpleType name="myDateTime">
    <xs:restriction base="xs:dateTime">
      <xi:include href="pattern.xsd#TZ-pattern" parse="xml"/>
    </xs:restriction>
  </xs:simpleType>
  <xs:element name="myDate" type="myDateTime"/>
</xs:schema>
```

Note that XInclude is still a work in progress, and that this syntax may change before XInclude reaches the status of W3C Recommendation. Also note that a parser implementing XInclude should be used to read such a schema.

Simplifying the Library

Our library, with its single instance document, doesn't really deserve redefinition, so we will just use inclusion to isolate simple and complex type definitions in their own schemas to keep these schemas shorter. To do this, we can create a partial schema to define all our simple types:

```
<?xml version="1.0"?>
<xs:schema xmlns:xs="http://www.w3.org/2001/XMLSchema">
  <xs:simpleType name="string255">
    <xs:restriction base="xs:token">
      <xs:maxLength value="255"/>
    </xs:restriction>
  </xs:simpleType>
  <xs:simpleType name="string32">
    <xs:restriction base="xs:token">
      <xs:maxLength value="32"/>
    </xs:restriction>
  </xs:simpleType>
  <xs:simpleType name="isbn">
    <xs:restriction base="xs:unsignedLong">
      <xs:totalDigits value="10"/>
      <xs:pattern value="\d{10}"/>
    </xs:restriction>
  </xs:simpleType>
  <xs:simpleType name="bookID">
    <xs:restriction base="xs:ID">
      <xs:pattern value="b\d{10}"/>
    </xs:restriction>
  </xs:simpleType>
  <xs:simpleType name="supportedLanguages">
    <xs:restriction base="xs:language">
      <xs:enumeration value="en"/>
      <xs:enumeration value="es"/>
```

```
      </xs:restriction>
    </xs:simpleType>
    <xs:simpleType name="date">
      <xs:restriction base="xs:date">
        <xs:pattern value="[^:Z]*"/>
      </xs:restriction>
    </xs:simpleType>
  </xs:schema>
```

We can then create a second schema containing all the complex type definitions (note that this second schema doesn't need to include the simple type definitions that will be included directly into the main schema):

```
<?xml version="1.0"?>
<xs:schema xmlns:xs="http://www.w3.org/2001/XMLSchema">
  <xs:complexType name="elementWithID">
    <xs:attribute ref="id"/>
  </xs:complexType>
  <xs:complexType name="bookTmp">
    <xs:complexContent>
      <xs:extension base="elementWithID">
        <xs:sequence>
          <xs:element ref="isbn"/>
          <xs:element ref="title"/>
          <xs:element ref="author" minOccurs="0"
            maxOccurs="unbounded"/>
          <xs:element ref="character" minOccurs="0"
            maxOccurs="unbounded"/>
        </xs:sequence>
        <xs:attribute ref="available"/>
      </xs:extension>
    </xs:complexContent>
  </xs:complexType>
  <xs:complexType name="personType">
    <xs:complexContent>
      <xs:extension base="elementWithID">
        <xs:sequence>
          <xs:element ref="name"/>
          <xs:element ref="born"/>
          <xs:element ref="dead" minOccurs="0"/>
          <xs:element ref="qualification" minOccurs="0"/>
        </xs:sequence>
      </xs:extension>
    </xs:complexContent>
  </xs:complexType>
</xs:schema>
```

We can leave all the other definitions in our main schema, which includes (using xs:include) the schemas containing the simple and complex type definitions:

```
<?xml version="1.0"?>
<xs:schema xmlns:xs="http://www.w3.org/2001/XMLSchema">
  <xs:include schemaLocation="simpleTypes.xsd"/>
  <xs:include schemaLocation="complexTypes.xsd"/>
```

```
<xs:element name="name" type="string32"/>
<xs:element name="qualification" type="string255"/>
<xs:element name="born" type="date"/>
<xs:element name="dead" type="date"/>
<xs:element name="isbn" type="isbn"/>
<xs:attribute name="id" type="xs:ID"/>
<xs:attribute name="available" type="xs:boolean"/>
<xs:attribute name="lang" type="supportedLanguages"/>
<xs:element name="title">
  <xs:complexType>
    <xs:simpleContent>
      <xs:extension base="string255">
        <xs:attribute ref="lang"/>
      </xs:extension>
    </xs:simpleContent>
  </xs:complexType>
</xs:element>
<xs:element name="library">
  <xs:complexType>
    <xs:sequence>
      <xs:element ref="book" maxOccurs="unbounded"/>
    </xs:sequence>
  </xs:complexType>
</xs:element>
<xs:element name="book">
  <xs:complexType>
    <xs:complexContent>
      <xs:restriction base="bookTmp">
        <xs:sequence>
          <xs:element ref="isbn"/>
          <xs:element ref="title"/>
          <xs:element ref="author" minOccurs="0"
            maxOccurs="unbounded"/>
          <xs:element ref="character" minOccurs="0"
            maxOccurs="unbounded"/>
        </xs:sequence>
        <xs:attribute name="id" type="bookID"/>
        <xs:attribute ref="available"/>
      </xs:restriction>
    </xs:complexContent>
  </xs:complexType>
</xs:element>
<xs:element name="author">
  <xs:complexType>
    <xs:complexContent>
      <xs:restriction base="personType">
        <xs:sequence>
          <xs:element ref="name"/>
          <xs:element ref="born"/>
          <xs:element ref="dead" minOccurs="0"/>
        </xs:sequence>
        <xs:attribute ref="id"/>
      </xs:restriction>
    </xs:complexContent>
```

```
        </xs:complexType>
    </xs:element>
    <xs:element name="character">
        <xs:complexType>
            <xs:complexContent>
                <xs:restriction base="personType">
                    <xs:sequence>
                        <xs:element ref="name"/>
                        <xs:element ref="born"/>
                        <xs:element ref="qualification"/>
                    </xs:sequence>
                    <xs:attribute ref="id"/>
                </xs:restriction>
            </xs:complexContent>
        </xs:complexType>
    </xs:element>
</xs:schema>
```

CHAPTER 9

Defining Uniqueness, Keys, and Key References

Like any storage system, a XML document needs to provide ways to identify and reference pieces of the information it contains. In this chapter, we will present and compare the two features that allow XML to do so with W3C XML Schema. One directly emulates the ID, IDREF, and IDREFs attribute types from the XML DTDs, while the other was introduced to provide more flexibility through the use of XPath expressions.

xs:ID and xs:IDREF

The first way to describe identifiers and references with W3C XML Schema is inherited from XML's DTDs. We already discussed this in Chapter 5: the xs:ID, xs:IDREF, and xs:IDREFS datatypes introduced in W3C XML Schema emulate the behavior of the XML DTD's ID, IDREF, and IDREFS attribute types.

Unlike their DTD counterparts, these simple types can be used to describe both elements and attributes, but inherit the other restrictions from the DTDs: their lexical space is the same as the unqualified XML name (known as the xs:NCName datatype), and they are global to a document, meaning that you won't be allowed to use the same ID value to identify, for instance, both an author and a character within the same document.

The restriction on the lexical space can often prevent you from using an existing node as an identifier. For instance, in our library, we will not be able to use an ISBN number as an ID since xs:NCName cannot start with a number and whitespace is prohibited. We will therefore need to create completely arbitrary IDs and derive their values from existing nodes. The ISBN number "0836217462" can, for instance, be used to build the ID isbn-0836217462, and the name "Charles M. Schulz" can become the ID au-Charles-M.-Schulz. Adding a prefix (ISBN, AU, etc.) is also a way to avoid a collision between IDs used for different element types.

These IDs can be used to define either attributes or elements; however, the Recommendation reminds us that if we want to maintain compatibility with XML 1.0 IDs and IDREFs, they should be used only for attributes. In both cases (elements or attributes), the contribution to the PSVI is done in a similar fashion through a "ID/IDREF table"; except for maintaining compatibility with the feature as it was previously defined in XML 1.0, there is no reason to avoid using ID, IDREF, and IDREFS to define elements.

For example, to show how these styles can be combined, a book element of our library can be written as:

```
<book identifier="isbn-0836217462">
  <isbn>
    0836217462
  </isbn>
  <title>
    Being a Dog Is a Full-Time Job
  </title>
  <author-ref ref="au-Charles_M._Schulz"/>
  <character-refs>
    ch-Peppermint_Patty ch-Snoopy ch-Schroeder ch-Lucy
  </character-refs>
</book>
```

The book element is identified by an identifier (ID) attribute, and references its author though the ref (IDREF) attribute of an author-ref element as well as a whitespace-separated list of characters through a character-refs (IDREFS) element. The piece of schema for this element can be:

```
<xs:element name="book">
  <xs:complexType>
    <xs:sequence>
      <xs:element name="isbn" type="xs:NMTOKEN"/>
      <xs:element name="title" type="xs:string"/>
      <xs:element name="author-ref">
        <xs:complexType>
          <xs:attribute name="ref" type="xs:IDREF" use="required"/>
        </xs:complexType>
      </xs:element>
      <xs:element name="character-refs" type="xs:IDREFS"/>
    </xs:sequence>
    <xs:attribute name="identifier" type="xs:ID" use="required"/>
  </xs:complexType>
</xs:element>
```

XPath-Based Identity Checks

The IDs and IDREFs are stored in the PSVI in a table (called the "ID/IDREF table") and can eventually be used by the applications to locate the corresponding nodes. We can expect XPath applications (including XPointer) to provide shortcuts and fast access to the nodes identified by W3C XML Schema, as is already the case with the DTD IDs.

Simple and easy to use within their domain, IDs and IDREFs keep the limitations of their DTDs ancestors. W3C XML Schema provides a more flexible feature for defining identity constraints without limitation on its lexical space and allowing local keys and references, as well as multinodes keys.

Another important difference is that the ID/IDREF checks are done on datatypes based on `xs:NMTOKEN` datatypes, while the checks that we will see hereafter can be performed on other datatypes, and the comparisons will be done on the actual value spaces rather than on their string representations from the lexical space. These checks are based on a set of *XPath* expressions and are defined through three different (but similar) constructs to test the uniqueness of a value, define a key, and define a key reference.

Uniqueness

The first of these constructs defines a simple check for uniqueness. We will spend some time explaining this in detail, since the two other constructs are based on the same pattern.

The definition of these constraints is done using two consecutive relative XPath expressions evaluated against the position of the element under which they are defined. We need a clear picture of the structure of the instance documents to define them. The starting point is the location of the element under which the check is defined. This location determines the scope of the test and must be carefully chosen, since it is the basis from which all the checks will be performed for this constraint.

For instance, in our library, we can choose to define a check for the uniqueness of the ISBN number of our books under the library element, since we need to check it within the scope of the whole library. However, within a book, we may also test that the reference to a character is unique within the scope of this book. We can define this second check inside the book element.

Once we have chosen the location of the test, we can start writing it at the end of the definition of the element:

```
<xs:element name="book" maxOccurs="unbounded">
  <xs:complexType>
    .../...
  </xs:complexType>
  <xs:unique name="book">
    .../...
  </xs:unique>
</xs:element>
```

The `name` attribute used here will be useful if we want to refer to this constraint through a `keyref`.

Now that we have defined the name and the root of the test, we will define the selector that is the relative path of the node being identified. In our example, the relative path to access a book element from library is book, so we write:

```
<xs:element name="library">
  <xs:complexType>
    .../...
  </xs:complexType>
  <xs:unique name="book">
    <xs:selector xpath="book"/>
    .../...
  </xs:unique>
</xs:element>
```

We have expressed the fact that a book must be unique within a library. To complete the description of this check, we need to define how a book is identified through field elements.

In our case, the identifier is the isbn subelement, and the complete definition is:

```
<xs:element name="library">
  <xs:complexType>
    .../...
  </xs:complexType>
  <xs:unique name="book">
    <xs:selector xpath="book"/>
    <xs:field xpath="isbn"/>
  </xs:unique>
</xs:element>
```

Translated into plain English, this definition can be read as "for each library, each book identified by its ISBN should be unique."

 A unique condition doesn't impose that the node used as an identifier (the field) is required. Selectors whose field is not available are just ignored. To define the same check when the field is required, a "key" should be defined instead of "unique."

Composite Fields

If the names of our authors were split in our library into first, middle, and last names, we may find it convenient to define a composite field to identify our authors. W3C XML Schema provides this feature by allowing definition of several fields within a single constraint—for instance:

```
<xs:element name="library">
  <xs:complexType>
    .../...
  </xs:complexType>
  <xs:unique name="author">
    <xs:selector xpath="author"/>
    <xs:field xpath="first-name"/>
```

```
      <xs:field xpath="middle-name"/>
      <xs:field xpath="last-name"/>
    </xs:unique>
  </xs:element>
```

The check is then done on the triple that is composed of the values of the three fields
(first-name, middle-name, last-name) that need to be unique as a combination.

Keys

A key is a unique constraint with the additional restriction that all the nodes corresponding to all the fields are required.

The syntax for defining a key is the same as the syntax for defining a unique condition, except the unique element is replaced by a key element:

```
<xs:element name="library">
  <xs:complexType>
    .../...
  </xs:complexType>
  <xs:key name="book">
    <xs:selector xpath="book"/>
    <xs:field xpath="isbn"/>
  </xs:key>
</xs:element>
```

There is clearly an overlap between the additional existence check
done by a key constraint and the other ways to control the number of
occurrences of an element or attribute. In our example, if the minimum number of occurrences for the author's name is set to one, using
xs:unique or xs:key is equivalent, except when the author's name can
have a "nil" value. (We will discuss the "nil" value in Chapter 11.)

Key References

Despite its name, xs:keyref can be used not only to define a reference to xs:key, but
also to xs:unique.

The usage of xs:keyref is straightforward and similar to the usage of xs:key or xs:
unique, with an important point worth mentioning: the refer attribute of xs:keyref
should refer to a xs:key or xs:unique element defined under the same element or
under one of their ancestors.

The reason for this rule is that the "identity-constraint tables" where
the keys and references are stored are local to an element and its
ancestors.

The definitions of matching xs:unique or xs:key and xs:keyref need to be done
within the same element, or else one of its ancestors has an impact on the choice of

this location. If, for instance, our books and authors are kept in separate sections of our document:

```
<library>
  <books>
    <book>
      .../...
      <author-ref ref="Charles M. Schulz"/>
      .../...
    </book>
    .../...
  </books>
  <authors>
    <author>
      <name>
        Charles M. Schulz
      </name>
      .../...
    </author>
    .../...
  </authors>
</library>
```

It's good practice to define a modular schema by locating the constraints as near as possible to the elements they control. A natural fit is to locate a key in the authors element and the matching keyref in the books element. However, since a xs:keyref needs to be in the same element as the matching xs:key or one of its ancestors, and books isn't an ancestor of authors, the xs:keyref definition can only be done in the library element. (The xs:key can be defined either in the library or in the authors element.)

In the previous example, locating the xs:key definition within library or authors was only a matter of style, since the authors are unique both within a library and within the authors elements. However, W3C XML Schema allows for situations in which this isn't the case and in which a key is unique within the scope of a subelement without being unique within the whole document.

Let's modify the previous example to define several categories of authors:

```
<library>
  <books>
    <book>
      .../...
      <author-ref ref="Charles M. Schulz"/>
      .../...
    </book>
    .../...
  </books>
  <authors>
    <category id="comics">
      <author>
        <name>
          Charles M. Schulz
```

```
        </name>
        .../...
      </author>
      .../...
    </category>
    <category id="novels">
      .../...
    </category>
    .../...
  </authors>
</library>
```

Defining a xs:key (or xs:unique) within library or authors specifies a uniqueness within the scope of the entire library. Defining a list of authors within category specifies a uniqueness within this category only, and allows authors with the same name to be defined under several categories.

It is perfectly valid, per W3C XML Schema, to define a xs:key under category and a matching xs:keyref under library (since library is an ancestor of category). By doing so, a new constraint is added to authors' names. When an author is referenced within a book, her name has to be unique within the scope of the xs:keyref. Applied to our instance document, this means that if "Charles M. Schulz" was not referenced in one of the books, he can be defined in several categories; since he is referenced in one book, his name must be defined once only.

 While this behavior is described in the Recommendation, the results may be surprising for schema designers. It is probably good practice to keep the definitions of the xs:key (or xs:unique) and their matching xs:keyref in the same elements.

Permitted XPath Expressions

The W3C XML Schema Recommendation states that "to reduce the burden on implementers, in particular implementers of streaming processors, only restricted subsets of XPath expressions are allowed" in xs:selector and xs:field. The result of this statement is a limited subset of XPath that allows only the selection of nodes that are descendants of or are part of the current locations.

The XPath expressions allowed in xs:selector must exclusively go deeper into the hierarchy of the XML element nodes, do not allow any tests in the XPath steps, and must match a set of elements. In addition, the XPath expressions allowed in xs:field can also select attributes.

The full BNF for this subset is given in the reference guide. Rather than giving a verbose explanation, let's see some examples of what is possible and what is not.

The following are allowed:

xpath="author"
 Selects the child elements named author that do not belong to any namespace.

xpath="author|character"
> Selects the child elements named `author` or `character` that do not belong to any namespace.

xpath="lib:author"
> Selects the child elements named `author` that belong to the namespace whose prefix is "lib".

xpath=""*
> Selects all the child elements.

xpath="lib:"*
> Selects all the child elements that belong to the namespace whose prefix is "lib".

xpath="authors/author"
> Selects all the authors/author child elements.

xpath=".//author"
> Selects all the elements that are descendants of the current node, named `author`, and don't belong to any namespace.

xpath="author/@id"
> Selects the `id` attribute of the `author` child element (allowed only for `xs:field`, and not for `xs:selector`).

xpath="@id|@name"
> Selects `@id` or `@name` (valid only in `xs:field`, since attributes are forbidden in `xs:selector`).

The following are forbidden:

xpath="/library/author"
> Absolute paths are not allowed.

xpath="../author"
> The parent axis is not allowed.

xpath=".//[@id]"*
> Tests are not allowed.

xpath="author[@type='comics']"
> Tests are not allowed.

xpath="substring-after(@xlink:href, '#')"
> Function calls are not allowed.

xpath="//author"
> Absolute paths are not allowed.

 Default namespaces do not apply within XPath expressions, and elements and attributes must always be qualified by a prefix if they belong to a namespace.

ID/IDREF Versus xs:key/xs:keyref

We have enumerated the features that key and key references provide beyond those of ID and IDREF: no constraint on datatypes, tests done on values rather than on lexical representation, and independent sets of values for each key. To get a complete picture, we need to see if key and key references can emulate ID and IDREF; in other words, we must determine which features of ID and IDREF are missing from key and key references.

First of all, the location of our key and keyref definition needs to be on the root of the document to fully emulate the ID and IDREF that is global to a document, whatever its document element is. Our best move with W3C XML Schema, which doesn't directly constrain the root node, is to locate our declaration in the global element that is likely to be used as a document element.

Then, to define the xs:selector, we will need to provide the list of all the elements holding ID attributes within a single XPath expression.

The last difference is that ID allows definition of a whitespace-separated list of ID references (through IDREFS datatypes), while there is no similar possibility with xs: key. (There is no xs:keyrefs!)

To use xs:key and xs:keyref, we, therefore, have to modify the instance document that is used in the section about ID and IDREF to transform the list of IDs referencing characters into a series of references, and to use the same convention for IDs and references in all our elements:

```
<library xsi:noNamespaceSchemaLocation="library-keys-id-key.xsd"
  xmlns:xsi="http://www.w3.org/2001/XMLSchema-instance">
  <book id="isbn-0836217462">
    <isbn>
      0836217462
    </isbn>
    <title>
      Being a Dog Is a Full-Time Job
    </title>
    <author-ref ref="au-Charles_M._Schulz"/>
    <character-ref ref="ch-Peppermint_Patty"/>
    <character-ref ref="ch-Snoopy"/>
    <character-ref ref="ch-Schroeder"/>
    <character-ref ref="ch-Lucy"/>
  </book>
  .../...
  <author id="au-Charles-M.-Schulz">
    <name>
      Charles M. Schulz
    </name>
    <nickName>
      SPARKY
    </nickName>
```

```
    <born>
      November 26, 1922
    </born>
    <dead>
      February 12, 2000
    </dead>
  </author>
  <character id="ch-Peppermint-Patty">
    <name>
      Peppermint Patty
    </name>
    <since>
      Aug. 22, 1966
    </since>
    <qualification>
      bold, brash and tomboyish
    </qualification>
  </character>
  ...
</library>
```

The definition follows:

```
<xs:element name="library">
  <xs:complexType>
    .../...
  </xs:complexType>
  <xs:key name="ID">
    <xs:selector xpath="book|author|character"/>
    <xs:field xpath="@id"/>
  </xs:key>
  <xs:keyref name="IDREF" refer="ID">
    <xs:selector xpath="book/author-ref|book/character-ref"/>
    <xs:field xpath="@ref"/>
  </xs:keyref>
</xs:element>
```

This example illustrates the main difference between the two mechanisms: ID/IDREF declarations are done at the level where they are used, and are, therefore, fully integrated with the pseudo-object-oriented features of W3C XML Schema, while key/keyref definitions are done at the level of a common ancestor and rely on the actual structure of the instance documents rather than on its object-oriented schema.

 Since key/keyref rely on the actual structure of the instance documents, they ignore features such as substitution groups. Their XPath expressions need to explicitly define each of the possible element names (except when they use a "*" to indicate "any element" at a particular level).

Using xs:key and xs:unique As Co-occurrence Constraints

Co-occurrence constraints are interdependent conditions given on the child elements or attributes of a node, such as "if this element is present, then this attribute must be absent." Under-implemented within W3C XML Schema, these constraints can be a workaround to the "Consistent Declaration rule," which forbids definition of two different content models for an element at the same location in an instance document. With co-occurrence constraints, one can define a superset of the two content models and add the constraints to forbid the unwanted combinations. This is frequently useful with vocabularies (such as RDF) in which some properties can be expressed either as an attribute or an element, and in which we may want to extend our book example to accept the ISBN number and the title to be expressed as elements or attributes. The two following instance documents are then valid (with their two remaining combinations):

```
<book id="b0836217462" available="true">
  <isbn>
    0836217462
  </isbn>
  <title lang="en">
    Being a Dog Is a Full-Time Job
  </title>
  ../..
</book>
```

or:

```
<book id="b0836217462" available="true" isbn="0836217462"
  title="Beinga Dog Is a Full-Time Job">
  .../...
</book>
```

The obvious way is to define the book element as a choice between the four different valid content models (with the four combinations of elements and attributes). However, this is forbidden by the Consistent Declaration rule, which states that only one content model may be used for a given element. The workaround is to define a content model that accepts both optional elements and attributes:

```
<xs:complexType>
  <xs:sequence>
    <xs:element ref="isbn" minOccurs="0"/>
    <xs:element ref="title" minOccurs="0"/>
    <xs:element ref="author" minOccurs="0" maxOccurs="unbounded"/>
    <xs:element ref="character" minOccurs="0" maxOccurs="unbounded"/>
  </xs:sequence>
  <xs:attribute ref="id"/>
  <xs:attribute ref="available"/>
  <xs:attribute ref="isbn"/>
  <xs:attribute ref="title"/>
</xs:complexType>
```

This definition allows instance documents with both a `title` (or `isbn`) element and attribute or instance documents without any `title` or `isbn` at all. We need to add co-occurrence constraints. In a more general case, these constraints cannot be expressed using W3C XML Schema, and we need to embed other languages (as shown in Chapter 14) but when we think about it, `xs:unique`, `xs:key`, and `xs:keyref` can be considered very specific co-occurrence constraints and they can be used here. If we want to insure that we have only one title and ISBN number, we can add a `xs:key` definition in the book element itself:

```
<xs:key name="isbn">
  <xs:selector xpath="."/>
  <xs:field xpath="isbn|@isbn"/>
</xs:key>

<xs:key name="title">
  <xs:selector xpath="."/>
  <xs:field xpath="title|@title"/>
</xs:key>
```

These keys are evaluated in the scope of a book element and won't have any effect outside each book element. They will consider the book invalid if the XPath expression in their `field` element returns either no nodes or multiple nodes. Note that if we had used `xs:unique` instead of `xs:key`, we would still have required that only one of the elements or attributes be present, but that would have made the property optional. For the record, the full definition of our book element would then be:

```
<xs:element name="book">
  <xs:complexType>
    <xs:sequence>
      <xs:element ref="isbn" minOccurs="0"/>
      <xs:element ref="title" minOccurs="0"/>
      <xs:element ref="author" minOccurs="0" maxOccurs="unbounded"/>
      <xs:element ref="character" minOccurs="0"
        maxOccurs="unbounded"/>
    </xs:sequence>
    <xs:attribute ref="id"/>
    <xs:attribute ref="available"/>
    <xs:attribute ref="isbn"/>
    <xs:attribute ref="title"/>
  </xs:complexType>
  <xs:key name="isbn">
    <xs:selector xpath="."/>
    <xs:field xpath="isbn|@isbn"/>
  </xs:key>
  <xs:key name="title">
    <xs:selector xpath="."/>
    <xs:field xpath="title|@title"/>
  </xs:key>
</xs:element>
```

CHAPTER 10

Controlling Namespaces

The W3C released *Namespaces in XML* about a year after XML 1.0. Namespaces provide a URI-based mechanism that helps differentiate XML vocabularies. Rather than update XML 1.0's DTDs to provide explicit namespace support, the W3C chose to implement namespace support in W3C XML Schema. Support of namespaces was eagerly awaited by the XML community and, thus, are especially well-polished by the W3C XML Schema editors.

Namespaces caused two problems to DTDs. One was how to recognize namespaces defined using different prefixes in instance documents. The other was how best to facilitate the definition of schemas with multiple namespaces. The problem of open schemas tightly controlling some namespaces while keeping the flexibility to add unknown elements and attributes from unknown namespaces, was especially difficult.

W3C XML Schema has gone beyond these expectations for its use of namespaces by associating a namespace to all the objects (elements and attributes, but also simple and complex types as well as groups of elements and attributes) defined in a schema, allowing the use of namespaces to build modular libraries of schemas.

Namespaces Present Two Challenges to Schema Languages

Namespace prefixes should only be considered to be local shortcuts to replace the URI references that are the real identifiers for a namespace. The following documents should, therefore, be considered strictly equivalent by namespace-aware applications:

```
<?xml version="1.0"?>
<library xmlns="http://dyomedea.com/ns/library">
  <book id="b0836217462">
    <title>
      Being a Dog Is a Full-Time Job
```

```
      </title>
      <authors>
        <person id="CMS">
          <name>
            Charles M Schulz
          </name>
        </person>
      </authors>
    </book>
  </library>
```

In the document above, the namespace "*http://dyomedea.com/ns/library*" is defined as the default namespace and applies to all the elements within the document. Next, we'll show a namespace-equivalent, but very different-looking, document:

```
<?xml version="1.0"?>
<!-- Namespace: http://dyomedea.com/ns/library -->
<lib:library xmlns:lib="http://dyomedea.com/ns/library">
  <lib:book id="b0836217462">
    <lib:title>
      Being a Dog Is a Full-Time Job
    </lib:title>
    <lib:authors>
      <lib:person id="CMS">
        <lib:name>
          Charles M Schulz
        </lib:name>
      </lib:person>
    </lib:authors>
  </lib:book>
</lib:library>
```

The namespace "*http://dyomedea.com/ns/library*" is defined as mapping to the prefix lib and is used as a prefix for all the elements within the document. Next, we'll create another namespace-equivalent document using a different prefix.

```
<?xml version="1.0"?>
<!-- Namespace: http://dyomedea.com/ns/library -->
<l:library xmlns:l="http://dyomedea.com/ns/library">
  <l:book id="b0836217462">
    <l:title>
      Being a Dog Is a Full-Time Job
    </l:title>
    <l:authors>
      <l:person id="CMS">
        <l:name>
          Charles M Schulz
        </l:name>
      </l:person>
    </l:authors>
  </l:book>
</l:library>
```

The namespace *"http://dyomedea.com/ns/library"* is defined as mapping to the prefix l and is used as a prefix for all the elements within the document. Finally, we'll mix all of these possibilities in a single document still namespace-equivalent to the others.

```
<?xml version="1.0"?>
<!-- Namespace: http://dyomedea.com/ns/library -->
<l:library xmlns:l="http://dyomedea.com/ns/library">
  <l:book id="b0836217462" xmlns:lib="http://dyomedea.com/ns/library">
    <l:title>
      Being a Dog Is a Full-Time Job
    </l:title>
    <lib:authors>
      <l:person id="CMS" xmlns="http://dyomedea.com/ns/library">
        <name>
          Charles M Schulz
        </name>
      </l:person>
    </lib:authors>
  </l:book>
</l:library>
```

The same namespace is defined and used as l, lib, and even as a default namespace, depending on its location in the document. This last example is, of course, an extreme case that isn't recommended. This document conforms to the namespaces recommendation, however, and the specification states that it is strictly equivalent to the three previous ones.

DTDs are not aware of the namespaces. Since the colon (:) is allowed in the XML names, lib:person, l:person, and person are three different, valid names for a DTD. Furthermore, a DTD sees namespace declaration attributes (xmlns, xmlns:l, xmlns: lib) as ordinary attributes that need to be declared.

A XML document using namespaces is a well-formed XML 1.0 document and it is perfectly possible to write a DTD to describe it. Nevertheless, you must define the prefixes that can be used and the location where the namespace declarations must be inserted. This is acceptable only if you can fully control or specify the authoring processes of the documents.

The second and larger issue is design. Since XML is often used as the glue between different applications, it is becoming increasingly important to be able to define modular vocabularies that can live together in the same document, and namespaces were invented to make this possible. To take advantage of this feature, it is often necessary to define open vocabularies that will define places where external elements and attributes from external namespaces may be included without breaking the applications.

Imagine a marketing department wants to add the type of cover and the number of pages to the information about a particular book. A neat way to do this—if this new information is specific to their needs and we don't want to break the existing applications—is to create a new namespace:

```
<?xml version="1.0"?>
<!-- Namespace: http://dyomedea.com/ns/library -->
<library xmlns="http://dyomedea.com/ns/library"
  xmlns:mkt="http://dyomedea.com/ns/library/mkt">
  <book id="b0836217462">
    <title>
      Being a Dog Is a Full-Time Job
    </title>
    <authors>
      <person id="CMS">
        <name>
          Charles M Schulz
        </name>
      </person>
    </authors>
    <mkt:cover>
      Paperback
    </mkt:cover>
    <mkt:pages>
      128
    </mkt:pages>
  </book>
</library>
```

However, if we want to keep our schema independent of the marketing application, we need a flexible way to open it and say "accept any element from the marketing namespace at the end of our book element." Also, even if there might be other applications that work with our vocabulary, we can say to accept any element from any other namespace at the end of our book element.

Namespace Declarations

Until now, we have seen schemas for documents that had no namespace declarations of any kind and, therefore, did not belong to any namespace. To match the documents without namespaces, the schemas had no namespace declaration either, except the one needed to identify the W3C XML Schema namespace itself.

To match the elements and attributes that belong to a namespace, we need to associate this namespace with our schema through the targetNamespace attribute of the xs: schema element.

If we modify our library to use a single namespace:

```
<library xmlns="http://dyomedea.com/ns/library">
  <book id="b0836217462" available="yes">
    <isbn>
      0836217462
    </isbn>
    <title>
      Being a Dog Is a Full-Time Job
    </title>
```

```
      .../...
    </book>
  </library>
```

We need to modify our schema to declare the namespace and to define it as the target namespace:

```
<xs:schema targetNamespace="http://dyomedea.com/ns/library"
   elementFormDefault="qualified" attributeFormDefault="unqualified"
   xmlns:lib="http://dyomedea.com/ns/library"
   xmlns:xs="http://www.w3.org/2001/XMLSchema">
   .../...
</xs:schema>
```

The definition of the namespaces is especially important here, since W3C XML Schema uses them for two purposes.

As for any XML document that conforms to the namespaces Recommendation, the first purpose of the namespace declaration is to associate a URI reference that is the identifier of a namespace to a prefix, which is a shortcut for this identifier.

In our example, we have two such declarations: xmlns:xs="http://www.w3.org/2001/XMLSchema" and xmlns:lib="http://dyomedea.com/ns/library".

The first declaration associates the W3C XML Schema namespace with the prefix xs. We could, of course, have chosen any prefix, or even used this namespace as the default namespace; the choice of xs is just common usage.

The second declaration defines the namespace used in our instance document, xmlns:lib="http://dyomedea.com/ns/library". Here we chose to use the lib prefix, even though this namespace is never used for any element or attribute of the schema itself. We could also have chosen any prefix for this namespace, or even have defined it as our default namespace.

This second declaration is needed for the second usage of namespace prefixes. W3C XML Schema uses the namespace prefixes to resolve all the references to the components of a schema (datatypes, elements, attributes, groups, etc.), as well as for the XPath expressions used in the xs:unique, xs:key, and xs:keyref declarations.

We haven't yet mentioned which namespace this schema describes. We must do so using the targetNamespace attribute that defines the URI reference that identifies the target namespace.

With this last piece of information, a schema processor knows what the target namespace is. With the two namespaces declarations already complete, it also knows which prefix we want to use for it and for the W3C XML Schema namespace. This is sufficient information to write our schema.

This use of the namespace prefixes, common to *W3C XML Schema* and *XSLT*, is very controversial, since it creates a dependency between *W3C XML Schema* (considered an application) and the prefixes chosen for the namespaces. This breaks the layered structure of the XML specifications: the markup and its content become interdependent and cannot be changed independently any longer.

Not unlike a communication protocol, the XML specifications may be seen as a set of envelopes. XML 1.0 is the outermost envelope into which the namespaces are included. While the applications should be independent of these envelopes, the fact that W3C XML Schema is making use of the namespace prefixes inside its own attributes glues the schema to its envelope. This is a very dangerous practice that should be discouraged for other vocabularies that define their own sets of prefixes.

One of the consequences of this practice is that Canonical XML has been obliged to remove namespace prefix rewriting from its requirements, meaning that the four flavors of our library that are strictly equivalent, per the namespace recommendation, will have four different canonical values, and different digital signatures as a result.

To Qualify Or Not to Qualify?

The schemas that we have written up to this point have had no target namespace declaration. We also could only describe elements and attributes that didn't belong to any namespace.

The declaration of a target namespace gives us the possibility of defining elements and attributes that belong to the target namespace (called "qualified") and elements and attributes that don't belong to any namespace (called "unqualified").

The purpose of a schema is to describe a vocabulary, in which top-level nodes belong to its target namespace. For this reason, it is forbidden to define global elements that are unqualified when a target namespace is declared.

The distinction between qualified and unqualified elements and attributes is made through their <form> attributes—for example:

```
<xs:element name="book" form="qualified"/>

<xs:attribute name="isbn" form="qualified"/>

<xs:attribute name="lang" form="unqualified"/>

<xs:element name="character" form="unqualified"/>
```

The default values of these form attributes are defined in the elementFormDefault and attributeFormDefault attributes that we have added in our xs:schema element.

These attributes both have default values of their own, which are: `elementFormDefault="unqualified"` and `attributeFormDefault="unqualified"`. These values are appropriate to the case in which only the document element uses a namespace:

```
<lib:library xmlns:lib="http://dyomedea.com/ns/library">
  <book id="b0836217462" available="yes">
    <isbn>
      0836217462
    </isbn>
    <title>
      Being a Dog Is a Full-Time Job
    </title>
  </book>
</lib:library>
```

Since global elements and attributes must be qualified, defining this schema as a single schema requires that all the elements and attributes are locally defined.

Another combination, `elementFormDefault="qualified"` and `attributeForm-Default="unqualified"` matches the common case in which a namespace is attached to the root element as the default namespace that will, by definition apply to the included elements but not to the attributes. (Per the Namespaces Recommendation, the default namespace does not apply to attributes.)

```
<library xmlns="http://dyomedea.com/ns/library">
  <book id="b0836217462" available="yes">
    <isbn>
      0836217462
    </isbn>
    <title>
      Being a Dog Is a Full-Time Job
    </title>
  </book>
</library>
```

The usage considers that unqualified attributes belong to the same vocabulary as their parent element, and the vocabularies that take advantage of qualified attributes are often vocabularies that supply attributes used in elements from other namespaces. Examples of such vocabularies include RDF and attribute-only vocabularies such as XLink and XML Base. The schemas for these vocabularies will benefit from an `attributeFormDefault` set to qualified.

One should pay attention to the special status of the attributes in the namespace specification. The default namespace does not apply to attributes. This means that an attribute without a prefix is considered to have no namespace.

Another confusing aspect of attributes with a prefix (which thus belong to a namespace) is these attributes are called "global attributes" in the namespaces recommendation. In *W3C XML Schema* the term global is used differently, in opposition to local elements or attributes. A global attribute, per namespaces, is therefore a qualified attribute per *W3C XML Schema*, and may be globally or locally defined.

 Remember that `<elementFormDefault>` and `<attributeFormDefault>` define default values and that you can specify—element by element and attribute by attribute—if they are qualified or not.

Before we see how we can bring more namespaces into the game, let's look at a simple instance document with a single namespace and unqualified attributes:

```
<?xml version="1.0"?>
<library xmlns="http://dyomedea.com/ns/library">
  <book id="b0836217462" available="yes">
    <isbn>
      0836217462
    </isbn>
    <title>
      Being a Dog Is a Full-Time Job
    </title>
    <authors>
      <person id="CMS">
        <name>
          Charles M Schulz
        </name>
        <born>
          1922-11-26
        </born>
        <dead>
          2000-02-12
        </dead>
      </person>
    </authors>
    <characters>
      <person id="PP">
        <name>
          Peppermint Patty
        </name>
        <born>
          1966-08-22
        </born>
        <qualification>
          bold, brash and tomboyish
        </qualification>
      </person>
      <person id="Snoopy">
        <name>
          Snoopy
        </name>
        <born>
          1950-10-04
        </born>
        <qualification>
```

```
          extroverted beagle
        </qualification>
      </person>
      <person id="Schroeder">
        <name>
          Schroeder
        </name>
        <born>
          1951-05-30
        </born>
        <qualification>
          brought classical music to the Peanuts strip
        </qualification>
      </person>
      <person id="Lucy">
        <name>
          Lucy
        </name>
        <born>
          1952-03-03
        </born>
        <qualification>
          bossy, crabby and selfish
        </qualification>
      </person>
    </characters>
  </book>
</library>
```

If we want to avoid confusion while writing a schema for this instance document, we can define prefixes in the schema for both our target namespace and for the W3C XML Schema namespace, leading to a schema such as:

```
<?xml version="1.0"?>
<xs:schema targetNamespace="http://dyomedea.com/ns/library"
  elementFormDefault="qualified" attributeFormDefault="unqualified"
  xmlns:lib="http://dyomedea.com/ns/library"
  xmlns:xs="http://www.w3.org/2001/XMLSchema">
  <xs:element name="library">
    <xs:complexType>
      <xs:sequence>
        <xs:element name="book" type="lib:bookType"/>
      </xs:sequence>
    </xs:complexType>
  </xs:element>
  <xs:element name="person">
    <xs:complexType>
      <xs:sequence>
        <xs:element name="name" type="xs:string"/>
        <xs:element name="born" type="xs:date"/>
        <xs:element name="dead" type="xs:date" minOccurs="0"/>
        <xs:element name="qualification" type="xs:string"
          minOccurs="0"/>
      </xs:sequence>
```

```
      <xs:attribute name="id" type="xs:ID" use="required"/>
    </xs:complexType>
  </xs:element>
  <xs:complexType name="bookType">
    <xs:sequence>
      <xs:element name="isbn" type="xs:NMTOKEN"/>
      <xs:element name="title" type="xs:string"/>
      <xs:element name="authors">
        <xs:complexType>
          <xs:sequence>
            <xs:element ref="lib:person" maxOccurs="unbounded"/>
          </xs:sequence>
        </xs:complexType>
      </xs:element>
      <xs:element name="characters">
        <xs:complexType>
          <xs:sequence>
            <xs:element ref="lib:person" maxOccurs="unbounded"/>
          </xs:sequence>
        </xs:complexType>
      </xs:element>
    </xs:sequence>
    <xs:attribute name="id" type="xs:ID" use="required"/>
    <xs:attribute name="available" type="xs:string" use="required"/>
  </xs:complexType>
</xs:schema>
```

In this example, the names of components defined by the schema are always unprefixed when they are defined. Because this schema only defines components in the single *http://dyomedea.com/ns/library* namespace (identified as the `targetNamespace` attribute of the `xs:schema` element), there isn't any risk of confusion. The only other namespaces used here are the namespace for W3C XML Schema itself, identified with an `xs` prefix, and another mapping for the *http://dyomedea.com/ns/library* namespace, using `lib` as the prefix. The `lib`-prefixed form is used for cross-references between declarations.

A strictly equivalent schema, defining the exact same data model, can be defined using the target namespace as the default namespace of the schema document:

```
<?xml version="1.0"?>
<xs:schema targetNamespace="http://dyomedea.com/ns/library"
  elementFormDefault="qualified" attributeFormDefault="unqualified"
  xmlns:xs="http://www.w3.org/2001/XMLSchema"
  xmlns="http://dyomedea.com/ns/library">
  <xs:element name="library">
    <xs:complexType>
      <xs:sequence>
        <xs:element name="book" type="bookType"/>
      </xs:sequence>
    </xs:complexType>
  </xs:element>
  <xs:element name="person">
    <xs:complexType>
```

```
      <xs:sequence>
        <xs:element name="name" type="xs:string"/>
        <xs:element name="born" type="xs:date"/>
        <xs:element name="dead" type="xs:date" minOccurs="0"/>
        <xs:element name="qualification" type="xs:string"
          minOccurs="0"/>
      </xs:sequence>
      <xs:attribute name="id" type="xs:ID" use="required"/>
    </xs:complexType>
  </xs:element>
  <xs:complexType name="bookType">
    <xs:sequence>
      <xs:element name="isbn" type="xs:NMTOKEN"/>
      <xs:element name="title" type="xs:string"/>
      <xs:element name="authors">
        <xs:complexType>
          <xs:sequence>
            <xs:element ref="person" maxOccurs="unbounded"/>
          </xs:sequence>
        </xs:complexType>
      </xs:element>
      <xs:element name="characters">
        <xs:complexType>
          <xs:sequence>
            <xs:element ref="person" maxOccurs="unbounded"/>
          </xs:sequence>
        </xs:complexType>
      </xs:element>
    </xs:sequence>
    <xs:attribute name="id" type="xs:ID" use="required"/>
    <xs:attribute name="available" type="xs:string" use="required"/>
  </xs:complexType>
</xs:schema>
```

In this version, all references to W3C XML Schema's own elements are still made using the xs prefix. Names of components are still unprefixed, but the lib prefix is now unnecessary, so all of those prefixes can disappear. Because the default namespace is defined in this document, W3C XML Schema will understand the connection between the components it defines and references to those components.

If you prefer to use prefixes on the components you are defining and use the W3C XML Schema vocabulary without prefixes, you can also define the W3C XML Namespace as the default namespace and declare a prefixed namespace (here, lib) for the components you're defining:

```
<?xml version="1.0"?>
<schema targetNamespace="http://dyomedea.com/ns/library"
  elementFormDefault="qualified" attributeFormDefault="unqualified"
  xmlns="http://www.w3.org/2001/XMLSchema"
  xmlns:lib="http://dyomedea.com/ns/library">
  <element name="library">
    <complexType>
      <sequence>
```

```
          <element name="book" type="lib:bookType"/>
        </sequence>
      </complexType>
    </element>
    <element name="person">
      <complexType>
        <sequence>
          <element name="name" type="string"/>
          <element name="born" type="date"/>
          <element name="dead" type="date" minOccurs="0"/>
          <element name="qualification" type="string" minOccurs="0"/>
        </sequence>
        <attribute name="id" type="ID" use="required"/>
      </complexType>
    </element>
    <complexType name="bookType">
      <sequence>
        <element name="isbn" type="NMTOKEN"/>
        <element name="title" type="string"/>
        <element name="authors">
          <complexType>
            <sequence>
              <element ref="lib:person" maxOccurs="unbounded"/>
            </sequence>
          </complexType>
        </element>
        <element name="characters">
          <complexType>
            <sequence>
              <element ref="lib:person" maxOccurs="unbounded"/>
            </sequence>
          </complexType>
        </element>
      </sequence>
      <attribute name="id" type="ID" use="required"/>
      <attribute name="available" type="string" use="required"/>
    </complexType>
  </schema>
```

The references to W3C XML Schema data types are now done without a prefix while the references to components defined in the target namespace are done with a "lib" prefix.

Disruptive Attributes

So far we have seen that W3C XML Schema treats global attributes and elements alike, requiring both types to be explicitly namespace-qualified to be global. Although this approach makes sense—there's little reason to treat elements and attributes differently—it's different from the approach the *Namespaces in XML* Recommendation took. Global attributes turn out to be a rather unusual, though useful, case.

To understand this phenomenon, we need to examine the *Namespaces in XML* Recommendation closely. This differentiates qualified and unqualified attributes, explaining that only attributes applied to elements from another namespace need to be qualified (these are also called global attributes), and that unqualified attributes are considered to belong to the vocabulary from their parent element without needing to belong to their namespace. In this case, they inherit the membership to the namespace of their parent element without needing to show it. This is tightly linked to the fact that default namespaces do not apply to attributes (they don't need to since attributes are considered members of the namespace of their parent without needing default namespaces). In practice, most XML vocabularies will use unqualified attributes, such as:

```
<book id="b0836217462" xmlns="http://dyomedea.com/ns/library"/>
```

or:

```
<lib:book id="b0836217462"
  xmlns:lib="http://dyomedea.com/ns/library"/>
```

Very few would use qualified attributes, such as:

```
<lib:book lib:id="b0836217462"
  xmlns:lib="http://dyomedea.com/ns/library"/>
```

Also, very few would use that or its equivalent if we use a default namespace for the element that doesn't apply to the attribute:

```
<book lib:id="b0836217462" xmlns="http://dyomedea.com/ns/library"
  xmlns:lib="http://dyomedea.com/ns/library"/>
```

Unfortunately, since the W3C XML Schema requires that all the global attributes be qualified, this means that global attributes can't be used for those unqualified attributes that are used most of the time in XML vocabularies, and that our unqualified id attribute cannot be declared as global. In practice, this means that most of the time we will just define local attributes within the element or complex type definitions. When we want to define unqualified attributes that may be reused in different elements, we will either define them in a specific schema without a target namespace, which will be imported (but there is risk of collision if we mix several schemas for different target namespaces following this policy), or "hide" those attributes inside of attribute groups, such as:

```
<xs:attributeGroup name="id">
  <xs:attribute name="id" form="unqualified" type="xs:ID"/>
</xs:attributeGroup>
```

Namespaces and XPath Expressions

It's time to remember that default namespaces do not apply to XPath expressions, and that a prefix needs to be defined for each namespace used in the XPath expressions of the xs:unique, xs:key, and xs:keyref declarations!

A prefix declaration is therefore required to write expressions that reference qualified elements and attributes, even if the target namespace is defined as the default namespace. It's also important to notice that the xs:keyref refer attribute is a QName that needs to be prefixed, and a xs:key/xs:keyref on the authors in (in our previous example) with a namespace could become:

```
<xs:schema targetNamespace="http://dyomedea.com/ns/library"
   elementFormDefault="qualified" attributeFormDefault="unqualified"
   xmlns:lib="http://dyomedea.com/ns/library"
   xmlns:xs="http://www.w3.org/2001/XMLSchema">
   <xs:element name="library">
     <xs:complexType>
       <xs:sequence>
         <xs:element name="book" type="lib:bookType"
           maxOccurs="unbounded"/>
         <xs:element name="author" type="lib:authorType"
           maxOccurs="unbounded"/>
         <xs:element name="characters" type="lib:characterType"
           maxOccurs="unbounded"/>
       </xs:sequence>
     </xs:complexType>
     <xs:key name="author">
       <xs:selector xpath="lib:author"/>
       <xs:field xpath="@id"/>
     </xs:key>
     <xs:keyref name="keyref" refer="lib:author">
       <xs:selector xpath="lib:book/lib:author-ref"/>
       <xs:field xpath="@ref"/>
     </xs:keyref>
   </xs:element>
</xs:schema>
```

Referencing Other Namespaces

One of the goals of the namespaces specification is to allow the use of documents mixing elements and attributes from different vocabularies. W3C XML Schema lets you take full advantage of this possibility.

Part of the library vocabulary describes persons. This could be reused by other applications, and we might want to define a specific namespace and give it the URI reference "http://dyomedea.com/ns/people":

```
<?xml version="1.0"?>
<library xmlns:ppl="http://dyomedea.com/ns/people"
  xmlns="http://dyomedea.com/ns/library">
  <book id="b0836217462" available="yes">
    <isbn>
      0836217462
    </isbn>
    <title>
      Being a Dog Is a Full-Time Job
```

```
    </title>
    <authors>
      <ppl:person id="CMS">
        <ppl:name>
          Charles M Schulz
        </ppl:name>
        <ppl:born>
          1922-11-26
        </ppl:born>
        <ppl:dead>
          2000-02-12
        </ppl:dead>
      </ppl:person>
    </authors>
    <characters>
      <ppl:person id="PP">
        <ppl:name>
          Peppermint Patty
        </ppl:name>
        <ppl:born>
          1966-08-22
        </ppl:born>
        <ppl:qualification>
          bold, brash and tomboyish
        </ppl:qualification>
      </ppl:person>
      <ppl:person id="Snoopy">
        <ppl:name>
          Snoopy
        </ppl:name>
        <ppl:born>
          1950-10-04
        </ppl:born>
        <ppl:qualification>
          extroverted beagle
        </ppl:qualification>
      </ppl:person>
      <ppl:person id="Schroeder">
        <ppl:name>
          Schroeder
        </ppl:name>
        <ppl:born>
          1951-05-30
        </ppl:born>
        <ppl:qualification>
          brought classical music to the Peanuts strip
        </ppl:qualification>
      </ppl:person>
      <ppl:person id="Lucy">
        <ppl:name>
          Lucy
        </ppl:name>
        <ppl:born>
          1952-03-03
```

```
      </ppl:born>
      <ppl:qualification>
        bossy, crabby and selfish
      </ppl:qualification>
    </ppl:person>
  </characters>
 </book>
</library>
```

To handle these two namespaces, we need to define two different schemas (one per namespace). One will describe our vocabulary about persons as well as include the definitions of the element person and its child elements:

```
<?xml version="1.0"?>
<xs:schema targetNamespace="http://dyomedea.com/ns/people"
  elementFormDefault="qualified" attributeFormDefault="unqualified"
  xmlns:ppl="http://dyomedea.com/ns/people"
  xmlns:xs="http://www.w3.org/2001/XMLSchema">
  <xs:element name="person">
    <xs:complexType>
      <xs:sequence>
        <xs:element name="name" type="xs:string"/>
        <xs:element name="born" type="xs:date"/>
        <xs:element name="dead" type="xs:date" minOccurs="0"/>
        <xs:element name="qualification" type="xs:string"
          minOccurs="0"/>
      </xs:sequence>
      <xs:attribute name="id" type="xs:ID" use="required"/>
    </xs:complexType>
  </xs:element>
</xs:schema>
```

This schema describes the namespace "http://dyomedea.com/ns/people", and this vocabulary doesn't include anything from any other namespace. The schema is then similar to the examples we've seen in this chapter so far. It can be used alone with documents that use only this namespace, but can also be "imported" by schemas that describe other namespaces but would like to use some of its definitions.

To do this, the schema that describes the including vocabulary needs two pieces of information. It must have a prefix for the namespaces that will be included; this is done by a usual namespace declaration. It also must have a hint on where it can find the schema for this namespace; this is done using a xs:import element:

```
<xs:import namespace="http://dyomedea.com/ns/people"
  schemaLocation="simple-2-ns-ppl.xsd"/>
```

The schema now has all the information it needs to resolve references to schema components that belong to the http://dyomedea.com/ns/people namespace. References can be made just using its prefix:

```
<xs:element ref="ppl:person"/>
```

A full schema for the library vocabulary can then be:

```xml
<?xml version="1.0"?>
<xs:schema targetNamespace="http://dyomedea.com/ns/library"
  elementFormDefault="qualified" attributeFormDefault="unqualified"
  xmlns:xs="http://www.w3.org/2001/XMLSchema"
  xmlns:ppl="http://dyomedea.com/ns/people"
  xmlns:lib="http://dyomedea.com/ns/library">
  <xs:import namespace="http://dyomedea.com/ns/people"
    schemaLocation="simple-2-ns-ppl.xsd"/>
  <xs:element name="library">
    <xs:complexType>
      <xs:sequence>
        <xs:element name="book" type="lib:bookType"/>
      </xs:sequence>
    </xs:complexType>
  </xs:element>
  <xs:complexType name="bookType">
    <xs:sequence>
      <xs:element name="isbn" type="xs:NMTOKEN"/>
      <xs:element name="title" type="xs:string"/>
      <xs:element name="authors">
        <xs:complexType>
          <xs:sequence>
            <xs:element ref="ppl:person"/>
          </xs:sequence>
        </xs:complexType>
      </xs:element>
      <xs:element name="characters">
        <xs:complexType>
          <xs:sequence>
            <xs:element ref="ppl:person" maxOccurs="unbounded"/>
          </xs:sequence>
        </xs:complexType>
      </xs:element>
    </xs:sequence>
    <xs:attribute name="id" type="xs:ID" use="required"/>
    <xs:attribute name="available" type="xs:string" use="required"/>
  </xs:complexType>
</xs:schema>
```

 When importing schemas from other namespaces, we can only refer to the global components defined in the imported schemas.

Schemas for XML, XML Base and XLink

XML Base, XLink, and XML 1.0 all define vocabularies that are composed only of attributes. Attributes such as xml:base, xlink:href, or xml:lang are designed to work with elements from any vocabulary, imparting their meaning to those elements and sometimes the descendants of those elements.

XML Attributes

In this section, we will discuss how to allow the use of a XML attribute in our document. To illustrate this, let's use a `xml:lang` attribute to qualify the language of several descriptions in several languages for our book:

```
<?xml version="1.0"?>
<library xmlns="http://dyomedea.com/ns/library">
  <book id="b0836217462">
    <title>
      Being a Dog Is a Full-Time Job
    </title>
    <description xml:lang="en">
      Its title says it all !
    </description>
    <description xml:lang="fr">
      Son titre le résume parfaitement !
    </description>
  </book>
</library>
```

Following Namespaces in XML 1.0, *W3C XML Schema* considers `xml:lang`, `xml: space` (from the XML 1.0 recommendation) and `xml:base` (from the XML Base specification) to belong to the *XML* 1.0 namespace identified by the URI reference "`http: //www.w3.org/XML/1998/namespace`".

 The XML 1.0 namespace is an exception in the namespaces world, since we don't need to declare it in the instance documents. Its prefix "xml" is reserved for this usage and has a special meaning, even for the parsers that do not support the namespaces. In theory, any other prefix can be assigned to the XML 1.0 namespace, but this practice is confusing and shouldn't be encouraged.

To use attributes from this namespace, we will declare the XML namespace, import a schema, and reference both of them, as we've done previously for the elements from our "people" namespace:

```
<?xml version="1.0"?>
<xs:schema targetNamespace="http://dyomedea.com/ns/library"
  elementFormDefault="qualified" attributeFormDefault="unqualified"
  xmlns:lib="http://dyomedea.com/ns/library"
  xmlns:xs="http://www.w3.org/2001/XMLSchema">
<xs:import namespace="http://www.w3.org/XML/1998/namespace"
  schemaLocation="xml.xsd"/>
<xs:element name="description">
  <xs:complexType>
    <xs:simpleContent>
      <xs:restriction base="xs:string">
        <xs:attribute ref="xml:lang"/>
      </xs:restriction>
    </xs:simpleContent>
```

```
    </xs:complexType>
  </xs:element>
  <xs:element name="library">
    <xs:complexType>
      <xs:sequence>
        <xs:element ref="lib:book"/>
      </xs:sequence>
    </xs:complexType>
  </xs:element>
  <xs:element name="book">
    <xs:complexType>
      <xs:sequence>
        <xs:element name="title" type="xs:string"/>
        <xs:element ref="lib:description" maxOccurs="unbounded"/>
      </xs:sequence>
      <xs:attribute name="id" type="xs:ID" use="required"/>
    </xs:complexType>
  </xs:element>
</xs:schema>
```

In this example, we import a local schema (xml.xsd) for the XML namespace. The W3C has defined its own schema for the xml:lang, xml:space, and xml:base attributes. This is available at *http://www.w3.org/2001/xml.xsd*:

```
<?xml version='1.0'?>
<!DOCTYPE xs:schema PUBLIC "-//W3C//DTD XMLSCHEMA 200102//EN" "XMLSchema.dtd" >
<xs:schema targetNamespace="http://www.w3.org/XML/1998/namespace" xmlns:xs="http://
www.w3.org/2001/XMLSchema" xml:lang="en">

 <xs:annotation>
  <xs:documentation>
   See http://www.w3.org/XML/1998/namespace.html and
   http://www.w3.org/TR/REC-xml for information about this namespace.
  </xs:documentation>
 </xs:annotation>

 <xs:annotation>
  <xs:documentation>This schema defines attributes and an attribute group
        suitable for use by
        schemas wishing to allow xml:base, xml:lang or xml:space attributes
        on elements they define.

        To enable this, such a schema must import this schema
        for the XML namespace, e.g. as follows:
        &lt;schema . . .>
         . . .
         &lt;import namespace="http://www.w3.org/XML/1998/namespace"
                schemaLocation="http://www.w3.org/2001/03/xml.xsd"/>

        Subsequently, qualified reference to any of the attributes
        or the group defined below will have the desired effect, e.g.

        &lt;type . . .>
         . . .
```

```
        &lt;attributeGroup ref="xml:specialAttrs"/>

        will define a type which will schema-validate an instance
        element with any of those attributes</xs:documentation>
</xs:annotation>

<xs:annotation>
 <xs:documentation>In keeping with the XML Schema WG's standard versioning
  policy, this schema document will persist at
  http://www.w3.org/2001/03/xml.xsd.
  At the date of issue it can also be found at
  http://www.w3.org/2001/xml.xsd.
  The schema document at that URI may however change in the future,
  in order to remain compatible with the latest version of XML Schema
  itself.  In other words, if the XML Schema namespace changes, the version
  of this document at
  http://www.w3.org/2001/xml.xsd will change
  accordingly; the version at
  http://www.w3.org/2001/03/xml.xsd will not change.
 </xs:documentation>
</xs:annotation>

<xs:attribute name="lang" type="xs:language">
 <xs:annotation>
  <xs:documentation>In due course, we should install the relevant ISO 2- and 3-
letter
        codes as the enumerated possible values . . .</xs:documentation>
 </xs:annotation>
</xs:attribute>

<xs:attribute name="space" default="preserve">
 <xs:simpleType>
  <xs:restriction base="xs:NCName">
   <xs:enumeration value="default"/>
   <xs:enumeration value="preserve"/>
  </xs:restriction>
 </xs:simpleType>
</xs:attribute>

<xs:attribute name="base" type="xs:anyURI">
 <xs:annotation>
  <xs:documentation>See http://www.w3.org/TR/xmlbase/ for
                    information about this attribute.</xs:documentation>
 </xs:annotation>
</xs:attribute>

<xs:attributeGroup name="specialAttrs">
 <xs:attribute ref="xml:base"/>
 <xs:attribute ref="xml:lang"/>
 <xs:attribute ref="xml:space"/>
</xs:attributeGroup>

</xs:schema>
```

Among the many controversial issues surrounding the usage of URIs, the decision to use a schema at its original location (on the W3C web site) versus using a local copy is not easy. Using a schema at its original location provides a guarantee of always accessing the most recent version, but this can be a problem if the schema becomes out of sync with the applications using it. It can also impact the ability to process documents when the hosting site is unreachable and may open a possibility of malicious substitutions of schemas.

XLink Attributes

To illustrate the usage of XLink attributes, we can replace the definition of the author that is currently within the description of a book under the authors element, with a reference to an author described as a "person" in another XML document:

```
<?xml version="1.0"?>
<library xmlns="http://dyomedea.com/ns/library"
  xmlns:xlink="http://www.w3.org/1999/xlink">
  <book id="b0836217462">
    <title>
      Being a Dog Is a Full-Time Job
    </title>
    <authors>
      <person xlink:href="authors.xml#CMS"/>
    </authors>
  </book>
</library>
```

Again, we need to define the namespace for XLink and to import a schema before referencing the XLink attributes:

```
<?xml version="1.0"?>
<xs:schema targetNamespace="http://dyomedea.com/ns/library"
  elementFormDefault="qualified" attributeFormDefault="unqualified"
  xmlns:xs="http://www.w3.org/2001/XMLSchema"
  xmlns:xlink="http://www.w3.org/1999/xlink"
  xmlns:lib="http://dyomedea.com/ns/library">
  <xs:import namespace="http://www.w3.org/1999/xlink"
    schemaLocation="xlink.xsd"/>
  <xs:element name="person">
    <xs:complexType>
      <xs:attribute ref="xlink:href" use="required"/>
      <xs:attribute ref="xlink:type" fixed="simple"/>
      <xs:attribute ref="xlink:show" fixed="embed"/>
      <xs:attribute ref="xlink:actuate" fixed="onLoad"/>
    </xs:complexType>
  </xs:element>
  <xs:element name="library">
    <xs:complexType>
      <xs:sequence>
        <xs:element ref="lib:book"/>
      </xs:sequence>
```

```
    </xs:complexType>
  </xs:element>
  <xs:element name="book">
    <xs:complexType>
      <xs:sequence>
        <xs:element name="title" type="xs:string"/>
        <xs:element ref="lib:authors"/>
      </xs:sequence>
      <xs:attribute name="id" type="xs:ID" use="required"/>
    </xs:complexType>
  </xs:element>
  <xs:element name="authors">
    <xs:complexType>
      <xs:sequence>
        <xs:element ref="lib:person"/>
      </xs:sequence>
    </xs:complexType>
  </xs:element>
</xs:schema>
```

 Following the suggestion of the XLink specification, we have defined additional XLink attributes (type, show, and actuate) as fixed values. While this is legitimate, one should note that these values are only available to the applications that use a *W3C XML Schema* post-schema validation infoset (PSVI).

Although the XLink specification doesn't provide a schema, creating the parts we need is very straightforward:

```
<?xml version="1.0"?>
<xs:schema targetNamespace="http://www.w3.org/1999/xlink"
  elementFormDefault="qualified" attributeFormDefault="qualified"
  xmlns:xs="http://www.w3.org/2001/XMLSchema"
  xmlns:xlink="http://www.w3.org/1999/xlink">
  <xs:attribute name="type">
    <xs:simpleType>
      <xs:restriction base="xs:NMTOKEN">
        <xs:enumeration value="simple"/>
        <xs:enumeration value="extended"/>
        <xs:enumeration value="locator"/>
        <xs:enumeration value="arc"/>
        <xs:enumeration value="resource"/>
        <xs:enumeration value="title"/>
      </xs:restriction>
    </xs:simpleType>
  </xs:attribute>
  <xs:attribute name="href" type="xs:anyURI"/>
  <xs:attribute name="role" type="xs:anyURI"/>
  <xs:attribute name="arcrole" type="xs:anyURI"/>
  <xs:attribute name="title" type="xs:string"/>
  <xs:attribute name="show">
    <xs:simpleType>
```

```
      <xs:restriction base="xs:NMTOKEN">
        <xs:enumeration value="new"/>
        <xs:enumeration value="replace"/>
        <xs:enumeration value="embed"/>
        <xs:enumeration value="other"/>
        <xs:enumeration value="none"/>
      </xs:restriction>
    </xs:simpleType>
  </xs:attribute>
  <xs:attribute name="label" type="xs:NMTOKEN"/>
  <xs:attribute name="actuate">
    <xs:simpleType>
      <xs:restriction base="xs:NMTOKEN">
        <xs:enumeration value="onLoad"/>
        <xs:enumeration value="onRequest"/>
        <xs:enumeration value="other"/>
        <xs:enumeration value="none"/>
      </xs:restriction>
    </xs:simpleType>
  </xs:attribute>
  <xs:attribute name="from" type="xs:NMTOKEN"/>
  <xs:attribute name="to" type="xs:NMTOKEN"/>
</xs:schema>
```

Namespace Behavior of Imported Components

You may be wondering about the different approaches used to identify the namespaces for the elements defined by the schema and the data types defined by *W3C XML Schema*. Importing schemas imposes certain restrictions on the use of namespaces in the imported schema.

When we define an element or attribute, we give it a namespace. That namespace must be the same as the target namespace of the schema doing the importing, even if the datatype of the element or attribute belongs to a different namespace.

The rules are slightly different when we define an element or attribute by reference to a component which is in a different namespace, rather than a datatype. In that case, the name of the referenced component is imported, and that namespace must be the target namespace of the imported schema.

To illustrate how this works, we'll take a closer look at two ways to create schemas described in this simple example:

```
<?xml version="1.0"?>
<!-- Namespace: http://dyomedea.com/ns/library -->
<library xmlns:ppl="http://dyomedea.com/ns/people"
  xmlns="http://dyomedea.com/ns/library">
  <book id="b0836217462">
    <title>
```

```
      Being a Dog Is a Full-Time Job
    </title>
    <authors>
      <ppl:person id="CMS">
        <ppl:name>
          Charles M Schulz
        </ppl:name>
      </ppl:person>
    </authors>
  </book>
</library>
```

This document contains two namespaces. Everything except the contents of the authors element is in the http://dyomedea.com/ns/library namespace. The contents of the authors element (ppl:person and ppl:name) are in the http://dyomedea.com/ns/people namespace.

We have two main options for representing this document using W3C XML Schema. Both approaches start by defining a schema for the elements in the http://dyomedea.com/ns/library namespace. The first approach imports the schema defining the http://dyomedea.com/ns/people namespace, and then uses a reference to the ppl:person element to use it inside the authors element:

```
<?xml version="1.0"?>
<xs:schema targetNamespace="http://dyomedea.com/ns/library"
  elementFormDefault="qualified" attributeFormDefault="unqualified"
  xmlns:xs="http://www.w3.org/2001/XMLSchema"
  xmlns:ppl="http://dyomedea.com/ns/people"
  xmlns:lib="http://dyomedea.com/ns/library">
  <xs:import namespace="http://dyomedea.com/ns/people"
    schemaLocation="very-simple-2-ns-ppl.xsd"/>
  <xs:element name="library">
    <xs:complexType>
      <xs:sequence>
        <xs:element name="book" type="lib:bookType"/>
      </xs:sequence>
    </xs:complexType>
  </xs:element>
  <xs:complexType name="bookType">
    <xs:sequence>
      <xs:element name="title" type="xs:string"/>
      <xs:element name="authors">
        <xs:complexType>
          <xs:sequence>
            <xs:element ref="ppl:person"/>
          </xs:sequence>
        </xs:complexType>
      </xs:element>
    </xs:sequence>
    <xs:attribute name="id" type="xs:ID" use="required"/>
  </xs:complexType>
</xs:schema>
```

The second approach does the same import, but defines the authors element as having the type ppl:authorType rather than defining its complex type explicitly, resulting in a shorter schema:

```
<?xml version="1.0"?>
<xs:schema targetNamespace="http://dyomedea.com/ns/library"
  elementFormDefault="qualified" attributeFormDefault="unqualified"
  xmlns:lib="http://dyomedea.com/ns/library"
  xmlns:ppl="http://dyomedea.com/ns/people"
  xmlns:xs="http://www.w3.org/2001/XMLSchema">
  <xs:import namespace="http://dyomedea.com/ns/people"
    schemaLocation="very-simple-2-ns-ppl.xsd"/>
  <xs:element name="library">
    <xs:complexType>
      <xs:sequence>
        <xs:element name="book" type="lib:bookType"/>
      </xs:sequence>
    </xs:complexType>
  </xs:element>
  <xs:complexType name="bookType">
    <xs:sequence>
      <xs:element name="title" type="xs:string"/>
      <xs:element name="authors" type="ppl:authorType"/>
    </xs:sequence>
    <xs:attribute name="id" type="xs:ID" use="required"/>
  </xs:complexType>
</xs:schema>
```

Although the two schemas will validate the same instance documents, the design style is quite different. Applications relying on the schema for information about the document will see it in two very different ways. The first approach provides a cleaner separation between the two namespaces. The use of the reference allows the ppl:person element to appear inside the authors element but does nothing to mix the authors element with the http://dyomedea.com/ns/people namespace directly. The second approach is briefer, but assigns a datatype in one namespace to an element in another namespace.

If you are using your schemas purely for validation, this distinction is unimportant. Both schemas will validate identical sets of documents. If, however, your applications rely on your schemas for type information (using the PSVI or perhaps compile-time data-binding based on the schema), the perspective shift may matter. Using the datatype approach will mean that your applications need to understand quite a bit more about the contents of your schema and creates new dependencies between your application and the details of W3C XML Schema processing.

Importing Schemas with No Namespaces

We have seen how we can reference components from other namespaces and how the elements and attributes included in these components keep their full name, namespaces, and form (in the section "To Qualify Or Not to Qualify?"). However, this mechanism has a restriction: you can only reference global elements and attributes, and global elements and attributes must always be qualified.

Therefore, the only solution to importing elements and attributes with no namespace is to import a schema without any target namespace. Let's say that we want to describe a document in which the vocabulary to describe people has no namespace:

```
<?xml version="1.0"?>
<lib:library xmlns:lib="http://dyomedea.com/ns/library">
  <lib:book id="b0836217462">
    <lib:title>
      Being a Dog Is a Full-Time Job
    </lib:title>
    <lib:authors>
      <person id="CMS">
        <name>
          Charles M Schulz
        </name>
      </person>
    </lib:authors>
  </lib:book>
</lib:library>
```

The import of the schema without a namespace is done exactly as we've seen earlier with schemas having target namespaces, except now we omit the namespace attribute. Another point to note is that to be able to reference the components from the schema you are including, you will have to keep the default namespace (unprefixed) available:

```
<?xml version="1.0"?>
<xs:schema targetNamespace="http://dyomedea.com/ns/library"
  elementFormDefault="qualified" attributeFormDefault="unqualified"
  xmlns:lib="http://dyomedea.com/ns/library"
  xmlns:xs="http://www.w3.org/2001/XMLSchema">
  <xs:import schemaLocation="very-simple-2-ns-ppl-nons.xsd"/>
  <xs:element name="library">
    <xs:complexType>
      <xs:sequence>
        <xs:element name="book" type="lib:bookType"/>
      </xs:sequence>
    </xs:complexType>
  </xs:element>
  <xs:complexType name="bookType">
    <xs:sequence>
      <xs:element name="title" type="xs:string"/>
      <xs:element name="authors">
        <xs:complexType>
          <xs:sequence>
            <xs:element ref="person"/>
          </xs:sequence>
        </xs:complexType>
      </xs:element>
```

```
    </xs:sequence>
    <xs:attribute name="id" type="xs:ID" use="required"/>
  </xs:complexType>
</xs:schema>
```

The included schema is:

```
<?xml version="1.0"?>
<xs:schema xmlns:xs="http://www.w3.org/2001/XMLSchema">
  <xs:element name="person" type="personType"/>
  <xs:complexType name="personType">
    <xs:sequence>
      <xs:element name="name" type="xs:string"/>
    </xs:sequence>
    <xs:attribute name="id" type="xs:ID" use="required"/>
  </xs:complexType>
</xs:schema>
```

In this case, all the components are considered unqualified. All the other behavior, including the difference between referencing elements or attributes and using datatypes, is relevant.

We see then that to define unqualified elements and attributes in a schema with a target namespace, we have to choose between defining them locally in the schema or defining them in a separate schema without an imported target namespace.

Chameleon Design

This chapter wouldn't be complete without a look at the impact of namespaces on the inclusion of schemas through xs:include and xs:redefine.

When we initially introduced these features, we didn't worry about namespaces. However, these features have some important interactions with namespaces, since *W3C XML Schema* restricts inclusion (or redefinition) to pieces of schema with either the same target namespace or without any target namespace (schemas for other languages being "imported" rather than "included").

When a piece of schema that has no target namespace is included in a schema with a target namespace, the included definition acquires the target namespace of the including schema and behaves exactly as if it added the same target namespace. This feature allows creation of libraries with pieces of schema that are "namespace-transparent," and which take the namespace of the schema in which they are imported. This method is often called "chameleon," since the included schema takes the "color" of the context in which it is included.

To illustrate this feature and see its implication, let's look again at the example that we've used throughout this chapter:

```
<?xml version="1.0"?>
<library xmlns="http://dyomedea.com/ns/library">
  <book id="b0836217462">
```

```
    <title>
      Being a Dog Is a Full-Time Job
    </title>
    <authors>
      <person id="CMS">
        <name>
          Charles M Schulz
        </name>
      </person>
    </authors>
  </book>
</library>
```

If we want a library of schema parts that describe a person and can be included within several vocabularies, we can include a piece of schema that has no target namespace. This piece of schema would be something like the following (note that we do not define any target namespace):

```
<?xml version="1.0"?>
<xs:schema elementFormDefault="qualified"
  xmlns:xs="http://www.w3.org/2001/XMLSchema">
  <xs:element name="person">
    <xs:complexType>
      <xs:sequence>
        <xs:element name="name" type="xs:string"/>
      </xs:sequence>
      <xs:attribute name="id" type="xs:string" use="required"/>
    </xs:complexType>
  </xs:element>
</xs:schema>
```

And the including schema would look similar to the following example:

```
<?xml version="1.0"?>
<xs:schema targetNamespace="http://dyomedea.com/ns/library"
  elementFormDefault="qualified"
  xmlns="http://dyomedea.com/ns/library"
  xmlns:xs="http://www.w3.org/2001/XMLSchema">
  <xs:include schemaLocation="very-simple-1-ns-ppl.xsd"/>
  <xs:element name="library">
    <xs:complexType>
      <xs:sequence>
        <xs:element name="book">
          <xs:complexType>
            <xs:sequence>
              <xs:element name="title" type="xs:string"/>
              <xs:element name="authors">
                <xs:complexType>
                 <xs:sequence>
                 <xs:element ref="person"/>
                 </xs:sequence>
                </xs:complexType>
              </xs:element>
            </xs:sequence>
```

```
            <xs:attribute name="id" type="xs:ID"/>
          </xs:complexType>
        </xs:element>
      </xs:sequence>
    </xs:complexType>
  </xs:element>
</xs:schema>
```

While this looks very easy and neat, we may wonder if we are really building something modular. Including a piece of schema is similar to including a C header file. While this is slightly better than a copy/paste, the level of modularity that can be achieved in this way is very restricted.

The namespace of the element person is the namespace given to our library. An application cannot guess from looking at the instance document that this element is the same as a person element that it will find in another document describing, for example, an employee.

Looking at the modified infoset and checking the datatype doesn't help either, since the datatype will be defined as a datatype from a schema with the target namespace of our library, and won't match other target namespaces, including the same piece of schema.

The fact that the same person element is used by different vocabularies is totally lost by the processing of the include (or redefine). Before using it, you may consider if it isn't more useful to include information in the instance document using a separate namespace, or at least include information in the modified infoset by importing datatypes from another namespace rather than including common definitions.

Allowing Any Elements or Attributes from a Particular Namespace

We are going to see how to accommodate any element or attribute from other namespaces using our marketing extension, the http://dyomedea.com/ns/library/mkt namespace, as an example:

```
<?xml version="1.0"?>
<!-- Namespace: http://dyomedea.com/ns/library -->
<library xmlns="http://dyomedea.com/ns/library"
  xmlns:mkt="http://dyomedea.com/ns/library/mkt">
  <book id="b0836217462">
    <title>
      Being a Dog Is a Full-Time Job
    </title>
    <authors>
      <person id="CMS">
        <name>
          Charles M Schulz
        </name>
```

```
        </person>
      </authors>
      <mkt:cover>
        Paperback
      </mkt:cover>
      <mkt:pages>
        128
      </mkt:pages>
    </book>
  </library>
```

To allow any elements from the http://dyomedea.com/ns/library/mkt namespace after the author element, we use a xs:any element:

```
<xs:any namespace="http://dyomedea.com/ns/library/mkt"
  processContents="skip"minOccurs="0" maxOccurs="unbounded"/>
```

xs:anyAttribute should be used to allow attributes:

```
<xs:anyAttribute namespace="http://dyomedea.com/ns/library/mkt"
  processContents="skip"/>
```

The two new attributes shown above are namespace and processContents.

namespace specifies the namespaces of the elements or attributes that will be accepted. The value should be a list of namespaces that URIs allow a number of wildcards. The wildcards permitted within the list are ##local (a nonqualified element) and ##targetNamespace (the target namespace). Two wildcards can also be used instead of the list: ##any (any namespace) and ##other (any namespace other than the target namespace).

 It is not possible to specify that the possible namespaces are all the namespaces not defined in a schema, or even all the namespaces except those in a list. This is a serious limitation for multi-namespace vocabularies that would like to restrict some of the imported namespaces while remaining open to undefined namespaces.

processContents specifies the behavior of the validator regarding the elements or attributes from the specified namespaces. The possible values are "skip" (no validation is attempted on these elements or attributes), "strict" (schemas for the namespaces that will be included need to be available, and validators will validate the elements and attributes against these schemas), or "lax" (validators will do their best to find a schema for the included elements and attributes, validate them when they have found one, and silently skip the validation when they haven't). For example:

```
<?xml version="1.0"?>
<xs:schema targetNamespace="http://dyomedea.com/ns/library"
  elementFormDefault="qualified"
  xmlns:xs="http://www.w3.org/2001/XMLSchema"
  xmlns="http://dyomedea.com/ns/library">
```

```
<xs:element name="library">
  <xs:complexType>
    <xs:sequence>
      <xs:element ref="book"/>
    </xs:sequence>
    <xs:anyAttribute namespace="http://dyomedea.com/ns/library/mkt"
      processContents="skip"/>
  </xs:complexType>
</xs:element>
<xs:element name="book">
  <xs:complexType>
    <xs:sequence>
      <xs:element name="title" type="xs:string"/>
      <xs:element name="authors">
        <xs:complexType>
          <xs:sequence>
            <xs:element name="person">
              <xs:complexType>
                <xs:sequence>
                <xs:element name="name" type="xs:string"/>
                </xs:sequence>
                <xs:attribute name="id" type="xs:string"
                  use="required"/>
              </xs:complexType>
            </xs:element>
          </xs:sequence>
        </xs:complexType>
      </xs:element>
      <xs:any namespace="http://dyomedea.com/ns/library/mkt"
        processContents="skip"minOccurs="0" maxOccurs="unbounded"/>
    </xs:sequence>
    <xs:attribute name="id" use="required">
      <xs:simpleType>
        <xs:restriction base="xs:hexBinary"/>
      </xs:simpleType>
    </xs:attribute>
  </xs:complexType>
</xs:element>
</xs:schema>
```

This schema has been opened to accept any element from a single namespace and can be further opened to accept any element from any namespace other than the target namespace:

```
<xs:anyAttribute namespace="##other" processContents="skip"/>
```

This mechanism is flexible enough (with the exception of the lack of support for any undefined namespaces already mentioned) to accommodate a large majority of applications, but we must note that these wildcards are considered particles and can't replace global element definitions. The unfortunate consequence is that document elements cannot be wildcarded because a schema needs to provide a closed list of possible document elements.

CHAPTER 11

Referencing Schemas and Schema Datatypes in XML Documents

So far, we have seen how W3C XML Schemas can be written outside XML documents without touching the actual instance documents. In this chapter, we will introduce a new namespace to be used inside XML documents to provide information for use by schema processors. This information may identify the location of the associated schemas, as well as further identify the schema types used, which opens a new level of flexibility and interaction between schemas and instance documents in the design of XML applications.

This namespace (which is the same for all W3C XML Schema meta-information located in the instance documents themselves) is *http://www.w3.org/2001/ XMLSchema-instance*. The prefix usually used to designate this namespace is xsi. This namespace uses only four attributes, which are considered valid in any element of any instance document without being declared in the schema.

Associating Schemas with Instance Documents

The first piece of information that may be useful for a schema processor is some hints about the locations where the schema processor might find schemas relevant to the instance document. This feature is similar to the SYSTEM identifier of the XML doctype declaration, but with some important differences. The first difference is that a schema may not be enough to describe a document, since each schema might describe only one namespace (or lack of a namespace), and the composition of the schemas can be done in the instance document. The second difference is that the locations indicated in the instance documents are only considered hints and may be overridden by the user or by the schema processor.

The hard link between a XML document and its DTD has fed many debates in the XML community. Many developers remember what happened when Netscape restructured their web site. The address of the DTD for RSS 0.91 (*http://my.netscape.com/*

publish/formats/rss-0.91.dtd) suddenly returned a 404 error, breaking hundreds of applications. Another motivation for "soft" links between instance documents and their schemas is they allow application of different schemas, depending on local business rules. For instance, a supplier receiving an order in a XML document may have specific rules to check the document with its own schema.

For all these reasons, the Recommendation states that if a schema processor finds such information in a document, it should try to retrieve the schemas at the locations indicated, but it could be directed otherwise by the invoking application or user. When such information is missing, a schema processor may also be directed by the invoking application to dereference specified locations. When no information is provided at all by the invoking application or in the instance document, the schema processor is free to try any method to find a schema. Among the methods mentioned in this case, a schema processor may try to load the resource that may be available at the namespace URI to see if a schema is published there, but it could use other techniques as well, such as RDDL or catalog systems.

W3C XML Schema defines two attributes to define a list of schema locations associated with target namespaces as well as the location of a schema without target namespace. The attribute to use when there is no target namespace is xsi:noNamespaceSchemaLocation, and its value is a URI pointing to the corresponding schema. Although this attribute can be used without a declaration in any element of any instance document, it must be found by the schema processor before it needs it to validate any element or attribute (i.e., at or before the last point in the first element without a namespace found in the document). Furthermore, its scope is global to the entire document and it cannot be redefined.

In practice, the xsi:noNamespaceSchemaLocation attribute will often be located in the document element. We can locate a schema named first.xsd in the same directory as the instance document in the example used in this chapter (which doesn't use any namespace) as:

```
<library xsi:noNamespaceSchemaLocation="first.xsd"
    xmlns:xsi="http://www.w3.org/2001/XMLSchema-instance">
    .../...
</library>
```

To reference schemas with a target namespace, lists of URIs must be provided in xsi:schemaLocation attributes. This list is, in fact, a list of pairs of URIs. In each pair, the first URI identifies a target namespace and the second URI identifies the location of a schema with this target namespace. The same rule that applied to xsi:noNamespaceSchemaLocation applies to the location of this attribute: for each target namespace for which you want to provide a schema location, you need to provide this information before a schema processor needs it to do its job.

To illustrate the usage of the `xsi:schemaLocation` attribute, let's examine a simplified version of an example with the two namespaces that are described in Chapter 10. The instance document is as follows (without any `xsi:schemaLocation`):

```
<?xml version="1.0"?>
<book id="b0836217462" xmlns="http://dyomedea.com/ns/library"
  xmlns:mkt="http://dyomedea.com/ns/library/mkt">
  <title>
    Being a Dog Is a Full-Time Job
  </title>
  <author>
    Charles M Schulz
  </author>
  <mkt:cover>
    Paperback
  </mkt:cover>
  <mkt:pages>
    128
  </mkt:pages>
</book>
```

We have an open schema for the main namespaces that allows arbitrary elements from other namespaces, such as:

```
<?xml version="1.0"?>
<xs:schema targetNamespace="http://dyomedea.com/ns/library"
  elementFormDefault="qualified" attributeFormDefault="unqualified"
  xmlns:lib="http://dyomedea.com/ns/library"
  xmlns:xs="http://www.w3.org/2001/XMLSchema">
  <xs:element name="book">
    <xs:complexType>
      <xs:sequence>
        <xs:element name="title" type="xs:token"/>
        <xs:element name="author" type="xs:token"
          maxOccurs="unbounded"/>
        <xs:any namespace="##other" processContents="lax"
          minOccurs="0"maxOccurs="unbounded"/>
      </xs:sequence>
      <xs:attribute name="id" type="xs:ID"/>
    </xs:complexType>
  </xs:element>
</xs:schema>
```

We also have a schema for the two elements that belong to the namespace for our marketing department:

```
<?xml version="1.0"?>
<xs:schema targetNamespace="http://dyomedea.com/ns/library/mkt"
  elementFormDefault="qualified" attributeFormDefault="unqualified"
  xmlns:xs="http://www.w3.org/2001/XMLSchema">
  <xs:element name="cover" type="xs:NMTOKEN"/>
  <xs:element name="pages" type="xs:nonNegativeInteger"/>
</xs:schema>
```

This example was carefully chosen to have two schemas for two namespaces that are not linked together: there is no reference to the marketing namespace from the library and vice versa. We have several possibilities, depending on the hints given to the schema processor. If we validate the instance document without any xsi: schemaLocation attribute or any other information from the command line or application, the schema validator is left alone to try to locate a schema. Depending on the algorithm implemented in the processor, it may try to dereference the namespace URIs of the document element (i.e., to attempt to load a resource that may be available here). In our case, this is *http://dyomedea.com/ns/library*. If there is no schema there, then it can't say whether the document is valid or not. Alternatively, the schema processor can try to dereference a RDDL document at this location, hoping to find a reference to a schema in the RDDL document.

More typically, the author of the instance document may be kind enough to give the location of the schema for the library namespace—for instance:

```
<?xml version="1.0"?>
<book xsi:schemaLocation="http://dyomedea.com/ns/library library.xsd"
  id="b0836217462" xmlns="http://dyomedea.com/ns/library"
  xmlns:xsi="http://www.w3.org/2001/XMLSchema-instance"
  xmlns:mkt="http://dyomedea.com/ns/library/mkt">
  <title>
    Being a Dog Is a Full-Time Job
  </title>
  <author>
    Charles M Schulz
  </author>
  <mkt:cover>
    Paperback
  </mkt:cover>
  <mkt:pages>
    128
  </mkt:pages>
</book>
```

We don't have any choice above the location of xsi:schemaLocation because the information is needed to validate the document element. If we want to include it, we must locate it in the document element. This attribute contains a single pair of values separated by a space:

```
"http://dyomedea.com/ns/library library.xsd"
```

As mentioned, the first value identifies the target namespace while the second value identifies the schema location. With this information at hand, the processor can read the schema and start validating the instance document. However, when it finds the marketing namespace that matches the xs:any wildcard, with a processContents attribute asking to validate when possible, it may again try to find a schema for this namespace by dereferencing the namespace URI. If it can find a schema, it validates the elements from the marketing namespace; if not, it considers them valid, since the processContents attribute is set to "lax."

If we want to improve our chances of finding a schema for the marketing library, we can also define its location in a xsi:schemaLocation attribute. The place in the instance document that we can provide the information is in the first element that uses this namespace, such as:

```
<?xml version="1.0"?>
<book id="b0836217462"
  xsi:schemaLocation="http://dyomedea.com/ns/library library.xsd"
  xmlns="http://dyomedea.com/ns/library"
  xmlns:xsi="http://www.w3.org/2001/XMLSchema-instance"
  xmlns:mkt="http://dyomedea.com/ns/library/mkt">
  <title>
    Being a Dog Is a Full-Time Job
  </title>
  <author>
    Charles M Schulz
  </author>
  <mkt:cover xsi:schemaLocation="http://dyomedea.com/ns/library/mkt
    marketing.xsd">
    Paperback
  </mkt:cover>
  <mkt:pages>
    128
  </mkt:pages>
</book>
```

The schema processor now has all the hints it needs to retrieve the schemas for both namespaces, and it should fully validate the elements that belong to the marketing namespace. Alternatively, we can place all the schema location hints in the same xsi: schemaLocation attribute:

```
<?xml version="1.0"?>
<book id="b0836217462"
  xsi:schemaLocation="http://dyomedea.com/ns/library library.xsd
  http://dyomedea.com/ns/library/mkt marketing.xsd"
  xmlns="http://dyomedea.com/ns/library"
  xmlns:xsi="http://www.w3.org/2001/XMLSchema-instance"
  xmlns:mkt="http://dyomedea.com/ns/library/mkt">
  <title>
    Being a Dog Is a Full-Time Job
  </title>
  <author>
    Charles M Schulz
  </author>
  <mkt:cover>
    Paperback
  </mkt:cover>
  <mkt:pages>
    128
  </mkt:pages>
</book>
```

In these examples, we used relative URIs to locate the schemas. This is a good solution only if you assume that the schemas will be moved with the instance documents, and in many cases, absolute URIs will be preferred. When this is the case, they can be mapped back into local resources by a mechanism such as XML Catalogs (*http://www.oasis-open.org/committees/entity/spec-2001-08-06.html*), an OASIS specification that is implemented by an increasing number of tools.

Defining Element Types

The next hint we can give to a schema processor helps it to determine the simple or complex type of an element. A schema validator usually guesses the type of an element from its name and the description of the content model of its parent. This guess can be overridden by the author of an instance document through the xsi:type attribute, as long as this new type is a derivation by restriction or extension of the type defined in the schema document. Since this type is defined using an attribute in the instance document, the definition is possible only for elements. (Attributes can't have attributes!)

At this point, the question is "why would we want to define a type in the instance document?". The answer is somewhat different for simple and complex types, as well as whether we are interested in a schema for validation purposes only or for data binding.

Defining Simple Types

An element (or attribute) can belong to several different simple types and a derivation by union is generally a good way to let a schema validator pick the right type without having to use xsi:type. We can go quite far in this direction. To illustrate this, now that we've seen both the principles of the derivation by union and the patterns, let's define a union type that can accept ISO 8601 dates, common English ("April 2nd, 1998"), and French ("2 avril 1998") formats. We can start by defining a ISO date without a time zone as discussed in Chapter 4:

```
<xs:simpleType name="dateISO">
  <xs:restriction base="xs:date">
    <xs:pattern value="[^:Z]*"/>
  </xs:restriction>
</xs:simpleType>
```

The English format can be described using different patterns for the months that have 31, 30, and 28 days (we do not cover leap years in this example). The following definition should give a fairly good approximation for years after AD with a maximum of four digits (the lines are split for readability but the patterns are on a single line):

```
<xs:simpleType name="EnglishDate">
  <xs:restriction base="xs:token">
```

```
<xs:pattern
  value="(January|March|May|July|August|October|December)
  ([1-3]?1st|[12]?2nd|[12]?3rd|(30|[12]?[4-9])th),[0-9]{0,4}"/>
<xs:pattern value="February
  ([1-2]?1st|[12]?2nd|[12]?3rd|[12]?[4-9]th),[0-9]{0,4}"/>
<xs:pattern value="(April|June|September|November)
  ([1-2]?1st|[12]?2nd|[12]?3rd|(30|[12]?[4-9])th),[0-9]{0,4}"/>
  </xs:restriction>
</xs:simpleType>
```

After the English format, the French one looks simple! The same principle can be applied (line breaks have been added to the patterns for readability):

```
<xs:simpleType name="dateFrançaise">
  <xs:restrictionbase="xs:token">
    <xs:pattern value="(1er|[1-3][01]|[12]?[2-9])
        (janvier|mars|mai|juillet|aout|octobre|décembre)\d{0,4}"/>
    <xs:pattern value="(1er|[12][01]|[12]?[2-9]) février \d{0,4}"/>
    <xs:pattern value="(1er|[12][01]|[12]?[2-9]|30)
        (avril|juin|septembre|novembre)\d{0,4}"/>
  <xs:restriction>
</xs:simpleType>
```

The last step is to derive our type by union as follows:

```
<xs:simpleType name="anydate">
  <xs:union memberTypes="dateISO EnglishDate dateFrançaise"/>
</xs:simpleType>
```

We now have a simple type that will accept three different date formats. A schema processor should not only validate these three formats, but it should also mention which type it has recognized in the PSVI. We've achieved this without adding anything in the instance document. Why do we want to give the information in the instance document, then? There are a couple of reasons for this. The first is that we want to convey the information to an application that is not able to get it from the PSVI. This is often the case with current tools, since there is no specification of the interface that will allow an application to read the PSVI. This reason does not apply if we are interested only in validation, but may be important if we want to avoid making applications that manipulate our instance documents check which format they get.

The second reason isn't shown in the previous example. Because the lexical spaces of the different member types have no overlap, there is no confusion possible. This is not always the case. We may want to override the choice made by the schema validator, or even to use a generic "universal" type in the schema and rely on the instance documents to define which type is used. One type of application that is a good prospect for this scenario is protocol or binding applications for which XML is only a transient serialization format. These applications often need to define generic elements that can be used to hold parameters of any type.

For instance, a schema-based XML-RPC can be defined by the first example of the XML-RPC specification:

```
<methodCall>
  <methodName>
    examples.getStateName
  </methodName>
  <params>
    <param>
      <value>
        <i4>
          41
        </i4>
      </value>
    </param>
  </params>
</methodCall>
```

In an imaginary W3C XML Schema-aware version of XML-RPC, this could be replaced by:

```
<methodCall xmlns:xsi="http://www.w3.org/2001/XMLSchema-instance">
  <methodName>
    examples.getStateName
  </methodName>
  <params>
    <param>
      <value xsi:type="xs:int">
        41
      </value>
    </param>
  </params>
</methodCall>
```

 Without imposing such usage, SOAP allows this practice in the case of "Polymorphic Accessor." The W3C Working Draft of 2 October 2001 mentions this:

> Many languages allow accessors that can polymorphically access values of several types, each type being available at run time. A polymorphic accessor instance MUST contain an xsi:type attribute that describes the type of the actual value. For example, a polymorphic accessor named "cost" with a value of type xs:float would be encoded as follows:
>
> ```
> <cost xsi:type="xs:float"
>   xmlns:xsi="http://www.w3.org/2001/XMLSchema-instance">
>   29.95
> </cost>
> ```

Defining Complex Types

Although the mechanism to forcibly identify a complex type in an instance document is similar to the one we saw for simple types, the motivations for using it can be completely different. If it is still possible to use this feature in case of a polymorphic accessor, to use the terminology taken by the W3C Protocols WG, this is probably a relatively marginal use case for complex types that do not have extension by union. The equivalent to the simple type derivation by union for complex types would be the ability to define several content models for a same element and to let the schema processor try all these content models and keep the first one that matches the fragment of the instance document. This would indeed be a nice feature, but this is exactly what the Consistent Declaration and Unique Particle Attribution rules explicitly forbid. Therefore, xsi:type for complex types has no competition in the schema itself and is often used as a workaround against these rules.

Another way to understand this is to consider this feature a hint given to the schema processor that will allow it to disambiguate the choice it could have and avoid violating one of these rules. A typical use is to work around the Unique Particle Attribution rule to allow two different content models for the same element. We have seen in Chapter 9 that xs:key might be used to allow our title to be expressed either as an attribute or as an element, but this workaround doesn't help if we want to allow more complex combinations, such as either a title expressed as an attribute or one or more titles expressed as elements:

```
<book id="b0836217462" available="true" title="Being a Dog Is a
  Full-TimeJob">
  .../...
</book>
```

or:

```
<book id="b0836217462" available="true" type="bookTitleElements">
  <isbn>
    0836217462
  </isbn>
  <title lang="en">
    Being a Dog Is a Full-Time Job
  </title>
  <title lang="fr">
    Etre un chien est un travail à plein temps.
  </title>
  .../...
</book>
```

To do so, we will define a base type that is a superset of both content models:

```
<xs:complexType name="bookBase">
  <xs:sequence>
    <xs:element ref="isbn"/>
    <xs:element ref="title" minOccurs="0" maxOccurs="unbounded"/>
    <xs:element ref="author" minOccurs="0" maxOccurs="unbounded"/>
```

```
      <xs:element ref="character" minOccurs="0" maxOccurs="unbounded"/>
    </xs:sequence>
    <xs:attribute ref="id"/>
    <xs:attribute ref="title"/>
    <xs:attribute ref="available"/>
  </xs:complexType>
```

This base type accepts book elements with optional titles defined as attributes or elements. We can derive by restriction a first type which will accept only title attributes:

```
<xs:complexType name="bookTitleAttribute">
  <xs:complexContent>
    <xs:restriction base="bookBase">
      <xs:sequence>
        <xs:element ref="isbn"/>
        <xs:element ref="author" minOccurs="0"
          maxOccurs="unbounded"/>
        <xs:element ref="character" minOccurs="0"
          maxOccurs="unbounded"/>
      </xs:sequence>
    </xs:restriction>
  </xs:complexContent>
</xs:complexType>
```

We can derive a second type that accepts only titles defined as one or more title elements:

```
<xs:complexType name="bookTitleElements">
  <xs:complexContent>
    <xs:restriction base="bookBase">
      <xs:sequence>
        <xs:element ref="isbn"/>
        <xs:element ref="title" minOccurs="1" maxOccurs="unbounded"/>
        <xs:element ref="author" minOccurs="0"
          maxOccurs="unbounded"/>
        <xs:element ref="character" minOccurs="0"
          maxOccurs="unbounded"/>
      </xs:sequence>
      <xs:attribute ref="title" use="prohibited"/>
    </xs:restriction>
  </xs:complexContent>
</xs:complexType>
```

Now that we have all our building blocks, we can use them in the schema to define the book element as having a type bookBase:

```
<xs:element name="book" type="bookBase"/>
```

Then we can use them in the instance documents to declare which derived type we are using:

```
<book id="b0836217462" available="true" xsi:type="bookTitleElements">
  <isbn>
    0836217462
  </isbn>
  <title lang="en">
```

```
      Being a Dog Is a Full-Time Job
    </title>
    <title lang="fr">
      Etre un chien est un travail à plein temps.
    </title>
    .../...
  </book>
```

or:

```
  <book id="b0836217462" available="true" title="Being a Dog Is a
    Full-TimeJob" xsi:type="bookTitleAttribute">
    .../...
  </book>
```

However, this allows instance documents to use the base type, which may not be something we want, since we can have either no title at all or an attribute and one or more elements (something we want to avoid). We can forbid the use of the base type by defining it as "abstract." Setting this attribute of the complex type definition blocks instance documents from using it. They will have to specify one of its derived types through a xsi:type attribute.

The feature of the abstract attribute is symmetrical to the block attribute we have already seen. While the block attribute was prevented from further derivation, abstract requires a derivation. The final definition of our base complex type is then:

```
  <xs:complexType name="bookBase" abstract="true">
    <xs:sequence>
      <xs:element ref="isbn"/>
      <xs:element ref="title" minOccurs="0" maxOccurs="unbounded"/>
      <xs:element ref="author" minOccurs="0" maxOccurs="unbounded"/>
      <xs:element ref="character" minOccurs="0" maxOccurs="unbounded"/>
    </xs:sequence>
    <xs:attribute ref="id"/>
    <xs:attribute ref="title"/>
    <xs:attribute ref="available"/>
  </xs:complexType>
```

Defining Nil (Null) Values

This feature was introduced into W3C XML Schema to map the notion of "null" values, which is one of the core requirements of the relational model as defined by Codd. The W3C makes a subtle distinction between an empty element and an element that is null (or "nil," to use the name chosen for the xsi attribute that conveys the information). The two notions are considered different, but related (an empty element is not always null, but a null element must be empty).

The fact that an element can be nil is defined in the element definition and short-circuits all the content type definitions. It may be used for simple types, complex content, and simple content complex types; and it may be used even if the content model forbids empty contents. In this case, the "nillable" character of the element

---

takes precedence over the content model, and empty contents will be accepted when marked as nil. Again, since the fact that a value is nil is expressed using an attribute in the instance document, the mechanism does not apply to attributes that cannot have a null value.

One last thing to note before we look at some examples is that attributes are not affected by the fact that an element is nil, and they are still allowed or required if defined in the element.

The usage of this feature is rather simple. For example, if we want to allow nil values for the author of a book, we just set the `nillable` attribute in the element definition (`nillable` attributes cannot be specified in an element reference):

```
<xs:element name="author" nillable="true">
  <xs:complexType>
    <xs:sequence>
      <xs:element ref="name"/>
      <xs:element ref="born"/>
      <xs:element ref="dead" minOccurs="0"/>
    </xs:sequence>
    <xs:attribute ref="id"/>
  </xs:complexType>
</xs:element>
```

This declaration lets us declare null values in the instance documents:

```
<author xsi:nil="true"
  xmlns:xsi="http://www.w3.org/2001/XMLSchema-instance"/>
```

This is possible despite the fact that the author element had not been declared as allowing empty content.

 The difference between nil and empty values is very slim. Assuming the author element is defined as nillable and has a content model allowing empty contents, the difference between:

```
<author xsi:nil="true"
    xmlns:xsi="http://www.w3.org/2001/XMLSchema-instance"/>
```

and:

```
<author/>
```

is only a xsi:nil flag in the PSVI.

Beware the Intrusive Nature of These Features...

The title of this section says it all! Using the xsi namespace creates a dependency between the instance documents and a specific schema technology, and this dependency is questionable as such. One of the major strengths of XML is the decoupling between the information available in the documents and the applications that retrieve and process this information. If we consider a schema validator one of these applications, including schema features in the instance documents breaks this rule.

Another reason why the use of these features is questionable is we've learned that the life span of data or information is longer than the life span of the applications. We can suppose in many cases that the XML documents we create today will outlive the W3C XML Schema 1.0 technology. The Working Group started thinking about XML Schema 1.1 before 1.0 became a Recommendation, and these dependencies are potential migration issues. XML 1.0 has already seen two generations of schema languages (DTD and W3C XML Schema 1.0), and functionality bundled with the DTDs that has not been included into W3C XML Schema (such as external parsed and unparsed entities) are at risk of becoming deprecated in common use. Furthermore, there are other schema technologies; integrating your documents tightly with W3C XML Schema may close some doors that might be needed for your application.

On the other hand, these attributes are available in the instance documents for non-schema-aware applications, and you can easily process a `xsi:type` or `xsi:nil` attribute using a simple XSLT transformation.

The last thing to note about these attributes is they are attributes! This may seem obvious, but attributes can't be included within attributes. This means that one cannot qualify an attribute with `xsi:nil` or `xsi:type`. This introduces a new differentiation between elements and attributes which XML application designers might need to consider.

CHAPTER 12

Creating More Building Blocks Using Object-Oriented Features

We have already seen many features that have been borrowed from object-oriented languages. In this chapter, we will see substitution groups (similar to subclasses), abstract elements and datatypes (similar to abstract classes), and final datatypes (similar to final classes).

Substitution Groups

In many cases, a vocabulary needs the ability to accept a variety of different content models. We have two options: we can try to do it using a single generic element name, or we can define a schema smart enough to deal with the possible content model. Since we cannot define multiple different content models for the same element (because of the Consistent Declaration Rule), we can either use xs:type attributes in the instance documents, or we can define a content model wide enough to accommodate all the possibilities. Such a model would likely be wide enough to also accept combinations that we do not want.

The easiest solution for accommodating different types with W3C XML Schema is to use a different element name for each case. We already saw that the xs:choice (outside a group) compositor allows us to build such constructs where a node in an instance document can accept an element chosen in a list. However, this list is fixed in the complex type definition. We have also seen that this list cannot be extended, since the rules for complex type derivations by extension do not allow it. Substitution groups offer a flexible way to create xs:choice (outside a group) compositors out of single element definitions or references, as well as a way to extend them. More simply, they are lists of elements that can be used in place of each other within documents. One important thing to note before we start, though, is that substitution groups apply only to global elements.

Substitution groups can be seen as extensible element groups. Before introducing them, let's look again at the "traditional" element groups to highlight the differences between these two concepts. Since the Recommendation is especially fuzzy on the extensibility of element groups and the restriction of substitution groups, I have chosen to present a conservative interpretation, which should be free of interoperability issues. I will discuss the different interpretations at the end of the chapter.

Using a "Traditional" Group

Let's come back to the definition of a name. (After all, universal names are one of the most controversial subjects in normalization spheres, so it's no surprise that we can use them as examples!) Instead of playing with datatypes, we may just use different element names, and say that a name is either a simple name, such as:

```
<simple-name>
  Snoopy
</simple-name>
```

or a full name, such as:

```
<full-name>
  <last>
    Schulz
  </last>
  <first>
    Charles
  </first>
  <middle>
    M
  </middle>
</full-name>
```

We have already seen how we can define a flexible schema that will match these documents. A good idea is to create a group with a `xs:choice` compositor that allows one of those two elements and can be reused in all the elements in which a name needs to be included. The logical steps are to define the two elements (full name and simple name), to create a group, and to use it in the definition of the author and character elements:

```
<xs:element name="full-name">
  <xs:complexType>
    <xs:all>
      <xs:element name="first" type="string32" minOccurs="0"/>
      <xs:element name="middle" type="string32" minOccurs="0"/>
      <xs:element name="last" type="string32"/>
    </xs:all>
  </xs:complexType>
</xs:element>

<xs:element name="simple-name" type="string32"/>

<xs:group name="name">
  <xs:choice>
    <xs:element ref="simple-name"/>
    <xs:element ref="full-name"/>
```

```
      </xs:choice>
    </xs:group>

    <xs:element name="author">
      <xs:complexType>
        <xs:sequence>
          <xs:group ref="name"/>
          <xs:element ref="born"/>
          <xs:element ref="dead" minOccurs="0"/>
        </xs:sequence>
        <xs:attribute ref="id"/>
      </xs:complexType>
    </xs:element>

    <xs:element name="character">
      <xs:complexType>
        <xs:sequence>
          <xs:group ref="name"/>
          <xs:element ref="born"/>
          <xs:element ref="qualification"/>
        </xs:sequence>
        <xs:attribute ref="id"/>
      </xs:complexType>
    </xs:element>
```

Note that we are able to use xs:all in this case because the elements involved are isolated in the full name element. This is also a good time to mention that xs:all doesn't mean the order is not significant, but only that all the combinations are valid. In this case, writing the following:

```
    <full-name>
      <first>
        Eric
      </first>
      <last>
        van der Vlist
      </last>
    </full-name>
```

or:

```
    <full-name>
      <last>
        van der Vlist
      </last>
      <first>
        Eric
      </first>
    </full-name>
```

may express whether I prefer to be called "Eric van der Vlist" or "van der Vlist Eric." Applications that want access to the components of this full-name can still have it, but those that need a full-name must respect the document order.

Substitution Groups

Using substitution groups

Let's see how we can define the same content model using substitution groups. The first thing to do is to define an element that both full-name and simple name can be derived from. In this case, we have a simple type on one hand and a complex type with complex content on the other, and we cannot find a type that can be extended to both. We have no other choice but to start with the universal type, which accepts any content model. Known as xs:anyType, this very special type is also the default value when no type is specified, and we can define a generic name element without giving any type definition to keep it as open as possible:

```
<xs:element name="name"/>
```

This element will be what is known as the head of the substitution group. Without declaring anything on this head element, other elements can declare that they can be used wherever the head element is referenced in the schema. These elements are known as the members of the substitution group. The one restriction on the members is their types must be valid derivations of the type of the head element. This declaration is made through a substitutionGroup attribute that references the head element in each interchangeable element—for instance:

```
<xs:element name="simple-name" type="string32"
  substitutionGroup="name"/>

<xs:element name="full-name" substitutionGroup="name">
  <xs:complexType>
    <xs:all>
      <xs:element name="first" type="string32" minOccurs="0"/>
      <xs:element name="middle" type="string32" minOccurs="0"/>
      <xs:element name="last" type="string32"/>
    </xs:all>
  </xs:complexType>
</xs:element>
```

The effect of these declarations is these two elements can be used every time the head is used in the schema, such as in the definition of the character and author elements:

```
<xs:element name="character">
  <xs:complexType>
    <xs:sequence>
      <xs:element ref="name"/>
      <xs:element ref="born"/>
      <xs:element ref="qualification"/>
    </xs:sequence>
    <xs:attribute ref="id"/>
  </xs:complexType>
</xs:element>

<xs:element name="author">
  <xs:complexType>
```

```
<xs:sequence>
  <xs:element ref="name"/>
  <xs:element ref="born"/>
  <xs:element ref="dead" minOccurs="0"/>
</xs:sequence>
<xs:attribute ref="id"/>
  </xs:complexType>
</xs:element>
```

Abstract elements

If we keep our schema like we've just seen it, the usage of the head in the instance documents is allowed, and since our head element allows any content, this is probably not something we would want. We need to use a mechanism similar to the abstract types we saw when we encountered the same kind of problem with xsi:type in Chapter 7. We will define the head element as abstract using the abstract attribute in the definition of the head element, which then becomes:

```
<xs:element name="name" abstract="true"/>
```

Trees of substitution groups

What if our French offices define a composed-name element that is similar to the full name without its middle subelement? We may just add this element directly to our substitution group, but defining it as having the name element as its head will not clearly show the similarities between this new element and the full-name element. Furthermore, some applications might need to specify that they accept either full-name or composed-name. The solution is to use full-name as the head of a new substitution group. To do this, we need to define the type of the full-name element as global to show the explicit derivation between the two elements:

```
<xs:complexType name="full-name-type">
  <xs:all>
    <xs:element name="first" type="string32" minOccurs="0"/>
    <xs:element name="middle" type="string32" minOccurs="0"/>
    <xs:element name="last" type="string32"/>
  </xs:all>
</xs:complexType>

<xs:element name="full-name" substitutionGroup="name"
  type="full-name-type"/>

<xs:element name="composed-name" substitutionGroup="full-name">
  <xs:complexType>
    <xs:complexContent>
      <xs:restriction base="full-name-type">
        <xs:all>
          <xs:element name="first" type="string32" minOccurs="0"/>
          <xs:element name="last" type="string32"/>
        </xs:all>
      </xs:restriction>
```

```
        </xs:complexContent>
      </xs:complexType>
    </xs:element>
```

We have now defined not only two substitution groups (with the name and full-name heads), but also a tree of substitution groups, since the allowed substitutions for name will include both full-name and simple-name, but also composed-name!

Traditional Declarations or Substitution Groups?

If we look back at the two solutions that we used to solve the same issue, we see that substitution groups are more extensible than a traditional group which uses a xs: choice compositor. While the element group can only be derived using a xs:redefine inclusion, the substitution group can be extended with new possible elements by just defining them. These elements can be defined in any namespace; the only constraint is that their types must be the same or valid derivations of the head element's type. (This restriction is justified to ensure that applications are not too surprised by an unexpected content model.)

There is another difference to note, though. We have seen that the derivation of a content model using a xs:choice compositor cannot extend the scope of the choice and add new alternatives. The situation for substitution groups is almost the opposite. Although the Recommendation says that substitution groups should be validated as choices, it doesn't define the order of the elements in the equivalent choice. I do not advise restricting substitution groups in practice, since it may lead to interoperability issues between schema processors.

We then have a paradoxical situation where one of the mechanisms (xs:choice) can only be restricted while the other (substitution groups) can only be extended, even though the Recommendation states that these two mechanisms are equivalent as far as validation is involved. This characteristic needs to be taken into account when choosing between them.

The differences between these two features are summarized in Table 12-1, "Not advised" stands for "may work with some schema processors but relies on a liberal interpretation of the Recommendation, which may lead to interoperability issues."

Table 12-1. Element versus substitution groups

Feature	Element groups with a xs:choice (outside a group) compositor.	Substitution groups.
Definition	Centralized, using xs:group (definition) and xs:choice (outside a group).	Spread over global element definitions, using the substitutionGroup attribute.
Constraints on the choices	No constraint: the elements can be totally different.	The type of the elements needs to be an explicit derivation of the type of the head.
Allows global elements	Yes.	Yes.
Allows local elements	Yes.	No.

Table 12-1. Element versus substitution groups (continued)

Restriction to remove choices	Yes, though `xs:redefine`.	Not advised.
Extension to add choices	Not advised.	Yes, by adding new elements with the same head element.
Extension to add new elements in sequence	Yes, through `xs:redefine`.	No.

Fuzzy Recommendation

Both the extension of `xs:choice` during element group redefinitions and the restriction of substitution groups are very fuzzy in the Recommendation and require some explanation.

Extension of xs:choice through group redefinitions

If we return to our group that is defined as:

```
<xs:group name="name">
  <xs:choice>
    <xs:element ref="simple-name"/>
    <xs:element ref="full-name"/>
  </xs:choice>
</xs:group>
```

There doesn't seem to be anything in the recommendation that explicitly forbids redefinition of this group to add another element in the choice by writing:

```
<xs:redefine schemaLocation="foo.xsd">
  <xs:group name="name">
    <xs:choice>
      <xs:group ref="name"/>
      <xs:element ref="bar"/>
    </xs:choice>
  </xs:group>
</xs:redefine>
```

However, the effect of this redefinition is to allow a new element (bar) to be accepted instead of simple-name and full-name. Although this would be a nice feature, the principles of redefinition by restriction (i.e., when the content of the group is restricted during a restriction) are the same as the principles of the complex type derivation by restriction. The intention of the Working Group seems to be to define the features of redefinitions by extension after the complex type derivation by extension, which explicitly forbids the addition of new particles in a xs:choice (outside a group).

Although some schema processors do support this feature and some specialists consider it fine, I do not advise using it, since it seems to violate the intent (if not the wording) of the Recommendation.

Restricting substitution groups

The restriction of the substitution groups is quite the opposite. The intent of the Working Group seems to be to allow such restrictions while the wording of the Recommendation makes its result undefined.

The Recommendation clearly specifies that during the check to determine if a particle is a valid restriction of another particle, substitution groups should be treated as xs:choice, which is a clear indication that substitution groups could be restricted through complex type derivations by restriction. To illustrate this, let's take the definition of the complex type of the element author, using the substitution group whose head is name, as defined previously:

```
<xs:complexType name="authorType">
  <xs:sequence>
    <xs:choice>
      <xs:element ref="name"/>
      <xs:element ref="simple-name"/>
      <xs:element ref="full-name"/>
    </xs:choice>
    <xs:element ref="born"/>
    <xs:element ref="dead" minOccurs="0"/>
  </xs:sequence>
  <xs:attribute ref="id"/>
</xs:complexType>
```

If substitution groups are treated like xs:choice, and assuming that our head isn't defined as abstract, this definition is equivalent to:

```
<xs:complexType name="authorType">
  <xs:sequence>
    <xs:element ref="name"/>
    <xs:element ref="born"/>
    <xs:element ref="dead" minOccurs="0"/>
  </xs:sequence>
  <xs:attribute ref="id"/>
</xs:complexType>
```

It should be possible to derive this complex type by restriction by writing, for instance:

```
<xs:complexType name="restrictedAuthorType">
  <xs:complexContent>
    <xs:restriction base="authorType">
      <xs:sequence>
        <xs:choice>
          <xs:element ref="simple-name"/>
          <xs:element ref="full-name"/>
        </xs:choice>
        <xs:element ref="born"/>
        <xs:element ref="dead" minOccurs="0"/>
      </xs:sequence>
    </xs:restriction>
  </xs:complexContent>
</xs:complexType>
```

However, the Recommendation also states that during the derivation by restriction of a xs:choice compositor, "there is a complete order-preserving functional mapping" between the particles used to define the derived and original xs:choice. However, it does not define the order of the particles when substitution groups are mapped into xs:choice. Depending on the order chosen by the schema validator to build the xs:choice out of the substitution group, our derivation can thus be either valid or invalid!

Controlling Derivations

It's time to come back to the features already discussed—and to introduce new ones—to explain how to control the usage of the derivations of the different compositors. Basically, these features are attributes that allow you to block further derivation or, on the contrary, allow you to require derivations, but their granularity varies depending on the compositor being used.

Attributes

There are no substitution groups for attributes and no mechanism to derive them or define their types in instance documents. This also means no features are needed to control their derivation. Actually, to be completely accurate, we need to note that it is possible to indirectly derive attributes through a derivation by restriction of their parent elements or redefinitions of attribute groups.

Elements

When speaking of a xs:element, we need to differentiate between global definitions and local definitions or references that behave differently in regard to derivation. Therefore, derivation control is maintained as shown in Table 12-2.

Table 12-2. Controls on element derivation

Attribute	Global element	Local element definition	Element reference
block	Yes	Yes	No
abstract	Yes	No	No
final	Yes	No	No

Block attribute

The block attribute controls type substitution in the instance documents through the xsi:type attribute and substitution groups. This single attribute holds a whitespace-separated list of tokens—of "restriction," "extension," and "substitution"—or the special value #all (which means all three values together and the attribute's default value can be defined through the blockDefault attribute of the xs:schema document element).

The first two values (restriction and extension) control any substitution through xsi:type or substitution groups, and block the substitution by datatypes that are derived by restriction or extension from the datatype defined in the element declaration. The third (substitution) is specific to the substitution groups, and defines if an element from the substitution group (for which the element is the head) is allowed. Since only global elements can participate in a substitution group, the last value is clearly meaningful for global definitions only.

The fact that the block attribute is used both for type substitution and for substitution groups can be misleading, especially with the values restriction and extension, which act on both aspects. A simple example makes this more concrete. Let's say that we have a complex type definition (personType) describing a person as having a name, a mandatory birth date, and optional death date and qualification:

```
<xs:complexType name="personType">
  <xs:sequence>
    <xs:element ref="name"/>
    <xs:element ref="born"/>
    <xs:element ref="dead" minOccurs="0"/>
    <xs:element ref="qualification" minOccurs="0"/>
  </xs:sequence>
  <xs:attribute ref="id"/>
</xs:complexType>
```

We can also derive by extension from this complex type a datatype that describes an author as a person with a list of books:

```
<xs:complexType name="authorType">
  <xs:complexContent>
    <xs:extension base="personType">
      <xs:sequence>
        <xs:element name="book" type="xs:token" minOccurs="1"
          maxOccurs="unbounded"/>
      </xs:sequence>
    </xs:extension>
  </xs:complexContent>
</xs:complexType>
```

We can derive by restriction a datatype that describes a character as a person with no death date and a mandatory qualification:

```
<xs:complexType name="characterType">
  <xs:complexContent>
    <xs:restriction base="personType">
      <xs:sequence>
        <xs:element ref="name"/>
        <xs:element ref="born"/>
        <xs:element ref="qualification"/>
      </xs:sequence>
    </xs:restriction>
```

```
      </xs:complexContent>
    </xs:complexType>
```

The first purpose of `block` attributes in element definitions is to control the type substitution through `xsi:type`, which controls substitutions in the instance documents such as the following (if the person element is defined as having a type `personType`):

```
<person xsi:type="authorType" id="CMS"
  xmlns:xsi="http://www.w3.org/2001/XMLSchema-instance">
  <name>
    Charles M Schulz
  </name>
  <born>
    1922-11-26
  </born>
  <dead>
    2000-02-12
  </dead>
  <book>
    Being a Dog Is a Full-Time Job
  </book>
</person>

<person xsi:type="characterType" id="Snoopy"
  xmlns:xsi="http://www.w3.org/2001/XMLSchema-instance">
  <name>
    Snoopy
  </name>
  <born>
    1950-10-04
  </born>
  <qualification>
    extroverted beagle
  </qualification>
</person>
```

The first substitution uses `authorType`, which is derived by extension from `personType`, and can be blocked by specifying a `block` attribute including the value extension. The second one uses `characterType`, which is derived by restriction from `personType` and can be blocked by specifying a `block` attribute including the value restriction. Both can be blocked together by specifying a block attribute with the value #all.

> This example shows that the impact of both derivation types on the applications is very different. A type substitution by restriction has virtually no impact on the applications, since the content model matching the restricted type must also match the original type. Alternatively, a type substitution by extension allows content models not allowed by the original type (such as the addition of the book element in the previous example), and the risk of breaking applications that do not expect these additions is higher. Thus, a conservative attitude might be to include extension in the default values of block in your schemas.

That being said, we've seen only one side of the block attribute. It serves a second, different, yet not independent, purpose and also restricts the usage of substitution groups. To illustrate this purpose, let's define three different element members of a substitution group whose head is person. There is also a fourth element member, which is just a synonym for the element person and has the same type:

```
<xs:element name="person" type="personType"/>

<xs:element name="author" type="authorType"
  substitutionGroup="person"/>

<xs:element name="character" type="characterType"
  substitutionGroup="person"/>

<xs:element name="human" type="personType"
  substitutionGroup="person"/>
```

After defining this substitution group and without blocking anything, we allow not only block and the type substitutions seen above, but also element substitutions, such as:

```
<author id="CMS">
  <name>
    Charles M Schulz
  </name>
  <born>
    1922-11-26
  </born>
  <dead>
    2000-02-12
  </dead>
  <book>
    Being a Dog Is a Full-Time Job
  </book>
</author>

<character id="PP">
  <name>
    Peppermint Patty
  </name>
  <born>
    1966-08-22
  </born>
  <qualification>
    bold, brash and tomboyish
  </qualification>
</character>
<human id="CMS.">
  <name>
    Charles M Schulz
  </name>
  <born>
    1922-11-26
```

```
    </born>
    <dead>
        2000-02-12
    </dead>
</human>
```

The first substitution is by an element of the substitution group whose type is derived by extension from the head. It can be blocked by specifying a block attribute including the value extension. The second one is a substitution by an element of the substitution group whose type is derived by restriction from the head. It can be blocked by specifying a block attribute including the value restriction. Those two are similar to the two substitutions given as examples for the type substitutions, with the difference that the element name is now used to differentiate the type instead of the xsi:type attribute. The third substitution is new, since the type is the same as the type of the head, and it is blocked only by specifying a block attribute that includes the value substitution. Note that including substitution in a block attribute blocks any element substitution, while stating that not all the combinations are possible to express. To block everything, you would define author as:

```
<xs:element name="author" type="authorType" block="#all"/>
```

I don't want to leave you with the impression than you can't block type substitution without blocking substitution groups. We need to mention that type substitution can also be blocked on complex type definitions, which is covered later on in this chapter in the section "Complex Types."

Final elements

Like block, final has an impact on substitution groups, but works on a different level: constraining the schema itself while block constrains the instance documents. final can take a list of restriction and extension or the special value #all, and its default value can be defined using the finalDefault attribute of xs:schema. However, a substitution value is not necessary, since unlike block, final is about substitution groups, and #all can block all the substitutions (and only the substitutions).

final's effect is more radical than block: while block blocks the effects of the usage of substitution groups, final prohibits the usage of the element as a head of a substitution group. If the person element is defined with a final attribute set, it isn't possible to use it as head of a substitution group for either author, character, or both.

Abstract elements

The last attribute is abstract, which is the opposite of block. It prohibits the element from being used directly in an instance document and must be substituted through a substitution group. Defining the person element as abstract forbids its use in the instance documents. You must use one of the elements from its substitution group (such as author, character, or even human).

Complex Types

The attributes are the same for complex types as they are for elements, but their meaning is slightly different since one of them (block) operates on the substitution of the elements that use the datatype (as we have seen in the previous section). The others (final and abstract) work on the derivation of the complex type itself.

Blocking complex types

When the block attribute is used on complex type definitions, the type substitutions in the elements defined with this type are still blocked. The difference is that this time block doesn't act on element substitutions through substitution groups, but it does act on type substitutions. These block attributes can be seen as electric switches installed in a series, and each of them can block the derivation in its own "line," as shown in Figure 12-1.

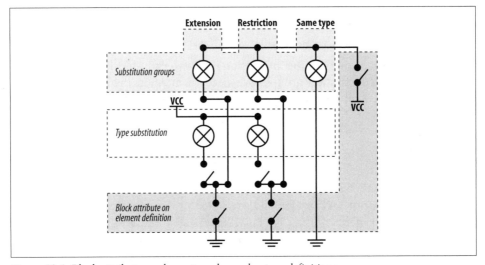

Figure 12-1. Block attribute on elements and complex type definitions

For each restriction and extension, the substitutions can first be switched off for both element and type substitutions by the block attribute of the element definition, and then the type substitutions can be blocked by the block attribute of the complex type definition. The value substitution in the block attribute of the element definition acts as a global switch to block all element substitutions, including a third line, which allows element substitutions with the same type and cannot be blocked separately.

The default value supplied in the schema element is used at both levels and may be different for the element and complex type definitions if they belong to different schemas and have a different xs:schema ancestor. The fact that the default value, when defined in the xs:schema ancestor, is applied to both levels means that it may block the derivation for those to levels (by "opening" two switches). To override such a nonempty default value, you need to define a block attribute both in the element and in the complex type definition.

Final complex types

The final attribute of complex type definitions controls whether the type can be derived by restriction and or extension to create new complex types.

Unlike the block attribute which is linked with its counterpart in the element definition, the final attribute in a complex type definition applies only to the complex type itself and, like the abstract attribute in the element definition, it acts at the level of the schema itself and has no impact on the instance documents.

Abstract complex types

The abstract attribute of complex type definitions works on the instance documents. When an abstract datatype is used to define elements, the type must be substituted in the instance documents through a xsi:type attribute.

We need to insist that abstract by itself doesn't mean that the complex type cannot be used in a content model. However, if it is used, it must be substituted through xsi:type in the instance documents. To define a complex type that will not be usable in a content model, we need to use both the final and block attributes; the complex type's only use is as a base type for derivations.

Simple Types

Simple types are, in fact, simpler, as far as controlling their derivation is concerned, since they can only be final. Their final attribute can take the values list, restriction, union, or the special value #all, which means the three of them and the default value are controlled through the finalDefault attribute of the schema element used for elements and complex types.

The fact that simple types cannot be abstract or blocked avoids potential issues when they are used to define attributes for which these notions are meaningless. When needed to define elements, a simple content complex type may be created using the simple type as its base. This complex type can hold the abstract and block attribute.

Even though final is the only attribute controlling simple type element derivation available on the xs:simpleType (global definition) element, a finer granularity of control may be achieved through the fixed attributes available on each of the facets (discussed in Chapter 5).

Other Components and Redefinitions

Other components, such as attributes and element and attribute groups, cannot be directly derived. Attributes can't be derived at all and groups can only be derived through redefinitions; therefore, no control is available to control their derivation. Similarly, the redefinitions of groups through xs:redefine escape this feature and cannot be controlled at all. Although the recommendation is fuzzy on this aspect, it is safer to consider that the final attribute of the complex types applies also to their redefinitions, which are processed as implicit derivations.

 The interpretation of the block attribute is subject to multiple interpretations. For the latest opinion of the W3C XML Schema Working Group, you should refer to the errata for the specification at *http://www.w3.org/2001/05/xmlschema-errata*.

CHAPTER 13

Creating Extensible Schemas

The X from XML stands for "extensible." The goal of any schema language is to control and limit this extensibility to help the applications deal with it. Extensibility and schemas pursue two opposite goals. Carelessly written schemas may significantly reduce extensibility, and we need to keep this in mind when we design our own schemas.

Here again, we find the duality between the schema and the instance documents, and we need to distinguish between two different forms of extensibility. The extensibility of the schema, is the ability to reuse its components to create other schemas, while the extensibility of the vocabulary, is the ability to add or modify the content models with a minimal impact on the applications, and is, in fact, the openness of the schema.

Extensible Schemas

The extensibility of a schema is essentially determined by its style, the choice of which components (elements and attributes, element and attribute groups, and simple and complex types) have been made global, the use of the `final` and `fixed` attributes, and the optional division of these components over different schema documents. We need to have a look at these three factors.

Global Components

A simple example is often better than a long explanation, so to illustrate the differences between the different schema styles, we will take some examples out of our library and study complex and simple type elements and attributes.

Elements

Let's consider the definition of the `book` element in the context of our library. We have four different basic ways of defining this element, and they all will validate the same set of instance elements—but not the same set of instance documents, since exposing an element as global allows its use as a document element. We can use a Russian doll design and define the book element and its type locally within the library element (I have used the same Russian doll design for the book's child elements to keep the schema concise as we will focus on the definition of book for this example):

```
<xs:element name="library">
  <xs:complexType>
    <xs:sequence>
      <xs:element name="book" maxOccurs="unbounded">
        <xs:complexType>
          <xs:sequence>
            <xs:element ref="isbn"/>
            <xs:element ref="title"/>
            <xs:element ref="author" minOccurs="0"
              maxOccurs="unbounded"/>
            <xs:element ref="character" minOccurs="0"
              maxOccurs="unbounded"/>
          </xs:sequence>
          <xs:attribute ref="id"/>
          <xs:attribute ref="available"/>
        </xs:complexType>
      </xs:element>
    </xs:sequence>
  </xs:complexType>
</xs:element>
```

We can also define a global book element and reference it in the content model of our library:

```
<xs:element name="book">
  <xs:complexType>
    <xs:sequence>
      <xs:element ref="isbn"/>
      <xs:element ref="title"/>
      <xs:element ref="author" minOccurs="0" maxOccurs="unbounded"/>
      <xs:element ref="character" minOccurs="0"
        maxOccurs="unbounded"/>
    </xs:sequence>
    <xs:attribute ref="id"/>
    <xs:attribute ref="available"/>
  </xs:complexType>
</xs:element>

<xs:element name="library">
  <xs:complexType>
    <xs:sequence>
      <xs:element ref="book" maxOccurs="unbounded"/>
    </xs:sequence>
  </xs:complexType>
</xs:element>
```

The third classical way is to define a complex type for the content model of our bookType element (note that I could have called it book, but I feel bookType is less confusing):

```
<xs:complexType name="bookType">
  <xs:sequence>
    <xs:element ref="isbn"/>
    <xs:element ref="title"/>
    <xs:element ref="author" minOccurs="0" maxOccurs="unbounded"/>
    <xs:element ref="character" minOccurs="0" maxOccurs="unbounded"/>
  </xs:sequence>
  <xs:attribute ref="id"/>
  <xs:attribute ref="available"/>
</xs:complexType>

<xs:element name="library">
  <xs:complexType>
    <xs:sequence>
      <xs:element name="book" type="bookType" maxOccurs="unbounded"/>
    </xs:sequence>
  </xs:complexType>
</xs:element>
```

Finally, we can define a group containing our book element:

```
<xs:group name="bookGroup">
  <xs:sequence>
    <xs:element name="book">
      <xs:complexType>
        <xs:sequence>
          <xs:element ref="isbn"/>
          <xs:element ref="title"/>
          <xs:element ref="author" minOccurs="0"
            maxOccurs="unbounded"/>
          <xs:element ref="character" minOccurs="0"
            maxOccurs="unbounded"/>
        </xs:sequence>
        <xs:attribute ref="id"/>
        <xs:attribute ref="available"/>
      </xs:complexType>
    </xs:element>
  </xs:sequence>
</xs:group>

<xs:element name="library">
  <xs:complexType>
    <xs:sequence>
      <xs:group ref="bookGroup" maxOccurs="unbounded"/>
    </xs:sequence>
  </xs:complexType>
</xs:element>
```

These four basic styles can, of course, be combined. The more extreme example is as follows:

```
<xs:complexType name="bookType">
  <xs:sequence>
    <xs:element ref="isbn"/>
    <xs:element ref="title"/>
    <xs:element ref="author" minOccurs="0" maxOccurs="unbounded"/>
    <xs:element ref="character" minOccurs="0" maxOccurs="unbounded"/>
  </xs:sequence>
  <xs:attribute ref="id"/>
  <xs:attribute ref="available"/>
</xs:complexType>

<xs:element name="book" type="bookType"/>

<xs:group name="bookGroup">
  <xs:sequence>
    <xs:element ref="book"/>
  </xs:sequence>
</xs:group>

<xs:element name="library">
  <xs:complexType>
    <xs:sequence>
      <xs:group ref="bookGroup" maxOccurs="unbounded"/>
    </xs:sequence>
  </xs:complexType>
</xs:element>
```

Although this example may seem excessive, we must acknowledge that it is also the most extensible, since it lets you use all the "reuse and derive" methods of our three compositors! Now that we've seen these four basic styles, let's see how they compare for re-usability and derivation.

The Russian doll is obviously the style that is the least extensible: both the definition of the book element and of its content model are local. They cannot be referenced to be reused in another part of a schema, they cannot be used as a document element, they cannot be modified by derivation, through xs:redefine, or through substitution groups. Using a Russian doll style here is thus a more efficient "blocking" feature than any blocking attribute is. Changing or reusing the book element or content model requires attaching a totally different schema to the instance document or using a xsi:type attribute in the instance document.

The flat model, which uses global element definitions, gives a basic level of flexibility since the element can now be reused in any location within any schema, can be used as a document element in an instance document, and can be used as the head of a substitution group. When used with a local complex type definition like in our example, the flat model doesn't allow you to change the content model of the book element. Among these three features, the flat model can be used as the head of a substitution group, and is the only one that can be blocked (using a block attribute). It can be used without restriction as a document element in an instance document or be used anywhere in a schema. We also need to note that elements cannot be redefined and that the content model of our book element cannot be changed, except through a substitution by means of xsi:type in the instance document.

The definition of a global complex type to describe the content model of the book element opens two different doors. The content model of the book element can now be reused to derive extended or restricted content models that may be used elsewhere, and the complex type can be redefined through xs:redefine. As seen in the previous chapter, the derivation can be blocked through the final attribute, but the redefinition cannot be controlled.

Last but not least, embedding the definition of the book element in a group allows the group to be reused elsewhere—for example, in our flat model—but can hide the definition of the book element, if needed, to avoid its usage as a document element in instance documents. (Incidentally, it also blocks its usage as the head of a substitution group.) Defining a group also opens the possibility to redefine it through xs:redefine to change the number of occurrences of the element, to add new elements, or even to change its content model if a global complex type has been used. Using an element group this way is very similar to the approach of RELAX NG and gives a bit of its flexibility. We need to note, though, that element groups cannot be recursive; this can be a limitation to using element groups to define recursive content models with element groups, since a global element still needs to be defined for use in a reference. This can be a problem when we can't, or don't want to, use a global element —for instance, when we have two different recursive content models using the same element name with different contents.

Which approach is appropriate? There is no single definite answer to this question, but we know that each of these styles has a different set of extensibility features. The choice between them or a combination of them has a major impact on the reusability and derivability of the definitions present in a schema. Table 13-1 may help with visualizing the differences between these styles, but keep in mind that combinations of all of them are allowed!

Table 13-1. Complex type styles

Style	Element reference	Content model reference	Derivation	Substitution group	Document element	Redefine
Russian doll	No	No	No	No	No	No
Flat	Yes	No	No	Yes	Yes	No
Complex type	No	Yes	Yes	No	No	Yes
Group	Yes	No	No	No	No	Yes

Simple type elements behave much like complex types, except that the complex type definitions are, of course, replaced by simple type definitions similar to those for attributes, discussed in the next section.

Attributes

As seen in Chapter 10, attributes behave differently from elements in that most of the time they are unqualified. This means then that they cannot be globally defined. Otherwise, we have a similar situation with attributes, simple types, and attribute groups as we had with elements and complex types (the other exception is there is no equivalent in attribute land to substitution groups or xsi:type). If we take the definition of a lang attribute restricted to en or fr in the title element, we can have a Russian doll design in which the attribute and its type will be locally defined:

```
<xs:element name="title">
  <xs:complexType>
    <xs:simpleContent>
      <xs:extension base="xs:token">
        <xs:attribute name="lang">
          <xs:simpleType>
            <xs:restriction base="xs:language">
              <xs:enumeration value="en"/>
              <xs:enumeration value="fr"/>
            </xs:restriction>
          </xs:simpleType>
        </xs:attribute>
      </xs:extension>
    </xs:simpleContent>
  </xs:complexType>
</xs:element>
```

We can also take a flat design in which the attribute is globally defined:

```
<xs:attribute name="lang">
  <xs:simpleType>
    <xs:restriction base="xs:language">
      <xs:enumeration value="en"/>
      <xs:enumeration value="fr"/>
    </xs:restriction>
  </xs:simpleType>
</xs:attribute>

<xs:element name="title">
  <xs:complexType>
    <xs:simpleContent>
      <xs:extension base="xs:token">
        <xs:attribute ref="lang"/>
      </xs:extension>
    </xs:simpleContent>
  </xs:complexType>
</xs:element>
```

A global simple type can also be defined:

```
<xs:simpleType name="langType">
  <xs:restriction base="xs:language">
    <xs:enumeration value="en"/>
    <xs:enumeration value="fr"/>
```

```
    </xs:restriction>
  </xs:simpleType>

  <xs:element name="title">
    <xs:complexType>
      <xs:simpleContent>
        <xs:extension base="xs:token">
          <xs:attribute name="lang" type="langType"/>
        </xs:extension>
      </xs:simpleContent>
    </xs:complexType>
  </xs:element>
```

The attribute may be "hidden" in an attribute group:

```
  <xs:attributeGroup name="langGroup">
    <xs:attribute name="lang">
      <xs:simpleType>
        <xs:restriction base="xs:language">
          <xs:enumeration value="en"/>
          <xs:enumeration value="fr"/>
        </xs:restriction>
      </xs:simpleType>
    </xs:attribute>
  </xs:attributeGroup>

  <xs:element name="title">
    <xs:complexType>
      <xs:simpleContent>
        <xs:extension base="xs:token">
          <xs:attributeGroup ref="langGroup"/>
        </xs:extension>
      </xs:simpleContent>
    </xs:complexType>
  </xs:element>
```

All can this can be used together:

```
  <xs:simpleType name="langType">
    <xs:restriction base="xs:language">
      <xs:enumeration value="en"/>
      <xs:enumeration value="fr"/>
    </xs:restriction>
  </xs:simpleType>

  <xs:attribute name="lang" type="langType"/>

  <xs:attributeGroup name="langGroup">
    <xs:attribute ref="lang"/>
  </xs:attributeGroup>

  <xs:element name="title">
    <xs:complexType>
      <xs:simpleContent>
        <xs:extension base="xs:token">
```

```
        <xs:attributeGroup ref="langGroup"/>
      </xs:extension>
    </xs:simpleContent>
  </xs:complexType>
</xs:element>
```

The impact of these design decisions is pretty much the same as those we've seen in complex type elements, except, of course, for substitution groups and usability as a document element. Table 13-2 explains the options these varying approaches provide.

Table 13-2. Attribute styles

Style	Attribute reference	Datatype reference	Derivation	Redefine
Russian doll	No	No	No	No
Flat	Yes	No	No	No
Simple type	No	Yes	Yes	Yes
Attribute group	Yes	No	No	Yes

final and fixed Attributes

These attributes were already covered in Chapter 12, and they have an obvious impact on the re-usability of simple and complex type definitions since they can block some or all the further derivations. This category of features affects the flexibility of the schema itself. Their friends block and abstract are features that impact the openness of the schema and have no impact on the set of instance documents.

Splitting Schema Components

The last factor that acts on the flexibility and re-usability of our schema (and schema libraries) is the split of the components among different documents. Some schema designers have gone as far as possible in this direction and advise the location of each class or component in its own schema document, and to include and import the components needed to create a full schema. This may seem excessive, but provides a very fine granularity and allows a workaround of the limitations of xs:redefine. (If a component needs to be redefined, just leave out the old definition and write a new one.)

The biggest issue with such a design is probably the management of a number of different documents that can rapidly grow, and the many dependencies between these documents. These dependencies must be considered when designing libraries of schemas since they can be tough to track because the links between the included and including documents are multidirectional. A component within an included schema can reference components defined in any other schema processed by the schema processor.

We need to reexamine how a schema processor will build a global schema using all the imported, included, and redefine instructions it will find. The schema processor initially builds a big consolidated schema with all the components defined in all the schema documents it has processed. It then resolves the references between components after building this consolidated schema. Although this simple and powerful mechanism applies to inclusions without restriction, we will see that things can get nastier with imports and redefinitions. Let's start with the simplest case and move on to the processing of xs:include.

The semantic of xs:include is slightly different from the semantic of the include statements used in languages such as C, and it should be considered a conditional include. A xs:include is actually a request to read a schema if it has not already been read, to add all the component declarations found in this schema to the consolidated schema if they have not already been defined, to ignore the components found in the new schema that are already defined in the global schema if they are identical, and to raise an error if they are different. This means it is perfectly legitimate to create loops and multiple inclusions, either directly (schema A includes schema B, which includes schema C) or indirectly (schema A includes schema B and schema C, which includes schema B) and we can create inclusion paths as complex as we wish.

The meaning of xs:redefine is similar, except that some components can be redefined. When used, this difference is enough to break the possibility of creating loops in which a schema A redefines components of a schema B, which redefines or includes schema A. This restriction actually means that while we can speak of inclusion graphs, the redefinitions would instead form a tree. The process of including or redefining is recursive, however, and when we include (or redefine) a schema, we include the consolidated schema resulting from the included document rather than the document itself. We can still create inclusion loops within the branches of the redefinition tree (schema A can redefine schema B, which includes schema C, which includes schema B).

Some designers rely on the fact that when a schema without target namespaces is included (or redefined) in a schema with a target namespace, the included schema "borrows" the target namespace of its "includer." This feature, already mentioned in Chapter 10, can be used to build "neutral" components with no namespaces that can be included and used as building blocks. Since these components take the namespace of the including schema like a chameleon takes the color of its environment, these schemas are called "chameleon schemas." Although this technique is simple and may be convenient in some cases, it can be confusing to define similar components (and, therefore, similar types and content models) in different namespaces instead of creating a common namespace for them, which would immediately identify these types and content models as identical.

xs:import behaves somewhat like xs:include: no redefinitions occur, which means that loops can be created where schema A (for namespace A) imports schema B (for namespace B), which itself imports schema A. It is a important to note that xs:import serves two different purposes: it is an instruction to import a schema and a declaration that components from a namespace can be referenced. If schema A for namespace A imports schema B for namespace B, and if schema B needs to reference components from the namespace A, an xs:import statement *must* be included in schema B to declare that namespace A can be used (the schemaLocation attribute is optional and can be omitted in such cases).

After working through the three mechanisms (include, redefine, and import), we can mix all of them together and note that chameleon schemas can be used together with imports. In this case, the same imported chameleon can contribute several times to a global schema under different namespaces. If schema A for namespace A includes schema B with no namespace, and imports schema C for namespace C with includes schema B, the two inclusions of schema B belong to different namespaces and are considered different.

We now have all the elements to find innovative ways to mix inclusion and import graphs with redefinition trees. Keep in mind that simple is beautiful, and if we don't restrict ourselves, we humans might get lost well before our favorite schema processor!

The Need for Open Schemas

In this chapter, we have discussed the features that may make the components defined in a schema reusable and flexible. This is definitely something to look for, but the impact of this effort is limited to the conception and maintenance of schemas and has little or no impact on the documents themselves. Even though application designers often see XML instance documents as tightly coupled to their schema and to the application for which they were first created, the life span of documents often exceeds the life span of their applications and schemas. XML documents or fragments are also often reused in other contexts, or serve as a container in which other information is added to create combinations that their original author never imagined.

Opening XML vocabularies to facilitate and control such evolution is quite challenging and goes beyond designing open schemas. It requires a different perspective on what an XML document is and has an impact on the way to code the applications (which should, for instance, be as tolerant as possible of unexpected elements and attributes). Grammar-based schemas, such as W3C XML Schema, have a basic problem with open vocabulary: everything that has not been explicitly allowed is forbidden, and the schemas are effectively "closed by default."

If we define the openness of a schema as the ability to modify the content model explicitly defined by the original schema without defining a new schema (we already covered the modification of the content model through a modification of the schema in the earlier section "Extensible Schemas"), the tools that we have at hand are the substitution of type through xsi:type and the wildcards.

xsi:type

This kind of openness is allowed by default. A number of applications that use complex type derivations by extension, simple type derivations by union, or are using building blocks that have not specified block or blockDefault attributes, could probably be quite surprised by a substitution of type in the instance document.

Beyond these cases of "unexpected" openness, defining extensions of the complex types used to define our elements that can be substituted in the instance documents through the xsi:type attribute can be an initial approach to open the schema while keeping control over surprises. In this case, the xsi:type attribute can be processed by the applications to determine which kind of extension they are facing.

Wildcards

Namespaces and wildcards are the most powerful tools we can use to create open schemas. Many vocabularies (such as W3C XML Schema) allow attributes that have a namespace other than the target namespace in all their elements, while keeping tight control over both unqualified attributes and attributes from their namespace. The values of the processContents attribute (lax, skip, and strict) can be adjusted to provide the level of openness you find best adapts to your schema. skip is completely open, strict requires supplying schemas for the namespaces that are found during the validation, and lax is a medium-level constraint.

Elements from other namespaces are often considered more intrusive than attributes and can be kept within containers. This is also what W3C XML Schema does for its own vocabulary, allowing any element from any namespace within xs:appinfo. Other vocabularies, such as Relax NG or RSS 1.0, simply accept any element that has a namespace other than its target namespace.

Although this practice allows a great deal of flexibility for embedding unexpected information in instance documents, note that the fact that there is no special value to specify "any namespace except those which are defined in the consolidated schema" limits its applicability when several namespaces are defined together.

And Substitution Groups?

If we mention xsi:type here, shouldn't we mention substitution groups also? Yes and no. Yes, because using them is a good way to define several alternative content models. However, no, because they can be used only if they have been defined in a schema. However, xsi:type can be used even if the schema makes no special provision for them. Despite similarities, substitution groups truly belong to flexible schemas much more than to open schemas.

CHAPTER 14

Documenting Schemas

The issue of documenting schemas—or any machine readable language—goes beyond simple additions of comments. The real challenge is to create schemas that are readable both directly by looking at their source code and by documentation extraction tools.

Style Matters

Writing schemas is much like writing programs. Two pieces of code may both work, but one is more readable and maintainable than the other. Readability is good.

Keep It Simple

Although W3C XML Schema has been carefully specified so that schema processors can find their way through the most complex and intricate combinations of its many features, the same can't be expected of the average human reader. I must confess that I, for one, am getting rapidly lost in the meanders of medium complexity schemas, such as the famous schema for schema.

"Keep it simple" is a useful principle. Although W3C XML Schema gives you a huge number of features, you don't need to use all of them in every schema. Each of them incurs a price in terms of readability of your schema.

Some of the rules for simplicity that we have used for some time with programming languages apply here, such as the conflicting rules for brevity ("If a function is more than one page long, split it"), and directness ("A function should be called more than once"). There are, of course, others such as "Put the code and the documentation in the same place," "If you can't say it in English, you can't say it in C/C++ (or Java, C#, Perl, Python, etc.)," and "Don't solve problems that don't exist."

Translated for the XML design world, these four could read as "If a declaration is more than one page long, split it," "A declaration should be referred to at least one time" (we will see next that there might be exceptions), "If you can't say it in

English, you can't say it in XML," and, of course, "Don't solve problems that don't exist."

Think Globally

When I started working with W3C XML Schema, I used to think that the Russian doll design was the simplest, since it's so close to the structure of the instance documents. Having written the W3C XML Schema reference manual, I am convinced that flat structures in which all the elements are global are much simpler to document and just as simple to write!

The Russian doll design relies on an analogy between object-oriented programming and markup. This is somewhat misleading: there is no such thing as a private or local object in an XML document (except maybe if you encode or encrypt some fragments); when you open an XML document, its whole content is exposed, and everything is public and needs to be documented with the same level of accuracy. To describe a concept, give it a name. W3C XML Schema enforces the attribution of unique names only for global elements. Although different content models are often presented as an advantage over the DTDs, defining them under the same element name is very confusing when reading an instance document. The most convenient way to create a reference manual for an XML vocabulary is through a dictionary of elements. Reusing the same element name for different purposes creates multiple entries that are confusing and difficult to read (like the entries for common words, such as "place" in an English dictionary); the example of W3C XML Schema and its very different meanings for xs:extension is enlightening. Therefore, the second piece of advice is to define the elements as global when possible. Note that this advice doesn't apply to unqualified attributes, which cannot be defined as global.

When It's Similar, Show It

The third and last piece of advice contradicts the first one, and a trade-off needs to be found between these two. The first two bits of advice lead to what I call flat schemas. These are similar to our very first example in Chapter 1, in which all the elements and attributes are global with local type definitions. This style is easy to read but doesn't highlight the similarities between elements such as the fact that authors and characters can be considered persons and share some properties. When strong similarities exist between different elements, using one of the techniques already discussed (either a complex type derivation or elements and attributes group composition) can enhance the readability of the schema.

The third bit of advice states you should use W3C XML Schema features to highlight the strong similarities when they are present.

The W3C XML Schema Annotation Element

The recommended way to add comments and documentation in a W3C XML Schema is through the xs:annotation element. This element can be added within pretty much all the W3C XML Schema elements (in fact, it can be added within all the schema elements except xs:annotation and its child elements, xs:documentation and xs:appinfo). It generally appears as the first child element (except for the xs:schema element in which xs:annotation can appear anywhere).

The xs:annotation element is a container for the xs:documentation and xs:appinfo elements that contain additional information. These two elements are dedicated to holding human readable documentation (xs:documentation) and machine-processable information (xs:appinfo). They accept any text and child elements. (These are the only W3C XML Schema elements that have a mixed content model.) Note, though, that the schema for schema specifies that the processing to apply to the content of these elements is lax. Concretely, this means that although W3C XML Schema elements can be included within these elements, they must be valid per the schema for schema. This mixed content model allows the inclusion of almost any content, such as text:

```
<xs:element name="author" type="author">
  <xs:annotation>
    <xs:documentation xml:lang="en">
      The author of a book.
    </xs:documentation>
    <xs:documentation xml:lang="fr">
      Designe l'auteur d'un livre.
    </xs:documentation>
  </xs:annotation>
</xs:element>
```

It also allows rich content, such as XHTML, which can be assembled to create more user friendly and readable documentation:

```
<xs:element name="author" type="author">
  <xs:annotation>
    <xs:documentation xml:lang="en">
      <p id="author" xmlns="http://www.w3.org/1999/xhtml">
        This element describes the
        <em>
          author
        </em>
        of a
        <a href="#book">
          book
        </a>
      </p>
      .
    </xs:documentation>
  </xs:annotation>
</xs:element>
```

It even allows SVG, such as the following, which provides a picture of what an author may look like:

```
<xs:element name="author" type="author">
  <xs:annotation>
    <xs:documentation>
      <svg xmlns="http://www.w3.org/2000/svg">
        <title>
          An author
        </title>
        <ellipse style="stroke:#000000; fill:#e3e000;
          stroke-width:2pt;" id="head" cx="280" cy="250" rx="110"
          ry="130"/>
        <ellipse style="stroke:none; fill:#7f7f7f; " id="leftEye"
          cx="240"cy="225" rx="18" ry="18"/>
        <ellipse style="stroke:none; fill:#7f7f7f; " id="rightEye"
          cx="320"cy="225" rx="18" ry="18"/>
        <path style="fill:none;stroke:#7F7F7F; stroke-width:5pt;"
          id="mouth"d="M 222 280 A 58 48 0 0 0 338 280"/>
      </svg>
    </xs:documentation>
  </xs:annotation>
</xs:element>
```

Dublin Core elements are a set of elements widely used on the Web to qualify web pages and supported by a large range of applications. They may be used as general purpose metadata embedded within annotations:

```
<xs:element name="author" type="author">
  <xs:annotation>
    <xs:appinfo xmlns:dc="http://purl.org/dc/elements/1.1/">
      <dc:creator>
        Eric van der Vlist (mailto:vdv@dyomedea.com)
      </dc:creator>
      <dc:date>
        2002-02-01
      </dc:date>
      <dc:subject>
        author,person,book
      </dc:subject>
      <dc:description>
        This element describes the author of a book.
      </dc:description>
    </xs:appinfo>
  </xs:annotation>
</xs:element>
```

Annotations are also a good container for application-specific metadata, such as those used by the schema for schema to describe the list of facets and properties of its primitive datatypes:

```
<xs:simpleType name="string" id="string">
  <xs:annotation>
    <xs:appinfo>
```

```
            <hfp:hasFacet name="length"/>
            <hfp:hasFacet name="minLength"/>
            <hfp:hasFacet name="maxLength"/>
            <hfp:hasFacet name="pattern"/>
            <hfp:hasFacet name="enumeration"/>
            <hfp:hasFacet name="whiteSpace"/>
            <hfp:hasProperty name="ordered" value="false"/>
            <hfp:hasProperty name="bounded" value="false"/>
            <hfp:hasProperty name="cardinality" value="countably
               infinite"/>
            <hfp:hasProperty name="numeric" value="false"/>
        </xs:appinfo>
        <xs:documentation
          source="http://www.w3.org/TR/xmlschema-2/#string"/>
    </xs:annotation>
    <xs:restriction base="xs:anySimpleType">
      <xs:whiteSpace value="preserve" id="string.preserve"/>
    </xs:restriction>
  </xs:simpleType>
```

The Schema Adjunct Framework (SAF) is a proposal to complement schemas with the information needed to generate applications. It is found at *http://www.extensibility.com/ saf/spec.* One of its syntaxes, "schema adornments," also uses xs:appinfo; although this syntax hasn't been adapted to the W3C XML Schema Recommendation yet, it could be something like this (note that this is my own unofficial adaptation given here just as an example):

```
<xs:element name="author" type="author">
  <xs:annotation>
    <xs:appinfo source="saf:meta-data-item"
      xmlns:sql="http://www.extensibility.com/saf/spec/safsample/sql-map.saf"
      >
      <sql:select>
        select
        <sql:elem>
          name
        </sql:elem>
        ,
        <sql:elem>
          birthdate
        </sql:elem>
        ,
        <sql:attr>
          deathdate
        </sql:attr>
        from tbl_author
      </sql:select>
    </xs:appinfo>
  </xs:annotation>
</xs:element>
```

SAF also defines a syntax to embed rules written as XPath expressions, which is also the domain of Schematron (which is discussed in Appendix A). Schematron rules can be embedded in xs:appinfo elements and used to test things that W3C XML Schema cannot—like ensuring that the birth of a person took place before their death.

How can this work, given that the XPath 1.0 on which Schematron is built can't interpret dates? This is a fairly dangerous practice, but assuming that the dates use four digits for the years, as well as the same time zone (which we saw how to impose through patterns in Chapter 6), this works because ISO 8601 dates are then following the alphabetical sort order!

```xml
<xs:element name="author" type="author">
  <xs:annotation>
    <xs:appinfo xmlns:sch="http://www.ascc.net/xml/schematron">
      <sch:pattern name="Born before dead">
        <sch:rule context="author">
          <sch:assert test="not(dead) or (dead > born)"
            diagnostics="bornAfterDead">
            An author should die after her or his death.
          </sch:assert>
          <sch:diagnostics>
            <sch:diagnostic id="bornAfterDead">
              Error, this author is born after her or his birth!
              Author=
              <sch:value-of select="name"/>
              Birth =
              <sch:value-of select="born"/>
              Death =
              <sch:value-of select="dead"/>
            </sch:diagnostic>
          </sch:diagnostics>
        </sch:rule>
      </sch:pattern>
    </xs:appinfo>
  </xs:annotation>
</xs:element>
```

Although not a common practice, it is also possible to embed code snippets, such as this XSLT template:

```xml
<xs:element name="book" type="book">
  <xs:annotation>
    <xs:appinfo xmlns:xsl="http://www.w3.org/1999/XSL/Transform">
      <xsl:template match="book">
        <xsl:apply-templates select="title"/>
        <xsl:apply-templates select="isbn"/>
        <p>
          Authors:
        </p>
        <ul>
          <xsl:apply-templates select="author"/>
        </ul>
        <p>
          Characters:
        </p>
```

```
      <ul>
        <xsl:apply-templates select="character"/>
      </ul>
    </xsl:template>
  </xs:appinfo>
 </xs:annotation>
</xs:element>
```

Instead of embedding resources, you can also link them using XLink. RDDL, a vocabulary aimed at describing namespaces may be diverted from its original goal to provide the glue for expressing these links:

```
<xs:element name="author" type="author">
  <xs:annotation>
    <xs:appinfo xmlns:xlink="http://www.w3.org/1999/xlink"
      xmlns:rddl="http://www.rddl.org/">
      <rddl:resource id="author-transform"
        xlink:arcrole="http://www.w3.org/1999/xhtml"
        xlink:role="http://www.w3.org/1999/XSL/Transform"
        xlink:title="Author template"
        xlink:href="library.xslt#author">
        <div class="resource">
          <h4>
            XSLT Transformation
          </h4>
          <p>
            This
            <a href="library.xslt#author">
              template
            </a>
            displays the description of an author.
          </p>
        </div>
      </rddl:resource>
      <rddl:resource id="CSS" xlink:title="CSS Stylesheet"
        xlink:role="http://www.isi.edu/in-notes/iana/assignments/media-types/text/css"
        xlink:href="author.css">
        <div class="resource">
          <h4>
            CSS Stylesheet
          </h4>
          <p>
            A
            <a href="author.css">
              CSS stylesheet
            </a>
            defining the styles which may be used to display an author.
          </p>
        </div>
      </rddl:resource>
    </xs:appinfo>
  </xs:annotation>
</xs:element>
```

RDDL should be pronounced "riddle," and its specification is available at *http:// rddl.org*.

 xs:documentation and xs:appinfo both accept an optional source attribute, which is a URI, and can identify the source or the nature of the included information. Since it's designed for human consumption, xs:documentation also accepts an optional xml:lang attribute.

Foreign Attributes

Although xs:annotation is certainly the most flexible way to embed any information within a schema, W3C XML Schema defines a second opening in its vocabulary that may be used either as an alternative or in conjunction with annotations. All the W3C XML Schema elements (except xs:documentation and xs:appinfo) accept any attribute that has a namespace other than the W3C XML Schema namespace (unprefixed attributes are forbidden). Such attributes may be used to document a schema:

```
<xs:element name="author" type="author" doc:doc="This element
   describes the author of a book."
   xmlns:doc="http://dyomedea.com/ns/doc"/>
```

This approach is also used by SAF adornments, whose simple form can be embedded in attributes:

```
<xs:element name="author" type="author" sql:table="TBL_AUTHOR"
   xmlns:sql="http://www.extensibility.com/saf/spec/safsample/sql-map.saf"
   />
```

The huge opening given to attributes is especially interesting with attribute-only vocabularies such as XLink, and simple XLinks can be directly embedded into W3C XML Schema. The following example links the definition of our author element directly to a XSLT template:

```
<xs:element name="author" type="author"
   xlink:arcrole="http://www.w3.org/1999/xhtml"
   xlink:role="http://www.w3.org/1999/XSL/Transform"
   xlink:title="Author template" xlink:href="library.xslt#author"
   xmlns:xlink="http://www.w3.org/1999/xlink"/>
```

Unfortunately, because of the exception for xs:appinfo and xs:documentation, which do not accept foreign attributes, metadata cannot be added through attributes in these elements, so the following example is invalid:

```
<xs:element name="author" type="author">
  <xs:annotation>
    <xs:appinfo
      xlink:arcrole="http://www.w3.org/1999/XSL/Transform"
      xlink:role="http://www.w3.org/1999/XSL/Transform"
      xlink:title="Author template" xlink:href="library.xslt#author"
      xmlns:xlink="http://www.w3.org/1999/xlink">
      <div class="resource">
```

```
      <h4>
        XSLT Transformation
      </h4>
      <p>
        This
        <a href="library.xslt#author">
          template
        </a>
        displays the description of an author.
      </p>
    </div>
  </xs:appinfo>
  <xs:appinfo title="CSS Stylesheet"
    role="http://www.isi.edu/in-notes/iana/assignments/media-types/text/css"
    href="author.css">
    <div class="resource">
      <h4>
        CSS Stylesheet
      </h4>
      <p>
        A
        <a href="author.css">
          CSS stylesheet
        </a>
        defining the styles which may be used to display an
        author.
      </p>
    </div>
  </xs:appinfo>
  </xs:annotation>
</xs:element>
```

Of course, the usual limitations of attributes apply here: attributes are less extensible than elements and they cannot include structured content.

XML 1.0 Comments

There is a general tendency among recent XML vocabularies to use special elements to add documentation or meta-information rather than general purpose XML 1.0 comments or processing instructions. W3C XML Schema follow this tendency with its xs:documentation and xs:appinfo elements. The arguments often used to justify this choice are the ease of use by applications and the fact that parsers are not obliged to transmit comments to applications. In practice, most parsers do transmit comments; comments are available to the applications and can be manipulated quite easily, even through XPath expressions. A more solid argument in favor of using elements is their ability to include structured content.

On the other hand, XML 1.0 comments (and processing instructions) are lighter weight and can be included at any location within any element—not only as the first child element of XML Schema components. With an XML 1.0 comment, our example becomes:

```
<xs:element name="author" type="author">
  <!-- This element describes the author of a book. -->
</xs:element>
```

Which One and What For?

If we recap the three different forms we have seen to include simple comments, we may use xs:documentation:

```
<xs:element name="author" type="author">
  <xs:annotation>
    <xs:documentation xml:lang="en">
      The author of a book.
    </xs:documentation>
    <xs:documentation xml:lang="fr">
      Designe l'auteur d'un livre.
    </xs:documentation>
  </xs:annotation>
</xs:element>
```

Or foreign attributes:

```
<xs:element name="author" type="author" doc:doc="This element
  describes the author of a book."
  xmlns:doc="http://dyomedea.com/ns/doc"/>
```

Or XML 1.0 comments:

```
<xs:element name="author" type="author">
  <!-- This element describes the author of a book. -->
</xs:element>
```

Which one is more appropriate? There is no simple answer, since it depends on which form is supported by the set of tools you choose, and on what you want to do out of these comments. That being said, does that really matter? The hard work is to include relevant comments in your schemas and to keep them up to date. The format itself is not really that important, and each approach is only one XSLT transformation away from the two other alternatives!

The same applies to all the meta-information that we included in our schemas: they do not break the schema and can be processed by any schema processor but will be ignored by most of them! Adding them is useful only if one has an application in mind, and the choice of the format will be determined by the constraints of this application.

Finally, we must note that we have only presented schema-centric options, in which information is added within W3C XML Schema that conforms to the Recommendation. Other options exist, which may be object-oriented design-centric (generating schemas from UML specifications) or adjunct-centric (describing the schema adjunct outside of the W3C XML Schema document). Also, some new inventive packaging could be invented, such as formats that would group different resources (schemas, transformations, stylesheets, etc.) for an information item under a single umbrella, and perhaps recompose the traditional "per function" packaging, depending on the composition done by the application.

CHAPTER 15

Elements Reference Guide

This chapter provides a quick reference to all of the elements W3C XML Schema uses to define components of XML Schemas. Some elements can be defined simply, while others require multiple entries reflecting usage in different contexts. If an element name is followed by a parenthetical phrase, you may want to examine following entries to determine which context is most appropriate for your use.

xs:all (outside a group)

Compositor describing an unordered group of elements.

```
<xs:all
        id                  = xs:ID
        maxOccurs           = "1" : "1"
        minOccurs           = ( "0" | "1" ) : "1"
        {any attributes with non-schema namespace}
        >
        Content: (xs:annotation?, xs:element*)
</xs:all>
```

May be included in: xs:complexType (local definition), xs:complexType (global definition), xs:extension (complex content), xs:restriction (complex content)

Description

xs:all is used to describe an unordered group of elements whose number of occurences may be zero or one..

Restrictions

xs:all is the only compositor that cannot be used as a particle and needs to be used by itself to describe a complete content model. Unlike xs:choice and xs:sequence, xs:all cannot be embedded within another compositor. It can, thus, only be embedded directly into an xs:complexType, xs:restriction, or xs:extension; furthermore, its number of occurrences may be only zero or one.

The particles included in xs:all are also limited: they can only be xs:element and their number of occurrences can only be zero or one.

Combining these two restrictions means xs:all may only be used to describe content models in which a group of unordered elements (mandatory or optional, but with a number of occurrences not greater than one) are the only child elements.

Situations describing unordered groups of optional elements that have the same number of maximum occurrences can be described using xs:choice or substitution groups, but other content models (such as groups of unordered elements with arbitrary and different maximum numbers of occurrences) cannot be described with W3C XML Schema.

Complex types defined using an xs:all compositor cannot be derived by extension.

Example

```
<xs:element name="author">
  <xs:complexType>
    <xs:all>
      <xs:element ref="name"/>
      <xs:element ref="born"/>
      <xs:element ref="dead" minOccurs="0"/>
    </xs:all>
    <xs:attribute ref="id"/>
  </xs:complexType>
</xs:element>


<xs:element name="full-name" substitutionGroup="name">
  <xs:complexType>
    <xs:all>
      <xs:element name="first" type="string32" minOccurs="0"/>
      <xs:element name="middle" type="string32" minOccurs="0"/>
      <xs:element name="last" type="string32"/>
    </xs:all>
  </xs:complexType>
</xs:element>
```

Attributes

id
    W3C XML Schema's element ID.

maxOccurs
    Maximum number of occurrences. Note that this value is fixed to one.

minOccurs
    Minimum number of occurrences. Note that this value can be only zero or one.

---

xs:all (within a group)

Compositor describing an unordered group of elements.
The number of occurrences cannot be defined when xs:all is used within a group.

```
<xs:all
        id          = xs:ID
        {any attributes with non-schema namespace}
        >
```

```
          Content: (xs:annotation?, xs:element*)
</xs:all>
```

May be included in: xs:group (definition)

Description

Used within a group, `xs:all` has the same meaning as when it is used directly under `xs:complexType`, except that the `minOccurs` and `maxOccurs` attributes have completely disappeared (i.e., it cannot be marked as optional).

Restrictions

The restrictions that apply to `xs:all` apply to the group embedding the `xs:all` compositor. This group cannot have a number of occurrences greater than one and cannot be used as a particle. It must be included directly under `xs:complexType`, `xs:restriction`, or `xs:extension`.

All other restrictions of `xs:all` apply here.

Example

```
<xs:group name="authorSubElements">
  <xs:all>
    <xs:element ref="name"/>
    <xs:element ref="born"/>
    <xs:element ref="dead" minOccurs="0"/>
  </xs:all>
</xs:group>
```

Attributes

id
    W3C XML Schema's element ID.

---

xs:annotation

Informative data for human or electronic agents.

```
<xs:annotation
          id          = xs:ID
          {any attributes with non-schema namespace}
          >
          Content: (xs:appinfo | xs:documentation)*
</xs:annotation>
```

May be included in: xs:all (outside a group), xs:all (within a group), xs:any, xs:anyAttribute, xs:attribute (reference or local definition), xs:attribute (global definition), xs:attributeGroup (reference), xs:attributeGroup (global definition), xs:choice (outside a group), xs:choice (within a group), xs:complexContent, xs:complexType (local definition), xs:complexType (global definition), xs:element (within xs:all), xs:element (reference or local definition), xs:element (global definition), xs:enumeration, xs:extension (complex content), xs:extension (simple content), xs:field, xs:fractionDigits, xs:group (reference), xs:group (definition), xs:import, xs:include, xs:key, xs:keyref, xs:length, xs:list, xs:maxExclusive, xs:maxInclusive, xs:maxLength, xs:minExclusive, xs:minInclusive, xs:minLength, xs:notation, xs:pattern,

> *xs:redefine, xs:restriction (complex content), xs:restriction (simple type), xs:restriction (simple content), xs:schema, xs:selector, xs:sequence (within a group), xs:sequence (outside a group), xs:simpleContent, xs:simpleType (local definition), xs:simpleType (global definition), xs:totalDigits, xs:union, xs:unique, xs:whiteSpace*

Description

xs:annotation is a container in which additional information can be embedded, either for human consumption (with xs:documentation) or for programs (xs:appinfo). xs:annotation can be added as a first element in almost any W3C XML Schema element. It can also be included anywhere as a top-level element (directly under xs:schema).

Restrictions

xs:annotation cannot be included within itself.

Example

```
<xs:element name="author" type="author">
  <xs:annotation>
    <xs:documentation xml:lang="en">
      The author of a book.
    </xs:documentation>
    <xs:documentation xml:lang="fr">
      Designe l'auteur d'un livre.
    </xs:documentation>
    <xs:appinfo xmlns:sch="http://www.ascc.net/xml/schematron">
      <sch:pattern name="Born before dead">
        <sch:rule context="author">
          <sch:assert test="not(dead) or (dead > born)"
            diagnostics="bornAfterDead">
            An author should die after her or his death.
          </sch:assert>
          <sch:diagnostics>
            <sch:diagnostic id="bornAfterDead">
              Error, this author is born after her or his birth!
              Author=
              <sch:value-of select="name"/>
              Birth =
              <sch:value-of select="born"/>
              Death =
              <sch:value-of select="dead"/>
            </sch:diagnostic>
          </sch:diagnostics>
        </sch:rule>
      </sch:pattern>
    </xs:appinfo>
  </xs:annotation>
</xs:element>
```

Attributes

id
    W3C XML Schema's element ID.

xs:any

```
<xs:any
        id              = xs:ID
        maxOccurs       = ( xs:nonNegativeInteger | "unbounded" ) : "1"
        minOccurs       = xs:nonNegativeInteger : "1"
        namespace       = ( ( "##any" | "##other" ) | list of ( xs:anyURI | (
                          "##targetNamespace" | "##local" ) ) ) : "##any"
        processContents = ( "skip" | "lax" | "strict" ) : "strict"
        {any attributes with non-schema namespace}
        >
        Content: (xs:annotation?)
</xs:any>
```

May be included in: xs:choice (outside a group), xs:choice (within a group), xs:sequence (within a group), xs:sequence (outside a group)

Description

xs:any is a wildcard that allows the insertion of any element belonging to a list of namespaces. This particle can be used like xs:element within choices (xs:choice) and sequences (xs:sequence), and the number of occurrences of the elements that are allowed can be controlled by its minOccurs and maxOccurs attributes.

The list of permitted namespaces is specified though the namespace attribute. The namespace attribute expects a list of namespace URIs. In this list, two values have a specific meaning: ##targetNamespace stands for the target namespace, and ##local stands for local elements (without namespaces). These values can be mixed in the list with regular namespaces URIs. The whole list may also be replaced by two other special values: ##any stands for any namespace at all and is the default value for the namespace attribute, and ##other stands for any namespace other than the target namespace. When ##other is used in a schema without a target namespace, all the namespaces are allowed and only elements without namespaces are forbidden.

The target namespace used to evaluate the special values ##targetNamespace and ##other is the target namespace (or lack of target namespace) of the schema in which the xs:any wildcard is found. This doesn't change when one schema is imported into another.

The behavior of the validator regarding the elements that will be allowed and their children can be specified using the processContent attribute. When processContent is set to strict (i.e., the default values), the schema processors must validate these elements against their schemas and report an error if they are not valid or if it hasn't been able to fetch the schemas for their namespaces. When set to skip, the processors do not attempt to validate these elements. When set to lax, the validator validates the elements if it can find a definition for them, and skips them if it can't.

When the processContent is skip (or when it is lax and the schema processor hasn't been able to locate a schema for an element, which is equivalent), the processor skips any further validation of the elements accepted that may have any content type. The processor eventually includes attributes and subelements of any namespace regardless of the value of the namespace attribute.

When the processContent is strict (or when it is lax and the schema validator has found a schema for them, which is equivalent), the elements that are accepted for the wildcard need to be defined as global elements in the schema for this namespace or have a valid datatype associated in the instance document through xsi:type attribute.

Restrictions

Some combinations of specifications of namespaces that are useful to define multi-namespaces open vocabularies are missing. These are the cases of "any namespace known in the current validation context" and its complementary "any namespace not defined in the current validation context."

The usual restrictions for nondeterministic content models apply to wildcards. While trying to track the risks of or reasons for a nondeterministic content model, pay attention to the value of the processContent attribute. Possible conflict may occur with any element declared as global in one of the permitted namespaces if processContent is strict, and it may occur with any element (global or local) if processContent is skip.

The behavior of the special value ##other on unqualified elements in schemas with target namespaces is contradictory in the W3C XML Schema Recommentation and should be clarified in a future addendum. The most likely interpretation is unqualified elements are not allowed when ##other is specified in these schemas, even though a passage of the Recommendation states the contrary.

Attributes

id
> W3C XML Schema's element ID.

maxOccurs
> Maximum number of elements permitted for this wildcard.

minOccurs
> Minimum number of elements permitted for this wildcard.

namespace
> Permitted namespaces.

processContents
> Type of validation required on the elements permitted for this wildcard.

---

xs:anyAttribute
Wildcard to replace any attribute.

```
<xs:anyAttribute
        id                   = xs:ID
        namespace            = ( ( "##any" | "##other" ) | list of ( xs:anyURI | (
                               "##targetNamespace" | "##local" ) ) ) : "##any"
        processContents      = ( "skip" | "lax" | "strict" ) : "strict"
        {any attributes with non-schema namespace}
        >
        Content: (xs:annotation?)
</xs:anyAttribute>
```

May be included in: xs:attributeGroup (global definition), xs:complexType (local definition), xs:complexType (global definition), xs:extension (complex content), xs:extension (simple content), xs:restriction (complex content), xs:restriction (simple content)

Description

xs:anyAttribute is a wildcard that allows the insertion of any attribute belonging to a list of namespaces. This particle must be used wherever an attribute local declaration of reference can be used (i.e., within complexType or attributeGroup definitions).

The list of permitted namespaces is specified though the namespace attribute. The namespace attribute expects a list of namespace URIs. In this list, two values have a specific meaning: ##targetNamespace stands for the target namespace, and ##local stands for local attributes (without namespaces). These values can be mixed in the list with regular namespaces URIs. The whole list may also be replaced by two other special values: ##any stands for any namespace at all and is the default value for the namespace attribute and ##other stands for any namespace other than the target namespace. When ##other is used in a schema without a target namespace, all the namespaces are allowed and only attributes without namespaces are forbidden.

The target namespace used to evaluate the special values ##targetNamespace and ##other is the target namespace (or lack of target namespace) of the schema in which the xs:anyAttribute wildcard is found. This doesn't change when one schema is imported into another.

The behavior of the validator regarding the attributes that will be allowed can be specified using the processContent attribute. When processContent is set to strict (i.e., the default values), the schema processors must validate these attributes against their schemas and report an error if they are not valid or if it hasn't been able to fetch the schemas for their namespaces. When set to skip, the processors do not attempt to validate these attributes. When set to lax, the validator validates the attributes if it can find a definition for them, and skips them if it can't.

When the processContent is skip (or when it is lax and the schema processor hasn't been able to locate a schema for an attribute, which is equivalent), the processor skips any further validation of the accepted attributes that may belong to any datatype.

When the processContent is strict (or when it is lax and the schema validator has found a schema for them, which is equivalent), the accepted attributes for the wildcard need to be defined as global attributes in the schema for this namespace.

Restrictions

Some combinations of specifications of namespaces used to define multi-namespace open vocabularies are missing. These include the cases of "any namespace known in the current validation context" and its complementary "any namespace not defined in the current validation context."

The behavior of the special value ##other on unqualified attributes in schemas with target namespaces is contradictory in the W3C XML Schema Recommmentation and should be clarified in a future addendum. The most likely interpretation is that unqualified attributes are not allowed when ##other is specified in these schemas, even though a passage of the Recommendation states the contrary.

Attributes

id
> W3C XML Schema's element ID.

namespace
> Permitted namespaces.

processContents
> Type of validation required on the elements permitted for this wildcard.

---

xs:appinfo

Information for applications.

```
<xs:appinfo
        source          = xs:anyURI
        >
        Content: ({any})*
</xs:appinfo>
```

May be included in: xs:annotation

Description

xs:appinfo is a container that embeds structured information that can be used by applications. Its content model is open and can accept any element from any namespace (with a lax validation; W3C XML Schema elements included here must be valid). xs:appinfo can be used to include any kind of information, such as metadata, processing directives, or even code snippets.

Its content is similar to xs:documentation (which is reserved for human-readable information), except for an xml:lang attribute (which is allowed in xs:documentation but forbidden for xs:appinfo).

Restrictions

Foreign attributes cannot be included in xs:appinfo.

The source attribute is underspecified in the Recommendation, which could lead to interoperability issues between applications relying on xs:appinfo if they use relative or shared URIs. For instance, one application may decide to use the XSLT namespace in the source attribute to indicate an XSLT snippet while another application could use the same URI to indicate a set of parameters to pass to an XSLT transformation.

Example

```
<xs:element name="author" type="author">
  <xs:annotation>
    <xs:appinfo xmlns:dc="http://purl.org/dc/elements/1.1/">
      <dc:creator>
        Eric van der Vlist (mailto:vdv@dyomedea.com)
      </dc:creator>
      <dc:date>
        2002-02-01
      </dc:date>
      <dc:subject>
```

```
       author,person,book
     </dc:subject>
     <dc:description>
       This element describes the author of a book.
     </dc:description>
   </xs:appinfo>
  </xs:annotation>
</xs:element>


<xs:element name="author" type="author">
  <xs:annotation>
    <xs:appinfo source="saf:meta-data-item"
      xmlns:sql="http://www.extensibility.com/saf/spec/safsample/sql-map.saf"
      >
      <sql:select>
        select
        <sql:elem>
          name
        </sql:elem>
        ,
        <sql:elem>
          birthdate
        </sql:elem>
        ,
        <sql:attr>
          deathdate
        </sql:attr>
        from tbl_author
      </sql:select>
    </xs:appinfo>
  </xs:annotation>
</xs:element>


<xs:element name="book" type="book">
  <xs:annotation>
    <xs:appinfo xmlns:xsl="http://www.w3.org/1999/XSL/Transform">
      <xsl:template match="book">
        <xsl:apply-templates select="title"/>
        <xsl:apply-templates select="isbn"/>
        <p>
          Authors:
        </p>
        <ul>
          <xsl:apply-templates select="author"/>
        </ul>
        <p>
          Characters:
        </p>
        <ul>
          <xsl:apply-templates select="character"/>
        </ul>
      </xsl:template>
```

```
        </xs:appinfo>
      </xs:annotation>
    </xs:element>
```

Attributes

source

> Can be used to provide a link to the source of the information when a snippet is included, or as a semantic attribute to qualify the type of information that is included.

xs:attribute (global definition)

Global attribute definition that can be referenced within the same schema by other schemas.

```
<xs:attribute
          default       = xs:string
          fixed         = xs:string
          id            = xs:ID
          name          = xs:NCName
          type          = xs:QName
          {any attributes with non-schema namespace}
          >
          Content: (xs:annotation?, xs:simpleType?)
</xs:attribute>
```

May be included in: xs:schema

Description

All the attributes defined at the top level of a schema (i.e., xs:attribute, which is included directly under the xs:schema document element) are considered globally defined.

Globally defined attributes have a global scope: they can be referenced through their qualified name everywhere in the schema in which they are defined as well as in any schema that imports or includes this schema.

Attributes are identified by their qualified name, but the local name is expected in the name attribute.

The definition is done by assigning a simple datatype to the element. This assignment can be done either by reference, using the type attribute to refer to a simple datatype by its qualified name, or "inline," by embedding the definition of the simple type (xs:simpleType element) within the xs:attribute element.

Restrictions

When a target namespace is defined, global attributes must be defined as qualified, i.e., they must be prefixed in the instance documents. Since most of the XML vocabularies do not prefix attributes except when they are "foreign attributes" immersed in elements from other namespaces, this means that global attributes are seldom used when a target namespace is defined. To work around this restriction, attribute groups (xs:attributeGroup) can be used to embed definitions of unqualified attributes that need to be included within multiple complex type definitions.

The identification of the global attributes by their qualified names makes it impossible to globally define multiple attributes having the same qualified name. When a schema must include multiple definitions of attributes that have the same qualified names (and different datatypes), all the definitions (except one) must be locally declared. In this case, it is possible to use simple types or attribute groups instead of global attributes to define reusable content models.

All the globally defined attributes must be qualified if a target namespace is defined for the schema—they must all belong to the target namespace. When no target namespace is defined, all the attributes that are globally or locally defined must be unqualified.

Example

```
<xs:schema xmlns:xs="http://www.w3.org/2001/XMLSchema">
  <xs:attribute name="id" type="xs:ID"/>
  <xs:attribute name="available" type="xs:boolean"/>
  <xs:attribute name="lang" type="xs:language"/>
  .../...
</xs:schema>
```

Attributes

default

> Default value. When specified, an attribute is added by the schema processor (if it is missing from the instance document) and it is given this value. The `default` and `fixed` attributes are mutually exclusive.

fixed

> When specified, the value of the attribute is fixed and must be equal to the value specified here. The `default` and `fixed` attributes are mutually exclusive.

id

> W3C XML Schema's element ID.

name

> Local name of the attribute (without namespace prefix).

type

> Qualified name of a simple type of the attribute (must be omitted when a simple type definition is embedded).

---

xs:attribute (reference or local definition)

Reference to a global attribute definition or local definition (local definitions cannot be referenced).

```
<xs:attribute
          default        = xs:string
          fixed          = xs:string
          form           = ( "qualified" | "unqualified" )
          id             = xs:ID
          name           = xs:NCName
          ref            = xs:QName
          type           = xs:QName
          use            = ( "prohibited" | "optional" | "required" ) : "optional"
          {any attributes with non-schema namespace}
          >
```

```
            Content: ((xs:annotation?), (xs:simpleType?))
</xs:attribute>
```

May be included in: xs:attributeGroup (global definition), xs:complexType (local definition), xs:complexType (global definition), xs:extension (complex content), xs:extension (simple content), xs:restriction (complex content), xs:restriction (simple content)

Description

This element serves two different purposes and has two different content models for these two purposes: it can either be a reference to a globally defined attribute or it can be a local attribute definition. These options are mutually exclusive.

When used as a reference to an attribute, the `ref` attribute must contain the qualified name of the attribute (with its namespace prefix).

When used as a local definition, the definition is done by assigning a simple datatype to the attribute. This assignment can be done either by reference, using the `type` attribute to refer to a simple datatype by its qualified name, or inline, by embedding the definition of the simple type (`xs:simpleType` element) within the `xs:attribute` element.

Restrictions

Locally defined attributes cannot be referenced.

Example

```
<xs:complexType>
  <xs:simpleContent>
    <xs:extension base="xs:string">
      <xs:attribute ref="lang"/>
    </xs:extension>
  </xs:simpleContent>
</xs:complexType>
              .../...


<xs:simpleContent>
  <xs:extension base="xs:string">
    <xs:attribute name="lang" type="xs:language"/>
  </xs:extension>
</xs:simpleContent>
```

Attributes

default
> Default value. When specified, an attribute is added by the schema processor, if missing from the instance document, and is given this value. The `default` and `fixed` attributes are mutually exclusive.

fixed
> When specified, the value of the attribute is fixed and must be equal to the value specified here. The `default` and `fixed` attributes are mutually exclusive.

form

 Specifies if the attribute is qualified (i.e., must have a namespace prefix in the instance document) or not. The default value for this attribute is specified by the `attributeFormDefault` attribute of the `xs:schema` document element—local definition only.

id

 W3C XML Schema's element ID.

name

 Local name (without namespace prefix)—local definition only.

ref

 Qualified name of a globally defined attribute—reference only.

type

 Qualified name of a simple datatype—definition only.

use

 Possible usage of the attribute. Marking an attribute "prohibited" is useful to exclude attributes during derivations by restriction.

---

xs:attributeGroup (global definition)   Global attributes group declaration that can be referenced within the same schema by other schemas.

```
<xs:attributeGroup
        id              = xs:ID
        name            = xs:NCName
        {any attributes with non-schema namespace}
        >
        Content: (xs:annotation?, ((xs:attribute | xs:attributeGroup)*,
                    xs:anyAttribute?))
</xs:attributeGroup>
```

May be included in: xs:redefine, xs:schema

Description

Attribute groups are global containers that embed groups of attributes. They can be used to manipulate groups of several attributes often used together, but also to provide global access to attributes that cannot be globally defined because they are unqualified or because several definitions cohabit in a single schema (see the example).

Attribute references or local definitions, attribute wildcards, and attribute group references may be included within attribute group definitions.

Attribute groups may be redefined through `xs:redefine` elements.

Restrictions

None.

Example

```
<xs:attributeGroup name="bookAttributes">
  <xs:attribute name="id" type="xs:ID"/>
```

```
    <xs:attribute name="available" type="xs:boolean"/>
  </xs:attributeGroup>
```

Attributes

id
> W3C XML Schema's element ID.

name
> Name of the attribute group.

xs:attributeGroup (reference)

Reference to a global attributes group declaration.

```
<xs:attributeGroup
        id              = xs:ID
        ref             = xs:QName
        {any attributes with non-schema namespace}
        >
        Content: (xs:annotation?)
</xs:attributeGroup>
```

May be included in: xs:attributeGroup (global definition), xs:complexType (local definition), xs:complexType (global definition), xs:extension (complex content), xs:extension (simple content), xs:restriction (complex content), xs:restriction (simple content)

Description

Any non-top-level occurrence of xs:attribute is a reference to an attribute group that acts like a replacement of the group by the attributes (or attribute group references) embedded in the group.

Restrictions

None.

Example

```
<xs:element name="book">
  <xs:complexType>
    <xs:sequence>
      <xs:element ref="isbn"/>
      <xs:element ref="title"/>
      <xs:element ref="author" minOccurs="0" maxOccurs="unbounded"/>
      <xs:element ref="character" minOccurs="0"
        maxOccurs="unbounded"/>
    </xs:sequence>
    <xs:attributeGroup ref="bookAttributes"/>
  </xs:complexType>
</xs:element>
```

Attributes

id
> W3C XML Schema's element ID.

ref

> Qualified name of the attribute group to reference.

---

xs:choice (outside a group) Compositor to define group of mutually exclusive elements or compositors.

```
<xs:choice
        id                   = xs:ID
        maxOccurs            = ( xs:nonNegativeInteger | "unbounded" ) : "1"
        minOccurs            = xs:nonNegativeInteger : "1"
        {any attributes with non-schema namespace}
        >
        Content: (xs:annotation?, (xs:element | xs:group | xs:choice |
                xs:sequence | xs:any)
        )*)
</xs:choice>
```

May be included in: xs:choice (outside a group), xs:choice (within a group), xs:complexType (local definition), xs:complexType (global definition), xs:extension (complex content), xs:restriction (complex content), xs:sequence (within a group), xs:sequence (outside a group)

Description

xs:choice is a compositor that defines a group of mutually exclusive particles. Only one can be found in the instance document per occurrence of the xs:choice compositor. The number of occurrences of the compositor itself is controlled by its minOccurs and maxOccurs attributes, while the number of occurrences of each particle within a single occurrence of xs:choice can be controlled by the minOccurs and maxOccurs attributes of the particles.

In addition to situations where simple choices are expressed (element "a" or "b" can be accepted here), xs:choice is often used to work around the limitations of xs:all and to define content models where an unlimited number of elements can be found in any order (see the example).

When the particle used in a xs:choice compositor is an element, a similar effect may be achieved using substitution groups.

Restrictions

The xs:choice compositor may cause violations of the Unique Particle Attribution and Consistent Declaration rules.

Example

```
<xs:choice>
  <!-- Allows either "name" or the sequence "first-name",
  "middle-name"and"last-name". -->
  <xs:element ref="name"/>
  <xs:sequence>
    <xs:element ref="first-name"/>
    <xs:element ref="middle-name" minOccurs="0"/>
    <xs:element ref="last-name"/>
  </xs:sequence>
</xs:choice>
```

Attributes

id

> W3C XML Schema's element ID.

maxOccurs

> Maximum number of occurrences of the choice compositor.

minOccurs

> Minimum number of occurrences of the choice compositor.

---

xs:choice (within a group)   Compositor to define group of mutually exclusive elements or compositors. The number of occurrences cannot be defined when xs:choice is used within a group.

```
<xs:choice
        id          = xs:ID
        {any attributes with non-schema namespace}
        >
        Content: (xs:annotation?, (xs:element | xs:group | xs:choice |
              xs:sequence | xs:any)
        )*)
</xs:choice>
```

May be included in: xs:group (definition)

Description

When embedded in a group definition, the xs:choice compositor has the same function as other contexts, except that the number of its occurrences is defined in the xs:group reference instead of by the minOccurs and maxOccurs attributes of the xs:choice compositor.

Restrictions

The minOccurs and maxOccurs attributes that are allowed in other contexts are forbidden.

Example

```
<xs:group name="author-or-character">
  <xs:choice>
    <xs:element ref="author"/>
    <xs:element ref="character"/>
  </xs:choice>
</xs:group>
```

Attributes

id

> W3C XML Schema's element ID.

---

xs:complexContent   Definition of a complex content by derivation of a complex type.

```
<xs:complexContent
        id          = xs:ID
        mixed       = xs:boolean
```

```
            {any attributes with non-schema namespace}
            >
            Content: ((xs:annotation?), (xs:restriction | xs:extension))
</xs:complexContent>
```

May be included in: xs:complexType (local definition), xs:complexType (global definition)

Description

This element allows you to define a complex content model by derivation of a complex type. It is not a component by itself (complex contents are not named), but rather the declaration of an intention to define a complex content model by derivation.

The derivation method is not defined by the xs:complexContent element itself, but by the choice of its child element (xs:restriction for a derivation by restriction, or xs:extension for a derivation by extension).

This element can be used to define if the content model is mixed or not—but this information can also be defined in the xs:complexType parent element, which has also a mixed attribute.

The mixed nature of the content model defined by xs:complexContent attribute is dependent on the derivation method and on the base type. If the base type is mixed, it can be restricted to become elements only; otherwise the mixed nature of the base type cannot be changed.

Restrictions

A base type whose elements cannot be extended to be mixed.

Example

```
<xs:element name="author">
  <xs:complexType>
    <xs:complexContent>
      <xs:extension base="basePerson">
        <xs:sequence>
          <xs:element ref="dead" minOccurs="0"/>
        </xs:sequence>
      </xs:extension>
    </xs:complexContent>
  </xs:complexType>
</xs:element>
```

Attributes

id
>   W3C XML Schema's element ID.

mixed
>   When set to true, the content model is mixed; when set to false, the content model is "element only"; when not set, the content model is determined by the mixed attribute of the parent xs:complexType element.

xs:complexType (global definition)   Global definition of a complex type that can be referenced within the same schema by other schemas.

```
<xs:complexType
        abstract     = xs:boolean : "false"
        block        = ( "#all" | list of ( "extension" | "restriction" ) )
        final        = ( "#all" | list of ( "extension" | "restriction" ) )
        id           = xs:ID
        mixed        = xs:boolean : "false"
        name         = xs:NCName
        {any attributes with non-schema namespace}
        >
        Content: (xs:annotation?, (xs:simpleContent | xs:complexContent | (,
                (xs:group | xs:all | xs:choice | xs:sequence)?,
                ((xs:attribute | xs:attributeGroup)*, xs:anyAttribute?
        ?))))
</xs:complexType>
```

May be included in: xs:redefine, xs:schema

Description

This component is used to create global complex types as direct descriptions of their content model, or by derivation from simple types or other complex types. The creation of a new complex type is done by a compositor (xs:sequence, xs:choice, or xs:all) that describes the child elements, followed by a list of attributes (or attribute groups or attribute wildcards). The derivation of a complex type through existing simple or complex types is done by including an xs:simpleContent (for simple contents) or an xs:complexContent (for complex contents) element. In both cases, when the content is not simple, the mixed attribute defines if the content model is mixed (i.e., allows both text and element nodes) or not.

Several controls are provided through attributes. Complex types can be declared "abstract," their substitution can be "blocked," and they can be "final" for derivation.

Restrictions

Constraints about keys (xs:key, xs:unique, and xs:keyref) cannot be defined at this level but need to be defined in the xs:element element. This means that, while in many cases referencing a global element definition or a global complex type definition can be considered as equivalent to define modular content models, complex types are no longer an option when these constraints need to be included in the content model.

Example

```
<xs:complexType name="title">
  <xs:simpleContent>
    <xs:extension base="tokenWithLang">
      <xs:attribute name="note" type="xs:token"/>
    </xs:extension>
  </xs:simpleContent>
</xs:complexType>
```

Attributes

abstract
> When set to true, this complex type cannot be used directly in the instance documents and needs to be substituted using a xsi:type attribute.

block
> Controls whether a substitution (either through a xsi:type or substitution groups) can be performed to a complex type, which is an extension or a restriction of the current complex type. This attribute can only block such substitutions (it cannot "unblock" them), which can also be blocked in the element definition. The default value is defined by the blockDefault attribute of xs:schema.

final
> Controls whether the complex type can be further derived by extension or restriction to create new complex types.

id
> W3C XML Schema's element ID.

mixed
> Defines if the content model will be mixed.

name
> Name of the complex type.

xs:complexType (local definition)

Complex type local definition
(local definitions cannot be referenced).

```
<xs:complexType
        id              = xs:ID
        mixed           = xs:boolean : "false"
        {any attributes with non-schema namespace}
        >
        Content: (xs:annotation?, (xs:simpleContent | xs:complexContent | (,
                (xs:group | xs:all | xs:choice | xs:sequence)?,
                ((xs:attribute | xs:attributeGroup)*, xs:anyAttribute?
        ?))))
</xs:complexType>
```

May be included in: xs:element (within xs:all), xs:element (reference or local definition), xs:element (global definition)

Description

Complex type definition can be created several ways. It can be done by derivation using an xs:simpleContent (for simple content models) or an xs:complexContent (for simple content model) element, or it can be described, using xs:sequence (for an ordered sequence of elements), an xs:choice (for an alternative beyond several elements), xs:all (for a unordered list of elements) or xs:group (to reference a group of elements), and xs:attribute, xs:attributeGroup, and xs:anyAttribute to define the list of its attributes.

Complex types describe all the constraints on the element, character, and attribute nodes that may be included within an element except those described by xs:unique, xs:key, and xs:keyref, which are defined directly under the xs:element element definitions.

Restrictions

Constraints defined by xs:unique, xs:key, and xs:keyref are not defined within complex types but directly under the xs:element element definitions.

Local definitions can neither be derived (by restriction or extension) nor substituted. In addition, the derivation by restriction of complex types and the redefinition by restriction of element groups, including elements defined with local complex type definitions, is limited since derivations by restriction need to redefine the elements that are kept using explicit derivations.

Unlike other components (xs:element, xs:attribute, xs:group, and xs:attributeGroup), local xs:complexType components cannot be used to reference global complex types. Reference to complex types is done through xs:element type attributes and xs:restriction and xs:extension base attributes.

Example

```
<xs:element name="title">
  <xs:complexType>
    <xs:simpleContent>
      <xs:extension base="xs:string">
        <xs:attribute ref="lang"/>
      </xs:extension>
    </xs:simpleContent>
  </xs:complexType>
</xs:element>
```

Attributes

id
> W3C XML Schema's element ID.

mixed
> Defines if the content type will be mixed.

xs:documentation   Human-targeted documentation.

```
<xs:documentation
        source          = xs:anyURI
        xml:lang        = xml:lang
        >
        Content: ({any})*
</xs:documentation>
```

May be included in: xs:annotation

Description

xs:documentation is a container for human-readable documentation in plain text or structured formats. Its content model is open and can accept any element from any namespace (with a lax validation only—W3C XML Schema elements included here must be valid). xs:documentation can be used to include any kind of information.

Its content is similar to xs:appinfo (which is reserved for application processable information), except that it has xml:lang attribute; this is allowed in xs:documentation, but
forbidden for xs:appinfo).

Restrictions

Foreign attributes cannot be included in xs:documentation. The source attribute is also
underspecified in the Recommendation. This could lead to interoperability issues between
applications that rely on xs:documentation.

Example

```
<xs:element name="author" type="author">
  <xs:annotation>
    <xs:documentation xml:lang="en">
      The author of a book.
    </xs:documentation>
    <xs:documentation xml:lang="fr">
      Designe l'auteur d'un livre.
    </xs:documentation>
  </xs:annotation>
</xs:element>
```

Attributes

source
> Can be used to provide a link to the source of the information when a snippet is
> included, or it can be used as a semantic attribute to qualify the type of information
> included.

xml:lang
> Language used for the documentation.

xs:element (global definition)

Global element definition that can be referenced
within the same schema by other schemas.

```
<xs:element
          abstract           = xs:boolean : "false"
          block              = ( "#all" | list of ( "extension" | "restriction" |
                                 "substitution" ) )
          default            = xs:string
          final              = ( "#all" | list of ( "extension" | "restriction" ) )
          fixed              = xs:string
          id                 = xs:ID
          name               = xs:NCName
          nillable           = xs:boolean : "false"
          substitutionGroup  = xs:QName
          type               = xs:QName
          {any attributes with non-schema namespace}
          >
          Content: (xs:annotation?, (xs:simpleType | xs:complexType)?, (xs:unique |
                   xs:key | xs:keyref)*)
</xs:element>
```

May be included in: xs:schema

Description

All the elements defined at the top level of a schema (i.e., xs:element, which is included directly under the xs:schema document element) are considered globally defined.

Globally defined elements have a global scope: they can be referenced through their qualified name everywhere in the schema in which they are defined, as well as in any schema that imports or includes this schema. They can also be used as document elements in instance documents.

Elements are identified by their qualified name, but the local name is expected in the name attribute. The type definition is performed by assigning a simple or complex datatype to the element.

This assignment can be done either by reference, using the type attribute to refer to a simple or complex datatype by its qualified name, or inline, by embedding the definition of the simple (xs:simpleType) element or the complex (xs:complexType) element that is within the xs:element element.

A default value may be defined using the default attribute, but note that the semantics of default values for elements are different than those of the default values for attributes. An element is not created if it is absent from the instance document; the default value is applied only if the element is present and empty.

Several control attributes are included in element definitions (see the attributes abstract, blocked, final, fixed, and nillable) .

Element definitions are also the place in which substitution groups are defined using the substitutionGroup attribute to refer to the head of the substitution group. Any global element that is not final may be chosen as the head of a substitution group. Any reference to the head of a substitution group may be replaced in the instance documents by any of the members of the substitution group (assuming these substitutions have not been blocked through block attributes). The relation is transitive, and if the head of a substitution "A" is a member of another substitution group "B," the members of "A" are also considered members of "B."

Restrictions

There is no feature that allows definition of global elements that cannot be used as document elements. When this is needed, the workaround is to define all the elements, save one, and use simple and complex types or element groups instead of global elements to define reusable content models, and then reference these types from a single globally-defined element.

The identification of the global elements by their qualified names makes it impossible to globally define multiple elements that have the same qualified name. When a schema must include multiple definitions of elements that have the same qualified name (and different datatypes), all the definitions except one must be locally declared. It is possible to use simple and complex types or element groups instead of global elements to define reusable content models.

All globally defined elements must be qualified if a target namespace has been defined for the schema; they must all belong to the target namespace. When no target namespace is defined, all the elements that are globally or locally defined must be unqualified.

The default and fixed values are defined in attributes and, therefore, can only apply to simple type elements.

Elements cannot be directly redefined. To redefine an element, one can either include it in a group and redefine the group, or use a global complex type to define the element and redefine the complex type.

Example

```
<xs:element name="name" type="xs:string"/>
```

Attributes

abstract
> Controls whether the element may be used directly in instance documents. When set to true, the element may still be used to define content models, but it must be substituted through a substitution group in the instance document.

block
> Controls whether the element can be subject to a type or substitution group substitution. #all blocks any substitution, substitution blocks any substitution through substitution groups, and extension and restriction block any substitution (both through xsi:type and substitution groups) by elements or types, derived respectively by extension or restriction from the type of the element. Its default value is defined by the blockDefault attribute of the parent xs:schema.

default
> Default value of the element. Defined in an attribute, element default values must be simple contents. Also note that default values apply only to elements that are present in the document and empty. The fixed and default attributes are mutually exclusive.

final
> Controls whether the element can be used as the head of a substitution group for elements whose types are derived by extension or restriction from the type of the element. Its default value is defined by the finalDefault attribute of the parent xs:schema.

fixed
> A simple content element may be fixed to a specific value using this attribute. This value is also used as a default value, and if the element is empty, it is supplied to the application. The fixed and default attributes are mutually exclusive.

id
> W3C XML Schema's element ID.

name
> Local name of the element (without namespace prefix).

nillable
> When this attribute is set to true, the element can be declared as nil using an xsi:nil attribute in the instance documents.

substitutionGroup
> Qualified name of the head of the substitution group to which this element belongs.

type

Qualified name of a simple or complex type (must be omitted when a simple or complex type definition is embedded).

---

xs:element (within xs:all)

Reference to a global element declaration or local definition (local definitions cannot be referenced). The number of occurrences can only be zero or one when xs:element is used within xs:all..

Synopsis

```
<xs:element
        block        = ( "#all" | list of ( "extension" | "restriction" |
                         "substitution" ) )
        default      = xs:string
        fixed        = xs:string
        form         = ( "qualified" | "unqualified" )
        id           = xs:ID
        maxOccurs    = ( "0" | "1" ) : "1"
        minOccurs    = ( "0" | "1" ) : "1"
        name         = xs:NCName
        nillable     = xs:boolean : "false"
        ref          = xs:QName
        type         = xs:QName
        {any attributes with non-schema namespace}
        >
        Content: (xs:annotation?, (xs:simpleType | xs:complexType)?, (xs:unique |
                  xs:key | xs:keyref)*)
</xs:element>
```

May be included in: xs:all (outside a group), xs:all (within a group)

Description

This element serves two different purposes and has two different content models for these purposes: it can either be a reference to a globally defined element or to a local element definition. These options are mutually exclusive.

When used as a reference to an element, the ref attribute must contain the qualified name of the element (with its namespace prefix).

When used as a local definition, the definition is done by assigning a simple or complex datatype to the element. This assignment can be done either by reference, using the type attribute to refer to a simple or complex datatype by its qualified name, or inline, by embedding the definition of the simple (xs:simpleType) element or complex (xs:complexType) element within the xs:element element.

Restrictions

Local element definitions or references cannot have a number of occurrences greater than one.

The default and fixed values are defined in attributes and, therefore, can only apply to simple type elements.

The fact that W3C XML Schema cannot describe the exclusive combinations of the attributes and elements of xs:element, which can be summarized as:

```
ref attribute xor name attribute, type attribute xor xs:simpleType element, xor
xs:complexType element
```

is an example that shows some of the restrictions of the language.

Example

```
<xs:all>
  <xs:element name="first" type="string32" minOccurs="0"/>
  <xs:element name="middle" type="string32" minOccurs="0"/>
  <xs:element name="last" type="string32"/>
</xs:all>
```

Attributes

block
> Controls whether the element can be subject to a type or substitution group substitution. #all blocks any substitution, substitution blocks any substitution through substitution groups, and extension and restriction block any substitution (both through xsi:type and substitution groups) by elements or types, derived respectively by extension or restriction from the type of the element. Its default value is defined by the blockDefault attribute of the parent xs:schema.

default
> Default value of the element. Defined in an attribute, element default values must be simple contents. Also note that default values apply only to elements that are present in the document and empty. The fixed and default attributes are mutually exclusive.

fixed
> A simple content element may be fixed to a specific value using this attribute. This value is also used as a default value, and if the element is empty, it is supplied to the application. The fixed and default attributes are mutually exclusive.

form
> Specifies whether the element must be qualified (i.e., belong to a namespace) in the instance documents or not. The default value of this attribute is determined by the xs:schema elementFormDefault attribute.

id
> W3C XML Schema's element ID.

maxOccurs
> Maximum number of occurrences of the element. Can take only the values 0 or 1 within a xs:all compositor.

minOccurs
> Minimum number of occurrences of the element. Can take only the values 0 or 1 within a xs:all compositor.

name
> Name of the element (mutually exclusive with the ref attribute).

nillable
> When this attribute is set to true, the element can be declared as nil using an xsi:nil attribute in the instance documents.

ref
>   Reference to a global element definition (mutually exclusive with the `name`, `block`, and type attributes and any embedded type definition.

type
>   Simple or complex type of the element (mutually exclusive with the `ref` attribute and any embedded type definition).

xs:element (reference or local definition)

Reference to a global element declaration or local definition (local definitions cannot be referenced).

```
<xs:element
        block         = ( "#all" | list of ( "extension" | "restriction" |
                            "substitution" ) )
        default       = xs:string
        fixed         = xs:string
        form          = ( "qualified" | "unqualified" )
        id            = xs:ID
        maxOccurs     = ( xs:nonNegativeInteger | "unbounded" ) : "1"
        minOccurs     = xs:nonNegativeInteger : "1"
        name          = xs:NCName
        nillable      = xs:boolean : "false"
        ref           = xs:QName
        type          = xs:QName
        {any attributes with non-schema namespace}
        >
        Content: (xs:annotation?, (xs:simpleType | xs:complexType)?, (xs:unique |
                    xs:key | xs:keyref)*)
</xs:element>
```

May be included in: xs:choice (outside a group), xs:choice (within a group), xs:sequence (within a group), xs:sequence (outside a group)

Description

This element serves two different purposes and has two different content models for these purposes: it can either be a reference to a globally defined element or to a local element definition. These options are mutually exclusive.

When used as a reference to an element, the `ref` attribute must contain the qualified name of the element (with its namespace prefix).

When used as a local definition, the definition is done by assigning a simple or complex datatype to the element. This assignment can be done either by reference, using the `type` attribute to refer to a simple or complex datatype by its qualified name, or inline, by embedding the definition of the simple (`xs:simpleType`) element or complex (`xs:complexType`) element within the `xs:element` element.

In all cases, the number of occurrences can be constrained using the `minOccurs` and `maxOccurs` attributes, whose default value is 1. The `maxOccurs` attribute can take the value unbounded, to define that an element may appear as many times as the author of the document wishes.

Restrictions

The default and fixed values are defined in attributes and, therefore, can only apply to simple type elements.

The fact that W3C XML Schema cannot describe the exclusive combinations of the attributes and elements of xs:element which could be summarized as:

```
ref attribute xor name attribute, type attribute xor xs:simpleType element, xor
xs:complexType element
```

is an example that shows some of the restrictions of the language.

Example

```
<xs:sequence>
  <xs:element name="book" maxOccurs="unbounded">
    <xs:complexType>
      <xs:sequence>
        <xs:element ref="isbn"/>
        <xs:element ref="title"/>
        <xs:element ref="author" minOccurs="0"
          maxOccurs="unbounded"/>
        <xs:element ref="character" minOccurs="0"
          maxOccurs="unbounded"/>
      </xs:sequence>
      <xs:attribute ref="id"/>
      <xs:attribute ref="available"/>
    </xs:complexType>
  </xs:element>
</xs:sequence>
```

Attributes

block

Controls whether the element can be subject to a type or substitution group substitution. #all blocks any substitution, substitution blocks any substitution through substitution groups, and extension and restriction block any substitution (both through xsi:type and substitution groups) by elements or types, derived respectively by extension or restriction from the type of the element. Its default value is defined by the blockDefault attribute of the parent xs:schema.

default

Default value of the element. Defined in an attribute, element default values must be simple contents. Also note that default values apply only to elements that are present in the document and empty. The fixed and default attributes are mutually exclusive.

fixed

A simple content element may be fixed to a specific value using this attribute. This value is also used as a default value, and if the element is empty, it is supplied to the application. The fixed and default attributes are mutually exclusive.

form

Defines if the element is "qualified" (i.e., belongs to the target namespace) or "unqualified" (i.e., doesn't belong to any namespace)—to be used only for local element definitions.

id
> W3C XML Schema's element ID.

maxOccurs
> Maximum number of occurrences ("unbounded" means "unlimited").

minOccurs
> Minimum number of occurrences.

name
> Local name (without namespace prefix)—to be use only for local element definitions.

nillable
> When this attribute is set to true, the element can be declared as nil using an xsi:nil attribute in the instance documents.

ref
> Reference to a global element—to be used only for references.

type
> Reference to a simple or complex type—to be used only for local element definitions.

---

xs:enumeration Facet to restrict a datatype to a finite set of values.

```
<xs:enumeration
        id              = xs:ID
        value           = anySimpleType
        {any attributes with non-schema namespace}
        >
        Content: (xs:annotation?)
</xs:enumeration>
```

May be included in: xs:restriction (simple type), xs:restriction (simple content)
May be used as facet for: xs:anyURI, xs:base64Binary, xs:byte, xs:date, xs:dateTime, xs:decimal, xs:double, xs:duration, xs:ENTITIES, xs:ENTITY, xs:float, xs:gDay, xs:gMonth, xs:gMonthDay, xs:gYear, xs:gYearMonth, xs:hexBinary, xs:ID, xs:IDREF, xs:IDREFS, xs:int, xs:integer, xs:language, xs:long, xs:Name, xs:NCName, xs:negativeInteger, xs:NMTOKEN, xs:NMTOKENS, xs:nonNegativeInteger, xs:nonPositiveInteger, xs:normalizedString, xs:NOTATION, xs:positiveInteger, xs:QName, xs:short, xs:string, xs:time, xs:token, xs:unsignedByte, xs:unsignedInt, xs:unsignedLong, xs:unsignedShort

Description

xs:enumeration is a facet that allows definition of a list of possible values for the value space of a datatype by enumerating all these values in separated xs:enumeration elements in a single restriction step (i.e., under a single rs:restriction parent element). This is one of the two facets (with xs:pattern) that are available for all the datatypes (atomic, lists, or unions), but unlike xs:pattern, xs:enumeration is not available for xs:boolean.

Restrictions

The values of the xs:enumeration facets must belong to the value space of the base datatype. When the base datatype is already restricted by enumeration, the new enumeration values must be a subset of the base datatype enumerations (even though they may have different lexical representations that correspond to the same logical values).

This facet cannot be fixed (i.e., it remains available in all the derived types).

This facet is not available for xs:boolean.

Example

```
<xs:simpleType name="schemaRecommendations">
  <xs:restriction base="xs:anyURI">
    <xs:enumeration value="http://www.w3.org/TR/xmlschema-0/"/>
    <xs:enumeration value="http://www.w3.org/TR/xmlschema-1/"/>
    <xs:enumeration value="http://www.w3.org/TR/xmlschema-2/"/>
  </xs:restriction>
</xs:simpleType>
```

Attributes

id
>   W3C XML Schema's element ID.

value
>   Value to be added to the list of possible values for this datatype.

xs:extension (simple content)   Extension of a simple content model.

```
<xs:extension
         base          = xs:QName
         id          = xs:ID
         {any attributes with non-schema namespace}
         >
         Content: (xs:annotation?, ((xs:attribute | xs:attributeGroup)*,
                  xs:anyAttribute?))
</xs:extension>
```

May be included in: xs:simpleContent

Description

This element is used to extend either a simple type or a simple content complex type into a simple content complex type (i.e., the content model of an element with a text nodes and some attributes). The type to extend is specified in the base attribute, and the list of the attributes to add to the content model is given as xs:attributes, xs:attributeGroup, and xs:anyAttribute embedded in the xs:extension element.

Such a derivation by extension of a simple type is the only way to create a complex type simple content content model.

Restrictions

The definition of the base type cannot be embedded in the xs:extension element, and the base type needs to be a global type.

The same element name (xs:extension) is used by W3C XML Schema for the extension of simple content and complex content complex types with a different content model.

Example

```
<xs:element name="title">
  <xs:complexType>
    <xs:simpleContent>
      <xs:extension base="string255">
        <xs:attribute ref="lang"/>
      </xs:extension>
    </xs:simpleContent>
  </xs:complexType>
</xs:element>
```

Attributes

base
> Qualified name of the base type (simple type or simple content complex type).

id
> W3C XML Schema's element ID.

xs:extension (complex content)

Extension of a complex content model.

```
<xs:extension
          base       = xs:QName
          id         = xs:ID
          {any attributes with non-schema namespace}
          >
          Content: ((xs:annotation?), (, (xs:group | xs:all | xs:choice |
                    xs:sequence)?, ((xs:attribute | xs:attributeGroup)*,
                    xs:anyAttribute?)))
</xs:extension>
```

May be included in: xs:complexContent

Description

Extension of a complex (or mixed) content complex type. This derivation method can be applied to another complex content complex base type, and allows the addition of elements and attributes to this base type. The additional elements are added after the compositor used in the base type.

When new elements are added during a derivation by extension, the resulting content model is equivalent to creating a sequence that contains the compositor used to define the base type and the one included in the xs:extension element.

Restrictions

Complex types that use a xs:all compositor cannot be used as base types for derivations by extension, except when those extensions add only attributes.

New elements added to base types using a xs:choice compositor are added in sequence after the xs:choice, rather than as new choices.

Example

```
<xs:element name="character">
  <xs:complexType>
```

```
    <xs:complexContent>
      <xs:extension base="basePerson">
        <xs:sequence>
          <xs:element ref="qualification"/>
        </xs:sequence>
      </xs:extension>
    </xs:complexContent>
  </xs:complexType>
</xs:element>
```

Attributes

base

> Qualified name of the base type.

id

> W3C XML Schema's element ID.

xs:field

Definition of the field to use for a uniqueness constraint.

```
<xs:field
        id              = xs:ID
        xpath           = xs:token
        {any attributes with non-schema namespace}
        >
        Content: (xs:annotation?)
</xs:field>
```

May be included in: xs:key, xs:keyref, xs:unique

Description

xs:field is used to define the location of the fields on which a uniqueness constraint or reference will be checked.

The fields are elements or attributes that are identified by relative XPath expressions (i.e., xpath attributes) evaluated against the nodes selected by the xs:selector element.

Concatenated keys can be expressed defining multiple fields under a xs:unique, xs:key, or xs:keyref element.

Restrictions

The xpath attribute uses a simple subset of XPath 1.0. The motivation of the W3C XML Schema Working Group for defining this subset is to simplify the work of the implementers of schema processors, and also to define a subset that constraints the path to stay within the scope of the current element.

This subset is restricted to using only the child, attribute, self, and descendant or self XPath axes through their abbreviated syntaxes without including any test in any of the XPath location steps, and without using any XPath functions. It is identical to the subset defined for xs:selector, except that attributes are allowed in xs:field and forbidden in xs:selector.

The formal extended BNF given in the W3C Recommendation is as follows:

```
Field ::= Path ( '|' Path )* Path ::= ('.//')? ( Step '/' )* ( Step | '@' NameTest )
Step ::= '.' | NameTest NameTest ::= QName | '*' | NCName ':' '*'
```

When concatenated keys are defined, the node sets identified by each field must have a single occurrence per iteration of locator. This means that on structures such as:

```
<sect num="1">
  <sub-sect num="1"> Sub section 1.1 </sub-sect>
  <sub-sect num="2"> Sub section 1.2 </sub-sect>
</sect>
<sect num="1">
  <sub-sect num="3"> Sub section 1.3 </sub-sect>
  <sub-sect num="4"> Sub section 1.4 </sub-sect>
</sect>
```

multilevel concatenated keys over the num attributes of sect and sub-sect cannot be defined with W3C XML Schema. This is because the locator would need to iterate on the sect element, and the num attribute of the sub-sect element then takes several values for each iteration.

Example

```
<xs:element name="library">
  <xs:complexType>
    .../...
  </xs:complexType>
  <xs:unique name="book">
    <xs:selector xpath="book"/>
    <xs:field xpath="isbn"/>
  </xs:unique>
</xs:element>
```

Attributes

id
> W3C XML Schema's element ID.

xpath
> Relative XPath expression identifying the field(s) composing the key, key reference, or unique constraint.

---

xs:fractionDigits
Facet to define the number of fractional digits of a numerical datatype.

```
<xs:fractionDigits
        fixed        = xs:boolean : "false"
        id           = xs:ID
        value        = xs:nonNegativeInteger
        {any attributes with non-schema namespace}
        >
        Content: (xs:annotation?)
</xs:fractionDigits>
```

May be included in: xs:restriction (simple type), xs:restriction (simple content)
May be used as facet for: xs:decimal

Description

xs:fractionDigits defines the maximum number of fractional digits (i.e., digits that are after the decimal point) of an xs:decimal datatype.

This facet constrains the value space, which means that the number of fractional digits is checked after the value is transformed to its canonical form, and the trailing zeros are removed.

Restrictions

Within a restriction step, xs:fractionDigits is dependent on xs:totalDigits, since using inconsistent values leads to datatypes with empty value spaces.

xs:fractionDigits must restrict the value space of its base type, and its value must be smaller than the value of xs:fractionDigits of its base type if defined.

It is possible to use xs:pattern to constrain the number of fractional digits in the lexical space.

Example

```
<xs:simpleType name="fractionDigits">
  <xs:restriction base="xs:decimal">
    <xs:fractionDigits value="2"/>
  </xs:restriction>
</xs:simpleType>
```

Attributes

fixed
> When set to true, the value of the facet cannot be modified during further restrictions.

id
> W3C XML Schema's element ID.

value
> Value of the facet.

---

xs:group (definition)

Global elements group declaration that can be referenced within the same schema by other schemas.

```
<xs:group
        name                = xs:NCName
        >
        Content: (xs:annotation?, (xs:all | xs:choice | xs:sequence))
</xs:group>
```

May be included in: xs:redefine, xs:schema

Description

Groups of elements can be globally defined and used as containers, which can be referenced elsewhere in this schema or in other schemas. These containers, which are almost free of semantics, are very flexible and may be used as building blocks for the definition of local or global complex types.

Being global components, they can also be used to encapsulate element definitions that cannot be made global, such as unqualified elements in a schema with target namespaces, multiple elements with the same name in a schema, elements that should not be used as document elements, or elements that should be redefined through xs:redefine in other schemas.

Element groups can be redefined through xs:redefine; the redefinition can be either a restriction (similar to a complex type derivation by restriction) or an extension. (This is more flexible than a complex type extension since the location where the base group is included in the new group can be chosen, while the new elements are always located after the base type during a derivation by extension.)

Any of the three compositors (xs:all, xs:sequence, or xs:choice) may be used to create an element group.

Restrictions

When a group is created using a xs:all compositor, this group inherits all the restrictions of xs:all. In other words, including a xs:all compositor in a group is not a workaround to avoid the fundamental restrictions of xs:all!

Group definition cannot be recursive.

Example

```
<xs:group name="name">
  <xs:choice>
    <xs:element ref="name"/>
    <xs:sequence>
      <xs:element ref="first-name"/>
      <xs:element ref="middle-name" minOccurs="0"/>
      <xs:element ref="last-name"/>
    </xs:sequence>
  </xs:choice>
</xs:group>
```

Attributes

name
>   Name of the group (unqualified).

---

xs:group (reference)

Reference to a global elements group declaration or local definition (local definitions cannot be referenced).

Synopsis

```
<xs:group
        id          = xs:ID
        maxOccurs              = ( xs:nonNegativeInteger | "unbounded" ) : "1"
        minOccurs              = xs:nonNegativeInteger : "1"
        ref         = xs:QName
        {any attributes with non-schema namespace}
        >
```

```
        Content: (xs:annotation?)
</xs:group>
```

May be included in: xs:choice (outside a group), xs:choice (within a group), xs:complexType (local definition), xs:complexType (global definition), xs:extension (complex content), xs:restriction (complex content), xs:sequence (within a group), xs:sequence (outside a group)

Description

Used in a local context, xs:group is a reference to an element group. The effect is a logical replacement of the group reference by the group's content.

When a group is being redefined (through xs:redefine), a self reference (i.e., a reference to the group being redefined) specifically means "include the original content of the group at this location."

Restrictions

Groups cannot be recursive (i.e., a group cannot be referred to either directly or indirectly within its definition).

Example

```
<xs:element name="author">
  <xs:complexType>
    <xs:sequence>
      <xs:group ref="name"/>
      <xs:element ref="born"/>
      <xs:element ref="dead" minOccurs="0"/>
    </xs:sequence>
    <xs:attribute ref="id"/>
  </xs:complexType>
</xs:element>
```

Attributes

id
    W3C XML Schema's element ID.

maxOccurs
    Maximum number of occurrences of the group.

minOccurs
    Minimum number of occurrences of the group.

ref
    Qualified name of the group to include.

xs:import

Import of a W3C XML Schema for another namespace.

```
<xs:import
        id              = xs:ID
        namespace       = xs:anyURI
        schemaLocation  = xs:anyURI
        {any attributes with non-schema namespace}
        >
```

```
        Content: (xs:annotation?)
</xs:import>
```

May be included in: xs:schema

Description

xs:import identifies the location at which a W3C XML Schema validator may find the definition corresponding to namespaces other than the target namespace of the current schema.

All the global definitions (elements, attributes, element and attribute groups, simple and complex types) and unique and key constraints of the imported schemas can be referenced using a namespace prefix defined for the corresponding namespace URI.

The schema locations indicated in xs:import elements are only hints provided to the schema validators and may be omitted. In this case, the Recommendation states that "the schema author is leaving the identification of that schema to the instance, application or user, via the mechanisms described in Layer 3: Schema Document Access and Web-interoperability."

xs:import may also be used to import components with no target namespaces into schemas with target namespaces.

Restrictions

xs:import must not be used to import component definitions from the target namespace since two other elements are available for this purpose (see the sections xs:include and xs:redefine).

Only global component definitions of the imported schemas can be referenced (local definitions can never be referenced).

The rules of scoping described for the xs:keyref element also apply to references between constraints for elements that belong to different namespaces (the root element of the keyref constraint must be an ancestor or self element of the root element for the unique or key constraint).

Example

```
<xs:schema targetNamespace="http://dyomedea.com/ns/library"
  elementFormDefault="qualified" attributeFormDefault="unqualified"
  xmlns:xs="http://www.w3.org/2001/XMLSchema"
  xmlns:ppl="http://dyomedea.com/ns/people"
  xmlns:lib="http://dyomedea.com/ns/library">
<xs:import namespace="http://dyomedea.com/ns/people"
  schemaLocation="simple-2-ns-ppl.xsd"/>
<xs:element name="library">
  <xs:complexType>
    <xs:sequence>
      <xs:element name="book" type="lib:bookType"/>
    </xs:sequence>
  </xs:complexType>
</xs:element>
<xs:complexType name="bookType">
  <xs:sequence>
```

```
            <xs:element name="isbn" type="xs:NMTOKEN"/>
            <xs:element name="title" type="xs:string"/>
            <xs:element name="authors">
              <xs:complexType>
                <xs:sequence>
                  <xs:element ref="ppl:person"/>
                </xs:sequence>
              </xs:complexType>
            </xs:element>
            <xs:element name="characters">
              <xs:complexType>
                <xs:sequence>
                  <xs:element ref="ppl:person" maxOccurs="unbounded"/>
                </xs:sequence>
              </xs:complexType>
            </xs:element>
          </xs:sequence>
          <xs:attribute name="id" type="xs:ID" use="required"/>
          <xs:attribute name="available" type="xs:string" use="required"/>
        </xs:complexType>
      </xs:schema>
```

Attributes

id

> W3C XML Schema's element ID.

namespace

> Namespace URI of the components to import. If this attribute is missing, the imported components are expected to have no namespace. When present, its value must be different than the target namespace of the importing schema.

schemaLocation

> Location of the schema to import. If this attribute is missing, the validator might expect to get the information from the application, or try to find it on the Internet.

---

xs:include

Inclusion of a W3C XML Schema for the same target namespace.

```
<xs:include
        id            = xs:ID
        schemaLocation = xs:anyURI
        {any attributes with non-schema namespace}
        >
        Content: (xs:annotation?)
</xs:include>
```

May be included in: xs:schema

Description

xs:include performs a straight inclusion of a schema within another schema that describes the same target namespace. It is possible, though, to include a schema that doesn't specify a target namespace. The included schema will be treated as adopting the target namespace of its includer in a schema with a target namespace. This possibility, often called "chameleon design," allows reuse of "transparent" schemas in the context of different namespaces.

The effect of a schema inclusion is a merge between the two schemas that are consolidated into a global schema. The schema that is included doesn't need to be a complete schema by itself.

Restrictions

It is not possible to use `xs:include` to include a schema describing another namespace. (`xs:import` should be used in this case.)

It is not possible to change the definitions of the included schemas. (`xs:redefine` should be used in this case.)

It is not possible to include a fragment of a schema. (General purpose inclusion mechanisms such as `XInclude` should be used in this case.)

Example

```
<xs:include schemaLocation="simple-types.xsd"/>
```

Attributes

id
> W3C XML Schema's element ID.

schemaLocation
> Location of the schema to include.

---

xs:key   Definition of a key.

```
<xs:key
          id              = xs:ID
          name            = xs:NCName
          {any attributes with non-schema namespace}
          >
          Content: ((xs:annotation?), (xs:selector, xs:field+))
</xs:key>
```

May be included in: xs:element (within xs:all), xs:element (reference or local definition), xs:element (global definition)

Description

`xs:key` is used to define simple or compound keys by unambiguously identifying each element of a selected list of subelements within the scope of a root element.

`xs:key` is very similar to `xs:unique`. Like the constraints defined with `xs:unique`, keys defined with `xs:key` are unique in the scope of their root element and may be referenced by `xs:keyref`. The only difference between `xs:key` and `xs:unique` is the keys must be defined for each of the elements in the selection list, while unique identifiers may be undefined for elements in the selection list.

The root element for the key is the element in which the key is defined. The location of the root element must be carefully chosen since the unicity of the key is checked only within the node elements that are the key's children. Defining a root element that has multiple occurrences within a document leaves the possibility to define local keys that are unique only in the scope of each occurrence of a document. When a key is global to a document, defining it using the document element as a root may cause it to be less error-prone.

The contribution of xs:key to the PSVI is a node table in each occurrence of the root key element that contains the list of the key sequences for this root element. The scope of these node tables is limited to the root element in which they are contained and its ancestors. This scope is used to determine the behavior of the key references and impacts the choice of the key root element when the key is referenced (see the section on xs:keyref).

Restrictions

These XPath-based features do not follow the object-oriented, namespace-aware general philosophy of W3C XML Schema. The XPath expressions are specified independently of the element's content model and the constraints for the elements of all the possible namespaces must be defined in the schema for the namespace of the constraint root element.

Example

```
<xs:element name="library">
  <xs:complexType>
    .../...
  </xs:complexType>
  <xs:key name="book">
    <xs:selector xpath="book"/>
    <xs:field xpath="isbn"/>
  </xs:key>
</xs:element>
```

Attributes

id
> W3C XML Schema's element ID.

name
> The name of the key.

---

xs:keyref
Definition of a key reference.

```
<xs:keyref
          id          = xs:ID
          name        = xs:NCName
          refer       = xs:QName
          {any attributes with non-schema namespace}
          >
          Content: ((xs:annotation?), (xs:selector, xs:field+))
</xs:keyref>
```

May be included in: xs:element (within xs:all), xs:element (reference or local definition), xs:element (global definition)

Description

xs:keyref is used to define a reference to a simple or compound key or to a unique constraint.

The syntax of xs:keyref is very similar to the syntax of xs:key or xs:unique. The only difference is the refer attribute, which must contain the name of the referred key or unique constraint.

The root element for the keyref is the element in which the key is defined. The key reference is often defined with the same root element as its referred key or unique constraint, in which case the matching is simple and straightforward.

The root element of the keyref may also be defined in any element for which it is in the scope of a matching constraint node table, i.e., in all the ancestors of the root element of the referred key or unique constraint. In this case, an additional check is performed; for each matching key reference, the validator should test that the key or unique value is defined only once in all the matching key or unique root elements.

Restrictions

Key references defined in an ancestor of their referenced key or unique constraint actually add additional constraints on the referenced key or the unique key, which may be unexpected. A set of identifiers that match a key or unique constraint may become invalid when a key reference is defined.

If, for instance, local keys are defined to identify characters within the scope of a book, these keys would allow the reuse of the same characters' identifiers in distinct books, such as in the following:

```
<book>
  <isbn> 0836217462 </isbn>
  <title> Being a Dog Is a Full-Time Job </title>
  <character id="PP">
    <name> Peppermint Patty </name>
    <qualification> bold, brash and tomboyish </qualification>
  </character>
  <character id="Snoopy">
    <name> Snoopy </name>
    <qualification> hero of the book </qualification>
  </character>
  <character id="Schroeder">
    <name> Schroeder </name>
    <qualification> brought classical music to the Peanuts strip</qualification>
  </character>
  <character id="Lucy">
    <name> Lucy </name>
    <qualification> bossy, crabby and selfish </qualification>
  </character>
</book>
<book>
  <isbn> 0805033106 </isbn>
  <title> Peanuts Every Sunday </title>
  <character id="Sally">
    <name> Sally Brown </name>
```

```
      <qualification> always looks for the easy way out </qualification>
    </character>
    <character id="Snoopy">
      <name> Snoopy </name>
      <qualification> extroverted beagle </qualification>
    </character>
  </book>
```

If we add a key reference to reference these keys from the books, using the same identifier for characters in different books will be allowed if, and only if, these keys are not referenced.

This example is then valid:

```
<library>
  <book>
    <isbn> 0836217462 </isbn>
    <title> Being a Dog Is a Full-Time Job </title>
    <character id="PP">
      <name> Peppermint Patty </name>
      <qualification> bold, brash and tomboyish </qualification>
    </character>
    <character id="Snoopy">
      <name> Snoopy </name>
      <qualification> hero of the book </qualification>
    </character>
    <character id="Schroeder">
      <name> Schroeder </name>
      <qualification> brought classical music to the Peanuts strip </qualification>
    </character>
    <character id="Lucy">
      <name> Lucy </name>
      <qualification> bossy, crabby and selfish </qualification>
    </character>
  </book>
  <book>
    <isbn> 0805033106 </isbn>
    <title> Peanuts Every Sunday </title>
    <character id="Sally">
      <name> Sally Brown </name>
      <qualification> always looks for the easy way out </qualification>
    </character>
    <character id="Snoopy">
      <name> Snoopy </name>
      <qualification> extroverted beagle </qualification>
    </character>
  </book>
  <comment about="Sally"> Sally is cute </comment>
</library>
```

Because "Sally" is a unique key, it becomes invalid if we add a comment element referring to "Snoopy," which is mentioned twice.

A complete schema for this document might be the following (note how the xs:keyref refers to a xs:unique constraint, which is defined for a child of the current node):

```
<xs:schema elementFormDefault="qualified" xmlns:xs=
  "http://www.w3.org/2001/XMLSchema">
```

```
<xs:element name="library">
  <xs:complexType>
    <xs:sequence>
      <xs:element name="book" maxOccurs="unbounded">
        <xs:complexType>
          <xs:sequence>
            <xs:element name="isbn" type="xs:NMTOKEN"/>
            <xs:element name="title" type="xs:string"/>
            <xs:element name="character" maxOccurs="unbounded">
              <xs:complexType>
                <xs:sequence>
                  <xs:element name="name" type="xs:string"/>
                  <xs:element name="qualification" type="xs:string"/>
                </xs:sequence>
                <xs:attribute name="id" type="xs:string"/>
              </xs:complexType>
            </xs:element>
          </xs:sequence>
        </xs:complexType>
        <xs:key name="character">
        <xs:selector xpath="character"/>
        <xs:field xpath="@id"/>
        </xs:key>
      </xs:element>
      <xs:element name="comment" minOccurs="0" maxOccurs="unbounded">
        <xs:complexType>
          <xs:simpleContent>
            <xs:extension base="xs:string">
            <xs:attribute name="about" type="xs:string"/>
            </xs:extension>
          </xs:simpleContent>
        </xs:complexType>
      </xs:element>
    </xs:sequence>
  </xs:complexType>
  <xs:unique name="book">
  <xs:selector xpath="book"/>
  <xs:field xpath="isbn"/>
  </xs:unique>
  <xs:keyref name="comment" refer="character">
  <xs:selector xpath="comment"/>
  <xs:field xpath="@about"/>
  </xs:keyref>
</xs:element>
</xs:schema>
```

Example

```
<xs:element name="library">
  <xs:complexType>
    .../...
  </xs:complexType>
  <xs:key name="ID">
    <xs:selector xpath="book|author|character"/>
```

```
    <xs:field xpath="@id"/>
  </xs:key>
  <xs:keyref name="IDREF" refer="ID">
    <xs:selector xpath="book/author-ref|book/character-ref"/>
    <xs:field xpath="@ref"/>
  </xs:keyref>
</xs:element>
```

Attributes

id
>   W3C XML Schema's element ID.

name
>   Name of the key reference.

refer
>   Name of the key or unique constraint referred by the key reference.

---

xs:length
Facet to define the length of a value.

Synopsis

```
<xs:length
        fixed          = xs:boolean : "false"
        id             = xs:ID
        value          = xs:nonNegativeInteger
        {any attributes with non-schema namespace}
        >
        Content: (xs:annotation?)
</xs:length>
```

May be included in: *xs:restriction (simple type), xs:restriction (simple content)*
May be used as facet for: *xs:anyURI, xs:base64Binary, xs:ENTITIES, xs:ENTITY, xs:hexBinary,*
    xs:ID, xs:IDREF, xs:IDREFS, xs:language, xs:Name, xs:NCName, xs:NMTOKEN,
    xs:NMTOKENS, xs:normalizedString, xs:NOTATION, xs:QName, xs:string, xs:token

Description

xs:length is a facet that allows the definition of the length expressed in a unit that depends on the datatype. For most of the datatypes, the unit is the character as defined in the XML 1.0 Recommendation (i.e., Unicode characters defined by ISO/IEC 10646 that may be represented on more than 8 bits). The exceptions are the binary datatypes (xs:hexBinary and xs:base64Binary), for which lengths are expressed in number of bytes (8 bits) of binary data, and all the list datatypes, for which lengths are expressed in number of list items.

xs:length constrains the value space. In practice, this means that it is checked after whitespace replacement and collapsing, as defined by the xs:whiteSpace facet.

Restrictions

This is a logical length that has often no direct relation to the size of storage needed for the value.

The value of this facet cannot be modified during further restrictions, and the value of the fixed attribute is meaningless (the behavior is always as if the facet were fixed).

Although also not specified in the Recommendation, xs:length interacts with the xs:minLength and xs:maxLength and shouldn't set the length to a value not in the range between xs:minLength and xs:maxLength of its base type.

Fixing the xs:length facet doesn't fix the xs:maxLength and xs:minLength facets. To fix the three facets, define two restriction steps, since it is forbidden to apply these facets in the same restriction step.

Example

```
<xs:simpleType name="standardNotations">
  <xs:restriction base="xs:NOTATION">
    <xs:length value="8"/>
  </xs:restriction>
</xs:simpleType>
```

Attributes

fixed
> When set to true, the value of the length cannot be modified during further restrictions (meaningless for this facet whose value can never be modified in further restrictions).

id
> W3C XML Schema's element ID.

value
> Value of the facet.

xs:list

Derivation by list.

```
<xs:list
          id                 = xs:ID
          itemType           = xs:QName
          {any attributes with non-schema namespace}
          >
          Content: ((xs:annotation?), (xs:simpleType?))
</xs:list>
```

May be included in: xs:simpleType (local definition), xs:simpleType (global definition)

Description

Derivation by list is the process of transforming a simple datatype (named the item type) into a whitespace-separated list of values from this datatype.

The item type can be defined inline by adding a simpleType definition as a child element of the list element, or by reference, using the itemType attribute (it is an error to use both).

The semantic and list of facets applicable on the item type are lost and the new datatype inherits a list of facets, which is common to all the list datatypes: xs:enumeration, xs:length, xs:maxLength, xs:minLength, and xs:pattern and its whitespaces are always collapsed.

After a derivation by list, the type of the resulting datatype is a list of whatever the item type was (atomic or union).

It is possible to define lists of atomic datatypes that allow whitespaces such as xs:string. In this case, the whitespaces are always considered separators.

Restrictions

The facets that can be applied to a list datatype are common to all the list datatypes, and add constraints to the list as a whole (rather than on the items composing the list). The constraints on the item composing the lists, therefore, need to be applied before the derivation by list.

The list separators cannot be chosen and are always whitespaces.

It is explicitly forbidden by the Recommendation to define lists of lists. Lists of unions and unions of lists are both allowed, so it should be possible to work around this limitation by defining a dummy union of a list and using this union as a list item if needed. However, lists of lists are effectively pointless, since all the list types have the same set of separators.

Example

```
<xs:simpleType name="integerList">
  <xs:list itemType="xs:integer"/>
</xs:simpleType>
```

Attributes

id
> W3C XML Schema's element ID.

itemType
> Reference to the item type when not defined inline by a xs:simpleType element.

---

xs:maxExclusive
Facet to define a maximum (exclusive) value.

```
<xs:maxExclusive
          fixed          = xs:boolean : "false"
          id             = xs:ID
          value          = anySimpleType
          {any attributes with non-schema namespace}
          >
          Content: (xs:annotation?)
</xs:maxExclusive>
```

May be included in: xs:restriction (simple type), xs:restriction (simple content)
May be used as facet for:xs:byte, xs:date, xs:dateTime, xs:decimal, xs:double, xs:duration, xs:float, xs:gDay, xs:gMonth, xs:gMonthDay, xs:gYear, xs:gYearMonth, xs:int, xs:integer, xs:long, xs:negativeInteger, xs:nonNegativeInteger, xs:nonPositiveInteger, xs:positiveInteger, xs:short, xs:time, xs:unsignedByte, xs:unsignedInt, xs:unsignedLong, xs:unsignedShort

Description

xs:maxExclusive defines an exclusive maximum value. To be valid, a value must be strictly less than the value of xs:maxExclusive. This facet constrains the value space.

Restrictions

It is forbidden to define both xs:maxExclusive and xs:maxInclusive in the same restriction step. Although not explicitly specified in the Recommendation, it doesn't make sense to define several xs:maxExclusive facets in a single restriction step also.

Within a restriction step, xs:maxExclusive is also dependent on xs:minExclusive and xs:minInclusive, since using inconsistent values leads to datatypes with empty value spaces.

xs:maxExclusive must restrict the value space of its base type, and its value must be in the value space of the base type.

Fixing the maxExclusive facet doesn't fix the xs:maxInclusive facet. To fix both facets, define two restriction steps since it is forbidden to apply these two facets in the same restriction step.

Example

```
<xs:simpleType name="myInteger">
  <xs:restriction base="xs:integer">
    <xs:minInclusive value="-2"/>
    <xs:maxExclusive value="5"/>
  </xs:restriction>
</xs:simpleType>
```

Attributes

fixed
> When set to fixed, the value of this facet cannot be changed in further restrictions.

id
> W3C XML Schema's element ID.

value
> Value of the facet (must be in the value space of the base type).

---

xs:maxInclusive

Facet to define a maximum (inclusive) value.

```
<xs:maxInclusive
        fixed         = xs:boolean : "false"
        id            = xs:ID
        value         = anySimpleType
        {any attributes with non-schema namespace}
        >
        Content: (xs:annotation?)
</xs:maxInclusive>
```

May be included in: xs:restriction (simple type), xs:restriction (simple content)
May be used as facet for: xs:byte, xs:date, xs:dateTime, xs:decimal, xs:double, xs:duration, xs:float, xs:gDay, xs:gMonth, xs:gMonthDay, xs:gYear, xs:gYearMonth, xs:int, xs:integer, xs:long, xs:negativeInteger, xs:nonNegativeInteger, xs:nonPositiveInteger, xs:positiveInteger, xs:short, xs:time, xs:unsignedByte, xs:unsignedInt, xs:unsignedLong, xs:unsignedShort

Description

xs:maxInclusive defines an inclusive maximum value. To be valid, a value must be less than or equal to the value of xs:maxInclusive.

This facet constrains the value space.

Restrictions

It is forbidden to define both xs:maxExclusive and xs:maxInclusive in the same restriction step. Although not explicitly specified in the Recommendation, it doesn't make sense to define several xs:maxInclusive facets in a single restriction step either.

Within a restriction step, xs:maxInclusive is also dependent on xs:minExclusive and xs:minInclusive, since using inconsistent values leads to datatypes with empty value spaces.

xs:maxInclusive must restrict the value space of its base type, and its value must be in the value space of the base type.

Fixing the maxInclusive facet doesn't fix the xs:maxExclusive facet. To fix both facets, define two restriction steps since it is forbidden to apply these two facets in the same restriction step.

Example

```
<xs:simpleType name="thousands">
  <xs:restriction base="xs:double">
    <xs:maxInclusive value="1e3"/>
  </xs:restriction>
</xs:simpleType>
```

Attributes

fixed
>   When set to fixed, the value of this facet cannot be changed in further restrictions.

id
>   W3C XML Schema's element ID.

value
>   Value of the facet (must be in the value space of the base type).

---

xs:maxLength

Facet to define a maximum length.

```
<xs:maxLength
        fixed           = xs:boolean : "false"
        id              = xs:ID
        value           = xs:nonNegativeInteger
        {any attributes with non-schema namespace}
        >
        Content: (xs:annotation?)
</xs:maxLength>
```

May be included in: xs:restriction (simple type), xs:restriction (simple content)

May be used as facet for:xs:anyURI, xs:base64Binary, xs:ENTITIES, xs:ENTITY, xs:hexBinary, xs:ID, xs:IDREF, xs:IDREFS, xs:language, xs:Name, xs:NCName, xs:NMTOKEN, xs:NMTOKENS, xs:normalizedString, xs:NOTATION, xs:QName, xs:string, xs:token

Description

xs:maxLength is a facet that allows the definition of the maximum length expressed in a unit that depends on the datatype. For most of the datatypes, the unit is a character as defined in the XML 1.0 Recommendation (i.e., Unicode characters defined by ISO/IEC 10646 that may be represented on more than 8 bits). The exceptions are the binary datatypes (xs:hexBinary and xs:base64Binary), for which lengths are expressed in number of bytes (8 bits) of binary data, and all the list datatypes, for which lengths are expressed in number of list items.

xs:maxLength constrains the value space. In practice, this means that it is checked after whitespace replacement and collapsing, as defined by the xs:whiteSpace facet.

Restrictions

This is a logical length, which often has no direct relation to the size of storage needed for the value.

It is forbidden to define both xs:maxLength and xs:length in the same restriction step. Although not explicitly specified in the Recommendation, it doesn't make sense to define several xs:maxLength facets in a single restriction step either.

Within a restriction step, xs:maxLength is also dependent on xs:minLength, since using inconsistent values leads to datatypes with empty value spaces.

xs:maxLength must restrict the value space of its base type, and its value must be smaller than the value of xs:maxLength of its base type, if defined.

Although not specified in the Recommendation, xs:maxLength interacts with the xs:length and shouldn't be used if xs:length is defined for its base type.

Fixing the xs:maxLength facet doesn't fix the xs:length facet. To fix both facets, define two restriction steps since it is forbidden to apply these two facets in the same restriction step.

Example

```
<xs:simpleType name="binaryImage">
  <xs:restriction base="xs:hexBinary">
    <xs:maxLength value="1024"/>
  </xs:restriction>
</xs:simpleType>
```

Attributes

fixed
 When set to true, the value of the facet cannot be modified during further restrictions.

id
 W3C XML Schema's element ID.

value
 Value of the facet.

xs:minExclusive

Facet to define a minimum (exclusive) value.

```
<xs:minExclusive
        fixed           = xs:boolean : "false"
        id              = xs:ID
        value           = anySimpleType
        {any attributes with non-schema namespace}
        >
        Content: (xs:annotation?)
</xs:minExclusive>
```

May be included in: xs:restriction (simple type), xs:restriction (simple content)
May be used as facet for: xs:byte, xs:date, xs:dateTime, xs:decimal, xs:double, xs:duration,
   xs:float, xs:gDay, xs:gMonth, xs:gMonthDay, xs:gYear, xs:gYearMonth, xs:int, xs:integer,
   xs:long, xs:negativeInteger, xs:nonNegativeInteger, xs:nonPositiveInteger, xs:positiveInteger,
   xs:short, xs:time, xs:unsignedByte, xs:unsignedInt, xs:unsignedLong, xs:unsignedShort

Description

xs:minExclusive defines an exclusive minimum value. To be valid, a value must be strictly greater than the value of xs:minExclusive.

This facet constrains the value space.

Restrictions

It is forbidden to define both xs:minExclusive and xs:minInclusive in the same restriction step. Although not explicitly specified in the Recommendation, it doesn't make sense to define several xs:minExclusive facets in a single restriction step either.

Within a restriction step, xs:minExclusive is also dependent on xs:maxExclusive and xs:maxInclusive, since using inconsistent values leads to datatypes with empty value spaces.

xs:minExclusive must restrict the value space of its base type, and its value must be in the value space of the base type.

Fixing the xs:minExclusive facet doesn't fix the xs:minInclusive facet. To fix both facets, define two restriction steps since it is forbidden to apply these two facets in the same restriction step.

Example

```
<xs:simpleType name="afterTeaTimeInParisInSummer">
  <xs:restriction base="xs:time">
    <xs:minExclusive value="17:00:00+02:00"/>
  </xs:restriction>
</xs:simpleType>
```

Attributes

fixed
    When set to fixed, the value of this facet cannot be changed in further restrictions.
id
    W3C XML Schema's element ID.

value
>	Value of the facet (must be in the value space of the base type).

---

xs:minInclusive
Facet to define a minimum (inclusive) value.

```
<xs:minInclusive
        fixed         = xs:boolean : "false"
        id            = xs:ID
        value         = anySimpleType
        {any attributes with non-schema namespace}
        >
        Content: (xs:annotation?)
</xs:minInclusive>
```

May be included in: xs:restriction (simple type), xs:restriction (simple content)
May be used as facet for: xs:byte, xs:date, xs:dateTime, xs:decimal, xs:double, xs:duration,
xs:float, xs:gDay, xs:gMonth, xs:gMonthDay, xs:gYear, xs:gYearMonth, xs:int, xs:integer,
xs:long, xs:negativeInteger, xs:nonNegativeInteger, xs:nonPositiveInteger, xs:positiveInteger,
xs:short, xs:time, xs:unsignedByte, xs:unsignedInt, xs:unsignedLong, xs:unsignedShort

Description

xs:minInclusive defines an inclusive minimum value. To be valid, a value must be greater than or equal to the value of xs:minInclusive.

This facet constrains the value space.

Restrictions

It is forbidden to define both xs:minInclusive and xs:minExclusive in the same restriction step. Although not explicitly specified in the Recommendation, it doesn't make sense to define several xs:minInclusive facets in a single restriction step either.

Within a restriction step, xs:minInclusive is also dependent on xs:maxExclusive and xs:maxInclusive, since using inconsistent values leads to datatypes with empty value spaces.

xs:minInclusive must restrict the value space of its base type, and its value must be in the value space of the base type.

Fixing the xs:minInclusive facet doesn't fix the xs:minExclusive facet. To fix both facets, define two restriction steps since it is forbidden to apply these two facets in the same restriction step.

Example

```
<xs:simpleType name="positive">
  <xs:restriction base="xs:double">
    <xs:minInclusive value="0"/>
  </xs:restriction>
</xs:simpleType>
```

Attributes

`fixed`
> When set to `fixed`, the value of this facet cannot be changed in further restrictions.

`id`
> W3C XML Schema's element ID.

`value`
> Value of the facet (must be in the value space of the base type).

---

xs:minLength
Facet to define a minimum length.

```
<xs:minLength
        fixed          = xs:boolean : "false"
        id             = xs:ID
        value          = xs:nonNegativeInteger
        {any attributes with non-schema namespace}
        >
        Content: (xs:annotation?)
</xs:minLength>
```

May be included in: xs:restriction (simple type), xs:restriction (simple content)
May be used as facet for: xs:anyURI, xs:base64Binary, xs:ENTITIES, xs:ENTITY, xs:hexBinary,
*   xs:ID, xs:IDREF, xs:IDREFS, xs:language, xs:Name, xs:NCName, xs:NMTOKEN,*
*   xs:NMTOKENS, xs:normalizedString, xs:NOTATION, xs:QName, xs:string, xs:token*

Description

`xs:minLength` is a facet that allows definition of the minimum length expressed in a unit that depends on the datatype. For most of the datatypes, the unit is the character as defined in the XML 1.0 Recommendation (i.e., Unicode characters defined by ISO/IEC 10646 that may be represented on more than 8 bits). The exceptions are the binary datatypes (`xs:hexBinary` and `xs:base64Binary`), for which lengths are expressed in number of bytes (8 bits) of binary data, and all the list datatypes, for which lengths are expressed in number of list items.

`xs:minLength` constrains the value space. In practice, this means that it is checked after whitespace replacement and collapsing, as defined by the `xs:whiteSpace` facet.

Restrictions

This is a logical length, which often has no direct relation on the size of storage needed for the value.

It is forbidden to define both `xs:minLength` and `xs:length` in the same restriction step. Although not explicitly specified in the Recommendation, it doesn't make sense to define several `xs:minLength` facets in a single restriction step either.

Within a restriction step, `xs:minLength` is also dependent on `xs:maxLength`, since using inconsistent values leads to datatypes with empty value spaces.

`xs:minLength` must restrict the value space of its base type, and its value must be greater than the value of `xs:minLength` of its base type if defined.

Although not specified in the Recommendation, xs:minLength interacts with xs:length and shouldn't be used if xs:length is defined for its base type.

Fixing the xs:minLength facet doesn't fix the xs:length facet. To fix both facets, define two restriction steps since it is forbidden to apply these two facets in the same restriction step.

Example

```
<xs:simpleType name="longName">
  <xs:restriction base="xs:NCName">
    <xs:minLength value="6"/>
  </xs:restriction>
</xs:simpleType>
```

Attributes

fixed
> When set to true, the value of the facet cannot be modified during further restrictions.

id
> W3C XML Schema's element ID.

value
> Value of the facet.

xs:notation

Declaration of a notation.

```
<xs:notation
        id            = xs:ID
        name          = xs:NCName
        public        = xs:token
        system        = xs:anyURI
        {any attributes with non-schema namespace}
        >
        Content: (xs:annotation?)
</xs:notation>
```

May be included in: xs:schema

Description

xs:notation is used to declare a notation just like the NOTATION declarations in DTDs. The main difference is that W3C XML Schema notations are namespace-aware and can be imported between schemas. When these declarations are used, the notations are used in xs:enumeration facets to create simple types.

Restrictions

Notations are very seldom used in real world applications.

Example

```
<xs:notation name="jpeg" public="image/jpeg"
  system="file:///usr/bin/xv"/>
```

```
<xs:notation name="gif" public="image/gif"
  system="file:///usr/bin/xv"/>

<xs:notation name="png" public="image/png"
  system="file:///usr/bin/xv"/>

<xs:notation name="svg" public="image/svg"
  system="file:///usr/bin/xsmiles"/>

<xs:notation name="pdf" public="application/pdf"
  system="file:///usr/bin/acroread"/>

<xs:simpleType name="graphicalFormat">
  <xs:restriction base="xs:NOTATION">
    <xs:enumeration value="jpeg"/>
    <xs:enumeration value="gif"/>
    <xs:enumeration value="png"/>
    <xs:enumeration value="svg"/>
    <xs:enumeration value="pdf"/>
  </xs:restriction>
</xs:simpleType>
```

Attributes

id
> W3C XML Schema's element ID.

name
> Name of the notation (unqualified).

public
> Public identifier (usually its content type).

system
> System identifier (typically the location of a resource that might be used to process the content type associated with the notation).

---

xs:pattern

Facet to define a regular expression pattern constraint.

```
<xs:pattern
        id              = xs:ID
        value           = anySimpleType
        {any attributes with non-schema namespace}
        >
        Content: (xs:annotation?)
</xs:pattern>
```

May be included in: xs:restriction (simple type), xs:restriction (simple content)

*May be used as facet for:xs:anyURI, xs:base64Binary, xs:boolean, xs:byte, xs:date, xs:dateTime,
    xs:decimal, xs:double, xs:duration, xs:ENTITY, xs:float, xs:gDay, xs:gMonth, xs:gMonthDay,
    xs:gYear, xs:gYearMonth, xs:hexBinary, xs:ID, xs:IDREF, xs:int, xs:integer, xs:language,
    xs:long, xs:Name, xs:NCName, xs:negativeInteger, xs:NMTOKEN, xs:nonNegativeInteger,
    xs:nonPositiveInteger, xs:normalizedString, xs:NOTATION, xs:positiveInteger, xs:QName,
    xs:short, xs:string, xs:time, xs:token, xs:unsignedByte, xs:unsignedInt, xs:unsignedLong,
    xs:unsignedShort*

Description

xs:pattern allows the definition of regular expression patterns over the lexical space. The syntax used for these patterns has been borrowed from Perl regular expressions, and has been enhanced to support the Unicode character blocks.

When multiple xs:pattern facets are defined in a single derivation step, a value is considered valid if it matches at least one of the patterns, meaning that a logical or is performed on all the patterns defined in a same derivation step.

Patterns are applied to the lexical space of the base datatype, meaning that a logical and is performed on patterns defined in different derivation steps.

The syntax of these patterns is explained in more detail in Chapter 6.

Restrictions

xs:pattern is a common workaround to define datatypes that look like datatypes missing from the list of predefined datatypes. It is possible, for instance, to simulate decimals using a separator other than the decimal point with a pattern. Such datatypes need to be based on xs:token, and will still not have the semantic of xs:decimal and its list of facets.

xs:pattern cannot be fixed.

Example

```
<xs:simpleType name="nonScientific">
  <xs:restriction base="xs:float">
    <xs:pattern value="[^eE]*"/>
  </xs:restriction>
</xs:simpleType>


<xs:simpleType name="noLeading0">
  <xs:restriction base="xs:float">
    <xs:pattern value="[^0].*"/>
  </xs:restriction>
</xs:simpleType>
```

Attributes

id
    W3C XML Schema's element ID.
value
    Value of the facet.

---

xs:redefine

Inclusion of a W3C XML Schema for the same namespace with possible override.

```
<xs:redefine
        id            = xs:ID
        schemaLocation = xs:anyURI
        {any attributes with non-schema namespace}
        >
        Content: (xs:annotation | (xs:simpleType | xs:complexType | xs:group |
```

```
                    xs:attributeGroup))*
</xs:redefine>
```

May be included in: xs:schema

Description

xs:redefine is similar to xs:include with one exception: the definition of simple and complex types and attribute and element groups can be changed. Changes performed on these components must lead to components that are valid restrictions or extensions of the original ones.

Simple and complex types are redefined using the usual mechanism of derivation: the new types must be defined as derivations by restriction or extension of their previous definition, which is considered to be the base type.

Element and attribute groups are redefined by giving a new definition, and may refer to themselves to indicate that the content of their original definition must be included. In this case, this self-reference is not considered a recursive definition (which is forbidden in element and attribute groups), but an extension of the original group.

When xs:redefine is used and no redefinitions are specified, its effect is similar to xs:include.

Restrictions

xs:redefine can be used only to include schemas with either the same target namespace or no target namespace. There is no equivalent to import and redefine schema definitions in a single operation. The schema must be redefined and imported in two different operations.

Arbitrary redefinitions are not allowed. After redefinition, the components must be valid derivations (by extension or restriction) of their definitions before redefinition.

xs:element, xs:attribute, and xs:notation cannot be redefined.

Example

```
<xs:redefine schemaLocation="complex-types2.xsd">
  <xs:complexType name="book">
    <xs:complexContent>
      <xs:restriction base="book">
        <xs:sequence>
          <xs:element ref="isbn"/>
          <xs:element ref="title"/>
          <xs:element ref="author" minOccurs="0"
            maxOccurs="unbounded"/>
          <xs:element ref="character" minOccurs="0"
            maxOccurs="unbounded"/>
        </xs:sequence>
        <xs:attribute name="id" type="bookID"/>
        <xs:attribute ref="available"/>
      </xs:restriction>
    </xs:complexContent>
  </xs:complexType>
</xs:redefine>
```

Attributes

`id`

> W3C XML Schema's element ID.

`schemaLocation`

> Location of the schema to redefine.

---

xs:restriction (simple type)

Derivation of a simple datatype by restriction.

```
<xs:restriction
        base        = xs:QName
        id          = xs:ID
        {any attributes with non-schema namespace}
        >
        Content: ((xs:annotation?), (xs:simpleType?, (xs:minExclusive |
                xs:minInclusive | xs:maxExclusive | xs:maxInclusive |
                xs:totalDigits | xs:fractionDigits | xs:length |
                xs:minLength | xs:maxLength | xs:enumeration |
                xs:whiteSpace | xs:pattern)*))
</xs:restriction>
```

May be included in: xs:simpleType (local definition), xs:simpleType (global definition)

Description

Deriving a simple datatype by restriction is the action of defining a new datatype by adding constraints (called facets) on a base datatype to restrict its lexical and value spaces.

The base datatype can be defined by reference (using the base attribute) or inline (through a `xs:simpleType` element defining a local datatype).

Each of the facets is defined as a child element after the optional embedded `xs:simpleType` definition.

Each facet has its own meaning and depending on the facet, acts on the lexical space, on the value space, or on the whitespace transformation performed between the lexical and value spaces. Depending on the base datatype, a facet may also have a different behavior. See the detailed description of each facet in this chapter for more information.

Derivations by restrictions can be applied to any type of datatype (atomic, list, or union), and don't change the type of the datatype (atomic, list, and union datatypes stay atomic, list, or union, after a derivation by restriction).

Restrictions

The same element name (`xs:restriction`) is used in three different contexts with highly different meanings. Be careful to distinguish restriction in the context of a simple datatype, a simple content model, and a complex content model.

The base attribute and the `xs:simpleType` embedded definition must not be used together (the base type is defined either by reference or embedded).

Example

```
<xs:simpleType name="myInteger">
  <xs:restriction base="xs:integer">
```

```
        <xs:minInclusive value="-2"/>
        <xs:maxExclusive value="5"/>
    </xs:restriction>
</xs:simpleType>
```

Attributes

base
> Qualified name of the base datatype when defined by reference.

id
> W3C XML Schema's element ID.

---

xs:restriction (simple content)
Derivation of a simple content model by restriction.

```
<xs:restriction
        base         = xs:QName
        id           = xs:ID
        {any attributes with non-schema namespace}
        >
        Content: (xs:annotation?, (xs:simpleType?, (xs:minExclusive |
                xs:minInclusive | xs:maxExclusive | xs:maxInclusive |
                xs:totalDigits | xs:fractionDigits | xs:length |
                xs:minLength | xs:maxLength | xs:enumeration | xs:whiteSpace |
                xs:pattern)*)?, ((xs:attribute | xs:attributeGroup)*,
                xs:anyAttribute?))
</xs:restriction>
```

May be included in: xs:simpleContent

Description

The restriction of simple content complex types is an operation that allows the addition of new constraints to both the attributes and the text node allowed in simple content elements (this reduces the set of valid instances structures). The restriction of the text node is done using the same facets that are available for restricting simple types; the restriction of the attributes is done by providing a list of modified attribute definitions or references. The attribute types used in this list must be identical or explicit derivations by restriction of the types used during the definition of the base type. The controls applied to the attributes must result in a restriction of their definition (for instance, a value may be fixed, an attribute that was optional may become either required or prohibited, etc.).

Restrictions

The same element name (xs:restriction) is used in three different contexts with highly different meanings. Be careful to distinguish restriction in the context of a simple datatype, a simple content model, and a complex content model.

Example

```
<xs:element name="title">
  <xs:complexType>
    <xs:simpleContent>
      <xs:restriction base="tokenWithLangAndNote">
```

```
            <xs:maxLength value="255"/>
            <xs:attribute name="lang">
              <xs:simpleType>
                <xs:restriction base="xs:language">
                  <xs:enumeration value="en"/>
                  <xs:enumeration value="es"/>
                </xs:restriction>
              </xs:simpleType>
            </xs:attribute>
          </xs:restriction>
        </xs:simpleContent>
      </xs:complexType>
    </xs:element>
```

Attributes

base

> Qualified name of the base type.

id

> W3C XML Schema's element ID.

xs:restriction (complex content)

Derivation of a complex content model by restriction.

```
<xs:restriction
        base        = xs:QName
        id          = xs:ID
        {any attributes with non-schema namespace}
        >
        Content: (xs:annotation?, (xs:group | xs:all | xs:choice | xs:sequence)?,
                ((xs:attribute | xs:attributeGroup)*, xs:anyAttribute?))
</xs:restriction>
```

May be included in: xs:complexContent

Description

The restriction of a complex content complex type is an operation that allows the addition of new constraints to both the attributes and child elements in complex content elements (this reduces the set of valid instances structures). It can be seen as a declaration of intention that a new content model is a subset of a base content model (the declaration by intention is checked by the schema processors). The new content model is entirely described under xs:restriction and must represent a restriction to what was allowed by the base content model (i.e., any content valid per the restricted type must also be valid per the base type). The only exception is attributes whose description may be skipped under xs:restriction, if not changed.

Restrictions

To facilitate the checking done by schema processors, the new derived content model must follow the definition of the base type particle per particle. Each of them must be explicit derivations by restriction.

The same element name (xs:restriction) is used in three different contexts with highly different meanings. Be careful to be able to distinguish restrictions in the context of a simple datatype, a simple content model, and a complex content model.

Example

```
<xs:element name="author">
  <xs:complexType>
    <xs:complexContent>
      <xs:restriction base="person">
        <xs:sequence>
          <xs:element ref="name"/>
          <xs:element ref="born"/>
          <xs:element ref="dead" minOccurs="0"/>
        </xs:sequence>
      </xs:restriction>
    </xs:complexContent>
  </xs:complexType>
</xs:element>
```

Attributes

base
    Qualified name of the base type.

id
    W3C XML Schema's element ID.

xs:schema

Document element of a W3C XML Schema.

```
<xs:schema
        attributeFormDefault = ( "qualified" | "unqualified" ) : "unqualified"
        blockDefault         = ( "#all" | list of ( "extension" | "restriction" |
                                 "substitution" ) ) : ""
        elementFormDefault   = ( "qualified" | "unqualified" ) : "unqualified"
        finalDefault         = ( "#all" | list of ( "extension" | "restriction" )
                                 ) : ""
        id                   = xs:ID
        targetNamespace      = xs:anyURI
        version              = xs:token
        xml:lang             = xml:lang
        {any attributes with non-schema namespace}
        >
        Content: ((xs:include | xs:import | xs:redefine | xs:annotation)*, (,
                ( | (xs:simpleType | xs:complexType | xs:group |
                xs:attributeGroup) | xs:element | xs:attribute |
                xs:notation), xs:annotation*)*)
</xs:schema>
```

May be included in: (must be root element)

Description

xs:schema is the document (root) element of any W3C XML Schema. It's both a container for all the declarations and definitions of the schema and a place holder for a number of default values expressed as attributes. The compositors embedded directly under xs:schema have a special role, since they are considered global definitions that can be referenced elsewhere.

Restrictions

A xs:schema element (and therefore a schema) is associated with a maximum of one namespace and must import the definitions of compositors for other namespaces if needed.

Example

```
<xs:schema xmlns:xs="http://www.w3.org/2001/XMLSchema">
  <xs:element name="name" type="xs:string"/>
  <xs:element name="qualification" type="xs:string"/>
  <xs:element name="born" type="xs:date"/>
  <xs:element name="dead" type="xs:date"/>
  <xs:element name="isbn" type="xs:NMTOKEN"/>
  <xs:attribute name="id" type="xs:ID"/>
  <xs:attribute name="available" type="xs:boolean"/>
  <xs:attribute name="lang" type="xs:language"/>
  .../...
</xs:schema>
```

Attributes

attributeFormDefault
> Default value for the form attributes of xs:attribute, determining whether attributes will be namespace-qualified by default.

blockDefault
> Default value of the block attribute of xs:element and xs:complexType.

elementFormDefault
> Default value for the form attributes of xs:element, determining whether attributes will be namespace-qualified by default

finalDefault
> Default value of the final attribute of xs:element and xs:complexType.

id
> W3C XML Schema's element ID.

targetNamespace
> Namespace attached to this schema. All the qualified elements and attributes defined in this schema will belong to this namespace. This namespace will also be attached to all the global components.

version
> Version of the schema (for user convenience).

xml
> Language of the schema.

xs:selector

Definition of the the path selecting an element for a uniqueness constraint.

```
<xs:selector
        id              = xs:ID
```

```
            xpath           = xs:token
            {any attributes with non-schema namespace}
            >
            Content: (xs:annotation?)
</xs:selector>
```

May be included in: xs:key, xs:keyref, xs:unique

Description

xs:selector is used to define the element on which a uniqueness constraint or reference is checked (it cannot be an attribute, since attributes are already unique per XML 1.0). It is identified by a relative XPath expression.

The constraint is checked while looping on the XPath expression is resolved relative to the root element of the constraint. It serves as the location from which xs:field XPath expressions are resolved.

Restrictions

The xpath attribute uses a simple subset of XPath 1.0. The motivation of the W3C XML Schema Working Group for defining this subset is to simplify the work of the implementers of schema processors, and also to define a subset that constrains the path to stay within the scope of the current element.

This subset is restricted to use the child only; self and descendant, and self XPath axes through their abbreviated syntaxes without including any test in any of the XPath location steps and without using any XPath functions. It is identical to the subset defined for xs:field, except that attributes are allowed in xs:field and forbidden in xs:selector.

The formal extended BNF given in the W3C Recommendation is as follow:

```
        Selector ::= Path ( '|' Path )* Path ::= ('.//')? Step ( '/' Step )* Step ::= '.' |
        NameTest NameTest ::= QName | '*' | NCName ':' '*'
```

Example

```
        <xs:element name="book" maxOccurs="unbounded">
          <xs:complexType>
            .../...
          </xs:complexType>
          <xs:unique name="book">
            <xs:selector xpath="book"/>
            .../...
          </xs:unique>
        </xs:element>
```

Attributes

id
    W3C XML Schema's element ID.

xpath
    Relative XPath expression identifying the element on which the constraint applies.

xs:sequence (outside a group)
Compositor to define an ordered group of elements.

```
<xs:sequence
        id                  = xs:ID
        maxOccurs           = ( xs:nonNegativeInteger | "unbounded" ) : "1"
        minOccurs           = xs:nonNegativeInteger : "1"
        {any attributes with non-schema namespace}
        >
        Content: (xs:annotation?, (xs:element | xs:group | xs:choice |
                xs:sequence | xs:any) )*)
</xs:sequence>
```

May be included in: xs:choice (outside a group), xs:choice (within a group), xs:complexType (local definition), xs:complexType (global definition), xs:extension (complex content), xs:restriction (complex content), xs:sequence (within a group), xs:sequence (outside a group)

Description

This compositor is used to define an ordered list or set of elements. It can hold its own minOccurs and maxOccurs attributes to define a number of occurrences of the whole sequence.

Restrictions

xs:sequence may not be included in an xs:all compositor, and xs:sequence may not include xs:all compositors.

When xs:sequence is included in an xs:group compositor, its content model is slightly different (see the section xs:sequence (within a group)).

Example

```
<xs:element name="library">
  <xs:complexType>
    <xs:sequence>
      <xs:element ref="book" maxOccurs="unbounded"/>
    </xs:sequence>
  </xs:complexType>
</xs:element>
```

Attributes

id
    W3C XML Schema's element ID.
maxOccurs
    Maximum number of occurrences.
minOccurs
    Minimum number of occurrences.

xs:sequence (within a group)
Compositor to define an ordered group of elements. The number of occurrences cannot be defined when xs:all is used within a group.

```
<xs:sequence
        id          = xs:ID
```

```
         {any attributes with non-schema namespace}
         >
         Content: (xs:annotation?, (xs:element | xs:group | xs:choice |
                   xs:sequence | xs:any) )*)
</xs:sequence>
```

May be included in: xs:group (definition)

Description

This compositor is used to define ordered list of elements.

Restrictions

xs:sequence may not include xs:all compositors.

When xs:sequence is used outside an xs:group compositor, its content model is slightly different (see the section xs:sequence (outside a group)).

Example

```
<xs:group name="name">
  <xs:sequence>
    <xs:element ref="name"/>
    <xs:sequence minOccurs="0">
      <xs:element ref="middle-name" minOccurs="0"/>
      <xs:element ref="last-name"/>
    </xs:sequence>
  </xs:sequence>
</xs:group>
```

Attributes

id
   W3C XML Schema's element ID.

---

xs:simpleContent   Simple content model declaration.

```
<xs:simpleContent
         id          = xs:ID
         {any attributes with non-schema namespace}
         >
         Content: ((xs:annotation?), (xs:restriction | xs:extension))
</xs:simpleContent>
```

May be included in: xs:complexType (local definition), xs:complexType (global definition)

Description

This element allows the definition of a simple content model by derivation of a simple type or of another simple content complex type. It is not a component by itself (simple contents are not named) but rather declaration of the intention to define a simple content model by derivation.

The derivation method is not defined by the xs:simpleContent element, but by the choice of its child element (which is xs:restriction for a derivation by restriction, or xs:extension for a derivation by extension).

Restrictions

None.

Example

```
<xs:element name="title">
  <xs:complexType>
    <xs:simpleContent>
      <xs:extension base="xs:string">
        <xs:attribute ref="lang"/>
      </xs:extension>
    </xs:simpleContent>
  </xs:complexType>
</xs:element>
```

Attributes

id
>   W3C XML Schema's element ID.

---

xs:simpleType (global definition)

Global simple type declaration that can be referenced within the same schema by other schemas.

```
<xs:simpleType
        final       = ( "#all" | ( "list" | "union" | "restriction" ) )
        id          = xs:ID
        name        = xs:NCName
        {any attributes with non-schema namespace}
        >
        Content: (xs:annotation?, (xs:restriction | xs:list | xs:union))
</xs:simpleType>
```

May be included in: xs:redefine, xs:schema

Description

Global user-defined simple datatypes are defined directly under the xs:schema document element (or redefined using xs:redefine) outside of the scope of any specific content model. They can be referenced through their qualified name in the same schema or by any other schema that has included or imported this schema.

Like local simple datatypes, these are defined by derivation from other simple datatypes (either predefined by W3C XML Schema or other user-defined datatypes) using one of the three derivation methods available for simple types: xs:restriction to add new constraints to a datatype, xs:list to define lists of values, and xs:union to perform the union of the lexical spaces of several datatypes).

The name attribute is unqualified since the datatype is considered to belong to the target namespace of the schema in which it is defined. During a reference, the prefix that has been defined for this namespace needs to be added.

Although simple datatypes are considered to belong to the target namespace of schema in which they are defined, they can be referenced to create new datatypes, attributes, or elements for any namespace.

Further derivations (by list, union, restriction, or all) can be blocked using the final attribute.

Restrictions

W3C XML Schema doesn't provide any mechanism to add new primary datatypes, new facets, or to act on the transformation performed between the lexical and value spaces (for instance, it is not possible to change the representation of the decimal point).

Example

```
<xs:simpleType name="totalDigits">
  <xs:restriction base="xs:integer">
    <xs:totalDigits value="5"/>
  </xs:restriction>
</xs:simpleType>
```

Attributes

final
> When set, this attribute blocks any further derivations of this datatype (by list, union, derivation, or all).

id
> W3C XML Schema's element ID.

name
> Unqualified name of this datatype.

---

xs:simpleType (local definition) Local simple type definition (local definitions cannot be referenced).

```
<xs:simpleType
        id           = xs:ID
        {any attributes with non-schema namespace}
        >
        Content: (xs:annotation?, (xs:restriction | xs:list | xs:union))
</xs:simpleType>
```

May be included in: xs:attribute (reference or local definition), xs:attribute (global definition), xs:element (within xs:all), xs:element (reference or local definition), xs:element (global definition), xs:list, xs:restriction (simple type), xs:restriction (simple content), xs:union

Description

Local simple datatypes are defined directly where needed (during element, attribute, or other simple type definitions) for local anonymous usage, and cannot be referenced as such in other places of a schema.

Like global simple datatypes, these are defined by derivation from other simple datatypes (either predefined by W3C XML Schema or other user-defined datatypes) using one of the three derivation methods available for simple types: xs:restriction to add new constraints to a datatype, xs:list to define lists of values, and xs:union to perform the union of the lexical spaces of several datatypes).

Restrictions

W3C XML Schema doesn't provide any mechanism for creating new primary datatypes, new facets, or to act on the transformation performed between the lexical and value spaces (for instance, it is not possible to change the representation of the decimal point).

Example

```
<xs:simpleType name="myInteger">
  <xs:restriction>
    <xs:simpleType>
      <xs:restriction base="xs:integer">
        <xs:maxExclusive value="5"/>
      </xs:restriction>
    </xs:simpleType>
    <xs:minInclusive value="-2"/>
  </xs:restriction>
</xs:simpleType>
```

Attributes

id
>   W3C XML Schema's element ID.

---

xs:totalDigits

Facet to define the total number of digits of a numeric datatype.

```
<xs:totalDigits
        fixed        = xs:boolean : "false"
        id           = xs:ID
        value        = xs:positiveInteger
        {any attributes with non-schema namespace}
        >
        Content: (xs:annotation?)
</xs:totalDigits>
```

May be included in: xs:restriction (simple type), xs:restriction (simple content)
May be used as facet for: xs:byte, xs:decimal, xs:int, xs:integer, xs:long, xs:negativeInteger,
*   xs:nonNegativeInteger, xs:nonPositiveInteger, xs:positiveInteger, xs:short, xs:unsignedByte,*
*   xs:unsignedInt, xs:unsignedLong, xs:unsignedShort*

Description

xs:totalDigits defines the maximum number of digits of decimal and derived datatypes (both after and before the decimal point, not counting the decimal point itself).

This facet constrains the value space, which means that the number of digits is checked after the value is transformed to its canonical form and the leading and trailing zeros are removed.

Restrictions

It is also possible to use xs:pattern to constrain the number of total digits in the lexical space.

Within a restriction step, xs:totalDigits is dependent on xs:fractionDigits since using inconsistent values leads to datatypes with empty value spaces.

xs:totalDigits must restrict the value space of its base type. Its value must be smaller than the value of the xs:totalDigits of its base type if defined.

Example

```
<xs:simpleType name="totalDigits">
  <xs:restriction base="xs:integer">
    <xs:totalDigits value="5"/>
  </xs:restriction>
</xs:simpleType>
```

Attributes

fixed
> When set to true, the value of the facet cannot be modified during further restrictions.

id
> W3C XML Schema's element ID.

value
> Value of the facet.

xs:union   Derivation of simple datatypes by union.

```
<xs:union
          id          = xs:ID
          memberTypes = list of xs:QName
          {any attributes with non-schema namespace}
          >
          Content: ((xs:annotation?), (xs:simpleType*))
</xs:union>
```

May be included in: xs:simpleType (local definition), xs:simpleType (global definition)

Description

Deriving a simple datatype by union merges the lexical spaces of several simple datatypes (called member types) to create a new simple datatype.

Whatever the type (atomic, list, or union) of the member types, the resulting datatype has a type union.

The member types can be defined either by reference (through the memberTypes attribute) or embedded as simple datatype local definitions in the xs:union element. Both styles can be mixed.

The semantic of the member datatypes is lost at least as far as validation is concerned, and the only facets that can be further applied to the resulting datatype are xs:pattern and xs:enumeration.

However, the semantic of the member datatypes isn't completely lost for an application built on a PSVI, since the validator needs to perform canonicalization according to the first member type that matches the instance value. This implies that order matters in the list of member types. When both styles are used, the datatypes referenced in the memberTypes are tested before the locally defined datatypes.

Restrictions

None.

Example

```
<xs:simpleType name="integerOrData">
  <xs:union memberTypes="xs:integer xs:date"/>
</xs:simpleType>
```

Attributes

id
    W3C XML Schema's element ID.

memberTypes
    List of member types (member types can also be embedded as xs:simpleType in the xs:union element).

---

xs:unique
Definition of a uniqueness constraint.

```
<xs:unique
        id              = xs:ID
        name            = xs:NCName
        {any attributes with non-schema namespace}
        >
        Content: ((xs:annotation?), (xs:selector, xs:field+))
</xs:unique>
```

May be included in: xs:element (within xs:all), xs:element (reference or local definition), xs:element (global definition)

Description

xs:unique is used to define simple or compound constraints, which unambiguously identify each element in which they are present, from a selected list of subelements within the scope of a root element.

xs:unique is very similar to xs:key. Like the constraints defined with xs:key, constraints defined with xs:unique are unique in the scope of their root element and may be referenced by xs:keyref. The only difference between xs:unique and xs:key is that the xs:unique keys may be undefined in any of the elements in the selection list, while xs:key identifiers must be defined for all the elements in the selection list.

The root element for the constraint is the element in which the constraint is defined. The location of the root element must be carefully chosen since the unity of the constraint is checked only within the node elements that are its children. Defining a root element that has multiple occurrences within a document leaves the possibility of defining local constraints that are unique only in the scope of each occurrence of a document. When a constraint is global to a document, defining it using the document element as a root may cause it to be less error-prone.

The contribution of xs:unique to the PSVI is a node table in each occurrence of the root key element that contains the list of the key sequences for this root element. The scope of these node tables is limited to the root element in which they are contained and all its ancestors. This scope is used to determine the behavior of the key references and impacts the choice of the constraint root element when the constraint is referenced (see the section xs:keyref).

Restrictions

These XPath-based features do not follow the object-oriented, namespace-aware general philosophy of W3C XML Schema. The XPath expressions are specified independently of the element's content model, and the constraints for the elements of all the possible namespaces must be defined in the schema for the namespace of the constraint root element.

Example

```
<xs:element name="library">
  <xs:complexType>
    .../...
  </xs:complexType>
  <xs:unique name="book">
    <xs:selector xpath="book"/>
    <xs:field xpath="isbn"/>
  </xs:unique>
</xs:element>
```

Attributes

id
    W3C XML Schema's element ID.
name
    Name of the unique constraint.

xs:whiteSpace

Facet to define whitespace behavior.

```
<xs:whiteSpace
        fixed           = xs:boolean : "false"
        id              = xs:ID
        value           = ( "preserve" | "replace" | "collapse" )
        {any attributes with non-schema namespace}
        >
        Content: (xs:annotation?)
</xs:whiteSpace>
```

May be included in: xs:restriction (simple type), xs:restriction (simple content)
May be used as facet for:xs:ENTITIES, xs:ENTITY, xs:ID, xs:IDREF, xs:IDREFS, xs:language, xs:Name, xs:NCName, xs:NMTOKEN, xs:NMTOKENS, xs:normalizedString, xs:string, xs:token

Description

This facet defines the treatment to perform on whitespace—i.e., #x20 (space), #x9 (tab), #xA (linefeed), and #xD (carriage return)—during the transformation between the lexical and value spaces.

Its values are preserve (whitespace characters are kept unchanged), replace (all instances of whitespace are replaced with a space), and collapse (leading and trailing whitespace is removed and all the other sequences of contiguous whitespace are replaced by a single space).

Restrictions

This is the only facet (or feature of W3C XML Schema) that interacts with the canonicalization transformation.

It is not possible to "relax" the whitespace behavior during a restriction: if a datatype has a whitespace set as preserve, its derived datatypes can have any whitespace behavior, but if its whitespace is set as replace, its derived datatypes can only have whitespace equal to replace or collapse. If its whitespace is equal to collapse, all its derived datatypes must have the same behavior.

This limitation is somewhat paradoxical since it allows the actual expansion of the lexical space of a datatype during a derivation by restriction.

Example

```
<xs:simpleType name="CapitalizedNameWS">
  <xs:restriction base="xs:string">
    <xs:whiteSpace value="collapse"/>
    <xs:pattern value="([A-Z]([a-z]*) ?)+"/>
  </xs:restriction>
</xs:simpleType>
```

Attributes

fixed
> When set to fixed, the value of this facet cannot be changed in further restrictions.

id
> W3C XML Schema's element ID.

value
> Value of the facet.

CHAPTER 16

Datatype Reference Guide

This chapter provides a quick reference to all of the datatypes W3C XML Schema defines. Each datatype is listed with its constraining facets, as well as information about what it represents and how.

Datatype

---

xs:anyURI

URI (Uniform Resource Identifier).

Derived from:	xs:anySimpleType
Primary:	xs:anyURI
Known subtypes:	none

Facets: xs:enumeration, xs:length, xs:maxLength, xs:minLength, xs:pattern, *xs:whiteSpace*

Definition

```
<xs:simpleType name="anyURI" id="anyURI">
  <xs:restriction base="xs:anySimpleType">
    <xs:whiteSpace value="collapse" fixed="true"/>
  </xs:restriction>
</xs:simpleType>
```

Description

This datatype corresponds normatively to the XLink href attribute. Its value space includes the URIs defined by the RFCs 2396 and 2732, but its lexical space doesn't require the character escapes needed to include non-ASCII characters in URIs.

Restrictions

Relative URIs are not "absolutized" by W3C XML Schema. A datatype defined as:

```
<xs:simpleType name="schemaRecommendations">
  <xs:restriction base="xs:anyURI">
    <xs:enumeration value="http://www.w3.org/TR/xmlschema-0/"/>
    <xs:enumeration value="http://www.w3.org/TR/xmlschema-1/"/>
    <xs:enumeration value="http://www.w3.org/TR/xmlschema-2/"/>
```

```
    </xs:restriction>
  </xs:simpleType>
```

should not validate the href attribute in this instance element:

```
  <a xml:base="http://www.w3.org/TR/" href="xmlschema-1/">
    XML Schema Part 2: Datatypes
  </a>
```

The Recommendation states that "it is impractical for processors to check that a value is a context-appropriate URI reference," freeing schema processors from having to validate the correctness of the URI.

Example

```
  <xs:simpleType name="httpURI">
    <xs:restriction base="xs:anyURI">
      <xs:pattern value="http://.*"/>
    </xs:restriction>
  </xs:simpleType>
```

---

xs:base64Binary

Binary content coded as "base64".

Derived from:	xs:anySimpleType	**Facets:**	xs:enumeration, xs:length, xs:maxLength,
Primary:	xs:base64Binary		xs:minLength, xs:pattern, *xs:whiteSpace*
Known subtypes:	none		

Definition

```
<xs:simpleType name="base64Binary" id="base64Binary">
  <xs:restriction base="xs:anySimpleType">
    <xs:whiteSpace value="collapse" fixed="true"/>
  </xs:restriction>
</xs:simpleType>
```

Description

The value space of xs:base64Binary is the set of arbitrary binary contents. Its lexical space is the same set after base64 coding. This coding is described in Section 6.8 of RFC 2045.

Restrictions

RFC 2045 has been defined to transfer binary contents over text-based mail systems. It imposes a line break at least every 76 characters to avoid the inclusion of arbitrary line breaks by the mail systems. Sending base64 content without line breaks is nevertheless a common usage for applications such as SOAP and the W3C XML Schema Working Group. After a request from other W3C Working Groups, the W3C XML Schema Working Group decided to remove the obligation to include these line breaks from the constraints on the lexical space. (This decision was made after the publication of the W3C XML Schema Recommendation and should be included in a release of the errata.)

Example

```
  <xs:element name="picture">
    <xs:complexType>
```

```
      <xs:simpleContent>
        <xs:extension base="xs:base64Binary">
          <xs:attribute name="type" type="graphicalFormat"/>
        </xs:extension>
      </xs:simpleContent>
    </xs:complexType>
  </xs:element>
```

xs:boolean

Boolean (true or false).

Derived from: xs:anySimpleType
Primary: xs:boolean
Known subtypes: none

Facets: xs:pattern, *xs:whiteSpace*

Definition

```
<xs:simpleType name="boolean" id="boolean">
  <xs:restriction base="xs:anySimpleType">
    <xs:whiteSpace value="collapse" fixed="true"/>
  </xs:restriction>
</xs:simpleType>
```

Description

The value space of xs:boolean is "true" and "false," and its lexical space accepts true, false, and also "1" (for true) and "0" (for false).

Restrictions

This datatype cannot be localized—for instance, to accept "vrai" and "faux" instead of "true" and "false".

Example

```
<book id="b0836217462" available="true"/>
```

xs:byte

Signed value of 8 bits.

Derived from: xs:short
Primary: xs:decimal
Known subtypes: none

Facets: xs:enumeration, *xs:fractionDigits*, xs:maxExclusive, xs:maxInclusive, xs:minExclusive, xs:minInclusive, xs:pattern, xs:totalDigits, *xs:whiteSpace*

Definition

```
<xs:simpleType name="byte" id="byte">
  <xs:restriction base="xs:short">
    <xs:minInclusive value="-128"/>
    <xs:maxInclusive value="127"/>
  </xs:restriction>
</xs:simpleType>
```

Description

The value space of xs:byte is the integers between -128 and 127, i.e., the signed values that can fit in a word of 8 bits. Its lexical space allows an optional sign and leading zeros before the significant digits.

Restrictions

The lexical space does not allow values expressed in other numeration bases (such as hexadecimal, octal, or binary).

Example

Valid values for byte include 27, -34, +105, and 0.

Invalid values include 0A, 1524, and INF.

---

xs:date

Gregorian calendar date.

		Facets:	
Derived from:	xs:anySimpleType		xs:enumeration, xs:maxExclusive, xs:maxInclusive,
Primary:	xs:date		xs:minExclusive, xs:minInclusive, xs:pattern,
Known subtypes:	none		*xs:whiteSpace*

Definition

```
<xs:simpleType name="date" id="date">
  <xs:restriction base="xs:anySimpleType">
    <xs:whiteSpace value="collapse" fixed="true"/>
  </xs:restriction>
</xs:simpleType>
```

Description

This datatype is modeled after the calendar dates defined in Chapter 5.2.1 of ISO 8601. Its value space is the set of Gregorian calendar dates as defined by this standard; i.e., a one-day-long period of time. Its lexical space is the ISO 8601 extended format "[-]CCYY-MM-DD[Z|(+|-)hh:mm]" with an optional timezone. Timezones that are not specified are considered "undetermined."

Restrictions

The basic format of ISO 8601 calendar dates "CCYYMMDD" is not supported.

The other forms of dates available in ISO 8601—ordinal dates defined by the year and the number of the day in the year and dates identified by calendar week and day numbers—are not supported.

As the value space is defined by reference to ISO 8601, there is no support for any calendar system other than Gregorian.

As the lexical space is also defined as reference to ISO 8601, there is no support for any localization such as different orders for date parts or named months.

The order relation between dates with and without timezone is partial: they can be compared only outside of a +/- 14 hours interval.

There is a dissension between ISO 8601 which defines a day as a period of time of 24 hours, and W3C XML Schema, which indicates that a date is a "one-day long, non-periodic instance…independent of how many hours this day has." Even though technically right (some days do not last exactly 24 hours because of leap seconds), this definition is not coherent with the definition of xs:duration for which a day is always exactly 24 hours long.

Example

Valid values include: "2001-10-26", "2001-10-26+02:00", "2001-10-26Z", "2001-10-26+00:00", "-2001-10-26", or "-20000-04-01".

The following values would be invalid: "2001-10" (all the parts must be specified), "2001-10-32" (the days part (32) is out of range), "2001-13-26+02:00" (the month part (13) is out of range), or "01-10-26" (the century part is missing).

---

xs:dateTime

Instant of time (Gregorian calendar).

Derived from:	xs:anySimpleType	Facets:	xs:enumeration, xs:maxExclusive, xs:maxInclusive,
Primary:	xs:dateTime		xs:minExclusive, xs:minInclusive, xs:pattern,
Known subtypes:	none		*xs:whiteSpace*

Definition

```
<xs:simpleType name="dateTime" id="dateTime">
  <xs:restriction base="xs:anySimpleType">
    <xs:whiteSpace value="collapse" fixed="true"/>
  </xs:restriction>
</xs:simpleType>
```

Description

This datatype describes instants identified by the combination of a date and a time. Its value space is described as a "combination of date and time of day" in Chapter 5.4 of ISO 8601. Its lexical space is the extended format "[-]CCYY-MM-DDThh:mm:ss[Z|(+|-)hh:mm]". The timezone may be specified as "Z" (UTC) or "(+|-)hh:mm." Timezones that are not specified are considered "undetermined."

Restrictions

The basic format of ISO 8601 calendar datetimes "CCYYMMDDThhmmss" is not supported.

The other forms of datetimes available in ISO 8601—ordinal dates defined by the year and the number of the day in the year and dates identified by calendar week and day numbers—are not supported.

As the value space is defined by reference to ISO 8601, there is no support for any calendar system other than Gregorian.

As the lexical space is also defined as reference to ISO 8601, there is no support for any localization such as different orders for date parts or named months.

The order relation between datetimes with and without timezone is partial: they can be compared only outside of a +/- 14 hours interval.

Example

Valid values for xs:dateTime include: "2001-10-26T21:32:52", "2001-10-26T21:32:52+02:00", "2001-10-26T19:32:52Z", "2001-10-26T19:32:52+00:00", "-2001-10-26T21:32:52", or "2001-10-26T21:32:52.12679".

The following values would be invalid: "2001-10-26" (all the parts must be specified), "2001-10-26T21:32" (all the parts must be specified), "2001-10-26T25:32:52+02:00" (the hours part (25) is out of range), or "01-10-26T21:32" (all the parts must be specified).

---

xs:decimal
Decimal numbers.

Derived from: xs:anySimpleType
Primary: xs:decimal
Known subtypes: xs:integer

Facets: xs:enumeration, xs:fractionDigits, xs:maxExclusive, xs:maxInclusive, xs:minExclusive, xs:minInclusive, xs:pattern, xs:totalDigits, *xs:whiteSpace*

Definition

```
<xs:simpleType name="decimal" id="decimal">
  <xs:restriction base="xs:anySimpleType">
    <xs:whiteSpace value="collapse" fixed="true"/>
  </xs:restriction>
</xs:simpleType>
```

Description

xs:decimal is the datatype that represents the set of all the decimal numbers with arbitrary lengths. Its lexical space allows any number of insignificant leading and trailing zeros (after the decimal point).

Restrictions

The decimal separator is always a point (".") and no thousand separator may be added. There is no support for scientific notations.

Example

Valid values include: "123.456", "+1234.456", "-1234.456", "-.456", or "-456".

The following values would be invalid: "1 234.456" (spaces are forbidden), "1234.456E+2" (scientific notation ("E+2") is forbidden), "+ 1234.456" (spaces are forbidden), or "+1,234.456" (delimiters between thousands are forbidden).

---

xs:double
IEEE 64 bit floating point.

Derived from: xs:anySimpleType
Primary: xs:double
Known subtypes: none

Facets: xs:enumeration, xs:maxExclusive, xs:maxInclusive, xs:minExclusive, xs:minInclusive, xs:pattern, *xs:whiteSpace*

Definition

```
<xs:simpleType name="double" id="double">
  <xs:restriction base="xs:anySimpleType">
```

```
      <xs:whiteSpace value="collapse" fixed="true"/>
   </xs:restriction>
</xs:simpleType>
```

Description

The value space of xs:double is "double" (64 bits) floating-point numbers as defined by the IEEE. The lexical space uses a decimal format with optional scientific notation. The match between lexical (powers of 10) and value (powers of 2) spaces is approximate and done on the closest value.

This datatype differentiates positive (0) and negative (-0) zeros, and includes the special values "-INF" (negative infinity), "INF" (positive infinity) and "NaN" (Not a Number).

Note that the lexical spaces of xs:float and xs:double are exactly the same; the only difference is the precision used to convert the values in the value space.

Restrictions

The decimal separator is always a point (".") and no thousands separator may be used.

Examples

Valid values include: "123.456", "+1234.456", "-1.2344e56", "-.45E-6", "INF", "-INF", or "NaN".

The following values would be invalid: "1234.4E 56" (spaces are forbidden), "1E+2.5" (the power of 10 must be an integer), "+INF" (positive infinity doesn't expect a sign), or "NAN" (capitalization matters in special values).

---

xs:duration   Time durations.

Derived from:	xs:anySimpleType	**Facets:**	xs:enumeration, xs:maxExclusive, xs:maxInclusive,
Primary:	xs:duration		xs:minExclusive, xs:minInclusive, xs:pattern,
Known subtypes:	none		*xs:whiteSpace*

Definition

```
<xs:simpleType name="duration" id="duration">
  <xs:restriction base="xs:anySimpleType">
    <xs:whiteSpace value="collapse" fixed="true"/>
  </xs:restriction>
</xs:simpleType>
```

Description

Durations may be expressed using all the parts of a datetime (from year to fractions of second) and are, therefore, defined as a "six-dimensional space." Note that because the relation between some of these date parts (such as the number of days in a month) is not fixed, the order relationship between durations is only partial and the result of a comparison between two durations may be undetermined.

The lexical space of xs:duration is the format defined by ISO 8601 under the form "PnYn-MnDTnHnMnS," in which the capital letters are delimiters and can be omitted when the corresponding member is not used.

Although some durations are undetermined, this is fixed as soon as a starting point is fixed for the duration. W3C XML Schema relies on this feature to define the algorithm to use to compare two durations. Four datetimes have been chosen, which produce the greatest deviations when durations are added. A duration will be considered bigger than another when the result of its addition to these four dates is consistently bigger than the result of the addition of the other duration to these same four datetimes. These datetimes are: "1696-09-01T00:00:00Z", "1697-02-01T00:00:00Z," "1903-03-01T00:00:00Z," and "1903-07-01T00:00:00Z."

Restrictions

The lexical space cannot be customized.

Example

Valid values include "PT1004199059S", "PT130S", "PT2M10S", "P1DT2S", "-P1Y", or "P1Y2M3DT5H20M30.123S".

The following values would be invalid: "1Y" (leading "P" is missing), "P1S" ("T" separator is missing), "P-1Y" (all parts must be positive), "P1M2Y" (parts order is significant and Y must precede M), or "P1Y-1M" (all parts must be positive).

---

xs:ENTITIES
Whitespace separated list of unparsed entity references.

Derived from:	xs:ENTITY	Facets:	xs:enumeration, xs:length, xs:maxLength,
Primary:	none		xs:minLength, xs:whiteSpace
Known subtypes:	none		

Definition

```
<xs:simpleType name="ENTITIES" id="ENTITIES">
  <xs:restriction>
    <xs:simpleType>
      <xs:list>
        <xs:simpleType>
          <xs:restriction base="xs:ENTITY"/>
        </xs:simpleType>
      </xs:list>
    </xs:simpleType>
    <xs:minLength value="1"/>
  </xs:restriction>
</xs:simpleType>
```

Description

xs:ENTITIES is derived by a list from xs:ENTITY. It represents lists of unparsed entity references. Each part of this entity reference is a nonqualified name (xs:NCName) and must be declared as an unparsed entity in an internal or external DTD.

Restrictions

Unparsed entities have been defined in XML 1.0 as a way to include non-XML content in a XML document, but most of the applications prefer to define links (such as those defined in (X)HTML to include images or other multimedia objects).

W3C XML Schema does not provide alternative ways to declare unparsed entities. A DTD is needed to do so.

---

xs:ENTITY

Reference to an unparsed entity.

Derived from:	xs:NCName	Facets:	xs:enumeration, xs:length, xs:maxLength,
Primary:	xs:string		xs:minLength, xs:pattern, xs:whiteSpace
Known subtypes:	xs:ENTITIES		

Definition

```
<xs:simpleType name="ENTITY" id="ENTITY">
  <xs:restriction base="xs:NCName"/>
</xs:simpleType>
```

Description

xs:ENTITY is an entity reference, i.e., a nonqualified name (xs:NCName) that has been declared as an unparsed entity in an internal or external DTD.

Restrictions

Unparsed entities are defined in XML 1.0 as a way to include non-XML content in XML document, but most of the applications prefer to define links (such as those defined in (X)HTML to include images or other multimedia objects).

W3C XML Schema does not provide alternative ways to declare unparsed entities. A DTD is needed to do so.

---

xs:float

IEEE 32 bit floating point.

Derived from:	xs:anySimpleType	Facets:	xs:enumeration, xs:maxExclusive, xs:maxInclusive,
Primary:	xs:float		xs:minExclusive, xs:minInclusive, xs:pattern,
Known subtypes:	none		*xs:whiteSpace*

Definition

```
<xs:simpleType name="float" id="float">
  <xs:restriction base="xs:anySimpleType">
    <xs:whiteSpace value="collapse" fixed="true"/>
  </xs:restriction>
</xs:simpleType>
```

Description

The value space of xs:float is "float" (32 bits) floating-point numbers as defined by the IEEE. The lexical space uses a decimal format with optional scientific notation. The match between lexical (powers of 10) and value (powers of 2) spaces is approximate and is done on the closest value.

This datatype differentiates positive (0) and negative (-0) zeros, and includes the special values "-INF" (negative infinity), "INF" (positive infinity), and "NaN" (Not a Number).

Note that the lexical spaces of xs:float and xs:double are exactly the same; the only difference is the precision used to convert the values in the value space.

Restrictions

The decimal separator is always a point (".") and no thousands separator may be added.

Example

Valid values include: "123.456", "+1234.456", "-1.2344e56", "-.45E-6", "INF", "-INF", or "NaN".

The following values would be invalid: "1234.4E 56" (spaces are forbidden), "1E+2.5" (the power of 10 must be an integer), "+INF" (positive infinity doesn't expect a sign), or "NAN" (capitalization matters in special values).

---

xs:gDay

Recurring period of time: monthly day.

Derived from: xs:anySimpleType
Primary: xs:gDay
Known subtypes: none

Facets: xs:enumeration, xs:maxExclusive, xs:maxInclusive, xs:minExclusive, xs:minInclusive, xs:pattern, *xs:whiteSpace*

Definition

```
<xs:simpleType name="gDay" id="gDay">
  <xs:restriction base="xs:anySimpleType">
    <xs:whiteSpace value="collapse" fixed="true"/>
  </xs:restriction>
</xs:simpleType>
```

Description

The value space of xs:gDay is the periods of one calendar day recurring each calendar month (such as the third of the month); its lexical space follows the ISO 8601 syntax for such periods (i.e., "---DD") with an optional timezone.

When needed, days are reduced to fit in the length of the months, so ---31 would occur on the the 28th of February of nonleap years.

Restrictions

The period (one month) and the duration (one day) are fixed, and no calendars other than the Gregorian are supported.

Example

Valid values include "---01", "---01Z", "---01+02:00", "---01-04:00", "---15", or "---31".

The following values would be invalid: "--30-" (the format must be "---DD"), "---35" (the day is out of range), "---5" (all the digits must be supplied), or "15" (missing leading "---").

---

xs:gMonth

Recurring period of time: yearly month.

Derived from: xs:anySimpleType
Primary: xs:gMonth
Known subtypes: none

Facets: xs:enumeration, xs:maxExclusive, xs:maxInclusive, xs:minExclusive, xs:minInclusive, xs:pattern, *xs:whiteSpace*

Definition

```
<xs:simpleType name="gMonth" id="gMonth">
  <xs:restriction base="xs:anySimpleType">
    <xs:whiteSpace value="collapse" fixed="true"/>
  </xs:restriction>
</xs:simpleType>
```

Description

The value space of xs:gMonth is the period of one calendar month recurring each calendar year (such as the month of April); its lexical space should follow the ISO 8601 syntax for such periods (i.e., "--MM") with an optional timezone. However, there is a typo in the W3C XML Schema Recommendation where the format is defined as "--MM--". Even though an erratum should be published to bring the W3C XML Schema inline with ISO 8601, most of the current schema processors will expect the (bogus) format "--MM--". In the example, we follow the correct ISO 8601 format.

Restrictions

The period (one year) and the duration (one month) are fixed, and no calendars other than the Gregorian are supported.

Because of the typo in the W3C XML Schema Specification, users must choose between a bogus format, which works on the current version of the tools, or a correct format, which conforms to ISO 8601.

Example

Valid values include "--05", "--11Z", "--11+02:00", "--11-04:00", or "--02".

The following values would be invalid: "-01-" (the format must be "--MM"), "--13" (the month is out of range), "--1" (both digits must be provided), or "01" (leading "--" are missing).

xs:gMonthDay

Recurring period of time: yearly day.

Derived from: xs:anySimpleType
Primary: xs:gMonthDay
Known subtypes: none

Facets: xs:enumeration, xs:maxExclusive, xs:maxInclusive, xs:minExclusive, xs:minInclusive, xs:pattern, *xs:whiteSpace*

Definition

```
<xs:simpleType name="gMonthDay" id="gMonthDay">
  <xs:restriction base="xs:anySimpleType">
    <xs:whiteSpace value="collapse" fixed="true"/>
  </xs:restriction>
</xs:simpleType>
```

Description

The value space of xs:gMonthDay is the period of one calendar day recurring each calendar year (such as the third of April); its lexical space follows the ISO 8601 syntax for such periods (i.e., "--MM-DD") with an optional timezone.

When needed, days are reduced to fit in the length of the months, so --02-29 would occur on the the 28th of February of nonleap years.

Restrictions

The period (one year) and the duration (one day) are fixed, and no calendars other than the Gregorian are supported.

Example

Valid values include "--05-01", "--11-01Z", "--11-01+02:00", "--11-01-04:00", "--11-15", or "--02-29".

The following values would be invalid: "-01-30-" (the format must be "--MM-DD"), "--01-35" (the day part is out of range), "--1-5" (the leading zeros are missing), or "01-15" (the leading "--" are missing).

---

xs:gYear

Period of one year.

Derived from:	xs:anySimpleType	Facets:	xs:enumeration, xs:maxExclusive, xs:maxInclusive,
Primary:	xs:gYear		xs:minExclusive, xs:minInclusive, xs:pattern,
Known subtypes:	none		*xs:whiteSpace*

Definition

```
<xs:simpleType name="gYear" id="gYear">
  <xs:restriction base="xs:anySimpleType">
    <xs:whiteSpace value="collapse" fixed="true"/>
  </xs:restriction>
</xs:simpleType>
```

Description

The value space of xs:gYear is the period of one calendar year (such as the year 2002); its lexical space follows the ISO 8601 syntax for such periods (i.e., "YYYY") with an optional timezone.

Restrictions

The duration (one year) is fixed, and no calendars other than the Gregorian are supported.

Example

Valid values include "2001", "2001+02:00", "2001Z", "2001+00:00", "-2001", or "-20000".

The following values would be invalid: "01" (the century part is missing) or "2001-12" (month parts are forbidden).

---

xs:gYearMonth

Period of one month.

Derived from: xs:anySimpleType
Primary: xs:gYearMonth
Known subtypes: none

Facets: xs:enumeration, xs:maxExclusive, xs:maxInclusive, xs:minExclusive, xs:minInclusive, xs:pattern, *xs:whiteSpace*

Definition

```
<xs:simpleType name="gYearMonth" id="gYearMonth">
  <xs:restriction base="xs:anySimpleType">
    <xs:whiteSpace value="collapse" fixed="true"/>
  </xs:restriction>
</xs:simpleType>
```

Description

The value space of xs:gYearMonth is the period of one calendar month (such as the month of February 2002); its lexical space follows the ISO 8601 syntax for such periods (i.e., "YYYY-MM") with an optional timezone.

Restrictions

The duration (one month) is fixed, and no calendars other than the Gregorian are supported.

Example

Valid values include "2001-10", "2001-10+02:00", "2001-10Z", "2001-10+00:00", "-2001-10", or "-20000-04".

The following values would be invalid: "2001" (the month part is missing), "2001-13" (the month part is out of range), "2001-13-26+02:00" (the month part is out of range), or "01-10" (the century part is missing).

---

xs:hexBinary

Binary contents coded in hexadecimal.

Derived from: xs:anySimpleType
Primary: xs:hexBinary
Known subtypes: none

Facets: xs:enumeration, xs:length, xs:maxLength, xs:minLength, xs:pattern, *xs:whiteSpace*

Definition

```
<xs:simpleType name="hexBinary" id="hexBinary">
  <xs:restriction base="xs:anySimpleType">
    <xs:whiteSpace value="collapse" fixed="true"/>
  </xs:restriction>
</xs:simpleType>
```

Description

The value space of xs:hexBinary is the set of all binary contents; its lexical space is a simple coding of each octet as its hexadecimal value.

Restrictions

This datatype should not be confused with another encoding called BinHex that is not supported by W3C XML Schema. Other popular binary text encodings (such as uuXX-code, Quote Printable, BinHex, aencode, or base85, to name few) are not supported by the W3C XML Schema.

The expansion factor is high since each binary octet is coded as two characters (i.e., four octets if the document is encoded with UTF-16).

Example

A UTF-8 XML header such as:

```
"<?xml version="1.0" encoding="UTF-8"?>"
```

encoded would be:

```
"3f3c6d78206c657673726f693d6e3122302e20226e656f636964676e6e223d54552d4622383e3f"
```

---

xs:ID

Definition of unique identifiers.

Derived from:	xs:NCName	Facets:	xs:enumeration, xs:length, xs:maxLength,
Primary:	xs:string		xs:minLength, xs:pattern, xs:whiteSpace
Known subtypes:	none		

Definition

```
<xs:simpleType name="ID" id="ID">
  <xs:restriction base="xs:NCName"/>
</xs:simpleType>
```

Description

The purpose of the xs:ID datatype is to define unique identifiers that are global to a document and emulate the ID attribute type available in the XML DTDs.

Unlike their DTD counterparts, W3C XML Schema ID datatypes can be used to define not only attributes, but also simple element content.

For both attributes and simple element content, the lexical domain of these datatypes is the lexical domain of XML nonqualified names (xs:NCName).

Identifiers defined using this datatype are global to a document and provide a way to uniquely identify their containing element, whatever its type and name is.

The constraint added by this datatype beyond the xs:NCName datatype from which it is derived is that the values of all the attributes and elements that have an ID datatype in a document must be unique.

Restrictions

Applications that need to maintain a level of compatibility with DTDs should not use this datatype for elements but should reserve it for attributes.

The lexical domain (xs:NCName) of this datatype doesn't allow the definition of numerical identifiers or identifiers containing whitespaces.

W3C XML Schema provides another mechanism to define unique and key constraints using the xs:unique or xs:key elements when more flexibility is needed.

Example

```
<xs:element name="book">
  <xs:complexType>
    <xs:sequence>
      <xs:element name="isbn" type="xs:int"/>
      <xs:element name="title" type="xs:string"/>
      <xs:element name="author-ref">
        <xs:complexType>
          <xs:attribute name="ref" type="xs:IDREF" use="required"/>
        </xs:complexType>
      </xs:element>
      <xs:element name="character-refs" type="xs:IDREFS"/>
    </xs:sequence>
    <xs:attribute name="identifier" type="xs:ID" use="required"/>
  </xs:complexType>
</xs:element>
```

xs:IDREF

Definition of references to unique identifiers.

		Facets:	
Derived from:	xs:NCName	Facets:	xs:enumeration, xs:length, xs:maxLength,
Primary:	xs:string		xs:minLength, xs:pattern, xs:whiteSpace
Known subtypes:	xs:IDREFS		

Definition

```
<xs:simpleType name="IDREF" id="IDREF">
  <xs:restriction base="xs:NCName"/>
</xs:simpleType>
```

Description

The xs:IDREF datatype defines references to the identifiers defined by the ID datatype and, therefore, emulates the IDREF attribute type of the XML DTDs, even though it can be used for simple content elements as well as for attributes.

The lexical space of xs:IDREF is, like the lexical space of xs:ID, nonqualified XML names (NCName).

The constraint added by this datatype beyond the xs:NCName datatype from which it is derived is the values of all the attributes and elements that have a xs:IDREF datatype must match an ID defined within the same document.

Restrictions

Applications that need to maintain a level of compatibility with DTDs should not use this datatype for elements but should reserve it for attributes.

The lexical domain (NCName) of this datatype doesn't allow definition of numerical key references or references containing whitespaces.

W3C XML Schema provides another mechanism to define key reference constraints using the xs:keyref elements when more flexibility is needed.

Example

```
<xs:element name="book">
  <xs:complexType>
    <xs:sequence>
      <xs:element name="isbn" type="xs:int"/>
      <xs:element name="title" type="xs:string"/>
      <xs:element name="author-ref">
        <xs:complexType>
          <xs:attribute name="ref" type="xs:IDREF" use="required"/>
        </xs:complexType>
      </xs:element>
      <xs:element name="character-refs" type="xs:IDREFS"/>
    </xs:sequence>
    <xs:attribute name="identifier" type="xs:ID" use="required"/>
  </xs:complexType>
</xs:element>
```

---

xs:IDREFS

Definition of lists of references to unique identifiers.

Derived from:	xs:IDREF	**Facets:** xs:enumeration, xs:length, xs:maxLength,
Primary:	none	xs:minLength, xs:whiteSpace
Known subtypes:	none	

Definition

```
<xs:simpleType name="IDREFS" id="IDREFS">
  <xs:restriction>
    <xs:simpleType>
      <xs:list>
        <xs:simpleType>
          <xs:restriction base="xs:IDREF"/>
        </xs:simpleType>
      </xs:list>
    </xs:simpleType>
    <xs:minLength value="1"/>
  </xs:restriction>
</xs:simpleType>
```

Description

xs:IDREFS is derived as a list from xs:IDREF and, thus, represents whitespace-separated lists of references to identifiers defined using the ID datatype.

The lexical space of xs:IDREFS is the lexical space of a list of xs:NCName values with a minimum length of one element (xs:IDREFS cannot be empty lists).

xs:IDREFS emulates the xs:IDREFS attribute type of the XML DTDs, even though it can be used to define simple content elements as well as attributes.

Restrictions

Applications that need to maintain a level of compatibility with DTDs should not use this datatype for elements but should reserve it for attributes.

The lexical domain (lists of xs:NCName) of this datatype doesn't allow definition of lists of numerical key references or references containing whitespaces.

Although the W3C XML Schema provides another mechanism to define unique, key, and key reference constraints (using the xs:unique, xs:key, and xs:keyref elements) when more flexibility is needed, this mechanism doesn't provide any alternative for lists of key references (similar to xs:IDREFS).

Example

```
<xs:element name="book">
  <xs:complexType>
    <xs:sequence>
      <xs:element name="isbn" type="xs:int"/>
      <xs:element name="title" type="xs:string"/>
      <xs:element name="author-ref">
        <xs:complexType>
          <xs:attribute name="ref" type="xs:IDREF" use="required"/>
        </xs:complexType>
      </xs:element>
      <xs:element name="character-refs" type="xs:IDREFS"/>
    </xs:sequence>
    <xs:attribute name="identifier" type="xs:ID" use="required"/>
  </xs:complexType>
</xs:element>
```

xs:int

32 bit signed integers.

Derived from:	xs:long	Facets:	xs:enumeration, *xs:fractionDigits*, xs:maxExclusive,
Primary:	xs:decimal		xs:maxInclusive, xs:minExclusive, xs:minInclusive,
Known subtypes:	xs:short		xs:pattern, xs:totalDigits, *xs:whiteSpace*

Definition

```
<xs:simpleType name="int" id="int">
  <xs:restriction base="xs:long">
    <xs:minInclusive value="-2147483648"/>
    <xs:maxInclusive value="2147483647"/>
  </xs:restriction>
</xs:simpleType>
```

Description

The value space of xs:int is the set of common single size integers (32 bits), i.e., the integers between -2147483648 and 2147483647, its lexical space allows any number of insignificant leading zeros.

Restrictions

The decimal point (even when followed only by insignificant zeros) is forbidden.

-0 and +0 are considered equal, which is different from the behavior of xs:float and xs:double.

Example

Valid values include "-2147483648", "0", "-0000000000000000000005", or "2147483647".
Invalid values include "-2147483649" and "1".

---

xs:integer

Signed integers of arbitrary length.

Derived from: xs:decimal
Primary: xs:decimal
Known subtypes: xs:nonPositiveInteger, xs:long, xs:nonNegativeInteger

Facets: xs:enumeration, *xs:fractionDigits*, xs:maxExclusive, xs:maxInclusive, xs:minExclusive, xs:minInclusive, xs:pattern, xs:totalDigits, *xs:whiteSpace*

Definition

```
<xs:simpleType name="integer" id="integer">
  <xs:restriction base="xs:decimal">
    <xs:fractionDigits value="0" fixed="true"/>
  </xs:restriction>
</xs:simpleType>
```

Description

The value space of xs:integer includes the set of all the signed integers, with no restriction on range. Its lexical space allows any number of insignificant leading zeros.

Restrictions

The decimal point (even when followed only by insignificant zeros) is forbidden.

-0 and +0 are considered equal, which is different from the behavior of xs:float and xs:double.

Example

Valid values for xs:integer include "-12345678901234567890123 4567890", "2147483647", "0", or "-0000000000000000000005".

Invalid values include "1.", "2.6", and "A".

---

xs:language

RFC 1766 language codes.

Derived from: xs:token
Primary: xs:string
Known subtypes: none

Facets: xs:enumeration, xs:length, xs:maxLength, xs:minLength, xs:pattern, xs:whiteSpace

Definition

```
<xs:simpleType name="language" id="language">
  <xs:restriction base="xs:token">
    <xs:pattern
      value="([a-zA-Z]{2}|[iI]-[a-zA-Z]+|[xX]-[a-zA-Z]{1,8})(-[a-zA-Z]{1,8})*"
    />
  </xs:restriction>
</xs:simpleType>
```

Description

The lexical and value spaces of xs:language are the set of language codes defined by the RFC 1766.

Restrictions

Although the schema for schema defines a minimal test to perform expressed as patterns (see the Definition), the lexical space is the set of existing language codes.

Example

Some valid values for this datatype are: "en", "en-US", "fr", or "fr-FR".

---

xs:long

64 bit signed integers.

Derived from:	xs:integer	Facets:	xs:enumeration, *xs:fractionDigits*, xs:maxExclusive,
Primary:	xs:decimal		xs:maxInclusive, xs:minExclusive, xs:minInclusive,
Known subtypes:	xs:int		xs:pattern, xs:totalDigits, *xs:whiteSpace*

Definition

```
<xs:simpleType name="long" id="long">
  <xs:restriction base="xs:integer">
    <xs:minInclusive value="-9223372036854775808"/>
    <xs:maxInclusive value="9223372036854775807"/>
  </xs:restriction>
</xs:simpleType>
```

Description

The value space of xs:long is the set of common double-size integers (64 bits), i.e., the integers between -9223372036854775808 and 9223372036854775807; its lexical space allows any number of insignificant leading zeros.

Restrictions

The decimal point (even when followed only by insignificant zeros) is forbidden.

Example

Valid values for xs:long include "-9223372036854775808", "0", "-0000000000000000000005", or "9223372036854775807".

Invalid values include "9223372036854775808" and "1.".

---

xs:Name

XML 1.0 names.

Derived from:	xs:token	Facets:	xs:enumeration, xs:length, xs:maxLength,
Primary:	xs:string		xs:minLength, xs:pattern, xs:whiteSpace
Known subtypes:	xs:NCName		

Definition

```
<xs:simpleType name="Name" id="Name">
  <xs:restriction base="xs:token">
    <xs:pattern value="\i\c*"/>
  </xs:restriction>
</xs:simpleType>
```

Description

The lexical and value spaces of xs:Name are the tokens (NMTOKEN) that conform to the definition of a name in XML 1.0.

Restrictions

Following XML 1.0, those names may contain colons (":"), but no special meaning is attached to these characters. Another datatype (xs:QName) should be used for qualified names when they use namespaces prefixes.

Example

Valid values include "Snoopy", "CMS", or "_1950-10-04_10:00".

Invalid values include "0836217462" (a xs:Name cannot start with a number) or "bold,brash" (commas are forbidden).

---

xs:NCName   Unqualified names.

Derived from:	xs:Name		Facets:	xs:enumeration, xs:length, xs:maxLength,
Primary:	xs:string			xs:minLength, xs:pattern, xs:whiteSpace
Known subtypes:	xs:ID, xs:IDREF, xs:ENTITY			

Definition

```
<xs:simpleType name="NCName" id="NCName">
  <xs:restriction base="xs:Name">
    <xs:pattern value="[\i-[:]][\c-[:]]*"/>
  </xs:restriction>
</xs:simpleType>
```

Description

The lexical and value spaces of xs:NCName are the names (Name) that conform to the definition of a NCName in the Recommendation "Namespaces in XML 1.0"—i.e., all the XML 1.0 names that do not contain colons (":").

Restrictions

This datatype allows characters such as "-" and may need additional constraints to match the notion of name in your favorite programming language or database system.

Example

Valid values include "Snoopy", "CMS", "_1950-10-04_10-00", or "bold_brash".

Invalid values include "_1950-10-04:10-00" or "bold:brash" (colons are forbidden).

---

xs:negativeInteger

Strictly negative integers of arbitrary length.

Derived from: xs:nonPositiveInteger
Primary: xs:decimal
Known subtypes: none

Facets: xs:enumeration, *xs:fractionDigits*, xs:maxExclusive, xs:maxInclusive, xs:minExclusive, xs:minInclusive, xs:pattern, xs:totalDigits, *xs:whiteSpace*

Definition

```
<xs:simpleType name="negativeInteger" id="negativeInteger">
  <xs:restriction base="xs:nonPositiveInteger">
    <xs:maxInclusive value="-1"/>
  </xs:restriction>
</xs:simpleType>
```

Description

The value space of xs:negativeInteger includes the set of all the strictly negative integers (excluding zero), with no restriction of range. Its lexical space allows any number of insignificant leading zeros.

Restrictions

The decimal point (even when followed only by insignificant zeros) is forbidden.

Example

Valid values for xs:negativeInteger include "-12345678901234567890123456789", "-1", or "-0000000000000000000005".

Invalid values include "0" or "-1.".

xs:NMTOKEN

XML 1.0 name token (NMTOKEN).

Derived from: xs:token
Primary: xs:string
Known subtypes: xs:NMTOKENS

Facets: xs:enumeration, xs:length, xs:maxLength, xs:minLength, xs:pattern, xs:whiteSpace

Definition

```
<xs:simpleType name="NMTOKEN" id="NMTOKEN">
  <xs:restriction base="xs:token">
    <xs:pattern value="\c+"/>
  </xs:restriction>
</xs:simpleType>
```

Description

The lexical and value spaces of xs:NMTOKEN are the set of XML 1.0 "name tokens," i.e., tokens composed of characters, digits, ".", ":", "-", and the characters defined by Unicode, such as "combining" or "extender".

Restrictions

This type is usually called a "token."

Example

Valid values include "Snoopy", "CMS", "1950-10-04", or "0836217462".

Invalid values include "brought classical music to the Peanuts strip" (spaces are forbidden) or "bold,brash" (commas are forbidden).

---

xs:NMTOKENS

List of XML 1.0 name token (NMTOKEN).

Derived from:	xs:NMTOKEN	**Facets:**	xs:enumeration, xs:length, xs:maxLength,
Primary:	none		xs:minLength, xs:whiteSpace
Known subtypes:	none		

Definition

```
<xs:simpleType name="NMTOKENS" id="NMTOKENS">
  <xs:restriction>
    <xs:simpleType>
      <xs:list>
        <xs:simpleType>
          <xs:restriction base="xs:NMTOKEN"/>
        </xs:simpleType>
      </xs:list>
    </xs:simpleType>
    <xs:minLength value="1"/>
  </xs:restriction>
</xs:simpleType>
```

Description

xs:NMTOKENS is derived by list from xs:NMTOKEN and represents whitespace-separated lists of XML 1.0 name tokens.

Restrictions

None.

Example

Valid values include "Snoopy", "CMS", "1950-10-04", "0836217462 0836217463", or "brought classical music to the Peanuts strip" (note that, in this case, the sentence is considered as a list of words).

Invalid values include "brought classical music to the "Peanuts" strip" (quotes are forbidden) or "bold,brash" (commas are forbidden).

---

xs:nonNegativeInteger

Integers of arbitrary length positive or equal to zero.

Derived from:	xs:integer	**Facets:**	xs:enumeration, *xs:fractionDigits*, xs:maxExclusive,
Primary:	xs:decimal		xs:maxInclusive, xs:minExclusive, xs:minInclusive,
Known subtypes:	xs:unsignedLong,		xs:pattern, xs:totalDigits, *xs:whiteSpace*
	xs:positiveInteger		

Definition

```
<xs:simpleType name="nonNegativeInteger" id="nonNegativeInteger">
  <xs:restriction base="xs:integer">
    <xs:minInclusive value="0"/>
  </xs:restriction>
</xs:simpleType>
```

Description

The value space of xs:nonNegativeInteger includes the set of all the integers greater than or equal to zero, with no restriction of range. Its lexical space allows any number of insignificant leading zeros.

Restrictions

The decimal point (even when followed only by insignificant zeros) is forbidden.

Example

Valid values include "+1234567890123456789012345678901234567890", "0", "00000000000000000000005", or "2147483647".

Invalid values include "1." or "-1.".

---

xs:nonPositiveInteger

Integers of arbitrary length negative or equal to zero.

Derived from:	xs:integer	Facets:	xs:enumeration, *xs:fractionDigits*, xs:maxExclusive,
Primary:	xs:decimal		xs:maxInclusive, xs:minExclusive, xs:minInclusive,
Known subtypes:	xs:negativeInteger		xs:pattern, xs:totalDigits, *xs:whiteSpace*

Definition

```
<xs:simpleType name="nonPositiveInteger" id="nonPositiveInteger">
  <xs:restriction base="xs:integer">
    <xs:maxInclusive value="0"/>
  </xs:restriction>
</xs:simpleType>
```

Description

The value space of xs:nonPositiveInteger includes the set of all the integers less than or equal to zero, with no restriction of range. Its lexical space allows any number of insignificant leading zeros.

Restrictions

The decimal point (even when followed only by insignificant zeros) is forbidden.

Example

Valid values include "-1234567890123456789012345678901234567890", "0", "-00000000000000000000005", or "-2147483647".

Invalid values include "-1." or "1.".

xs:normalizedString

Whitespace-replaced strings.

Derived from:	xs:string	Facets:	xs:enumeration, xs:length, xs:maxLength,
Primary:	xs:string		xs:minLength, xs:pattern, xs:whiteSpace
Known subtypes:	xs:token		

Definition

```
<xs:simpleType name="normalizedString" id="normalizedString">
  <xs:restriction base="xs:string">
    <xs:whiteSpace value="replace"/>
  </xs:restriction>
</xs:simpleType>
```

Description

The lexical space of xs:normalizedString is unconstrained (any valid XML character may be used), and its value space is the set of strings after whitespace replacement (i.e., after any occurrence of #x9 (tab), #xA (linefeed), and #xD (carriage return) have been replaced by an occurrence of #x20 (space) without any whitespace collapsing).

Restrictions

This is the only datatype that performs whitespace replacement without collapsing. When whitespaces are not significant, xs:token is preferred.

This datatype corresponds to neither the XPath function normalize-space() (which performs whitespace trimming and collapsing) nor to the DOM "normalize" method (which is a merge of adjacent text objects).

Example

The value of the element:

```
<title lang="en">
  Being a Dog Is
  a Full-Time Job
</title>"
```

is the string: " Being a Dog Is a Full-Time Job ", where all the whitespaces have been replaced by spaces if the title element is a type xs:normalizedString.

xs:NOTATION

Emulation of the XML 1.0 feature.

Derived from:	xs:anySimpleType	Facets:	xs:enumeration, xs:length, xs:maxLength,
Primary:	xs:NOTATION		xs:minLength, xs:pattern, *xs:whiteSpace*
Known subtypes:	none		

Definition

```
<xs:simpleType name="NOTATION" id="NOTATION">
  <xs:restriction base="xs:anySimpleType">
    <xs:whiteSpace value="collapse" fixed="true"/>
  </xs:restriction>
</xs:simpleType>
```

Description

The value and lexical spaces of xs:NOTATION are references to notations declared though the xs:notation element. The use of this element and datatype is, therefore, a namespace-aware emulation of the NOTATION feature of XML 1.0.

Restrictions

Notations are very seldom used in real-world applications.

One cannot use xs:notation directly, but must derive it as shown in the Example.

Example

```
<xs:schema xmlns:xs="http://www.w3.org/2001/XMLSchema">
  <xs:notation name="jpeg" public="image/jpeg"
    system="file:///usr/bin/xv"/>
  <xs:notation name="gif" public="image/gif"
    system="file:///usr/bin/xv"/>
  <xs:notation name="png" public="image/png"
    system="file:///usr/bin/xv"/>
  <xs:notation name="svg" public="image/svg"
    system="file:///usr/bin/xsmiles"/>
  <xs:notation name="pdf" public="application/pdf"
    system="file:///usr/bin/acroread"/>
  <xs:simpleType name="graphicalFormat">
    <xs:restriction base="xs:NOTATION">
      <xs:enumeration value="jpeg"/>
      <xs:enumeration value="gif"/>
      <xs:enumeration value="png"/>
      <xs:enumeration value="svg"/>
      <xs:enumeration value="pdf"/>
    </xs:restriction>
  </xs:simpleType>
  <xs:element name="picture">
    <xs:complexType>
      <xs:simpleContent>
        <xs:extension base="xs:base64Binary">
          <xs:attribute name="type" type="graphicalFormat"/>
        </xs:extension>
      </xs:simpleContent>
    </xs:complexType>
  </xs:element>
</xs:schema>
```

---

xs:positiveInteger

Strictly positive integers of arbitrary length.

		Facets:	
Derived from:	xs:nonNegativeInteger		xs:enumeration, *xs:fractionDigits*, xs:maxExclusive,
Primary:	xs:decimal		xs:maxInclusive, xs:minExclusive, xs:minInclusive,
Known subtypes:	none		xs:pattern, xs:totalDigits, *xs:whiteSpace*

Definition

```
<xs:simpleType name="positiveInteger" id="positiveInteger">
  <xs:restriction base="xs:nonNegativeInteger">
    <xs:minInclusive value="1"/>
  </xs:restriction>
</xs:simpleType>
```

Description

The value space of xs:positiveInteger includes the set of the strictly positive integers (excluding zero), with no restriction of range. Its lexical space allows any number of insignificant leading zeros.

Restrictions

The decimal point (even when followed only by insignificant zeros) is forbidden.

Example

Valid values include "12345678901234567890123456789890", "1", or "0000000000000000000000005".

Invalid values include "0" or "1.".

---

xs:QName   Namespaces in XML qualified names.

Derived from:	xs:anySimpleType	Facets:	xs:enumeration, xs:length, xs:maxLength,
Primary:	xs:QName		xs:minLength, xs:pattern, *xs:whiteSpace*
Known subtypes:	none		

Definition

```
<xs:simpleType name="QName" id="QName">
  <xs:restriction base="xs:anySimpleType">
    <xs:whiteSpace value="collapse" fixed="true"/>
  </xs:restriction>
</xs:simpleType>
```

Description

The lexical space of xs:QName is the qualified names per Namespace in XML, i.e., a local name (which is a xs:NCName) with an optional prefix (itself a xs:NCName), separated by a colon (":"), where the prefix is declared a namespace prefix in the scope of the element carrying the value. Its value space comprises the pairs (namespace URI, local name) in which the namespace URI is the URI associated to the prefix in the namespace declaration.

This dissociation between lexical and value spaces makes a lot of difference when using facets such as xs:pattern (which acts on the lexical space only and thus constrains the namespace prefix) and xs:enumeration (which acts on the value space and thus constrains the namespace URI).

Restrictions

It is impossible to apply a pattern on the namespace URI.

The usage of QNames in elements and attributes is controversial since it creates a dependency between the content of the document and its markup. However, the official position of the W3C doesn't discourage this practice.

Example

W3C XML Schema itself has already given us some examples of QNames. When we wrote "`<xs:attribute name="lang" type="xs:language"/>`", the type attribute was a xs:QName and its value was the tuple {"`http://www.w3.org/2001/XMLSchema`", "`language`"} because the URI "`http://www.w3.org/2001/XMLSchema`" had been assigned to the prefix "`xs:`". If there had been no namespace declaration for this prefix, the type attribute would have been considered invalid.

---

xs:short

32 bit signed integers.

Derived from:	xs:int		Facets:	xs:enumeration, *xs:fractionDigits*, xs:maxExclusive,
Primary:	xs:decimal			xs:maxInclusive, xs:minExclusive, xs:minInclusive,
Known subtypes:	xs:byte			xs:pattern, xs:totalDigits, *xs:whiteSpace*

Definition

```
<xs:simpleType name="short" id="short">
  <xs:restriction base="xs:int">
    <xs:minInclusive value="-32768"/>
    <xs:maxInclusive value="32767"/>
  </xs:restriction>
</xs:simpleType>
```

Description

The value space of xs:short is the set of common short integers (16 bits), i.e., the integers between -32768 and 32767; its lexical space allows any number of insignificant leading zeros.

Restrictions

The decimal point (even when followed only by insignificant zeros) is forbidden.

Example

Valid values include "-32768", "0", "-00000000000000000000005", or "32767".
Invalid values include "32768" and "1.".

---

xs:string

Any string.

Derived from:	xs:anySimpleType		Facets:	xs:enumeration, xs:length, xs:maxLength,
Primary:	xs:string			xs:minLength, xs:pattern, xs:whiteSpace
Known subtypes:	xs:normalizedString			

Definition

```
<xs:simpleType name="string" id="string">
  <xs:restriction base="xs:anySimpleType">
    <xs:whiteSpace value="preserve"/>
  </xs:restriction>
</xs:simpleType>
```

Description

The lexical and value spaces of xs:string are the set of all possible strings composed of any character allowed in a XML 1.0 document without any treatment done on whitespaces.

Restrictions

This is the only datatype that leaves all the whitespaces. When whitespaces are not significant, xs:token is preferred.

Example

The value of the following element:

```
<title lang="en">
  Being a Dog Is
  a Full-Time Job
</title>
```

is the full string "Being a Dog Is a Full-Time Job", with all its tabulations and CR/LF if the title element is a xs:string type .

---

xs:time   Point in time recurring each day.

Derived from:	xs:anySimpleType	Facets:	xs:enumeration, xs:maxExclusive, xs:maxInclusive,
Primary:	xs:time		xs:minExclusive, xs:minInclusive, xs:pattern,
Known subtypes:	none		*xs:whiteSpace*

Definition

```
<xs:simpleType name="time" id="time">
  <xs:restriction base="xs:anySimpleType">
    <xs:whiteSpace value="collapse" fixed="true"/>
  </xs:restriction>
</xs:simpleType>
```

Description

The lexical space of xs:time is identical to the time part of xs:dateTime ("hh:mm:ss[Z|(+|-)hh:mm]"); and its value space is the set of points in time recurring daily.

Restrictions

The period (one day) is fixed and no calendars other than the Gregorian are supported.

Example

Valid values include "21:32:52", "21:32:52+02:00", "19:32:52Z", "19:32:52+00:00", or "21:32:52.12679".

Invalid values include "21:32" (all the parts must be specified), "25:25:10" (the hour part is out of range), "-10:00:00" (the hour part is out of range), or "1:20:10" (all the digits must be supplied).

---

xs:token
Whitespace-replaced and collapsed strings.

Derived from:	xs:normalizedString	Facets:	xs:enumeration, xs:length, xs:maxLength,
Primary:	xs:string		xs:minLength, xs:pattern, xs:whiteSpace
Known subtypes:	xs:language, xs:NMTOKEN,		
	xs:Name		

Definition

```
<xs:simpleType name="token" id="token">
  <xs:restriction base="xs:normalizedString">
    <xs:whiteSpace value="collapse"/>
  </xs:restriction>
</xs:simpleType>
```

Description

The lexical and value spaces of xs:token are the sets of all the strings after whitespace replacement—i.e., after any occurrence of #x9 (tab), #xA (linefeed), and #xD (carriage return) is replaced by an occurrence of #x20 (space) and collapsing (i.e., the contiguous occurrences of spaces are replaced by a single space, and leading and trailing spaces are removed).

More simply said, xs:token is the most appropriate datatype to use for strings that do not care about whitespaces.

Restrictions

The name xs:token is misleading since whitespaces are allowed within xs:token. xs:NMTOKEN is the type corresponding to what is usually called "tokens."

Example

The element:

```
<title lang="en">
  Being a Dog Is
  a Full-Time Job
</title>
```

is a valid xs:token and its value is the string "Being a Dog Is a Full-Time Job", where all the whitespaces have been replaced by spaces, leading and trailing spaces have been removed and contiguous sequences of spaces have been replaced by single spaces.

---

xs:unsignedByte
Unsigned value of 8 bits.

Derived from:	xs:unsignedShort	Facets:	xs:enumeration, *xs:fractionDigits*, xs:maxExclusive,
Primary:	xs:decimal		xs:maxInclusive, xs:minExclusive, xs:minInclusive,
Known subtypes:	none		xs:pattern, xs:totalDigits, *xs:whiteSpace*

Definition

```
<xs:simpleType name="unsignedByte" id="unsignedBtype">
  <xs:restriction base="xs:unsignedShort">
    <xs:maxInclusive value="255"/>
  </xs:restriction>
</xs:simpleType>
```

Description

The value space of xs:unsignedByte is the integers between 0 and 255, i.e., the unsigned values that can fit in a word of 8 bits. Its lexical space allows an optional "+" sign and leading zeros before the significant digits.

Restrictions

The lexical space does not allow values expressed in other numeration bases (such as hexadecimal, octal, or binary).

The decimal point (even when followed only by insignificant zeros) is forbidden.

Example

Valid values include "255", "0", "+00000000000000000000005", or "1".

Invalid values include "-1" and "1.".

---

xs:unsignedInt

Unsigned integer of 32 bits.

		Facets:	xs:enumeration, *xs:fractionDigits*, xs:maxExclusive,
Derived from:	xs:unsignedLong		xs:maxInclusive, xs:minExclusive, xs:minInclusive,
Primary:	xs:decimal		xs:pattern, xs:totalDigits, *xs:whiteSpace*
Known subtypes:	xs:unsignedShort		

Definition

```
<xs:simpleType name="unsignedInt" id="unsignedInt">
  <xs:restriction base="xs:unsignedLong">
    <xs:maxInclusive value="4294967295"/>
  </xs:restriction>
</xs:simpleType>
```

Description

The value space of xs:unsignedInt is the integers between 0 and 4294967295, i.e., the unsigned values that can fit in a word of 32 bits. Its lexical space allows an optional "+" sign and leading zeros before the significant digits.

Restrictions

The decimal point (even when followed only by insignificant zeros) is forbidden.

Example

Valid values include "4294967295", "0", "+00000000000000000000005", or "1".

Invalid values include "-1" and "1.".

---

xs:unsignedLong

Unsigned integer of 64 bits.

Derived from: xs:nonNegativeInteger
Primary: xs:decimal
Known subtypes: xs:unsignedInt

Facets: xs:enumeration, *xs:fractionDigits*, xs:maxExclusive, xs:maxInclusive, xs:minExclusive, xs:minInclusive, xs:pattern, xs:totalDigits, *xs:whiteSpace*

Definition

```
<xs:simpleType name="unsignedLong" id="unsignedLong">
  <xs:restriction base="xs:nonNegativeInteger">
    <xs:maxInclusive value="18446744073709551615"/>
  </xs:restriction>
</xs:simpleType>
```

Description

The value space of xs:unsignedLong is the integers between 0 and 18446744073709551615, i.e., the unsigned values that can fit in a word of 64 bits. Its lexical space allows an optional "+" sign and leading zeros before the significant digits.

Restrictions

The decimal point (even when followed only by insignificant zeros) is forbidden.

Example

Valid values include "18446744073709551615", "0", "+000000000000000000005", or "1". Invalid values include "-1" and "1.".

xs:unsignedShort

Unsigned integer of 16 bits.

Derived from: xs:unsignedInt
Primary: xs:decimal
Known subtypes: xs:unsignedByte

Facets: xs:enumeration, *xs:fractionDigits*, xs:maxExclusive, xs:maxInclusive, xs:minExclusive, xs:minInclusive, xs:pattern, xs:totalDigits, *xs:whiteSpace*

Definition

```
<xs:simpleType name="unsignedShort" id="unsignedShort">
  <xs:restriction base="xs:unsignedInt">
    <xs:maxInclusive value="65535"/>
  </xs:restriction>
</xs:simpleType>
```

Description

The value space of xs:unsignedShort is the integers between 0 and 65535, i.e., the unsigned values that can fit in a word of 16 bits. Its lexical space allows an optional "+" sign and leading zeros before the significant digits.

Restrictions

The decimal point (even when followed only by insignificant zeros) is forbidden.

Example

Valid values include "65535", "0", "+000000000000000000005", or "1".

Invalid values include "-1" and "1.".

XML Schema Languages

What Is a XML Schema Language?

Roughly speaking, XML schema languages describe XML documents. Different approaches to that task, however, provide a wide range of functionality.

XML Schema Languages Are Not Schemas

The first thing we can say about XML schema languages is they are not schemas. At least they do not match the definition of a schema as given by Webster's dictionary, which states: "an outline or image universally applicable to a general conception, under which it is likely to be presented to the mind; as, five dots in a line are a schema of the number five; a preceding and succeeding event are a schema of cause and effect."

This definition does not apply to the languages known as "XML schema languages"; most of these are more complex than the documents they describe and are too difficult to "be presented to the mind." They focus on defining validation rules more than on representing or modeling a class of documents. When they do model a class of documents, they often want to add information to the documents they model.

Looking past the formal label of schemas, how can we classify so-called "XML schema languages"? Looking at all XML schema languages (DTDs, W3C XML Schema, RELAX NG, and also languages such as Schematron), the one thing they have in common is being transformations, which take a "schema" and an instance document as an input and transform them into a validation report, and optionally, into a PSVI (Post Schema Validation Infoset), a set of information added to the XML infoset of the source document. This PSVI (when it exists) includes information such as default values, datatypes, etc.

Changing the category of XML schema languages not only alters our perception of what they are, but also opens the game, since general-purpose transformations or programming languages, such as XSLT, Prolog, Java, C# and friends, can be considered XML schema languages.

Firewalls Against Diversity

The "X" in XML stands for Extensibility. XML is, in fact, so extensible and diverse that few if any applications are able to support this diversity. XML schema languages were created as firewalls against diversity and protect applications from meeting unexpected information and formats.

This analogy provides us our first classification of schema languages. These, like firewalls, can be open and allow any construction that isn't forbidden (as in the case of Schematron), or they can be closed and forbid anything that has not been allowed. (This is the case for most of the other schema languages, including W3C XML Schema.)

Closed firewalls are certainly much safer than open ones, but also much less extensible, since any new traffic must be allowed by the administrator before it can pass through. This is one of the reasons for the failure of protocols such as CORBA, as well as one the reasons web services has chosen to use HTTP. Closed XML schema languages can represent the same kind of threat against the diversity of XML vocabularies as closed firewalls do against the diversity of IP protocols.

Therefore, there is a trade-off: being able to check whether a document we have received or are about to send is valid and won't blow up our applications is not only useful but even necessary. However, our schemas should stay open whenever possible to remain extensible. (Chapter 13 presents the techniques available with the W3C XML Schema to limit the danger of "closedness.")

Intrusive Modeling Tools

Schematron is the only XML schema language that doesn't base its validation on a model of the class of the documents that are considered valid. All the other XML schema languages describe the structure of the valid documents (which is where the name "schema" comes from). The lack of expressiveness of their description languages can be another threat to the diversity of XML vocabularies since the structures, which cannot be described with one of the major XML schema languages, might become deprecated automatically. Unfortunately, this will likely be the case with the W3C XML Schema, in which expressiveness can be considered medium. Some existing vocabularies, such as RSS 1.0 and WebDAV, cannot be described with W3C XML Schema.

One may argue whether such and such a structure, which cannot be described by such and such a language, is good practice or not. However, I think that XML schema languages should be as neutral as possible and not add constraints to those defined by the XML 1.0 and Namespaces in XML Recommendations. XML is still a young technology, and many innovative ways of using it are still to be discovered. Some of them may be jeopardized by the lack of expressiveness of W3C XML Schema.

On the other hand, modeling activity is valuable by itself and its outcome, expressed as a XML schema, can be used to automate or enhance the processing of the XML document or the generation of applications and generic tools, such as Version 2 of XPath and XSLT. The initial version of XQuery will rely on the information provided by XML schemas for advanced features, but also for things as basic as knowing which sort order should be used for each node.

In modeling, we find the same basic differences that can be found between an API (such as the DOM, in which each node is manipulated individually and is highly differentiated) and a model such as XPath, which enables splitting XML documents into sets of nodes ("nodesets"). While RELAX NG (co-authored by James Clark, who was also the editor of XPath 1.0) is based on the definition of patterns (classes of undifferentiated nodesets or containers encapsulating elements, attributes, and text nodes) W3C XML Schema has defined differentiated and different constructions to define elements, attributes, their content (called simple or complex types), and groups of elements or attributes.

Although this differentiation will seem natural when we get used to the W3C XML Schema, it is often useful to remember that those different constructions can be seen as a difference of perspective. Also, elements, attributes, types, and groups are "patterns," as defined by RELAX NG with a different granularity, and can be embedded within each other.

There is also a second consequence to any modeling activity, which is to change our perception of what is modeled. As the outside world is seen differently after Aristotle, Newton, and Einstein, your perception of a given XML document will vary depending upon which XML schema language you use.

Early Binding Tools

Another often mentioned quality of XML is its ability to serve as a base for late binding and highly decoupled systems in which the sender and receiver applications are independent of each other. This late binding ability has two major advantages. The first, which is very practical, is a complete independence between the systems and applications that create the XML document on one side and those that use it on the other side. The second, which is more abstract, allows the receiver to apply its own treatment and project its own semantic to "understand" the document, leaving the possibility of adding some value to the sent message.

XML Schema languages may be a danger for late binding approaches, especially those like the W3C XML Schema, which produce a PSVI, since the association of information from the schema is a form of early binding that binds a document to a specific XML schema language (necessary to interpret the document). Here again, this danger seems to be the price of automating the writing of applications to process the documents.

Classification of XML Schema Languages

In the previous section, we saw several classifications for XML schema languages (open or closed, with or without PSVI, etc.). Here, we will follow the classification done by the DSDL (Document Schema Definition Language) ISO project and define a more layered and structured classification.

Rule-Based XML Schema Languages

The XML schema languages that have the finest granularity for controlling how an instance document may look are the rule-based schema languages such as Schematron. Since any constraint may be expressed as a set of rules of some kind, rule-based schema languages may be considered as lower-level than the other XML schema languages that can be built on top of them. Though I am not aware of any implementation that does so, a W3C XML Schema processor could generate a set of Schematron rules to express its constraints. They can be used alone or to finish any work that cannot be finished with other XML schema languages that do not have their level of granularity. Embedding their rules in the W3C XML Schema seems very promising (as discussed in Chapter 14).

Grammar-Based XML Schema Languages

Grammar-based XML Schema languages act at another level and attempt to describe the structure of the instance documents. In a sense, they may be compared to a BNF (Backus-Naur Notation or Form, used to describe the syntax of programming languages) for XML. They describe the possible patterns of XML nodes as BNF describes possible patterns of characters. The most popular grammar-based XML schema languages are DTDs and RELAX NG. Focusing on the structure, those languages do not attach a lot of importance to the notions of datatype and PSVI. Those languages may also be seen as a concise way to define the rules that constrain the structure of a document, and may be used in conjunction with rule-based languages needed to express nonstructural rules.

Object-Oriented XML Schema Languages

It's clear that W3C XML Schema is something more than just a grammar-based XML schema language. It is also an attempt to describe instance documents in a way that is as close as possible to an object oriented design. One consequence is the importance of type. If elements and attributes are assimilated to objects, the types are the closest thing to object-oriented classes and are crucial to express the similarity between objects. The other object-oriented features of the W3C XML Schema are the derivation and substitution mechanisms defined to match the inheritance between object-oriented classes. And finally, since it is anticipated that object-oriented applications will benefit from this mapping between hierarchical XML and the object-oriented paradigm, the PSVI is key to communication between the schema processor and the applications.

A Short History of XML Schema Languages

The list of schema languages is long and needs to include languages developed for SGML (the language used before XML was born) to be complete. The list that I propose is far from exhaustive, and includes only the major proposals that have influenced the schema languages I see as the most promising.

The DTD Family

Mandatory for any SGML application, a simplified version of the SGML DTDs was introduced in the XML 1.0 Recommendation. Even though a DTD is not mandatory for an application to read and understand a XML document, many developers highly recommend writing DTDs for any XML application.

The W3C XML Schema Family

The W3C XML Schema Working Group received many proposals that were contributed as notes:

- XML-Data, submitted as a note (*http://www.w3.org/TR/1998/NOTE-XML-data*) in January 1998 by Microsoft, DataChannel, Arbortext, Inso Corporation, and the University of Edinburgh, included most of the basic concepts later developed by W3C XML Schema. Although the details were not fully developed, the note covered a lot of ground that was kept out of W3C XML Schema, such as internal and external entity definitions and the mapping to RDF (Resource Description Framework) and OOP structures.

- XML-Data-Reduced (XDR), submitted in July 1998 (*http://www.ltg.ed.ac.uk/~ht/ XMLData-Reduced.htm*) by Microsoft and the University of Edinburgh was presented to "refine and subset those ideas down to a more manageable size in order to allow faster progress toward adopting a new schema language for XML" (mappings were left out). XDR was implemented by Microsoft and used by the BizTalk framework.

- DCD (Document Content Description for XML), also submitted in July 1998 (*http://www.w3.org/TR/NOTE-dcd*) by Textuality, Microsoft, and IBM, was a "subset of the XML-Data Submission (XML-Data) and expressed it in a way which is consistent with the ongoing W3C RDF (Resource Description Framework) effort." Mapping considerations were left out, but the language took care to be consistent with RDF through features such as "Interchangeability of Elements and Attributes."

- SOX (Schema for Object-Oriented XML) was developed by Veo Systems/Commerce One and submitted as a note in September 1998 (a second version was submitted in July 1999 (see *http://www.w3.org/TR/NOTE-SOX*) as "informed by the XML 1.0 specification as well as the XML-Data submission (XML-Data), the Document Content Description submission (DCD), and the EXPRESS language reference manual (ISO-10303-11)." SOX was very influenced by OOP language design and included concepts of interface and implementation, but it was also influenced by DTDs and included support for "parameters." SOX is widely used by Commerce One.

- DDML (Document Definition Markup Language or XSchema) was the "result of contributions from a large number of people on the XML-Dev mailing list, coordinated by a smaller group of editors" (Ronald Bourret, John Cowan, Ingo Macherius, and Simon St. Laurent) and was submitted as a note in January 1999 (*http://www.w3.org/TR/NOTE-ddml*). Its purpose was to "encode the logical (as opposed to physical) content of DTDs in an XML document." Great attention is paid to the definition of the back and forward conversions between DTDs and DDML, and the document also includes an "experimental" chapter proposing "Inline DDML Elements." DDML made a clear distinction between structures and data and left datatypes out.

- W3C XML Schema, published as a Recommendation in May 2001 (*http://www.w3.org/TR/xmlschema-0*, *http://www.w3.org/TR/xmlschema-1* and *http://www.w3.org/TR/xmlschema-2*) acknowledges the influence of DCD, DDML, SOX, XML-Data, and XDR in its list of references. It appears to have picked pieces from each of these proposals but is also a compromise between them. The main sponsors of the two languages still actively used and developed (Microsoft for XDR and Commerce One for SOX) both announced that they would support the W3C XML Schema for their new developments. W3C XML Schema will most likely become the only surviving member of this family in the long-term.

The RELAX NG Family

The RELAX NG family is a more traditional marriage between grammar-based XML Schema languages that have chosen to unite their strengths.

- First published in March 2000 as a Japanese ISO Standard Technical Report written by Murata Makoto, Regular Language description for XML Core (RELAX; see *http://www.xml.gr.jp/relax*) is both simple ("Tired of complicated specifications? You just RELAX !") and built on a solid mathematical foundation (the adaptation of the hedge automata theory to XML trees). It was approved as an ISO/IEC Technical Report in May 2001.

- XDuce (*http://xduce.sourceforge.net*) was first announced in March 2000. "XDuce ('transduce') is a typed programming language that is specifically designed for processing XML data. One can read an XML document as an XDuce value, extract information from it or convert it to another format, and write out the result value as an XML document." Although it is not meant to be a schema language, its typing system has influenced the schema languages.

- Published by James Clark in January 2001, TREX (Tree Regular Expressions for XML; see *http://thaiopensource.com/trex*) is "basically the type system of XDuce with an XML syntax and with a bunch of additional features." The names and content models of the elements used to define the tree patterns of a TREX schema have been carefully chosen, and TREX schemas are usually as easy to read as a plain text description. The simplicity of the structure of the language also allows the resurrection of a consistent treatment between elements and attributes, a feature lost since DCD.

- Announced in May 2001, RELAX NG (RELAX New Generation) is a merger of RELAX and TREX, developed by an OASIS TC (*http://www.oasis-open.org/ committees/relax-ng*), coedited by James Clark and Murata Makoto. "The key features of RELAX NG are that it is simple, easy to learn, uses XML syntax, does not change the information set of an XML document, supports XML namespaces, treats attributes uniformly with elements so far as possible, has unrestricted support for unordered content, has unrestricted support for mixed content, has a solid theoretical basis, and can partner with a separate datatyping language (such W3C XML Schema Datatypes)." RELAX NG is now an official specification of the OASIS RELAX NG Technical Committee and will probably progress to become an ISO/IEC International Standard as part of DSDL.

Schematron

Schematron (*http://www.ascc.net/xml/resource/schematron/schematron.html*), which was first proposed in September 1999 by Rick Jelliffe of the Academia Sinica Computing Centre, is an unusual schema language. It defines validation rules using XPath expressions. Schematron is also described in the ISO DSDL project.

Examplotron

Starting from the observations that instance documents are usually much easier to understand than the schemas that describe them, and that schema languages often need to give examples of instance documents to help human readers to understand their syntax, I proposed Examplotron (*http://examplotron.org*) in March 2001, to define "schemas by example" using sample instance documents as actual schemas.

Sample Application

In the remainder of this appendix, we use the following simple library application, adapted from our first example in Chapter 1 to illustrate the use of the various schema languages:

```
<library>
  <book id="-0836217462">
    <isbn>
      0836217462
    </isbn>
    <title>
      Being a Dog Is a Full-Time Job
    </title>
    <author-ref id="Charles-M.-Schulz"/>
    <character-ref id="Peppermint-Patty"/>
    <character-ref id="Snoopy"/>
    <character-ref id="Schroeder"/>
    <character-ref id="Lucy"/>
  </book>
  <book id="-0805033106">
    <isbn>
      0805033106
    </isbn>
    <title>
      Peanuts Every Sunday
    </title>
    <author-ref id="Charles-M.-Schulz"/>
    <character-ref id="Sally-Brown"/>
    <character-ref id="Snoopy"/>
    <character-ref id="Linus"/>
    <character-ref id="Snoopy"/>
  </book>
  <author id="Charles-M.-Schulz">
    <name>
      Charles M. Schulz
    </name>
    <nickName>
      SPARKY
    </nickName>
    <born>
      November 26, 1922
    </born>
    <dead>
      February 12, 2000
    </dead>
  </author>
  <character id="Peppermint-Patty">
    <name>
      Peppermint Patty
    </name>
    <since>
      Aug. 22, 1966
    </since>
```

```
      <qualification>
        bold, brash and tomboyish
      </qualification>
    </character>
    <character id="Snoopy">
      <name>
        Snoopy
      </name>
      <since>
        October 4, 1950
      </since>
      <qualification>
        extroverted beagle
      </qualification>
    </character>
    <character id="Schroeder">
      <name>
        Schroeder
      </name>
      <since>
        May 30, 1951
      </since>
      <qualification>
        brought classical music to the Peanuts strip
      </qualification>
    </character>
    <character id="Lucy">
      <name>
        Lucy
      </name>
      <since>
        March 3, 1952
      </since>
      <qualification>
        bossy, crabby and selfish
      </qualification>
    </character>
    <character id="Sally-Brown">
      <name>
        Sally Brown
      </name>
      <since>
        Aug, 22, 1960
      </since>
      <qualification>
        always looks for the easy way out
      </qualification>
    </character>
    <character id="Linus">
      <name>
        Linus
      </name>
      <since>
        Sept. 19, 1952
```

```
      </since>
      <qualification>
        the intellectual of the gang
      </qualification>
    </character>
  </library>
```

XML DTDs

Inherited from SGML, the XML DTD is the most widely deployed means of defining an XML schema. Defined in the XML 1.0 Recommendation, DTDs do not support namespaces, which were specified later. This, together with the fact that its datatype system is weak and applies only to attributes, is one of the main motivations for the W3C to develop a new schema language. Table A-1 provides the fact sheet for XML DTDs.

Table A-1. XML DTD fact sheet

Author:	W3C.
Status:	Recommendation ("embedded" in XML 1.0).
Location:	*http://www.w3.org/TR/REC-xml.*
Type:	Grammar-based.
PSVI:	Yes (weak).
Structures:	Yes.
Datatypes:	Yes (weak).
Integrity:	Yes (internal through ID/IDREF/IDREFS attributes).
Rules:	No.
Vendor support:	Excellent.
Miscellaneous:	Non-XML syntax; no support for namespaces. Schema definition is only one of the features of DTDs. Requires deterministic content models.

Example

```
<!ELEMENT author (name, nickName, born, dead)>
<!ATTLIST author
  id ID #REQUIRED
>
<!ELEMENT author-ref EMPTY>
<!ATTLIST author-ref
  id IDREF #REQUIRED
>
<!ELEMENT book (isbn, title, author-ref*, character-ref*)>
<!ATTLIST book
  id ID #REQUIRED
>
<!ELEMENT born (#PCDATA)>
<!ELEMENT character (name, since, qualification)>
<!ATTLIST character
  id ID #REQUIRED
>
```

```
<!ELEMENT character-ref EMPTY>
<!ATTLIST character-ref
  id IDREF #REQUIRED
>
<!ELEMENT dead (#PCDATA)>
<!ELEMENT isbn (#PCDATA)>
<!ELEMENT library (book+, author*, character*)>
<!ELEMENT name (#PCDATA)>
<!ELEMENT nickName (#PCDATA)>
<!ELEMENT qualification (#PCDATA)>
<!ELEMENT since (#PCDATA)>
<!ELEMENT title (#PCDATA)>
```

W3C XML Schema

As we have seen, the W3C XML Schema is a strongly typed schema language that eliminates any nondeterministic design from the described markup to insure that there is no ambiguity in the determination of the datatypes, and that the validation can be performed by a finite state machine. Table A-2 provides the fact sheet for W3C XML Schema.

Table A-2. W3C XML Schema fact sheet

Author:	W3C.
Status:	Recommendation.
Location:	*http://www.w3.org/TR/xmlschema-0*.
Type:	object-oriented
PSVI:	Yes.
Structures:	Yes.
Datatypes:	Yes.
Integrity:	Yes (internal through *ID/IDREF/IDREFS* and *xs:unique/xs:key/xs:keyref*).
Rules:	No.
Vendor support:	Potentially excellent but currently still immature.
Miscellaneous:	Borrows many ideas from OOP design; considered complex; requires deterministic content models; part of the foundation of XML in the vision of the W3C.

Example

```
<xs:schema xmlns:xs="http://www.w3.org/2001/XMLSchema">
  <xs:element name="library">
    <xs:complexType>
      <xs:sequence>
        <xs:element name="book" maxOccurs="unbounded">
          <xs:complexType>
            <xs:sequence>
              <xs:element name="isbn" type="xs:string"/>
              <xs:element name="title" type="xs:string"/>
```

```
            <xs:element name="author-ref" minOccurs="0"
              maxOccurs="unbounded">
             <xs:complexType>
             <xs:attribute name="id" type="xs:IDREF"
               use="required"/>
             </xs:complexType>
            </xs:element>
            <xs:element name="character-ref" minOccurs="0"
              maxOccurs="unbounded">
             <xs:complexType>
             <xs:attribute name="id" type="xs:IDREF"
               use="required"/>
             </xs:complexType>
            </xs:element>
          </xs:sequence>
          <xs:attribute name="id" type="xs:ID" use="required"/>
        </xs:complexType>
      </xs:element>
      <xs:element name="author" minOccurs="0"
        maxOccurs="unbounded">
        <xs:complexType>
          <xs:sequence>
            <xs:element ref="name"/>
            <xs:element name="nickName" type="xs:string"/>
            <xs:element name="born" type="xs:string"/>
            <xs:element name="dead" type="xs:string"/>
          </xs:sequence>
          <xs:attribute name="id" type="xs:ID" use="required"/>
        </xs:complexType>
      </xs:element>
      <xs:element name="character" minOccurs="0"
        maxOccurs="unbounded">
        <xs:complexType>
          <xs:sequence>
            <xs:element ref="name"/>
            <xs:element name="since" type="xs:string"/>
            <xs:element name="qualification" type="xs:string"/>
          </xs:sequence>
          <xs:attribute name="id" type="xs:ID" use="required"/>
        </xs:complexType>
      </xs:element>
    </xs:sequence>
  </xs:complexType>
 </xs:element>
 <xs:element name="name" type="xs:string"/>
</xs:schema>
```

RELAX NG

Its editors (James Clark and Murata Makoto) define RELAX NG as "the next generation schema language for XML: clean, simple, and powerful." RELAX NG appears to
be closer to a description of the instance documents in ordinary English as well as

---

simpler than the W3C XML Schema, to which it might become a serious alternative. Many constraints, especially those on the fringe of nondeterministic models, can be expressed by RELAX NG and not by the W3C XML Schema. Some combinations in document structures forbidden by the W3C XML Schema can be described by RELAX NG. Even though RELAX NG seems to be technically superior to the W3C XML Schema, support by software vendors and XML developers is uncertain given that W3C XML Schema is a W3C Recommendation. Table A-3 provides the fact sheet for RELAX NG.

Table A-3. RELAX NG fact sheet

Author:	OASIS and possibly ISO/DSDL.
Status:	OASIS RELAX NG Committee Specification.
Location:	*http://relaxng.org*.
Type:	Grammar-based.
PSVI:	No.
Structures:	Yes.
Datatypes:	No, but a modular mechanism has been defined to plug in datatype systems (W3C XML Schema Part 2 and others if needed).
Integrity:	No.
Rules:	No.
Vendor support:	To be seen.
Miscellaneous:	Result of the merge between RELAX and TREX, might become an ISO IS. Strong mathematical grounding. Alternate non-XML syntax proposed by James Clark.

Example

```
<grammar
  datatypeLibrary="http://www.w3.org/2001/XMLSchema-datatypes"
  xmlns="http://relaxng.org/ns/structure/1.0">
  <start>
    <ref name="library"/>
  </start>
  <define name="library">
    <element name="library">
      <oneOrMore>
        <ref name="book"/>
      </oneOrMore>
      <zeroOrMore>
        <ref name="author"/>
      </zeroOrMore>
      <zeroOrMore>
        <ref name="character"/>
      </zeroOrMore>
    </element>
  </define>
  <define name="author">
    <element name="author">
```

```
      <attribute name="id">
        <data type="ID"/>
      </attribute>
      <element name="name">
        <text/>
      </element>
      <element name="nickName">
        <text/>
      </element>
      <element name="born">
        <text/>
      </element>
      <element name="dead">
        <text/>
      </element>
    </element>
  </define>
  <define name="book">
    <element name="book">
      <ref name="id-attribute"/>
      <ref name="isbn"/>
      <ref name="title"/>
      <zeroOrMore>
        <element name="author-ref">
          <attribute name="id">
            <data type="IDREF"/>
          </attribute>
          <empty/>
        </element>
      </zeroOrMore>
      <zeroOrMore>
        <element name="character-ref">
          <attribute name="id">
            <data type="IDREF"/>
          </attribute>
          <empty/>
        </element>
      </zeroOrMore>
    </element>
  </define>
  <define name="id-attribute">
    <attribute name="id">
      <data type="ID"/>
    </attribute>
  </define>
  <define name="character">
    <element name="character">
      <ref name="id-attribute"/>
      <ref name="name"/>
      <ref name="since"/>
      <ref name="qualification"/>
    </element>
  </define>
  <define name="isbn">
```

```
        <element name="isbn">
          <text/>
        </element>
      </define>
      <define name="name">
        <element name="name">
          <text/>
        </element>
      </define>
      <define name="nickName">
        <element name="nickName">
          <text/>
        </element>
      </define>
      <define name="qualification">
        <element name="qualification">
          <text/>
        </element>
      </define>
      <define name="since">
        <element name="since">
          <data type="date"/>
        </element>
      </define>
      <define name="title">
        <element name="title">
          <text/>
        </element>
      </define>
    </grammar>
```

Schematron

Schematron is a XPath/XSLT-based language for defining context-dependent rules. Schematron doesn't directly support structure or datatype validation, but a schema author may write rules that implement these checks. To write a full schema with Schematron, the author needs to take care to include all the rules needed to qualify the structure of the document. Table A-4 provides the fact sheet for Schematron.

Table A-4. Schematron fact sheet

Author:	Rick Jelliffe and other contributors. Will be described by ISO/DSDL.
Status:	Unofficial.
Location:	*http://www.ascc.net/xml/schematron.*
Type:	Rule-based.
PSVI:	No.
Structures:	No (although the structure can be controlled by rules).
Datatypes:	No (although the datatypes can be controlled by rules).

Integrity:	No (although the integrity can be controlled by rules).
Rules:	Yes.
Vendor support:	Low but increasing.
Miscellaneous:	Pure rule expression. Can be embedded in W3C XML Schema and RELAX NG.

Example

```
<sch:schema xmlns:sch="http://www.ascc.net/xml/schematron">
  <sch:title>
    Schematron Schema for library
  </sch:title>
  <sch:pattern>
    <sch:rule context="/">
      <sch:assert test="library">
        The document element should be "library".
      </sch:assert>
    </sch:rule>
    <sch:rule context="/library">
      <sch:assert test="book">
        There should be at least a book!
      </sch:assert>
      <sch:assert test="not(@*)">
        No attribute for library, please!
      </sch:assert>
    </sch:rule>
    <sch:rule context="/library/book">
      <sch:assert test="not(following-sibling::book/@id=@id)">
        Duplicated ID for this book.
      </sch:assert>
      <sch:assert test="@id=concat('-', isbn)">
        The id should be derived from the ISBN.
      </sch:assert>
    </sch:rule>
    <sch:rule context="/library/*">
      <sch:assert test="name()='book' or name( )='author' or
        name( )='character'">
        This element shouldn't be here...
      </sch:assert>
    </sch:rule>
  </sch:pattern>
</sch:schema>
```

Note that the previous Schematron is a partial schema meant as a supplement.

Examplotron

Examplotron is an experiment to define a schema language based on sample trees, much like early proposals for XPath. Table A-5 provides the fact sheet for Examplotron.

Table A-5. Examplotron fact sheet

Author:	Eric van der Vlist.
Status:	Unofficial.
Location:	*http://examplotron.org*.
Type:	Grammar-based with native rules support.
PSVI:	No.
Structures:	Yes.
Datatypes:	No (although datatypes can be checked as rules).
Integrity:	No (although integrity can be checked as rules).
Rules:	Yes.
Vendor support:	Low.
Miscellaneous:	Schema by example (a sample document is a schema) with rule checking (syntax borrowed from Schematron).

Example

```
<library xmlns:eg="http://examplotron.org/0/">
  <book id="-0836217462" eg:occurs="+"
    eg:assert="not(following-sibling::book/@id=@id) and
    @id=concat('-',isbn)">
    <isbn>
      0836217462
    </isbn>
    <title>
      Being a Dog Is a Full-Time Job
    </title>
    <author-ref id="Charles-M.-Schulz" eg:occurs="*"/>
    <character-ref id="Peppermint-Patty" eg:occurs="*"/>
  </book>
  <author id="Charles-M.-Schulz" eg:occurs="*">
    <name>
      Charles M. Schulz
    </name>
    <nickName>
      SPARKY
    </nickName>
    <born>
      November 26, 1922
    </born>
    <dead>
      February 12, 2000
    </dead>
  </author>
  <character id="Peppermint-Patty" eg:occurs="*">
    <name>
      Peppermint Patty
    </name>
    <since>
      Aug. 22, 1966
```

```
    </since>
    <qualification>
      bold, brash and tomboyish
    </qualification>
  </character>
</library>
```

Decisions

The choice is open. XML schema languages are still a young technology and none of the candidates are perfect. In these conditions, the diversity allows you to choose the best tool adapted to each task: Schematron for the finishings or for very open applications, RELAX NG when the diversity and flexibility of the instance documents is critical, and W3C XML Schema when the mapping to object oriented applications is important or your partners require it!

Work in Progress

Although W3C XML Schema was approved as a W3C Recommendation in May 2001, it is still just getting started. This chapter identifies a short list of schema-related projects that seem either promising, useful, or just on the way.

W3C Projects

Edited by the W3C, the W3C XML Schema is considered by the consortium to belong to the very foundation of XML—together with XML 1.0 and namespaces in XML—and it does impact virtually all the other XML specifications. The most heavily affected seem to be the triumvirate XPath/XSLT/XQuery (and by consequence, XPointer- and XPointer-based specifications), DOM, and RDF.

XPath, XSLT, and XQuery

One of the most amazing things about XPath and XSLT 1.0 is that queries and transformations can be executed by applications with no prior knowledge of the structure of the documents on which they work. This is a major difference from previous information systems, such as RDBMS, in which the layout of the tables needs to be defined before any query can be run. Even though this works just fine in many circumstances, there are two main areas in which improvements can be obtained if the structure of the instance documents is known.

The first of these areas is optimization. This is not crucial for small documents, but as soon as the size of the document grows (which is typically the case in a XML database), any optimizer will need food for thought to perform his job. The first piece of basic information that is required is about the structure of the documents. The second is typed-aware comparisons and sorts. In XPath and XSLT 1.0, the sort order (numerical or string) is indicated in the XSLT style sheet and the comparisons are always done character by character. Sorting or comparing dates with different time zones is practically impossible in these conditions, and some type information coming out of a schema can help a lot.

For these reasons, XSLT 2.0, which will use XPath 2.0 like XSLT 1.0 uses XPath 1.0, and XQuery 1.0, which is a superset of XPath 2.0, both rely on the W3C XML Schema and use the information coming out of the PSVI.

This will indirectly impact a specification that relies on XPath, and XPointer (a specification that defines how fragments of XML documents can be addressed). It will also affect specifications using XPointer, such as XLink (definition of links between document fragments) and XInclude (inclusion of XML fragments). The case of XInclude is a good illustration of the need to define an overall processing model: XInclude relies on XPointer; XPointer relies on XPath, and XPath relies on the W3C XML Schema. This means that a XInclude processor will need the PSVI of the document containing the fragment to include, but this document may only be a container for the fragments and be invalid or even have no W3C XML Schema. On the contrary, from the schema viewpoint, the schema should be applied after the inclusion when the document is complete. Do we need to apply the schema processing before or after the inclusion (or both) ? This question is open.

 XPath 2.0, XSLT 2.0, XQuery 1.0, XPointer, XLink, and XInclude are either works in progress or published recommendations; their specifications can be found on the W3C web site (*http://www.w3.org*).

DOM

The W3C DOM Working Group is creating the "Document Object Model (DOM) Level 3 Abstract Schemas and Load and Save Specification." This will define an abstract API to access either DTDs or the W3C XML Schema schemas. This API will be read/write, allowing reading, updating, and writing schemas in the same way DOM Core allows you to read, update, and write XML documents. It also provides extensions to DOM Core interfaces (the Element interface, for instance, is extended into an ElementEditAS interface) to access some information determined by the analysis of the schema.

The DOM Working Group has been very careful to make sure their "Abstract Schemas" remain abstract and as independent of the schema language as possible. The DOM work cannot be considered an API to the PSVI since it does not expose the PSVI but rather objects that are containers to query the schema implementation (to find out if an action such as adding, updating, or removing content from a DOM tree is allowed or not).

RDF

RDF (Resources Description Framework) can be seen as a way to express graphs in XML by splitting these graphs into elementary elements of information named "statements" or "triples." Each triple is a logic assertion associating a subject, verb, and object, such as in the phrase "The book 0836217462 (subject) has been written by Charles M Schulz (object)." RDF has its own schema language (RDF Schema) to model and constrain the relations themselves and define the inheritance between them. Since it's defined as a level on top of XML, a XML schema language does not act at the right level to model a set of RDF triples. However, RDF recognizes two kind of objects, resources identified by a URI and literals (i.e., raw values), and needs a simple datatype system to define constraints on those literals.

Although the idea of associating a W3C XML Schema simple datatype to RDF literals looks simple, it raises several issues. One is the lack of a way to identify W3C XML Schema simple datatypes that would be acceptable for RDF. As we've seen, RDF identifies any resource by a URI. To be coherent with the RDF data model, the simple types associated to the literals should be identified by URIs. On the other hand, the W3C XML Schema does not use the URIs to identify its datatypes but rather uses qualified names (QNames). Furthermore, it decided that elements, attributes, simple and complex types, and groups have independent sets of QNames. The QName bib:book can thus refer to an element, an attribute, a complex and simple type, and an element and attribute group of the same schema. The simple approach of identifing the simple type book through its expanded QName (replacing the prefix by the namespace URI) isn't yet implemented.

ISO: DSDL

ISO (ISO/IEC JTC 1/SC34, to be precise) launched a work named "Document Schema Definition Language" (DSDL) in December 2001, which will be "a multi-part International Standard defining a modular set of specifications for describing the document structures, datatypes, and data relationships in structured information resources." DSDL includes efforts to classify the different XML schema languages into "path-based," "grammar-based," and "object-oriented" schema languages, to define a generic semantic for simple datatypes, and to define a common framework in which these languages may be used.

Working from the specifications of existing schema languages (Schematron, RELAX NG, DTDs, and W3C XML Schema), DSDL should clarify the situation by documenting their differences and how they might fit together. More information about DSDL is available at *http://www.jtc1.org/FTP/Public/SC34/DOCREG/0275.htm* and *http://www.dsdl.org*.

Other

W3C XML Schema is inspiring some new technologies all its own.

PSVI Serialization

The PSVI (Post Schema Validation Infoset) is one of the most obscure features of the W3C XML Schema. Although present throughout the Recommendation, its specification is scattered into small sections describing the "PSVI contribution" of each feature. These contributions are described as plain text even when they are very abstract and difficult to visualize, like those of the ID/IDREF or unique/key/keyref tables. These may eventually be exposed through APIs that haven't been specified yet.

This level of abstraction appears to be due to the organization of the W3C divided into independent working groups. Since the charter of the W3C XML Schema Working Group is hidden on the private members' only section of the W3C web site, we may think it did not include the definition of the processing model of a schema validation and only focused on the definition of the language itself.

However, the effects of this lack of formal specification are similar to those of the unpublished APIs practices that some software editors are famous for: the lack of a concrete description is an obstacle for most users to understand the PSVI, and it creates a kind of "vendor lock-in," since generating the PSVI using another tool instead of W3C XML Schema involves emulating these unspecified APIs and may prove difficult for many developers.

Four years of XML have taught us that there is an easy way to serialize abstract concepts, and the definition of a XML serialization for the PSVI would have a lot of advantages. Assuming the format is simple enough, it would let us visualize what the PSVI is, allow us to process a PSVI using the standard set of XML APIs (DOM, SAX, and friends) and tools (including XSLT), make it easy to include into XML processing pipelines, allow us to save it for reuse, and permit us to generate it out of any application or tool able to generate XML documents.

A proposal has been written by Richard Tobin and Henry S. Thompson and informally published on the W3C web site (*http://www.w3.org/2001/05/serialized-infoset-schema.html*), but the format is heavyweight and difficult to read.

APIs

Even though the PSVI is produced by W3C XML Schema processors and used by XPath/XSLT 2.0 and XQuery 1.0, no API has been defined to communicate between these applications. The traditional XML APIs (DOM and SAX) have not yet been adapted yet to support this additional amount of information. The most advanced open implementation in this area seems to be the Xerces Native Interface (XNI; see *http://xml.apache.org/xerces2-j/xni.html*), which is a general framework to add information to the stream of basic events supported by SAX. While it is more generic than it needs to be to support the PSVI, XNI can be used when working with Xerces to expose the information from the PSVI. There is also a Microsoft implementation that similarly exposes information from the PSVI.

The need is there, applications will follow soon, and the general-purpose XML APIs (DOM, SAX and friends) need to take the PSVI into account if they do not want to be replaced by new APIs which will become de facto standards!

Schema Extensions: Error Messages

While the extension mechanisms through foreign attributes and xs:annotation are highly extensible, it might be useful to define a set of commonly used schema extensions that could become interoperable between schema processors. The principle would be similar to the EXSLT extensions (see *http://www.exslt.org*) proposed by an informal group of XSLT experts, which are now supported by a number of XSLT processors.

The error messages sent by schema processors are often very obscure and difficult for an end user to understand. A schema designer can often provide context-aware messages that are much clearer. Associated with a template, an extension for error messages could look like the following (the namespace URI is just an example):

```
<xs:simpleType name="dateTimeWithTimezone">
  <xs:restriction base="xs:dateTime">
    <xs:pattern value=".+T.+(Z|[+-].+)">
      <xs:annotation>
        <xs:appinfo>
          <exsd:error xmlns:exsd="http://dyomedea.com/ns/esxd">
            This date should specify a timezone.
          </exsd:error>
        </xs:appinfo>
      </xs:annotation>
    </xs:pattern>
  </xs:restriction>
</xs:simpleType>
```

or (simpler but less extensible):

```
<xs:simpleType name="dateTimeWithTimezone">
  <xs:restriction base="xs:dateTime">
    <xs:pattern value=".+T.+(Z|[+-].+)" exsd:error="This date
      should specify a timezone."
      xmlns:exsd="http://dyomedea.com/ns/esxd"/>
  </xs:restriction>
</xs:simpleType>
```

Glossary

abstract

A type of element or complex datatype that cannot be used directly in the instance documents. An abstract element must be substituted and is usually the head of a substitution group. An abstract complex type may be used to define content models, in which case the type will have to be substituted in the instance documents using xsi:type. There is no feature to define simple types as abstract (even though the predefined type xs:NOTATION could be considered abstract).

atom

In a regular expression, an atom expresses a condition on a substring. Atoms may be followed by a quantifier defining the expected number of the atom's occurrences. The atom, with its optional number of occurrences, constitutes a "piece." An atom may be a character, a wildcard, a special character, a character class, or a regular expression.

atomic type

A simple type that is not derived by list or union from another simple type.

attributes

Pieces of information attached to an element and defined in its start tag. Considered child nodes by the XPath data model, and considered property nodes by the DOM, attributes are "information items" to the XML Infoset.

attribute groups

Containers that allow you to define, reference, and redefine groups of attributes.

base type

The datatype that is used as the starting point to define a new datatype by derivation by restriction or extension.

Berners-Lee, Tim

Inventor of HTML and HTTP, and Director of the W3C; he is considered the father of the World Wide Web (see *http://www.w3.org/People/all#timbl*).

block

Elements and complex datatypes that cannot be substituted in the instance documents. A blocked element or complex type is restricted in the substitutions that may occur in the instance documents. There is no feature to block simple types.

canonical lexical representation

When a value in the value space may have different lexical representations in the lexical space, the W3C XML Schema Recommendation provides (when possible) a canonical representation, which is the most "normal" or "classical" and may be used as a reference. Although most of the types have canonical representations, some such as xs:duration or xs:QName, do not have one.

chameleon design

Importing a schema without a namespace into a schema with a target namespace is known as "chameleon design." This is because the imported schema takes the target namespace of the schema in which it is imported like a chameleon takes the color of the environment in which it is placed.

character class

In a regular expression, a character class is an atom matching a set of characters. Character classes may be classical Perl character classes, Unicode character classes, or user-defined character classes.

classical Perl character class

A set of character classes designated by a single letter, for which upper- and lower-cases of the same letter are complementary (for instance, "\d" is all the decimal digits, and "\D" is all the characters that are not decimal digits).

complex content

An element has a complex content model when it has child element nodes only (and no text node).

component

Something that can be defined and referenced in a schema. Elements, attributes, simple and complex types, and element and attribute groups are components.

compositor

Containers that allow the manipulation of a set of elements as a whole and defines their relative order. Compositors include xs:sequence, xs:choice, and xs:all. Compositors may be included in other compositors to form complex combinations (with some limitations). Most can also be used as particles and have minOccurs and maxOccurs attributes, which allow definition of the number of repetitions expected for the whole group of elements that they define. The child elements of a compositor are "particles." A restriction applies to xs:all as a compositor: it can only include xs:element particles.

Consistent Declaration rule

This states that an element referenced by one "location" in a schema cannot be associated with two different simple or complex types.

content model

A description of the structure of children elements and text nodes (independent of attributes). The content model is "simple" when there is a text node but no elements, "complex" when there are element nodes but no text, "mixed" when there are text and element nodes, and "empty" when there are neither text nor element nodes. These definitions are commonly used by XML developers and slightly different from those of W3C XML Schema, for which there are only simple and complex content models. (Mixed models are considered special cases of complex contents, and empty models are considered either simple or complex contents with no child nodes.)

datatype

A term used by W3C XML Schema to qualify both the content and the structure of an element or attribute. Datatypes can be either simple (when they describe an attribute or an element without an embedded element or attribute) or complex (when they describe elements with embedded child elements or attributes). W3C XML Schema datatypes should not be confused with XML 1.0 element types, which are called element names by W3C XML Schema.

default value

A value that is used when no value is provided in the instance document. Default values apply to attributes that are either empty or missing in the instance documents and that apply to empty elements.

derivation

The action of defining a datatype by using the definition of one or several other datatypes. Simple datatypes may be defined by derivation by restriction, list, or union, while complex datatypes can be defined by derivation by restriction or extension.

derivation by extension

The action of adding attributes or elements to a complex type.

derivation by list

The action of using a simple datatype (called the list type) to define a new simple datatype as a whitespace-separated list of values of the list type. Derivation by list applies only to simple datatypes.

derivation by restriction

For simple datatypes, a derivation by restriction is the action of defining a simple datatype by adding new constraints (called facets) on the lexical or value space of an existing datatype (called the base type). For complex datatypes, a derivation by restriction is the action of giving a new content model for the datatype that is a restriction of the base type.

derivation by union

The action of using a set of simple datatypes (called the member types) to define a new simple datatype whose lexical space is the union of the lexical spaces of the member types.

derived datatype

A datatype that is defined by derivation from other datatypes. They can be user-defined when defined in a schema, or predefined when defined in the W3C XML Schema Recommendation.

DOM

Document Object Model. An object-oriented model of XML documents, including the definition of the API allowing its manipulation. The third version of DOM (DOM Level 3) will include an API named "Abstract Schemas" to facilitate schema-guided editions of XML documents (see *http://www.w3.org/TR/DOM-Level-3-Core*).

DSDL

Document Schema Definition Language (DSDL) is a project undertaken by the ISO (ISO/IEC JTC 1/SC 34/WG 1, to be precise) whose objective is "to create a framework within which multiple validation tasks of different types can be applied to an XML document in order to achieve more complete validation results than just the application of a single technology" (see *http://dsdl.org*). DSDL has classified

W3C XML Schema as "object-oriented schema language."

DTD

Document Type Definition. XML 1.0 DTDs are inherited from SGML, in which rules were included that allow the customization of the markup itself and played a very central role. Because of the syntactical rules included in their DTDs, SGML applications need a DTD to be able to read an SGML document. One of the simplifications of XML is to state that a XML parser should be able to read a document without needing a DTD. DTDs have therefore been simplified over their SGML ancestors and remain the first incarnation of what is today called a XML Schema language.

element

One of the basic type of nodes in the tree represented by a XML document. An element is delimited by start and end tags. In the corresponding tree, an element is a nonterminal node, which may have subnodes of type element, character (text), and namespace and attribute, as well as comment and processing instruction nodes.

element type

Term used in the XML 1.0 Recommendation, which is equivalent to the notion of element names in W3C XML Schema and should not be confused with the simple or complex datatype of an element.

element groups

Containers that allow you to define, reference, and redefine groups of elements.

empty content

An element that has neither child element nor text nodes (with or without attributes).

facet

A constraint added to the lexical or value space of a simple datatype during a derivation by restriction. The list of facets that can be used depends on the simple datatype. Facets can be "fixed" to disable their use during further derivations.

final

Elements and datatypes that cannot be substituted or derived any longer in the schema. A final element may not be chosen as the head of a substitution group while a final complex or simple type cannot be used as a base for further derivation.

fixed facets

Facets that are "fixed" during a derivation by restriction cannot be used during further derivations by restriction.

fixed values

A value that must match the value found in the instance document. Used as default values if no value is supplied.

global definition

All the components (elements, attributes, simple and complex types, element and attribute groups) can be defined at the top level of the schema, directly under the xs:schema document element. Their definition is said to be "global," and they can be referenced elsewhere in the schema, as well as in any schema that has imported or included this schema.

Infoset

XML Information Set. A formal description of the information that may be found in a well-formed XML document.

instance document

A XML document that is a candidate to be validated by a schema. Any well-formed XML 1.0 document that conforms to the Namespaces in XML 1.0 Recommendation can be considered a valid or invalid instance document.

item type

The simple datatype that is used as the starting point to define a new simple datatype using a derivation by list.

lexical space

The set of all representations (after parsing and whitespace processing) allowed for a simple datatype.

local definition

Most of the components (elements, attributes, simple and complex types) can be defined inside of other components where they are used. Their definition is said to be "local" and they cannot be referenced in other parts of the schema.

local name

The name of a component in its namespace, i.e., the part of the qualified name that comes after the namespace prefix.

member types

The simple datatypes used as the starting point to define a new simple datatype using a derivation by union.

mixed content

The content of an element that contains both child element and text nodes.

namespace

A unique identifier that can be associated with a set of XML elements and attributes. This identifier is a URI, which is not required to point to an actual resource but must "belong" to the author of these elements and attributes. Since this full URI can't be included in the name of each element and attribute, a namespace prefix is assigned to the namespace URI through a namespace declaration. This prefix is added to the local name of the elements and attributes to form a qualified name. Namespaces are optional and elements and attributes may have no namespaces attached. W3C XML Schema has extended the scope of namespaces by using them not only for elements and attributes but also for all the components of a schema. A schema identifies the namespace of the components described in a schema as a target namespace. When these components do not have a namespace, the schema is said to have no target namespace.

parsed space

The set of values that are sent by the parser to the applications. It is at the interface between the parser and the schema validator. Values from the parsed space undergo whitespace processing, as defined by their simple datatype, to feed the lexical space. The parsed space is, therefore, not visible by the facets.

particle

An element, such as a compositor, a group of elements (`xs:group`), an element definition or reference (`xs:element`), or an element wildcard (`xs:any`), which is included in a compositor to define a list of elements. A restriction applies to `xs:all`, which cannot be used as a particle even though it is defined as a compositor. The number of occurrences of particles may be constrained using their `minOccurs` and `maxOccurs` attributes.

pattern

A facet that allows definition of a regular expression, which will be applied to the lexical space to check its validity. By extension, the regular expression defined in a pattern is often called "pattern" as well.

piece

Regular expressions (or patterns) are composed of pieces. Each piece is itself composed of an atom describing a condition on a substring and an optional quantifier defining the expected number of occurrences of the atom.

predefined datatype

The simple datatypes (both primitive and derived) that are defined in the W3C XML Schema Recommendation.

primitive datatype

A simple datatype that cannot be defined by derivation from other datatypes. There is no way to create primitive datatypes, so all the primitive datatypes are therefore predefined.

PSVI

The Post Schema Validation Infoset. The Infoset after the information gathered during a schema validation is added.

qualified element or attribute

Elements and attributes that belong to a namespace; i.e., a namespace URI is defined for them. The name of qualified elements may have no prefix if a default namespace is defined, but the name of qualified attributes must be prefixed.

qualified name

The complete name of a component, including the prefix associated to its target namespace if one is defined.

RDBMS

Relational DataBase Management System. Developed in the late 70s, this system has taken most of the database market and hosts a significant amount of the data of many organizations. XML Schema languages may help to insure the interface between that information and XML documents.

Recommendation

Specifications published by the W3C. They cannot be officially called "standards," since the W3C is a consortium that does not have the status of the standard body reserved for the ISO and national standard bodies. The specifications, which are finalized and approved by the Director, are then called "W3C Recommendations."

reference

All of the components (elements, attributes, simple and complex types, element and attribute groups) that have been created with a global definition can be referenced when needed in the schema in which they are defined, and in any schema that has imported or included this schema. Their definition is used at the location where they are referenced.

regular expression

A syntax to express conditions on strings. The syntax used by the W3C XML Schema for its patterns is very close to the syntax introduced by the Perl programming language. A regular expression is composed of elementary "pieces."

RELAX

A grammar-based XML Schema language developed by Murata Makoto and published in March 2000 as a Japanese ISO Standard (see *http://www.xml.gr.jp/relax*).

RELAX NG

A grammar-based XML Schema language resulting from a merger between RELAX and TREX (see *http://relaxng.org*).

SAX

Simple API for XML. A streaming event-based API used between parsers and applications. Its streaming nature means that pipelines of XML processing may be created using SAX (see *http://www.saxproject.org*).

Schematron

A rule-based XML Schema language, developed by Rick Jelliffe, using XPath expressions to describe validation rules (see *http://www.ascc.net/xml/resource/schematron/schematron.html*).

serialization space

The set of values as they are stored in a document. These values are transformed by the parser, as defined in the Recommendation XML 1.0, before reaching the application. The serialization space is not visible to the schema processors.

SGML

Standard Generalized Markup Language. Created in 1980, the ancestor of XML. XML was designed as a simplified subset of SGML to be used on the Web.

simple content

An element has a simple content model when it has a child text node only (and no subelements). A simple content element has a simple type if it has no attributes, and it has a complex type if it has any attributes.

simple datatype

A datatype that accepts only a text value. Simple datatypes can be directly assigned to attributes and simple content elements that do not accept any attribute. Simple datatypes can be used to define complex datatypes by extension.

SOAP

The major XML protocol used by Web Services; relies on W3C XML Schema to describe the messages exchanged (see *http://www.w3.org/TR/SOAP*).

space

W3C XML Schema uses the term "space" to mean a set of values (lexical versus value spaces). For completeness, we introduced two additional spaces in this book (the serialization and parsed spaces).

special character

A character that may be used as an atom after a "\" to accept a specific character, either for convenience or because this character is interpreted differently in the context of a regular expression.

substitution group

A feature of W3C XML Schema, allowing you to define groups of elements that may be used interchangeably in instance documents. They are not declared as element groups, but through the substitutionGroup attribute of xs:element global definitions.

target namespace

The namespace of the components described in a schema. When these components do not have a namespace, the schema is said to have no target namespace.

TREX

A grammar-based XML Schema language developed by James Clark (see *http://www.thaiopensource.com/trex*).

Unicode block

A set of characters classified by their "localization" (Latin, Arabic, Hebrew, Tibetan, and even Gothic or musical symbols).

Unicode category

A set of characters classified by their usage (letters, uppercase, digit, punctuation, etc.).

Unicode character class

A set of character classes defined based on the Unicode blocks and categories.

unqualified element or attribute

Elements and attributes that don't belong to a namespace; i.e., no namespace URI is defined for them. Any unprefixed attribute is unqualified, but unprefixed elements are unqualified only if no default namespace is defined.

UPA rule

The UPA (Unique Particle Attribution) rule states that at any given moment, a W3C XML Schema processor must know—without ambiguity and without needing any forward reference in the document—which particle in the schema describes an element in the instance document. This rule is roughly equivalent to the restrictions known as "non-deterministic content models" for the XML 1.0 DTDs and as "ambiguous content models" by SGML. The UPA rule is often associated with the "Consistent Declaration rule."

URI

Uniform Resource Identifier. Defined by the RFCs 2396 and 2732. URIs were created to extend the notion of URLs (Uniform Resource Locators) to include abstract identifiers that do not necessarily need to "locate" a resource.

URL

Uniform Resource Locator, a common identifier used on the Web. URLs are absolute when the full path to the resource is indicated, and relative when a partial path is given that needs to be evaluated in relation with a base URL.

user-defined character class

A set of characters defined by the schema author.

user-defined datatype

Datatypes that are defined in a schema. All the datatypes can be defined by derivation or, for the complex datatypes only, by definition.

valid

A XML document that is well-formed and conforms to a schema (DTD, W3C XML Schema, etc.) of some kind.

value space

The set of all the possible values for a simple datatype, independent of their actual representation in the instance documents.

W3C

World Wide Web Consortium. Originally created to settle HTML and HTTP as de facto standards. The main specification body for the core specifications of the World Wide Web and the keeper of the core XML specifications (see *http://www.w3.org*).

Web Services

An approach to using the Web for applications, as opposed to the Web for human consumption that we use on a daily basis. Those services rely on the same infrastructure as the Web, and exchange XML documents over HTTP though a layer of protocols (such as SOAP or XML-RPC), which are themselves based on XML. XML Schema languages are used by these services to describe and control the XML documents that are exchanged.

well-formed

An XML document that meets the conditions defined in the XML 1.0 Recommendation: it must be readable without ambiguity. Syntax errors will be detected by a XML parser without schema of any type.

whitespace

Characters #x9 (tab), #xA (linefeed), #xD (carriage return), and #x20 (space). These are often used to indent the XML documents to give them a more readable aspect, and are filtered by an operation named "whitespace processing."

whitespace collapsing

The action of applying the whitespace replacement, trimming the leading and trailing spaces, and replacing all the sequences of contiguous whitespaces by a single space between the parsed and lexical spaces. Most of the simple datatypes apply whitespace collapsing.

whitespace preservation

The action of preserving all the whitespaces from the parsed to the lexical space. The xs:string datatypes and the user-defined simple types derived from xs:string (which do not change the value of the xs:whitespace facet) are the only datatypes applying whitespace preservation.

whitespace processing

The operation of filtering that is done on the whitespaces present in the value of a simple datatype. The whitespace processing is done during the transformation between parsed and lexical spaces. W3C XML Schema defines three whitespace processing approaches (depending on the simple type): whitespace preservation, whitespace replacement, and whitespace collapsing.

whitespace replacement

The action of replacing all the occurrences of the characters #x9 (tab), #xA (linefeed), and #xD (carriage return) by a #x20 (space) between the parsed and the lexical space. Whitespace replacement doesn't change the length of the string. xs:normalizedString and the user-defined simple types derived from xs:string and xs:normalizedString (for which the value of the xs:whitespace facet is "replace") are the only datatypes that apply whitespace replacement.

wildcard

A character used as an atom in a regular expression to accept a set of characters. W3C XML Schema supports only one such wildcard: the character ".", which means "any character." This expression is also used to designate the xs:any and xs:anyAttribute particles.

Xerces

The XML parser developed by the XML Apache project (see *http://xml.apache.org/xerces2-j/index.html*).

XInclude

A W3C specification defining a general purpose inclusion mechanism for XML documents (see *http://www.w3.org/TR/xinclude*).

XLink

XML Linking Language is a W3C Recommendation (*http://www.w3.org/TR/xlink*) "which allows elements to be inserted into XML documents in order to create and describe links between resources."

XML

Extensible Markup Language. A subset of SGML created to be used on the Web. Its core specification (XML 1.0) was published by the W3C in February 1998. New specifications have been added since this date, and the W3C considers that, with the addition of W3C XML Schema, the core specifications are now complete.

XML-RPC

Considered the ancestor of SOAP, XML-RPC is a simple XML protocol that may be used to implement Web Services. It does not rely on the W3C XML Schema to describe the content of its messages but has defined a simpler binding mechanism (see *http://www.xmlrpc.com*).

XPath

A query language used to identify a set of nodes within a XML document. Originally defined to be used with XSLT, it is also used by XPointer and a simple subset is used in the xs:key, xs:keyref, and xs:unique W3C XML Schema elements. The XQuery specification will be a superset of the second version of XPath. This version will use type information provided by W3C XML Schema (see *http://www.w3.org/TR/xpath*).

XQuery

XML Query language. This will be a superset of XPath 2.0 that will use type information provided by the W3C XML Schema to optimize its queries, and for features such as sort orders (see *http://www.w3.org/TR/xquery*).

XSLT

Extensible Stylesheet Language Transformations. A programming language specialized for the transformation of XML documents (see *http://www.w3.org/TR/xslt*).

XSV

An open source W3C XML Schema implementation available at *http://www.w3.org/2001/03/webdata/xsv*.

Index

We'd like to hear your suggestions for improving our indexes. Send email to *index@oreilly.com*.

About the Author

Eric van der Vlist is an independent XML consultant, developer, and writer. He is a contributing editor to *XML.com* and *xmlhack*, creator and chief editor of *XMLfr.org*, and editor of the ISO DSDL Part 5 specification (work in progress) describing "Object Oriented XML Schema Languages."

Colophon

Our look is the result of reader comments, our own experimentation, and feedback from distribution channels. Distinctive covers complement our distinctive approach to technical topics, breathing personality and life into potentially dry subjects.

The animal on the cover of *XML Schema* is a Reeves's pheasant. Reeves's pheasants originated in north and central China. They are named after the man who first introduced the species in England to be bred for game. The species is one of the most popular types of pheasant to be held in captivity and can be found all over the world.

Reeves's pheasants are black, white, and bronze in color. Male pheasants have white heads with black stripes across their eyes resembling masks, while females have gold heads with light brown masks. Most remarkable are the birds' tail feathers, which can reach six feet long. These long tail feathers have historically been used in ceremonies.

Hens produce two or more clutches of 8 to 14 eggs per season. The eggs are olive brown or cream color, and hatch after 24 days. They have to be separated from other chicks, especially of different species, soon after birth, as they tend to be quite aggressive. Dominant male Reeves's pheasants are also quite aggressive and need to be separated when held in captivity.

Darren Kelly was the production editor, Mary Brady was the copyeditor, and Tatiana Diaz was the proofreader for *XML Schema*. Mary Anne Weeks Mayo and Claire Cloutier provided quality control. Interior composition was done by Philip Dangler, Matt Hutchinson, and Emily Quill. Judy Hoer wrote the index.

Hanna Dyer designed the cover of this book, based on a series design by Edie Freedman. The cover image is a 19th-century engraving from the Dover Pictorial Archive. Emma Colby produced the cover layout with QuarkXPress 4.1 using Adobe's ITC Garamond font.

David Futato designed the interior layout. This book was converted to FrameMaker 5.5.6 with a format conversion tool created by Erik Ray, Jason McIntosh, Neil Walls, and Mike Sierra that uses Perl and XML technologies. The text font is Linotype Birka; the heading font is Adobe Myriad Condensed; and the code font is Lucas-

Font's TheSans Mono Condensed. The illustrations that appear in the book were produced by Robert Romano and Jessamyn Read using Macromedia FreeHand 9 and Adobe Photoshop 6. The tip and warning icons were drawn by Christopher Bing. This colophon was written by Linley Dolby.